Integrating the Rural Poor into Markets

BIBEK DEBROY is Director of the Rajiv Gandhi Institute for Contemporary Studies, Rajiv Gandhi Foundation, New Delhi. He is a professional economist and was educated in Presidency College (Calcutta), Delhi School of Economics and Trinity College (Cambridge). He has worked at Presidency College (Calcutta), Gokhale Institute of Politics and Economics (Pune), Indian Institute of Foreign Trade (Delhi), National Council of Applied Economic Research (Delhi) and as Consultant, Department of Economic Affairs, Ministry of Finance, Government of India. He was also the Director for a project known as LARGE, set up by the Ministry of Finance and UNDP to examine legal reforms. He has been a member of several government committees. He is the author and editor of several books, papers and popular articles and is also Consulting Editor with Financial Express. Bibek Debroy's special interests are international trade (in particular the WTO), law reform and the political economy of liberalization in India.

AMIR ULLAH KHAN graduated in Electronics Engineering from Osmania and studied at IRMA. For his PhD he has worked on Intellectual Property Issues. In 1993, he joined the Indian Civil Service, quit and worked with Project LARGE of the UNDP. He taught Economics and Management at the Indian School of Finance and Management in New Delhi, Madras and London. He then worked as Executive Director, Encyclopaedia Britannica India. He is now a Fellow at the India Development Foundation.

INDIA DEVELOPMENT FOUNDATION (IDF) is a privately funded, non-profit, non-partisan think tank set up as a Trust on April 2, 2003. Its objective is to develop awareness about how markets work, why they are desirable and how to develop them. IDF helps policymakers transform emerging economies into market based societies. Its recommendations are derived from research and analysis. IDF then generates a blue-print of how to implement the recommendations. These are worked out through interaction with practitioners and stakeholders. IDF's work is disseminated through publications in peer-reviewed journals, workshops, seminars and various media to reach out to practitioners, policymakers and the general public. It also undertakes pilot projects to demonstrate how its recommendations can be realized.

INTERNATIONAL DEVELOPMENT ENTERPRISES, INDIA (IDEI) is an Indian not-for-profit organisation. IDEI's approach to rural development focuses on market opportunities as the driving force for poverty reduction. Development interventions are required to remove basic market constraints, enabling the rural poor to participate in markets both as customers of purchased inputs and as suppliers of high-value products. The *income generation* through market participation will allow smallholders to access food, education, health, housing, water etc. and thus escape *income poverty*. Having successfully increased the annual incomes of a customer base of half a million smallholder farmers and small businessmen and women, IDEI continues to work with private enterprises to Integrate Poor into Market Systems (IPMAS).

Integrating the Rural Poor into Markets

Editors:

Bibek Debroy
Amir Ullah Khan

Academic Foundation
NEW DELHI
www.academicfoundation.com

International Development Enterprises, India (IDEI)
www.ide-india.org

I·D·F
India Development Foundation (IDF)
www.idfresearch.org

Reprint 2005

First Published in 2004 by

ACADEMIC FOUNDATION

4772-73 / 23 Bharat Ram Road, (23 Ansari Road),
Darya Ganj, New Delhi - 110 002.
INDIA.

Phones : 23245001, 02, 03, 04.
Fax : +91-11-23245005.
e-mail : academic@vsnl.com
www : academicfoundation.com

Published in association with
India Development Foundation (IDF)
www.idfresearch.org
and
International Development Enterprises, India (IDEI)
www.ide-india.org

Photographs courtesy
International Development Enterprises, India (IDEI)

Integrating the Rural Poor into Markets
edited by Bibek Debroy and Amir Ullah Khan

ISBN 81-7188-390-7

Designed and typeset by Italics India, New Delhi
and printed at Print Perfect, New Delhi.

Contents

...Contd....

Editors' Introduction

There will be various attempts to interpret and understand the results of the 2004 Central elections. It is doubtful that voting takes place on the basis of economic issues alone. However, to the extent this hypothesis is true, the overall message is not one that is anti reform. Instead, the message is one about composition of reforms and about making reforms more broad-based. Agriculture may account for only 25% of GDP. But 70% of India's population earns a living from the rural sector. If there is a perception in India that liberalization has been anti-poor and pro-rich, that is largely because the agricultural cum rural sector has been untouched. Unlike a country like China, where in the first flush of reforms, the rural sector was addressed and that made income and consumption growth much more broad-based. In contrast, the NSS (National Sample Survey) large-sample data show that between 1993-94 and 1999-2000, the employment elasticity of GDP growth declined and that was largely because of agriculture's failure to create new jobs. Consequently, the Tenth Plan's (2002-07) promised 10 million new jobs a year also failed to materialize. The Tenth Plan also promised 8% real GDP growth. That too, is impossible to ensure without agriculture and allied sectors growing by 4%, a rate that is considerably above the trend rate of growth.

The reform agenda for agriculture is fairly vast, encompassing rural infrastructure, public investments (needed as a catalyst to stimulate private investments), credit, insurance, extension services, research and development, revamping land ownership and tenancy legislation, scrapping outdated controls on production, control and distribution on small-scale sector reservations, improving regulatory oversight, dis-intermediating the distribution chain and extending the Green or Rainbow Revolutions to parts of India other than Punjab, Haryana and Uttar Pradesh. The 17 papers in this volume address this agenda in different ways and taken collectively, one obtains a very good idea about what needs to be done to integrate the rural poor into markets. If there is one underlying strand that knits these papers together, that is in a belief in markets (not unregulated) and in a pro-poor focus.

Any discussion of Indian agriculture inevitably brings in the WTO and the agreement on agriculture (AoA). The AoA has three strands of disciplines on domestic support, export subsidies and market access, although agreements on trade-related intellectual property rights (TRIPs) and SPS (sanitary and phytosanitary) measures also have a bearing on agriculture. Discussions on further liberalization, beyond the Uruguay Round's AoA, are stuck at WTO and the DDA (Doha Development Agenda) is heading nowhere. EU and US offers on reducing domestic and export subsidies have been perceived to be inadequate by the G-20 group of developing countries. The G-20 group is a mixed bag, with members from the Cairns group possessing a strong export interest in agro products. Given supply-side constraints, India is not one of those and India's negotiating interests are presently restricted to containing the possible negative effects of market access liberalization in sectors like dairy and edible oils. Nevertheless, in a long-term sense, assuming domestic reforms ease supply-side constraints, India has an export interest, especially because many of India's agro exports are price competitive, notwithstanding infrastructure problems. Shaswat Mody's paper discusses US agricultural subsidies and their impact on developing countries. If tariffs are disciplined, policy substitution of protectionism surfaces through various means. Standards operating as non-tariff barriers (NTBs) are one example. Samrat Bose's paper is on the SPS agreement and Mohammed Saqib discusses instances of where standards operate as NTBs. While Sugata Ghosh's paper is on organic farming, it too covers some of this terrain.

The trigger for agro reform may indeed be border trade and resultant price signals. However, the source for agro reform should be endogenous and domestic. Income and consumption growth in agricultural and rural sectors is a prerequisite for addressing problems of poverty and unemployment. N.C. Saxena's paper is a sketch of what has happened to agricultural policy and rural poverty in the reform decade of the 1990s, highlighting policy failures. Amir Ullah Khan's paper reiterates some of the arguments, while the Satyaprakash and

Teli paper focus on institutional and technological policy issues. Amitabha Sadangi discusses IDEI's approach and interventions of integrating the poor into market systems. Phansalkar discusses similar instances of what may be called case studies. Some papers are on specific issues. The water problem, of both the drinking and irrigation variety, plagues India. Drip irrigation may indeed be the answer in some geographical areas and successful cases are presented in Shagun Krishnan's paper. Soil degradation is related to the water management problem and this is covered by Bhattacharya, Khan and Riyazuddin. Credit is a perennial problem and absence of land markets creates a collateral problem. Micro finance is a promising alternative and Rajesh Chakrabarti sketches the accomplishments and constraints on this count. Often, the problem is not lack of entrepreneurship or skills, but an inability to handle risk. Notwithstanding Kisan Credit Cards, the issue of insurance for the rural poor is often neglected and this is covered by Saleema Razvi. With technology increasingly in the private domain, regulatory issues assume significance. Globally, genetic engineering is a controversial area and the issue of Bt Cotton in India has been extremely contentious. Irrespective of the detailed figures, the case of regulatory failure in this sector is probably unambiguously established. Shabana Zahoor discusses this episode.

The remaining three papers cover different ground. Too often, absence of reforms has mean that agriculture has been equated with the rural sector, although this need not be the case. Information technology (IT) can be a promising tool, not only for removing or reducing asymmetry of information and collapsing the distribution chain, but also for improving public governance. Having covered the conceptual issues, Nirvikar Singh discusses some recent IT initiatives. Bibek Debroy's paper is on ICT (information and communication technology) and its links with poverty. Finally, the Gangopadhyay and Wadhwa paper set out a formal model for the incidence of child labour and also test it on the basis of empirical data.

After the recent elections, negative expectations about reforms concern privatization and labour market reforms. On the positive side, there are expectations that agro and rural reforms will finally get off the ground, after having been talked about *ad nauseam*, although many such reforms are actually State government subjects.

If these expectations materialize, parts of India that are hitherto bypassed and marginalized in the growth process, will be mainstreamed. If one is looking for a reform agenda for such liberalization, this volume provides it. The agenda set out in these 17 papers is by no means exhaustive. But collectively, one obtains a very good idea of what needs to be done to bring the rural poor into interaction with markets, so that they can tap the opportunities that market-based liberalization throws up.

— **Bibek Debroy**
Amir Ullah Khan

Contributors to this Volume

Amitabha Sadangi has spent 22 years in various aspects of rural development work. He first joined IDE International in 1992, served as the Country Director of IDE Sri Lanka, and served as Deputy Country Director of IDE International's India programme till September 2001. He has worked in all aspects of IDE India – programme design, field programme management, staffing, finances, marketing, strategic planning, fund raising, donor relations and new product development. He has represented IDE in a number of international settings. He is a founding member of the IDE (India) board, and has been selected to serve as the first Executive Director of IDE (India).

Amir Ullah Khan, currently at the Indian Development Foundation, studied at the Osmania University, Hyderabad and the Institute of Rural Management at Anand. For his PhD he has worked on Intellectual Property Issues in International Trade In 1993, he joined the Indian Civil Service after which he worked for five years with project LARGE of the UNDP. He taught Economics and Management at the School of Finance and Management and subsequently worked as Executive Director and Editor, Encyclopaedia Britannica India.

Ashutosh A.T. is an IAS officer of the 2002 batch and is currently serving as Assistant Collector in Jodhpur, Rajasthan. He has done his BA in Economics and holds a Management degree. He has previously served as a journalist with the Grand Forks Gazette, Canada. He writes on various developmental issues concerning rural India.

Bibek Debroy is Director, Rajiv Gandhi Institute for Contemporary Studies, Rajiv Gandhi Foundation, New Delhi. He is a professional economist and was educated in Presidency College (Calcutta), Delhi School of Economics and Trinity College (Cambridge). He has worked at Presidency College (Calcutta), Gokhale Institute of Politics and Economics (Pune), Indian Institute of Foreign Trade (Delhi), National Council of Applied Economic Research (Delhi) and as Consultant, Department of Economic Affairs, Ministry of Finance, Government of India. He was also the Director for a project known as LARGE, set up by the Ministry of Finance and UNDP to examine legal reforms. He has been a member of several government committees. He is the author and editor of several books, papers and popular articles and is also Consulting Editor with *Financial Express*. Bibek Debroy's special interests are international trade (in particular the WTO), law reform and the political economy of liberalization in India.

Naresh C. Saxena is currently advising several international donors on food security, poverty alleviation, natural resource management, good governance, and peoples' participation. He is a member of Royal Swedish Academy of Agriculture and Forestry, Stockholm, and of the ADB Institute Advisory Council, Tokyo. Earlier, he was awarded a senior Post-Doctorate Fellowship from the Rockefeller Foundation to do research at the University of Oxford (1989-92), which resulted in Ph.D on Agro-forestry in India. He has been a Visiting Fellow to the IDS, Sussex, and CIFOR, Indonesia. Dr. Saxena also worked for Government of India as Secretary, Planning Commission (1999-2002) Secretary, Rural Development (1997-99), and Director, LBS National Academy of Administration, Mussoorie (1993-96).

Nirvikar Singh is currently Director of the Business Management Economics Programme at the University of California, Santa Cruz, where he is Professor of Economics. He was a founding co-director of the Santa Cruz Center for International Economics (SCCIE), and served as coordinator (lead co-director) of SCCIE in 2001-03. He served as Chair of the Department of Economics from 1992 to 1995. He has held visiting research appointments at Stanford, Australian National University, and several institutions in India. He has served as an advisor for several high-tech start-ups. He received his PhD from the University of California, Berkeley, and his BSc and MSc from the London School of Economics, where he was awarded the Allyn Young Prize, Gonner Prize and Ely Devons Prize. His current research topics include information technology and development, governance and economic reform in India, federalism, electronic commerce, business strategy, and innovation. He has authored over 70 research papers on these and related topics in economics.

Qamar Iqbal Khan is a senior officer in the Department of Agriculture, Andhra Pradesh. He is a postgraduate in Agriculture with specialization in Soil & Water Management with a Ph.D in Remote Sensing Applications in Watershed Management. He has also obtained a PG Diploma in Remote Sensing for Agriculture & Soils from Indian Institute of Remote Sensing, Dehradun. He has vast experience in Soil Survey and Land Use Planning using Remote Sensing and GIS techniques.

Rajesh Chakrabarti, Assistant Professor of Finance at Georgia Tech's College of Management, is also the Chief Economist for the Kolkata-based microfinance research and training organization, Creditwatch and a scholar at the India Development Foundation, Gurgaon. Educated at Presidency College, Kolkata and IIM, Ahmedabad, Rajesh has a Ph.D. in Management from the University of California, Los Angeles. He has previously been with IFCI, New Delhi, taught at the University of Alberta, Canada and at IIM, Calcutta, and has been a visiting scholar at the Federal Reserve Bank of Atlanta. He publishes regularly in reputed academic journals and has co-authored *The Asian Manager's Handbook of E-Commerce.*

Riyazuddin Ahmed is a Principal Scientist in the Division of Soil Science and Agriculture Chemistry, ANGR Agricultural University, Rajendranagar, Andhra Pradesh. He has pursued his Masters and Doctorate degrees in Soil Science and Agricultural Chemistry. He is a co-author of the Extension

Bulletin, Soil Test Based Fertiliser Applications, published by ANGR Agricultural University. He is currently working on the conjunctive use of organic manure and inorganic fertilizers in appropriate dozes for various crops.

Saleema Razvi works for GE Capital at Gurgaon. After her schooling at La Martiniere in Calcutta, she studied at the Women's Christian College, Chennai, where she did her Masters in Nutrition and Dietetics. She then completed her M.Phil in Public Health and is currently a Research Scholar at the Centre for Social Medicine and Community Health, Jawaharlal Nehru University. She has worked with the National Council for Applied Economic Research and EPOS Health Consultants, both in Delhi. Her areas of interest include Health insurance, Public Health, Health Economics, Maternal and Child health, Consumer issues, and Food safety regulation.

Samrat Bose is a Masters in Economics from Jamia Millia Islamia. His research projects have included constructing indicators on national highways, analyzing effects of tariffs in the manufacturing sector and studying the impact of taxes on handlooms. At present, he is working on taxation modeling, food security and resource generation in agriculture.

Sanjiv J. Phansalkar was trained in management in the Indian Institute of Management Ahmedabad from which he first completed PGP in 1979 and then his Doctorate in 1989. He taught at the Institute of Rural Management, Anand. His publications include three books, several research papers and a number of cases, case studies and newspaper articles. Based in Nagpur, he works now as a consultant specializing in the issues connected with enhancement of rural livelihoods in the country.

Shabana Zahoor graduated from Aligarh Muslim University with Botany (Hons.). She obtained her Master's degree in Environmental Botany from Jamia Hamdard, New Delhi in 2003. She has with Gene Campaign, a Delhi-based non-governmental organization. Her areas of work in Gene Campaign were genetic engineering and genetically modified foods (GM Foods) and their implications. There she also contributed in preparing a resource guide for the Consumers International Asia Pacific Office under the Food and Nutrition Programme, 2002-2005.

Shagun Krishnan did her M.A. in Economics from Jamia Milia Islamia, Delhi. Prior to joining IDF in Bangalore, she was a senior researcher with Deepak Talwar Associates, Delhi, working in market research for various sectors. During this tenure she was involved in analysing the insurance, telecom and automobile sectors and was also involved in industry updates to the Indian arm of various global companies and company websites. She was with the Indian Council of Research on International Economic Relations (ICRIER), focusing primarily on trade and international relations. She has also taught economics at the graduate level. Her areas of interest are environment and health.

Shashwat Mody graduated from Hiram College, Ohio, USA with a Bachelor's of Arts Degree. His majors included Economics and Management with a minor in Mathematics. His research and academic interests include agricultural economics, developmental economics and financial markets. He was a visitor at IDF and worked on issues related to the SPS agreement of the WTO, the tax structure in India and the competitiveness of Indian agriculture.

Shubhashis Gangopadhyay did his Ph.D. in Economics from Cornell University, Ithaca, New York, USA. He joined the Delhi Centre of the Indian Statistical Institute as a lecturer in 1983. He became a full Professor in 1991. He took over as founder-director of IDF in July 2002. He has published widely in journals on development economics, international trade, industrial organization, regulatory economics and finance. He has also co-authored and co-edited a number of books in economics and finance. He is the Chief Editor of the Journal of Emerging Market Finance and is the President of two professional societies, the Society for Economic Research and Financial Analysis (SERFA) and the Society for the Promotion of Game Theory and its Applications (SPGTA). He has been on many government committees and consulted with various ministries and private business.

Sugata Ghosh is currently Head (Commissioning) at Macmillan India. He has previously worked at Esconet, Britannica India and the Financial Express. After his M Phil he was a Ford Foundation fellow at the University of Reading. Sugata's interests cover issues related to the health sector, the agriculture policy, and the industrial and political environment.

Sutirtha Bhattacharya is a senior IAS officer of the Andhra Pradesh cadre. He is a postgraduate in Physics and Operations Research from Presidency College, Kolkata. Apart from serving in district administration, he has served in the field of jute development. Currently he is the Commissioner for Agriculture, Government of Andhra Pradesh, working for the development of agriculture and sustainable land management through watershed development, soil health management, land reclamation etc.

Wilima Wadhwa did her Ph.D. in Economics from the University of California, Irvine (UCI), USA. She is the Executive Director of Society for Economic Research and Financial Analysis (SERFA) and teaches at UCI in their spring quarter. She has also taught at the Delhi Centre of the Indian Statistical Institute and Jawaharlal Nehru University. She is an applied econometrician working in the areas of macroeconomics, monetary economics, and development. She has consulted with various ministries and international organizations on macro-econometric and other studies on the Indian economy.

1

Integrating the Poor into Market Systems (IPMAS)

A Blueprint

AMITABHA SADANGI

"The future lies with those companies who see the poor as their customers"

— **Prof. C.K. Prahlad**

(While speaking to Indian CEOs, Jan 2000)

Background

Hunger persists because the poor are unable to obtain access to food at reasonable prices. 35 per cent of India's population lives on the equivalent of less than US$1 a day, and is too poor to be able to afford food and other necessities on a sustainable basis. The rural poor, especially women, are most affected by poverty. 75 per cent of people facing poverty live in rural areas. And three out of four poor people living in rural areas are dependent on agriculture. Also, the rural poor are the world's forgotten smallholder farmers. They have even been bypassed in most development assistance.

Smallholder poor farmers face many problems. Low soil fertility and lack of access to quality inputs along with salinated and waterlogged soils contribute to low yield, production risks and natural resource degradation. Inadequate infrastructure, land tenure biased against the poor, under developed markets, and lack of access to credit and technical assistance add impediments. Low agricultural productivity results in high unit costs of food, poverty, food insecurity, poor nutrition, and low farm incomes. Given the rural centre of gravity of poverty, broad-based agricultural and rural development is essential for reducing poverty and assuring food security.

Even those people in rural areas who are neither farmers nor farm workers work in jobs closely related to agriculture, hence the following conclusions. "A 1 per cent increase in agriculture GDP per capita led to a 1.6 per cent gain in the per capita incomes of the lowest income quintile of the population in 35 countries" (Timmer, 1997). "A 10 per cent increase in crop yield leads to a reduction between 6 per cent and 10 per cent of people living on less than $1 a day" (Irz, *et al*, 2001). "The average real income of small farmers in southern India rose by 90 per cent and that of landless labourers by 125 per cent between 1973 and 1994, as a result of the green revolution" (World Bank, 2001).

The poor self-employed producers of tradable agricultural commodities are constrained on account of limited access to land and capital and relatively low farm incomes. Therefore, there is a need to optimize productivity with the limited resources at hand. There is considerable potential for the landless to benefit directly (from increased labour demand when poor farmers produce more) and indirectly (through increased demand for services). The challenge is to improve the access of poor farmers to the skills, capital and market institutions.

Markets play an important role in pro-poor livelihood development and poverty reduction. This premise follows from four different observations. Firstly, livelihoods of most poor people are directly dependent on their involvement in a range of markets. Secondly, poverty reduction processes have historically depended on equitable private sector economic growth. Thirdly, the poor themselves identify problems they encounter because of the absence of, or the underdevelopment of, markets as factors that critically affect their livelihoods. And fourthly, markets provide a highly efficient mechanism for exchange, coordination and allocation of many resources, goods and services, *but they are prone to failure*. Recognition of failures and their harmful effects on the poor is central to any discussion on markets. It is often very convenient and facile to blame failures on marketisation. What is required is an understanding of the importance of institutional development, with markets being only one part of an enabling system that regulates, guards against risk and provides information to all players.

For more than 12 years, IDEI has successfully pursued its mission to reduce hunger and poverty through promotion of affordable irrigation technology leading to additional wealth for the rural poor. Our products are used by the rural poor to boost agricultural productivity and overall food production and to better manage the water resources that support production. The rationale for IDEI's task, still valid and compelling in 2004, is simple: most poor people live in rural areas where the daily struggle for survival depends largely on productive farming and wise stewardship of land, labour and water.

The imperative to fight poverty through higher agricultural production has been a constant preoccupation of development agencies for many years. Yet, the global context in which solutions must be planned and applied to local or regional realities is rapidly changing. At this juncture, IDEI's perspective plan takes into account emerging trends, explores the potential for wealth creation for the rural poor, and envisions a future of sustainable rural livelihoods. In support of this vision, the IPMAS approach outlines new directions and organizational arrangements, including partnerships needed and the regional and national scope of future work.

Table 1

How Growth Helps in Reducing Rural Poverty

Activity	*Gains*
Farm activities	Direct gains if high labour content required by poor producers. Large upstream/downstream linkages have high labour content
	Indirect gains if high labour content by the non-poor. The poor benefit from expenditure linkages
Non-farm activities	Apart from mining, other activities and migrant labour/ remittances. Unlikely without good communication infrastructure and strong urban or export markets, features generally absent from poorer rural areas.

International Development Enterprises (India) is a not-for-profit company which has demonstrated its commitment to identifying, developing and disseminating affordable technologies to the rural poor. IDEI believes that access to markets and related agro-inputs are crucial in fighting poverty. Over the years, IDEI has worked towards reducing poverty in India by helping the rural poor increase their agricultural productivity and income. IDEI has applied business practices and principles in facilitating markets where the rural poor can participate effectively as micro-entrepreneurs. IDEI has helped empower more than 450,000 rural poor and enabled them to progress from subsistence agriculture to small-scale commercial farming, thus beginning an upward spiral out of poverty.

IDEI does not conform to the myths that state: Poor people are helpless; the poor cannot co-operate, cannot plan ahead, cannot decide for themselves, and cannot help themselves and that massive state sponsored projects constitute the best form of economic development. IDEI believes in increasing the access of the poor to productive assets as customers, not as beneficiaries, ensuring a return on productive assets to make surplus income a reality and relying on the poor farmer to use her own initiative and enterprise to increase his income further and fulfill her own aspirations. IDEI's mission is "To improve equitably the social, economic and environmental conditions of families in need with special emphasis on the rural poor, by identifying developing and marketing affordable, appropriate and environmentally sustainable solutions through market forces".

Poverty in India

It is estimated that one-third of the world's poor live in India, and there are more poor people in India alone than the whole of Sub-Saharan Africa. Of the poor in India, three-quarters are dependent on agriculture as a livelihood. The policy approach to agriculture, particularly in the 1990s, has been to secure increased production through subsidies on inputs such as power, water and fertilizer, and by increasing the minimum support price rather than through building new capital assets in irrigation, power and rural infrastructure. This has shifted the production base from low-cost regions to high-cost regions, causing an increase in the cost of production, regional imbalance, and increasing the burden of storage and transport of food grains.

The equity, efficiency and sustainability of the current approach are questionable. The subsidies do not improve income distribution or the demand for labour. The boost in output from subsidy-stimulated use of fertilizer, pesticides and water has the potential to damage aquifers and soils – an environmentally unsustainable approach that may partly explain the rising costs and slowing growth and productivity in agriculture, notably in Punjab and Haryana. Instead of promoting low cost options that have a higher capital-output ratio; present policies have resulted in excessive use of capital on the farms, such as too many tube wells in water scarce regions. The situation is however changing and is clearly reflected in the Union Budget, *Economic Survey* etc. of the current financial year:

"But neither in agriculture, nor in industry, shall we be able to attain our objective, if infrastructure, both physical and social, is not rapidly and efficiently developed. For this, private and public interest must combine so as to generate maximum social welfare. ..... We have to recognize the need to address a reduction of not just our social but economic inequalities, too. .... This is a collective need, for the nation's growth, which all of us have to address together." (Extract from Budget Speech 2003-2004, of the Minister of Finance, GoI)

"Liberalization of world trade in agriculture has provided new opportunities to the farm sector to access markets for agricultural commodities world-wide. However, to make this happen, reforms have to be brought about in agriculture sector to remove all barriers, whether legal or policy induced, which introduce inefficiencies and monopoly rents in the functioning of agricultural markets. At present, though agricultural production is largely free from controls, the same is not true for marketing of agricultural commodities. Under the APMC Act, State Governments alone are empowered to initiate the process of setting up markets for agri-products within a defined area. As a result, private and cooperative sectors cannot take initiative in setting up markets equipped with more modern facilities....... Government's role should be that of a facilitator rather than that of exercising control over management of markets." (Extract from Budget Speech 2003-2004, of the Minister of Finance, GoI)

"Encouraged by the success of the scheme of funding rural roads under the *Pradhan Mantri Gram Sadak Yojana* (Prime Ministers' Village Road Scheme) by earmarking 50 per cent of the cess on diesel, it is proposed that the resources for rural roads be augmented. Accordingly, apart from allocating the anticipated Rs. 2,325 crore from the existing cess on diesel for 2003-04, additional funds will be made available for rural roads from the proposed additional cess on diesel of 50 paise."

"Agriculture, the life-blood of our economy, after giving the country adequate food security, is now again at cross roads, as it prepares to diversify and move up the value chain. It also needs to respond robustly to second generation issues such as land degradation and water logging. Diversification, resonance with market-forces, and a swift adoption of sunrise technologies are the other needs." (Extract from Budget Speech 2003-2004, of the Minister of Finance, GoI)

"The recent drought again brings into sharp focus the need for conserving our water resources. A number of initiatives have already been taken to conserve land and water resources. States are also encouraged to promote drip and sprinkler irrigation through supply of equipment at subsidized rates. But these efforts have to be intensified. Therefore, a bipartisan task force, headed by the Chief Minister of Andhra Pradesh, and with a Minister of Agriculture from another State, as one of the members, will be constituted to recommend measures needed to be adopted firstly, to expand the coverage of such irrigation, thereafter to also suggest safeguards so that the intended benefits actually reach the target." (Extract from Budget Speech 2003-2004, of the Minister of Finance, GoI)

The terms of reference for the taskforce on micro irrigation is as follows:

1. To suggest strategies to expand coverage of area under micro irrigation in the country.
2. To suggest institutional mechanism needed for promoting micro irrigation including quality assurance, regionally differentiated technologies and interventions.
3. To suggest technological support for regions and crop specific interventions on micro irrigation.
4. To suggest measures so that the intended benefits reach the target group.

"Till the year 1999-2000, the Government of India (GoI) provided assistance for drip installation for horticultural crops @ 90 per cent of the cost of the system or Rs. 25,000 per ha, whichever is less for Small & Marginal, SC/ST and Women farmers and 70 per cent of the total cost or Rs. 25,000 per ha, whichever is less for other category of farmers. Assistance was also provided for drip demonstration @ of Rs. 22,500 or 75 per cent of the system cost per hectare whichever is less. ....Thereafter, with effect from 2002-03 during the Tenth Plan, the assistance has been reduced to 25 per cent of the cost of the system to all category of farmers."

IDEI and its impact

The basic idea around which IDEI's efforts were focussed was that if water related constraints were to be removed, agricultural production and incomes will increase. Experience has shown that this assumption was correct, but not totally conclusive. To date about 450,000 small holders have adopted micro-irrigation systems and are earning, on an average, INR 6,000 in additional net income each year (which is 33 per cent to 50 per cent of their annual income prior to adopting these technologies). About 20 per cent of the IDEI technology users, however, earn over 30,000 INR per year, which begs the question: why the great disparity between the average and high earners? Studies show that the high-earning families are those who are self-sufficient in their staple food crops and also have been able to overcome the barriers, i.e. the *market constraints* after the *water constraints*. They have been able to enhance their market participation by purchasing right inputs, making effective use of technical knowledge and market information, and developing stable linkages to output markets.

From the experience of IDEI programme in Sangola, in Solapur District of Maharashtra, it is quite evident that with horticulture, it is possible to lift the poor above the poverty line. Under the World Bank definition, the poverty line is at about Rs. 30,000. However, the average actual net income from cultivating pomegranate (4,000 Sq. meters) in Sangola was Rs. 43,000. It is therefore quite evident that this poverty reduction objective of IPMAS (Rs. 30,000) is possible to achieve. Based on the Sangola experience, the following aspects need to be included in the implementation strategy of the other IDEI projects:

Lead the Coalition: It is amply clear that the success of Sangola is a result of multiple agencies, since it is nearly impossible for a single agency to achieve such a degree of success in such a short period of time and on such a significant scale. To achieve such a result, IDEI must play a lead role in identifying the agencies that could join together for a common objective: "poverty reduction", each contributing as per their core competency. The key to success lies in identifying such a coalition of agencies and making them work together.

Aim at the Goal Level Impact: Sangola has proved that if one aims at the goal level impact (creating wealth for the poor), the purpose level impacts (no. of poor who enhanced their market participation) will automatically be achieved. This requires a paradigm shift in thinking, as it also implies that many a times if one aims at the purpose level indicators (number of poor who enhanced their market participation), it may not be possible to achieve the goal level impact (creating wealth for the poor).

Aim for the sky: The Sangola experience also showed that it was aiming at a very high level of impact at the poor farmer level of about Rs. 1,00,000 per family per year through irrigated pomegranate and probably because of this it could very easily achieve Rs. 43,000, which is more than 25 per cent higher than the poverty line. Hence for impact, it is advisable to set a very high standard.

Do a proper comparison: Internally, IDEI team was comparing horticulture (the new intervention) with agriculture. But the farmers were comparing this with their wage labour. They accepted it because irrigated pomegranate gave them significantly more income than wage labour, which they had to forgo to take up horticulture.

Manage the gestation period: Horticulture in general is probably the most profitable agricultural activity, but it requires a gestation period. In the first year of plantation, the farmers had to dig a well. Many farmers used this water to grow crops like cotton, sugarcane to get over the gestation period, while many resorted to wage labour. Hence in horticulture, this plan is extremely important, otherwise farmers will not take it up, no matter how profitable it may be in the long run.

Manage high initial investment: Horticulture also requires high initial investment. In case of pomegranate, the investment required was Rs. 20,000 to Rs. 40,000, which was 3-4 times higher than the annual income of the farmers. But they managed this investment in several ways (i.e. excessive wage labour, sale of other assets, credit from NGOs, clubbing investments etc.). Hence, it is also important to have a proper plan to meet such high initial investments.

Prioritize most profitable crop: As horticulture requires high initial investment, it is extremely important to identify region specific profitable crops. This will require a thorough technology search and market research. All this means that the final crop should be selected on the basis of sub-sector analysis.

Facilitators and Providers: The entire programme will require specific agencies to play the role of facilitators (Government, NGOs, Agri-universities, Research centers etc.) to kick start the process and agencies to play the role of direct service providers (dealers, fruit merchants, manufacturers, agents etc.). It is also important to make sure that these agencies don't get into each other's roles (i.e. NGO not to be used as dealers). The aim is to ensure that the role of facilitators is for a specific period or for a specific task and the role of providers is to remain for a long term on profit basis. Profits also must be worked out well for attractive margins for the service providers.

A Clear Implementation and Business Plan: One of the successes of Sangola was the way the field team had developed the implementation plan, internalized it and following it up. A well made plan and proper implementation are absolute prerequisites for success in other locations.

Liberating Market Forces

Feasible solutions for overcoming the marketing constraints should be sought primarily through involvement of the private sector as well as through central and local governments and other structures within the civil society (*Gram Panchayats*, Community Based Organizations, and NGOs). IPMAS advocates an indirect approach to reducing constraints by highlighting the underlying causes of market imperfections and failure and suggests appropriate partners, their entry points, expected actions or outputs. An initial investment in enabling market institutions is required to remove constraints that smallholders face. This donor led initiative would ensure the integration of the small holder into pro-poor markets.

IPMAS defines institutions as 'rules of the game', that put into place the incentives and sanctions affecting people's behaviour. Key concepts relevant to this argument are the distinctions between the institutional environment and institutional (or contractual) arrangements; the interaction of these with property rights, information flows, transaction costs, transaction risks, market access failures affecting different market participants and processes whereby institutions evolve. Less developed economies are characterised by high transaction costs and risks, weak information flows, and weak institutional environments. Market participants with little bargaining power and low financial and social capital bear high costs of information and experience problems in the enforcement of property rights. This inhibits access to markets and reduces the pace of market development, which in turn inhibits economic and technological development. Low levels of economic activity lead to thin markets, high transaction costs, and high unit costs of infrastructural development. The result is a 'low level equilibrium trap'. We are faced with critical questions about (a) the processes by which institutional, technological, social and economic development can proceed and (b) the roles of different stakeholders in promoting such a development, particularly that which involves and benefits the poor.

One important approach to follow in addressing this question is to consider the political economy processes of institutional change. Institutional change is explained in terms of responses of powerful groups to changes in relative prices, technologies and transaction costs. These groups respond by modifying institutions in ways that serve their interests. It is quite possible that in different regions the same set of changes in relative prices and in transactions technology could stimulate radically different types of institutional change. Much depends upon (a) the perception by different groups of the possible opportunities and threats posed to their interests by alternative paths of institutional change or stagnation, and (b) their political effectiveness (locally, nationally and internationally) in influencing the paths and pace of institutional change.

In broad terms, institutional change can take an "anti-development" form (structuring transactions to create rents), or a "pro-development" (structuring transactions to reduce costs, thereby providing incentives for more trade and investment). There is a strong "path dependency" in these processes of institutional change, as development history plays an important role in determining both the relative perceptions and power of different groups on the one hand, and the institutional and technological options that they face on the other.

Why IPMAS? Problems & Justification

The benefits of people-centered change to livelihood thinking and approaches are widely recognised. However, in much of the conceptualization and application of 'livelihood approaches', there is an acute lack of emphasis on "*markets*". Failure to address the roles played by markets and market relationships leads to an inability to identify and act on (a) livelihood opportunities and constraints and (b) institutional issues that are important for pro-poor market development.

IDEI believes that poverty reduction must be addressed directly as a separate issue, distinct from economic growth. Poverty-reduction strategies must be aimed at increasing the ability of rural poor to generate wealth. The driving force for wealth creation is to spot new market opportunities. For rural livelihoods to be truly sustainable, it is not enough for rural poor to work as wage labourers or produce only for home consumption. They must also earn cash to pay for life's other necessities, like health and education. Selling a part of their harvest is a key livelihood strategy.

With rapid urbanization, domestic markets for agricultural products are growing. The rural poor need to gain access to markets other than traditional rural markets and thus respond to demand from cities as well. In this expanding economic arena, rural poor compete against large, well-capitalized agribusinesses. And with the emergence of freer international trade, both through regional trading blocs and globally through the WTO, the pressure of competition has increased. Many of these issues are easily overlooked in livelihood approaches that focus on the more immediate situations, opportunities and constraints facing rural poor. Such analysis can easily overlook the dynamic opportunities and constraints posed by wider market interactions.

Intensification, diversification, and value addition are mutually reinforcing tactics that make rural poor more competitive. Intensification boosts the productivity of land, labour, and other limiting factors through higher yields, better on-farm nutrient cycling, and more effective pest control. It does not necessarily imply heavier reliance on off-farm inputs, like purchased agrochemicals, since proven management methods are available to exploit on-farm renewable resources more efficiently.

Diversification helps rural poor manage risk. Options include cultivating different varieties of the same crop species, introducing higher value species to their existing mix of staple crops, and integrating livestock with crop production. Diversity is essential at different scales: from the level of the farm field (crops and animals), to household level (different productive activities), to the landscape level (diversity in land use). The risks involved in sustainable remunerative agricultural crop production (greater market exposure, higher input costs) suggest that intervention strategies leading to market participation must be accompanied by strategies that ensure adequate staple foods production.

The basis of value creation in the agriculture sector can be reduced to three primary resources: people, land, and water. People make use of land and water to create value that is then exchanged through markets. Pro-poor market development is a mechanism by which the relationships between people, land, and water can be enabled so that the rural poor participate more effectively in these transactions.

In many areas in India, land and water resources are under increased stress due to population pressure. As rural economies move from subsistence farming to commercial agriculture, the situation gets exacerbated, especially where large numbers of rural poor are involved. The sustainability of pro-poor market systems depends on minimizing or mitigating harmful impacts and encouraging proactive stewardship of land and water resources. Market development can have a beneficial environmental impact, if a portion of the income generated by rural poor is invested in the protection and maintenance of the limited resources available to them.

Creation of Pro-Poor Markets

IDEI has been promoting micro irrigation technologies (both lifting and application devices) for the last 12 years and has developed village market places to make these technologies available to rural poor. IDEI has also learnt that while these technologies have benefited the rural poor significantly, many are yet unable to enhance their participation in markets resulting in lower returns. The IPMAS approach for poverty reduction will allow the rural poor to not only overcome the water constraint, but enhance their market participation also.

Pro-poor Markets - The Nexus of People, Land and Water

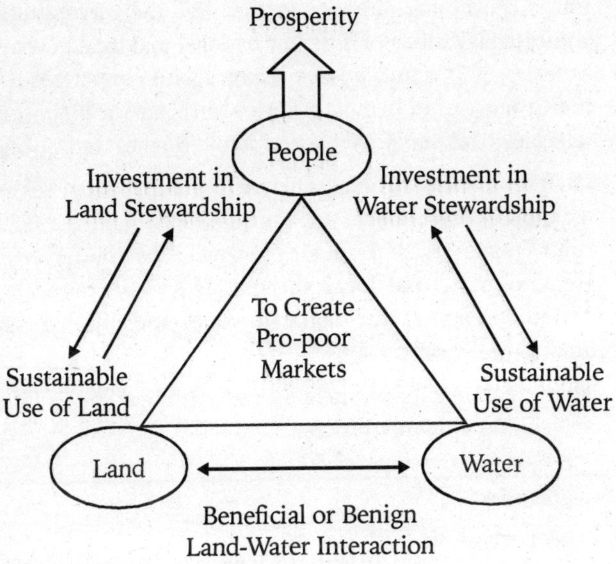

This framework focuses on market opportunities as the driving force in poverty reduction. Publicly funded initiatives are required to remove basic market constraints, thus enabling smallholders to participate in markets both as consumers of inputs, and as suppliers of remunerative agricultural products. The wealth creation through market participation will allow rural poor to access food, education, health, housing, water, etc., and thus escape "poverty".

A set of steps necessary for developing a programme to address marketing constraints and opportunities facing the rural poor are:

- Identify markets that are important for the rural poor.
- Understand the potential for improvement.
- Identify critical opportunities and constraints.
- Assess how these may be addressed, and identify the stakeholders involved.
- Relate opportunities and constraints to stakeholders' resources, objectives and existing activities.
- Prioritize issues for action and identify sources of further information. Consult stakeholders.

This process should take note of

- Issues concerning different sectors, and the varying interests and responsibilities of different national and local government agencies, NGOs and private sector agents. Important sectors identified, in addition to agriculture, are transportation, telecom, banking, governance, public finance and policy.
- Different roles of external parties (advocacy, technical assistance, investment, and coordination), and the different roles, resources and constraints faced by the government (federal, state and local authorities and *parastatals*), civil society, private sector, donor agencies and different groups among the rural poor.
- The importance of partnership and participation by different stakeholders in this process.

Rural Poor – Stratified	*Markets with Direct Impacts*
Poor agricultural producers	*Crop sales* Crop purchases *Agricultural inputs & technologies* Water Land *Seasonal finance and savings*
Poor agricultural processors	*Crop sales* Crop purchases *Processing inputs & equipment* Financial services
Agricultural labourers	Labour Food purchases Financial services
Rural artisans	Labour Food purchases *Financial services*
Petty trade, services, etc.	Local goods & services Production inputs (raw foods, processing equipment, etc) *Crop purchases* Micro-finance/financial services
Migrant labour & remittances	*Migrant labour markets* *Money transfer, & other financial services*

Note: Italics indicate missing markets and markets where the poor lack access.

The Importance of Markets

A primary cause for persistent poverty is limited interaction with markets by the rural poor. They cannot afford to purchase required inputs for their small plots or invest in production technologies, resulting in production that does not rise above subsistence levels. Trapped in a subsistence economy, a majority of rural poor do not have an opportunity to improve their livelihoods. IDEI's thesis is poverty can be addressed on a large scale by helping rural poor overcome the barriers that keep them from participation in "markets". Markets develop gradually. The challenge is to allow the evolution of pro-poor *markets* that enable the poor to be members of both input and output markets, and to derive significant additional income from their micro-entrepreneurship. It is precisely this enabling that IDEI seeks to promote and facilitate.

The Rural Poor as Participants in Markets

IDEI estimates that people earning below INR 18,000 per annum (at current price) would constitute the poorest, though official poverty lines are drawn from anywhere between INR 18,000 to 24,000 – varying from state to state. Even within this category, it would be easier to work with people who are just below the figure of 18,000, i.e. whose annual incomes would be in the range of 16,000 to 18,000 at the peril of ignoring the poorest of the poor. IDEI recognizes the fact that even within the poorest in rural India, there could be various categories of people who may not be differentiated by income only, but by other factors like poor access to resources, locational and geographical disadvantages and other market related factors.

A net additional income of at least Rs. 10,000 per participant per year (at current prices) is sufficient to allow a poor household to gradually pull itself out of poverty. At the same time, an increase of just Rs. 5,000 for people earning Rs. 10,000 would dramatically change their lives. To reach this income level, rural poor must increasingly concentrate on sustainable remunerative crops, which generate higher returns to both land and labour. The risks involved in sustainable remunerative agricultural crop production (greater market exposure, higher input costs) suggest that intervention strategies leading to market participation must be accompanied by strategies that ensure adequate staple crops production.

In doing the above, Pro-poor market development should also recognize and provide a framework which would help (a) reduce vulnerability to shocks and stresses (b) to invest in assets to improve future livelihoods (c) reduce uncertainty which will help lower the threshold for risk-taking. Risk may be in the following forms:

Supply Risk – affects the ability to participate in the market as a seller of produce or services, e.g. climatic fluctuations.

Market Risk – may result from ineffective institutions or weak or absence of linked markets, e.g. insurance market.

Price Risk – arises from paucity of information and also from lack of assurance for receiving the price that is stated as the market price at a particular time and location.

IDEI expects that markets (local, national, regional, and global) will be able to absorb the additional production of millions of rural poor, because of a) expanding markets due to increasing population and incomes; b) increasing rural poor market share based on their comparative advantage and c) technology development.

IPMAS Strategy

In order to create the conditions necessary for large numbers of rural poor to work their way out of poverty, IDEI is moving beyond the development of technology and supply chains and adopting "market" as an institution approach to rural economic development and thereby poverty reduction. The IPMAS programme proposed by IDEI aims at strengthening the participation of rural poor in to markets, both as buyers of their choice and sellers by strengthening their bargaining power.

An important concept in the IPMAS Programme is the idea of a 'marketshed' that has been referred to in several places in the project document. The concept of a marketshed is based on an analogy with the concept of a watershed in hydrology. A marketshed is a unit encompassing the population that interacts with markets. Just as streams join together to make rivers that eventually flow to the ocean, so local markets are connected to regional, national, and global markets. However, unlike water in a watershed, economic activity in a marketshed flows in both directions; goods, services, information, and credit flow from markets to the surrounding population, and surplus production is sold by the population to the markets. For the purpose of IPMAS Programme geographical extent of the field programmes are delineated by *marketsheds*. IDEI, will do this by working in specific districts (marketsheds) within states, concentrating on marketsheds with a) the highest potential for our micro irrigation (lifting, storage and application devices) products and b) large number of rural poor living below US$1 day.

IPMAS programme purpose is to develop an intervention for creating micro-irrigation-driven market systems for rural poor. The resulting intervention will be applicable to diverse settings and will provide guidelines for the creation of replicating markets within a period of not more than six years in a given marketshed. A sustainable market is defined as one that continues to engage new and existing rural poor in market activities, by providing affordable and expanding markets for increasing agricultural output with external subsidies that do not surpass those granted to the medium and large-scale farming sector in the same market environment.

During this phase, field-based pilot programmes will be implemented in 50 to 150 marketsheds (depending on the size of the marketsheds, the number of marketsheds can increase to 150 or the current marketsheds can be expanded to cover more number of villages and thereby more number of rural poor), a concept unique to the IPMAS programme. By the end of the project period, IDEI expects that 120-150,000 rural poor households will be integrated into marketsheds. Those rural poor who have participated in the process for the whole project will have reached an average extra net income of approximately Rs. 2,500 to 10,000 per year (depending on their base income of participation). These marketsheds are designed to be fully self-sufficient after six years, and in fact to have the capacity to grow larger or expand to incorporate an ever-increasing number of rural poor.

The IPMAS Approach for Pro-poor Market Development

The IPMAS approach envisions the rural poor as a potential micro-entrepreneur who transforms natural resources (land and water), human resources (labour and know-how), and purchased inputs into high-value agricultural products that can be marketed at economically rewarding prices. The rural poor is seen as a rational, capable, and proactive member of an integrated system of private-sector

The IPMAS Approach for Pro-poor Market Development

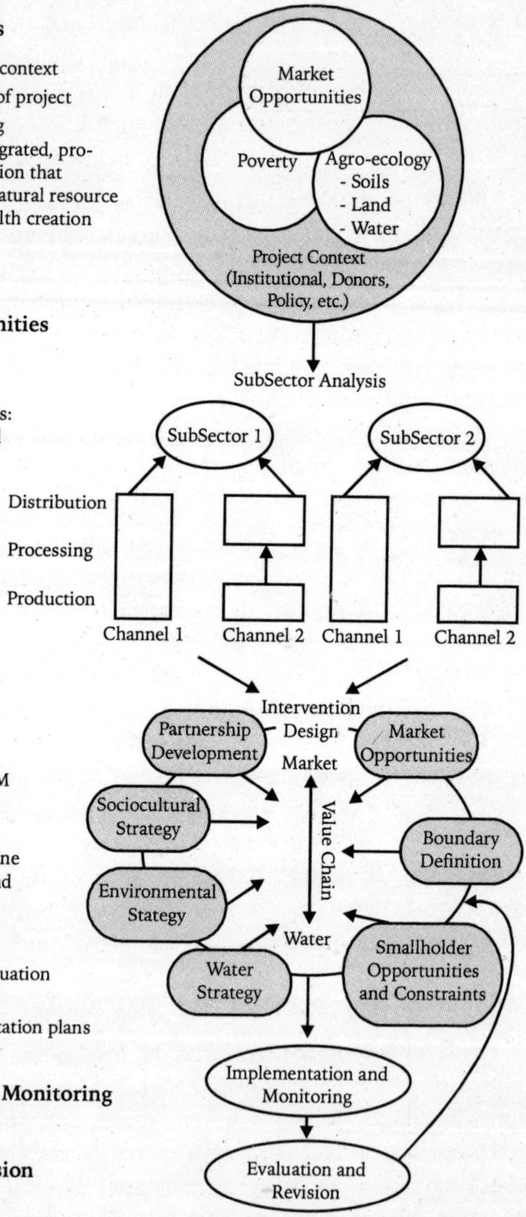

Situational Analysis

a. Macro-assessment of context

b. Strategic orientation of project

c. Identify 2-3 promising opportunities for integrated, pro-active poverty alleviation that ensures sustainable natural resource management and wealth creation

Assessment of 2-3 Promising Opportunities

a. Identify and involve potential partners

b. Collect data and assess:
- Key constraints and opportunities
- Sociocultural
- Sustainability of natural resources
- Potential partners

c. Select opportunity

Intervention Design

a. Design intervention:
- Vertical integration of value chain
- Integration of PRISM strategies

b. Implementation plan
- Activities and timeline
- Baseline measure and anticipated impact
- Financial, costs and benefits
- Monitoring and evaluation
- Reporting

c. Consolidate implementation plans

Implementation and Monitoring

Evaluation and Revision

enterprises—including suppliers, smallholders, and output handlers—that coordinate themselves to fulfill specific market demands.

The process that IDEI has developed for facilitating such Pro-poor markets can be summarized in seven tasks as represented in the following diagram. The first five tasks are performed in a non-linear fashion with some or all of the tasks being performed simultaneously and/or iteratively. Among these five tasks, the starting point and sequence of execution are not fixed, but will vary, depending on the level of prior knowledge, the existence of pre-selected partners, and to large extent donor priorities (IDEI is a donor dependent organization, and the notion of its' sustainability comes from the fact that IDEI is a force multiplier).

Integrating Poor into Market Systems (IPMAS) Approach

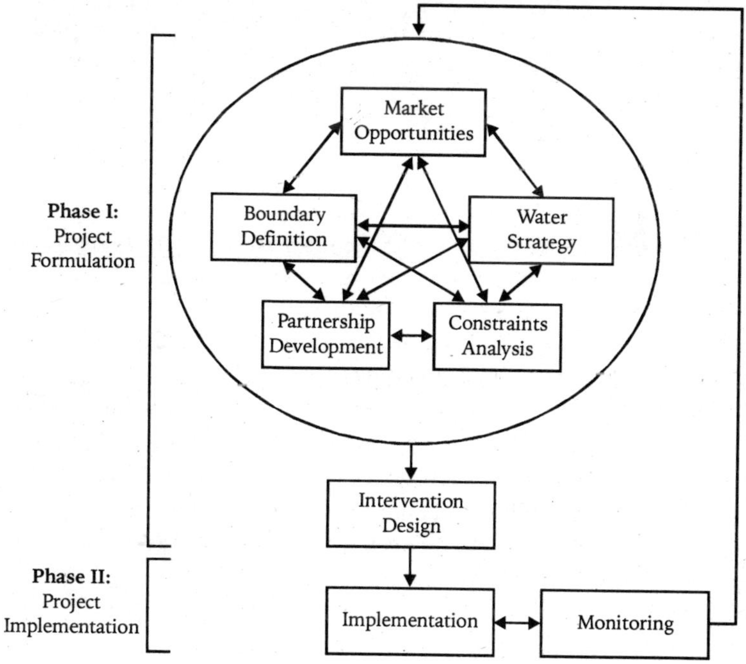

Boundary Definition

A single area may comprise anywhere from several thousand to several hundred thousand rural poor households that share a degree of uniformity in hydrology, agro-ecology, socio-cultural characteristics, and potential market opportunities. Boundary definition is an iterative process, starting with the selection of a broad region and progressively focusing in as more is learned about local needs, opportunities, and constraints. It is also likely to be influenced by donor priorities and the availability of suitable partners and support services.

Market Opportunities

Identify three to six market opportunities that have potential to provide significant income for rural poor. Ideal opportunities will have large and growing demand, high income potential, low start-up costs, rapid turnaround on investment, and will make use of the rural poors' existing agricultural asset base and family labour advantage. The search for market opportunities focuses on high-value crops for which the smallholder has or can develop a comparative advantage. Opportunities in staple crops, livestock, aquaculture, etc., may also be appropriate in some cases.

Water Strategy

Identify a water strategy that will enable rural poor to ensure access to and control over water for crop irrigation. Water is usually the most critical limiting factor for rural poor production, as it affects directly the intrinsic fertility of their land and the impact of any fertilizer applied to it. Emphasis is placed on low-cost, household-level, affordable-irrigation systems for accessing, storing, and controlling irrigation water. Such systems are consistent with the ideal of maximizing water-use efficiency, minimizing social transaction costs for the users, and targeting benefits to the poor. In developing the water strategy, it will be important to consider the influence of water policy, customary water-use arrangements, power relations (including gender issues), potential water-use conflicts, and potential environmental impacts. Naturally, given India's heterogeneity, the model used will vary from region to region.

Constraints Analysis

Identify constraints that hinder rural poors' ability to take advantage of the market opportunities identified above.

The following grouping has been done for the marketing constraints identified above into a set of principal causes of market imperfection and failure as follows:

Physical access is of considerable importance, and poor roads and other infrastructure raise marketing costs of transport inputs and products, increase post-harvest losses, and create a rationale for high margins.

Information (like many of the issues raised) is a complex issue both in respect of its kind, collection and delivery. It is here above all that the interests of the private sector firms to extend operations into rural areas can help to overcome informational imperfections and increase the competitiveness of the trading system.

External agencies may have an important role in supporting this, as both technology and institutional innovations (such as private/public partnerships and community participation) are needed. Current commercial environment and the rate of technological change offer both opportunities and threats for poverty reduction.

There was evidence of the micro, medium and small business sector suffering from over-regulation that imposes high costs on entrepreneurship and prevents starts-ups and business growth. This element of the regulatory framework needs to be studied, leading, if necessary to deregulation or re-regulation in a more business-friendly way.

IPMAS perceives three ways in which the market organization is weak:

- Competition within and linkages to the wider economy (for example the non-competitive practices of trader associations);
- Provision of utilities which are normally considered to be 'public goods'
- Provision of local marketsheds, infrastructure, which is normally considered to be a 'public good', and trading space.

Some of the competitive issues could be addressed by improved business skills, by promoting alternative (and competing) market channels, and by reducing over-regulation. Other ways to mitigate the inevitable inequities in market power included the development and implementation of customary (traditional) and modern contract law. Contracts may serve to enhance business attitudes and ethics, and reduce transaction costs. Public market information systems could also have a limited but real function in improving competitiveness. This is a difficult area that needs more attention.

Questions also arise in the provision of 'public good' utilities of power and water that make small-scale agro-industry possible, and that creates a healthy and congenial trading environment, particularly in traditional market places. These need to be tackled initially in government. Privatization policies may lead to the introduction of private sector involvement and coordination is needed between donors and government approaches to removing these constraints.

Finally, the need for physical infrastructure in market places needed to be tackled at local government level, together with the participation of civil organizations such as *Gram Panchayats*, CBOs and trader organizations. The collection of local market fees suggested the potential for government resources to be invested in appropriate infrastructure. Local governments should be in a position to ensure that spatial planning and land use takes account of the need for small-scale industrial development and environmental concerns.

Finance is always a constraint to input and output marketing activities, and financial assets of the poorest are the most difficult to address. Facilitating finance to intermediary agencies – private firms, CBOs, traders and associations - is an important strategy in its own right to increase scale and scope of business enterprise, and upgrade technology. Facilitating finance to intermediary agencies also can improve the delivery of inputs to farmers and introduce liquidity into output marketing. Moreover, delivery of credit can be linked to savings, the other important element in rural finance. There is currently no workable sustainable mechanism for the direct delivery of seasonal finance to rural poor. However, finance can sometimes be delivered successfully to rural poor – at a cost – through intermediate agencies such as traders, and there is scope for imaginative institutional innovations here.

Business Skills: Because rural poor often have to await buyers' visits, because of lower levels of educational attainment, and possibly because of intimidation at market places, entrepreneurial skills are expected to be relatively undeveloped among many poor households. IPMAS did not envisage direct interventions to bring about better grading and standardization of products, but more emphasis on consumer satisfaction, quality control and safety of food products. This could be encouraged by better coordination of efforts to channel expertise in business skills through universities, technical institutes, NGOs and school curricula. Developing appropriate teaching materials and delivering them through various channels is not a complex task, and could lead to long term improvements in trading and serve somewhat to redress the imbalance in economic power between rural poor and trader.

Macro-economic and Trade Conditions: It had been noted that private sector activity and in particular food crop production (and marketing) were inhibited by the unpredictable macro-economic and policy environment. A major task facing the government is to promote transparent, accountable and consistent policy making processes that support rather than inhibit more equitable private sector investment in productive and trading activities.

A thorough analysis of constraints at each market level and in each constraint category will normally result in a long and daunting list of market constraints, some of which can be addressed by the IPMAS project and some which will fall outside the scope of the project. In order to limit and focus the potential areas of intervention, constraints are prioritized to identify the "key logs in the logjam" that can unleash growth potential for large numbers of rural poor. Such leverage points may be found by identifying nodes in the value chain where a small number of firms act as intermediaries for large numbers of rural poor, or by taking advantage of geographic clustering of similar enterprises or production systems, or by identifying policy levers that will remove constraints for many market actors at once. Constraints are ranked and prioritized based on the potential impact on rural poor households' income and the number of rural poor people affected.

IDEI's experience in the past has been that rural poor people have successfully understood the constraints that they face and built up strategies to move into higher income brackets on a sustainable basis. At the same time, this information is either unknown or not understood properly or very often thought that it cannot be implemented by other people. If organizations like IDEI are to act as agents of change in the development process, they have to be knowledge based organizations driven by a passion for acquiring, assimilating, contextualizing and disseminating this knowledge across its larger focus group.

Leaving aside formal agriculture extension systems as implemented by the government or Universities or tried out on a pilot basis by civil society organizations or on a commercial basis by private sector organizations, there exists a yawning gap when it comes to transfer of information between people in the same village or adjoining villages. It is this gap which needs to be filled during the implementation of IPMAS.

IDEI also recognizes that in countries that suffer from a high level of illiteracy, diffidence towards modern technology, huge gaps in information availability and a large digital divide, the challenge of disseminating knowledge becomes even more formidable. Gathering these learnings and dissemination of them would need to use some of the promotional strategies that IDEI has fine tuned in the past as well as use traditional forms of village level information transfer which is part of their culture.

Partnership

Identify and develop partnerships with organizations that can contribute complementary expertise or provide necessary services to the development of marketsheds. It is clear *a priori* that IDEI will not be able to perform all the functions necessary to facilitate sustainable marketsheds within a given project area. Nor will IDEI be able to take a leadership role in every marketsheds development effort that is eventually undertaken in a given location. Careful selection of partners will ensure that the full range of constraints are adequately resolved to develop sustainable marketsheds, and that the process of market sheds development itself will continue in the long run.

A distinction is made between two types of partners:

Direct Service Providers are the market actors who are aligned with the objectives of the project and receive support from the project to increase their efficiency and effectiveness in their roles within the marketsheds. These actors will remain in the project area and continue to function within the marketsheds, providing affordable, appropriate, and sustainable goods and services to rural poor. These partners primarily consist of local organizations, including private enterprises, micro-finance institutions, business associations, farmer groups, and government agencies.

Facilitators assist in the development of smallholder markets by supporting Direct Service Providers. Support may take the form of training, research and development, establishing market and information linkages, awareness raising, demand creation, and policy advocacy, for example. Facilitator partners will include organizations that are able to provide facilitation services outside of IDEI's areas of expertise. Some of these will receive strategic support from the project during the start-up phase. The role of facilitators is time limited; they will phase-out their activities as marketsheds begin to function on their own. Facilitators may be national, regional, or global in scope and may include NGO, government, donor, or research organizations.

The procedure for partnership development will be highly flexible in order to respond to local needs and capabilities. Different partner types and different partner organizations may be brought into the process at different points of the project cycle. They may participate to a greater or lesser extent in individual project formulation and implementation activities. Also, their official relationship and working agreement with the project may take different forms. Facilitators will tend to be involved earlier and in a broader range of activities, while Direct Service Providers will tend to be involved later and in more specialized areas. In all cases, the objectives in developing partnerships will be to ensure that indigenous knowledge and experience is fully incorporated into the project design, to encourage local organizations to understand and take ownership of the IPMAS process, and to build local capacity to continue applying the IPMAS approach in the future.

Capacity Building of Partners

IDEI will design, implement and continually fine tune comprehensive, user friendly and highly effective modules to train IDEI's partners in production, quality assurance, marketing-demand creation/promotion, installation, repairs and maintenance and on developing poverty reduction strategies. The primary target groups are manufacturers, dealers/retailers/distributors, self-employed mechanics (SEMs), rural poor, extension officers, bankers and non-governmental organizations.

IDEI will continue to prepare comprehensive training modules. Some of these are as follows:

- Manufacturers are trained to fabricate quality (quality does not increase prices, products and in marketing techniques.
- *Mistries* (Self Employed Mechanics) are trained to promote and correctly install and repair IDEI products.
- Dealers/retailers/distributors are trained to identify good quality IDEI products and in marketing techniques.
- NGOs are trained in marketing and to be trainer of trainers for installation, repair and maintenance.
- Bankers are trained on the credit needs of smallholders and methods of simplifying loan procedures.
- Training modules and programs will be constantly evaluated for short and long term efficiency and efficacy.

Capacity Development of Staff

As an organization, IDEI is committed to work with rural poor and for sustainable development and in order to achieve this goal it realizes the need for the following:

- Human resource development to create a vibrant organization.
- Operating sound personnel policies.
- Investing in staff through skill development and training.
- Conduct training on gender mainstreaming in the organization.

A strong human resource development policy will help retain IDEI's staff and keep motivation high in the organization. It will also contribute to building a corpus of qualified professionals to work in the development sector in India. IDEI will develop this policy in collaboration with other organization. IDEI will also continue its efforts at hiring women at all levels.

IDEI will utilize the following strengths it has developed over the past decade which are listed:

- Holistic understanding of the peoples' problems.
- Good repository of skills in problem solving on the input side particularly in water related solutions.
- The field force has extraordinary knowledge of local conditions.
- The field force also has excellent relations with supply chain as well as with the rural poor.
- IDEI has a very large physical supply chain network and also more than 1200 *mistries* which give it tremendous reach into villages.
- IDEI has a working relationship with a large number of NGOs, as well as multiple donors.

In addition to the above mentioned strengths, IDEI will develop capacities in the following areas:

- IDEI has worked as a solution provider to the rural poor on the input side of agriculture and particularly focused on water technology.
- Understanding "local conditions" on the output as well as the input side to tailor make the approach in every market shed. For example in Maharashtra, there is no salinity problem, but there is a severe salinity problem in Gujarat.
- Need to sharpen focus on the rural poor in ADITI (affordable drip irrigation technology innovations) where self selection does not happen from the poorest of poor as opposed to the treadle Pump.

Mechanisms for Learning

Workshops

IDEI proposes to organize and/or participate in several workshops as a key learning and sharing platform. Some of these workshops are listed below. Strategy for developing and disseminating micro-irrigation technologies to rural poor families through a market-driven, private-sector supply chain. Special attention to be paid to where watershed development programs have increased available water so that the productivity of each drop of water used is maximized.

Strategy for linking rural poor families to output markets, increasing the flow of information from those markets to the rural poor, developing and disseminating post-harvest technologies, and increasing the peoples' capacity to analyze and plan their activities based on market information.

Strategy for increasing production and productivity of highly remunerative crops by the rural poor through design and implementation of sustainable information-flow methodologies, a focus on off-season and specialized crop production, and linkages to a strengthened private-sector input supply chain.

- Increased access to formal and informal credit opportunities for the rural poor, especially through expansion of linkages to micro-credit institutions and savings and credit groups.
- Advocacy of government and donor policies to support these efforts, especially through rational allocation of resources to the targeted activities and removal of market-distorting policies and practices.

Strategy to promote the orderly development of water markets in those areas with minimal penetration. This would involve promotion of the use of treadle pumps, introduction of low-cost diesel operated pumping sets, and facilitation of the establishment of orderly markets for purchasing water from these pumping sets. Establishment and support of a private sector network to deliver, install, and maintain these technologies in a sustainable manner would accomplish all this. Promotion of the technologies would be carried out by government, NGO's, and the private sector acting in partnership.

Monitoring Developments and Disseminating Learnings

The IPMAS approach has an inbuilt mechanism for self monitoring. This monitoring exercise not only enables a concurrent revision of activities and steps undertaken, it also enables an online dissemination of key learnings. This allows the larger community of interested people to simultaneously comment and critique the project as it gets along. IDEI recognizes the responsibility it carries in terms of being able to spread its learning and knowledge to a wider audience. The knowledge an organization acquires through its implementation and its analysis gives rise to an understanding and an insight that it then shares with others. This management of knowledge focuses on developing mechanisms for storing, adding value, disseminating and collecting comments from various target groups. This dissemination is optimally distributed among various mechanisms that on occasion demand getting people together, but in a majority of cases obviate the need to physically collect an audience.

As the IPMAS approach gets developed and is put into place, what is envisaged is a substantial change in the dynamics at the marketshed. While individual stakeholders get affected at the micro level, there are immediate fallouts that affect the community and the hinterland. These changes could be in the form of both negative and positive externalities. The monitoring mechanism captures these changes and adds them to the knowledge database that is generated through the duration of the project.

New market linkages develop as information flows are enabled, and as new institutions come up to take care of missing levels of activity. These linkages would in some case replace existing inefficient bands of activities. Also, these would extend present market boundaries beyond the immediate vicinity to tie up localized markets with larger areas. The development of a transport network and service providers would be essential for this greater reach. Factors that encourage small farmers to diversify their sale options and factors that inhibit the same would add to the learnings obtained. The baseline data would capture the *ab initio* status of virgin marketsheds, and then periodic collection of information as the project gets along dynamically observes the changes effected. The *post facto* analysis then measures the impact of actions taken. It gives IDEI the basis to argue for reforms in policy and in government institutions.

Geographical Focus

IDEI has till date worked in over 20 states in India at different points of time and in different projects. While planning the IPMAS approach we have kept in mind that since we are going through a major shift in approach, it is necessary to focus our approach both in terms of geographical approach and in terms of the various intervention areas. Therefore, during this phase we will limit the IPMAS intervention to a maximum of 150 marketsheds in a phased manner.

A lot of time and resources was spent on going through a set of exploratory questions which was posed to farmers, partners and internally among staff. A sample of these questions is recorded as follows:

- Who are the poor, what are the assets that they hold, what activities are they engaged in, what are their aspirations and livelihood strategies?
- What markets are important for the livelihoods of the poor (or should be important for them) now or in the future, directly or indirectly?
- How well do these markets currently serve the poor, in terms of ease of access, security of access and conditions of access?
- How do these markets fit into supply and value chains? How do these chains operate: where are the constraints, where are the high returns being made?
- What stakeholders are involved in these markets and what are their roles, their interests, their strengths, weaknesses, opportunities and threats?
- What are the barriers to entry and the transaction costs and risks for different stakeholders?
- What is the institutional environment like and what are its effects on key markets – is it enabling or disabling? How could these be developed or modified to improve market access for the poor?
- What institutional arrangements are currently in place? Why are they in their current form? How could these be developed or modified to improve market access for the poor?
- How these markets change and how are they likely to change as a result of wider, external processes of change? What opportunities are there for support to wider process of growth?

Based on the findings of these we have identified 50 marketsheds which will be taken up during the first year of this phase and subsequently these marketsheds would either be expanded or new ones added on.

Monitoring Mechanisms

Aim: To continually monitor the process for purposes of fine tuning the actual implementation of the IPMAS programme.

The key deliverables under this exercise are:

- A data set of initial conditions against which the final outcome will be bench-marked.
- A time line describing the points at which data will be collected for interim reviews of the IPMAS implementation process.
- A set of indicators, one set for each of the three objectives listed above, that will be used to evaluate the progress of implementation; these indicators will be observable at corresponding points along the time line.
- A system for objective evaluation of the indicators (scoring system).
- A set of actions to be undertaken based on the analysis of the indicators.
- A system of revising targets based on the interim evaluations.

Methodology

The purpose of the monitoring process is not simply to evaluate the IPMAS programme, but to ensure its success. The time frame of this programme does not allow immediate conclusions regarding its efficacy. On the other hand, given that the target groups are the poor and small farmers, finding out at the end of the day that the programme has failed will be devastating. Consequently, one needs to devise a method of early warning systems so that corrective measures can be undertaken to prevent failures. For each marketshed, a time line and the milestones on that line will have to be put in place before the project gets under way. All staff, whether at the planning stage or the implementation stage, will be made aware of these milestones.

The success of the programme can be measured by observable variables like the price received by the small farmer for the crops marketed, volume of sales, input costs, transport cost, etc., to arrive at estimates of income received. Early warning systems, to be effective, have to be triggered by observations of data well before income calculations are arrived at. While income is an *ex post* variable — after the programme has been completed — the monitoring variables will have to be *ex ante* — before the completion of the programme. To make the monitoring process objective, the monitoring variables should be observable by third parties (outside the farmers and the programme implementer).

The monitoring process will have to continually keep gathering information. For its success, such information will have to be easily observable, the number of items of information will have to be small and, they should be easily comparable across the different marketsheds. After the information at each stage is collected and collated, they will be compared to the milestones already in place.

Defining Incentives

All programme implementers need to be specifically aware of what the monitoring process is looking for and why. At the same time, they must be convinced that the monitoring variables cannot be manipulated by any direct action by either the farmer, or the implementer, or the monitor. Only then, proper targets, or incentives, can be set for the staff. Inability to reach milestones may be the result of faulty planning, inappropriate choice of market organization, unforeseen external shocks, or plain lack of effort. The monitoring variables should be such that one can distinguish among the causes. The associated incentive structures should be such that they enhance the learning process and do not encourage the manipulation of data.

This is the most important aspect of the monitoring process for it defines not only the variables to be observed, but also the analysis and the subsequent course of action. For instance, to monitor the growth of a crop, we will get more relevant information from the rate of growth (height) of the crop, or the color of the leaves (quality), rather than the amount of seed sowed. Alternatively, the information on leaf color must be taken at a time when controlling the water supply, or fertilizer use, can reverse the ill-health of the crop. It is obvious that different market-sheds, for different types of crops, catering to different market organizations will require different time lines. For instance, the timing of the information on market prices will depend crucially on whether the farmer produces a highly perishable or a more storable commodity.

Choice of Indicators

We have already stated that the indicators have to be observable by a third party. There are two types of indicators on which information need to be collected — those that are the outcomes of factors outside the system and those that depend on the activities of the target groups or the field staff. A third type of indicators will be those that are outcomes of the way the implementation plan has been worked out. A market price shock will be an outside variable. Density of cropping is, often, an outcome of the target farmer's effort. The rate at which a crop is lifted and moved to the market, will be determined by the transport activity planned for in the programme.

The three types of indicators will need different levels of corrective action. A bad market price shock has to be anticipated and fall-back options planned for well in advance. These fall-back options will have to be in place before the price shock is observed, and implemented as soon as the "bad" information comes in. Choice of the other two types of variables as monitoring indicators can be justified on either one of two grounds. First, these can be corrected by enhanced effort; second, the plan is flexible enough to be modified when the information is made available.

The advantage of this monitoring process is that it generates a wealth of information on how things can go wrong, where they can go wrong, when they can go wrong and, finally, how they can be corrected. This is because the movement of all the monitoring variables can be correlated to the final achievement of targets. These variables give a chronology of events that led to the final outcomes. Since the entire monitoring is done through the use of observable variables, the knowledge gained from the process is easily transferable. In particular, one group of project implementers and target farmers can learn from the experiences of some other group. More importantly, this knowledge can be transferred to other similar organizations.

Conclusion

In this evolving context, IDEI seeks to be a socially progressive force for change, effectively implementing programs which is relevant to the current and emerging problems of the disadvantaged people. We also recognize that pressing problems like low income from agriculture, high-input costs, unstable markets, poverty and hunger are not amenable to simple solutions. The complexity of these issues is beyond the ability of any single organization. Effective solutions that are across borders require a multidimensional multi-partner approach. To this end IDEI works, and will continue to work, through institutional alliances.

2

Agricultural Policy and Rural Poverty Reduction in India

N.C. SAXENA

Who are the Poor in India?

It is estimated that one-third of the world's poor live in India, and there are more poor people in India alone than in the whole of Sub-Saharan Africa. Although official estimates of the Government of India indicate that every fourth Indian is poor, the estimates of the internationally recognized poverty line of "a dollar a day" reveal that 39 per cent people in India were already living with incomes below "a dollar a day" in 1999-00 (the current figure is 34.7 – editors).

Indian poverty is predominantly rural, where landless labourers and casual workers are the worst-off economic groups. Scheduled castes and scheduled tribes, women and female-headed families, old people, and female children face more deprivation than others. The rural poor are primarily those with limited ownership of assets – including land. The vast majority of the rural poor in India are engaged in agriculture (including fishery and livestock) either as agricultural wage labourers or marginal farmers. Table 1 gives a breakdown of the occupational characteristics of the rural poor in India in 1993–94.

Table 1 reveals several important characteristics of the rural poor. First, almost 42 per cent of the rural poor fall into the most economically disadvantaged group of agricultural labour. Another 33 per cent of the poor are farmers. Thus, three-fourths of the rural poor are in the agriculture sector. Overall, the SC and ST communities constitute about 25 per cent of the rural population, but account for more than 42 per cent of the poor.

Table 1

Livelihood Characteristics of the Rural Poor in 1993-94

(In Percentage)

Livelihood Category	*Scheduled Tribe (ST)*	*Scheduled Caste (SC)*	*Others*	*All Households in the Livelihood Category*
Self-employed households in agriculture	5.6	4.8	22.5	32.9
Agricultural labour households	6.5	16.2	18.9	41.6
Self-employed households in non-agriculture	0.8	2.4	7.7	10.8
Other rural labour households	1.5	2.4	4.0	7.8
Other (residual households)	0.7	1.5	4.7	6.9
All households	15.0	27.2	57.8	100.0

Source: N.C. Saxena and John Farrington, 2003, *Trends and Prospects for Poverty Reduction in Rural India: Context and Options*, Working Paper 198, ODI, London.

Measurement of Poverty

The Planning Commission estimates poverty from the consumption distribution data reported by the National Sample Survey (NSS). These results obtained from the consumer expenditure data of the 55th Round are compared with the previous estimates in Table 2.

According to Table 2, the strongest decline in poverty took place during 1994–2000, by 1.7 per cent annually, as opposed to only 0.4 per cent during 1987–94.

Table 2

Poverty as Assessed by the Planning Commission

Year	*Percentage Below Poverty Line*	*Year*	*Annual Decline in Percentage Points During the Period*
1973–74	56.4		
1987–88	39.1	1974–87	1.3
1993–94	36.2	1987–94	0.4
1999–2000	26.1	1994–2000	1.7

Source: N.C. Saxena and John Farrington, 2003, *Trends and Prospects for Poverty Reduction in Rural India: Context and Options*, Working Paper 198, ODI, London.

However, the large ('thick') sample survey of 1999–2000 (55th Round) on which these figures are based, made a significant departure by canvassing information on consumption using two different reference periods on all sample households, and reported two sets of distributions of consumer expenditure. This makes it difficult to compare the estimates obtained not only from the 1999–2000 survey with those of earlier 'thick' estimates such as the 50th and 43rd rounds, but also with the thin rounds from the 51st to the 54th.

The claim of a very fast decline in poverty during the period 1994–2000 is not supported by data gathered by other agencies, or even by NSS for other purposes. For instance, the National Sample Survey Organization also carried out Employment-Unemployment Surveys (EUS) in 1993–94 and 1999–2000. These included consumption modules, which were not contaminated by the mixture of recall periods within one survey, as in the expenditure survey for the 1999–2000 NSS. Sundaram (2001) analyzed the consumption distributions from the EUS, and found that the average annual rate of poverty reduction was only 0.43 points per year, as opposed to 1.7 points declared by the Planning Commission on the basis of the Consumption Survey. This means that the annual rate of poverty reduction has broadly remained the same as in the earlier 1987-88 to 1993-94 period, and that the 1999-2000 level of poverty would be around 30 per cent, and not 26.1 per cent as claimed by the Planning Commission.

To take a further set of evidence, the data on per capita Net State Domestic Product (NSDP) of the poorer states, which contain almost 60 per cent of India's poor, show that the rate of growth during 1990–2000 has not been encouraging. In fact, it has hardly improved in Bihar, while in the other States, the rate has generally been below 2 per cent per annum. Out of the total number of people falling below the poverty line, the proportion in the five states of Uttar Pradesh (UP), Bihar, Madhya Pradesh, Orissa, and Assam has gone up from less than 50 per cent in 1973–74 to more than 65 per cent in 1999–2000. Given the poor growth record of these States, it is difficult to believe that the overall poverty would have declined rapidly.

Poverty in India is closely correlated with food consumption. However, macro-figures of overall food consumption are not available in India. But, availability, defined as 87.5 per cent of production plus imports minus exports plus changes in government stocks, can be taken as a good approximation for studying changes in consumption. While the growth rate in the availability of foodgrains per capita was 1.20 per cent per annum during the 1980s, the growth rate has come down to minus 0.28 per cent per annum during the 1990s. The drop in the availability has been very steep in the last five years, when grain production remained stagnant, but government stocks skyrocketed.

Per Capita Daily Foodgrain Availability in Grams

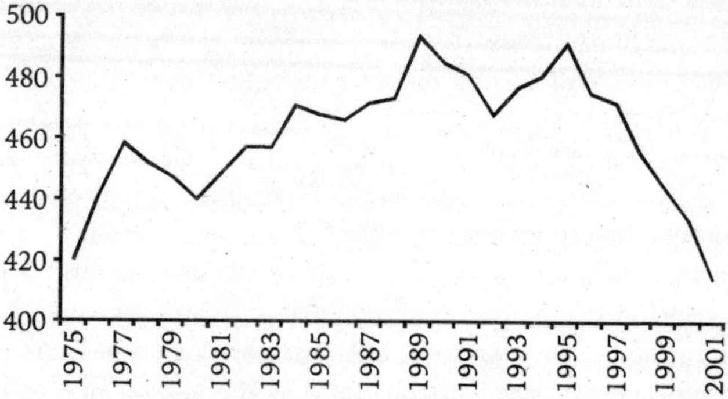

Source: MTA 2000, *Mid-term Review of the Ninth Plan*, Planning Commission, New Delhi

The poorest three deciles of the population in 1993-1994 consumed 11.76 kg of foodgrains per month as against 14.77 kg for the top three deciles.[1] So long as a significant cereal gap between the top and bottom end of the rural population persists, falling foodgrain availability must be taken seriously. As lower consumption by the poor cannot be a matter of choice, it must be viewed in terms of distress. Since the number of officially declared poor people is only 261 million in the country, bridging the gap of 3 kg between the top 30 per cent and the bottom 40 per cent would require only 261×3×12/1000, or less than 10 million tonnes of foodgrains to wipe off hunger and food-based poverty from India.

Nor do data on employment and wages support claims of a fast decline in poverty during the period 1993–94 to 1999–2000. There has been a long-term decline in the proportion of the working population dependent on agriculture – from 69.5 per cent in 1961 to 59.8 per

1. Anamitra Saha, 2000, "Puzzle of Declining Rural Foodgrains Consumption," *EPW*, July 1.

cent in 2001. The latest available national-level NSS for 1999–2000 shows an absolute decline in the number employed in agriculture, between 1993–94 and 1999–2000 at the all-India level. Whether this is due to a fast growth in modern non-agricultural sector employment or due to labour-displacing trends in agriculture remains to be seen. According to the NSS, on the basis of Current Daily Status (CDS), unemployment increased in India from 5.2 per cent in 1987-88 to 7.1 per cent in 1999–2000. This trend was even sharper in rural areas, where unemployment increased in the same period from 4.6 per cent to 7.2 per cent. The growth rate of employment dropped sharply from about 2 per cent per year in the period 1983 to 1993 to less than 1 per cent in the period 1993–94 to 1999–2000.

The analysis of the 1999–2000 National Consumption Survey by Sundaram (2001) cited above, together with the persuasive modelling by Dutt and Ravaillon (2002) suggests a 'guesstimate' for this paper of the current proportion of the population below the poverty line to be approximately 30 per cent. This is not inconsistent with the estimate of 28.6 per cent by Deaton and Drèze (2002), arrived at through a careful adjustment of official estimates to reduce the influence of methodological shortcomings.

Table 3

Employment Growth in the Last Two Decades

Period	*Annual Rate of Growth (%)*	
	Rural	*Urban*
1983 to 1987–88	1.36	2.77
1987–88 to 1993–94	2.03	3.39
1993–94 to 1999–2000	0.67	1.34

Source: Chandrashekhar and Ghosh (2001).

This analysis is not inconsistent with the recent slowdown in agricultural growth (see below) or with stagnation in other indicators, such as infant mortality, which has remained at around 70 per 1000 live births over the last several years.

Need for Agriculture and Food Policy Reforms

During the 1980s, the yields of crops such as rice, oilseeds, and pulses registered a high growth in India. Even the States with high incidence of poverty – Assam, Bihar, Madhya Pradesh, Orissa, Rajasthan, Uttar Pradesh, and West Bengal – registered a significant improvement in the crop yields, thus contributing to a decline in poverty. However, this trend did not continue in the 1990s. During the 1990s (1989-90 to 1999-2000), the growth of agriculture decelerated as compared to the 1980s (1979-80 to 1989-90). The overall growth rate of crop production declined from 3.72 per cent per annum to 2.29 per cent per annum, and productivity from 2.99 per cent per annum to 1.21 per cent per annum. During the 1990s, the growth rate of foodgrains production declined to 1.92 per cent per annum from 3.54 per cent per annum during 1980s. Similarly, the growth rate of productivity in foodgrains decelerated to 1.32 per cent per annum as compared to 3.33 per cent per annum during the 1980s (GoI 2002). This has also resulted in a slower increase of real agricultural wages from 4.68 per cent during 1981–91 to 2.04 per cent in 1991–99, with the poorer States showing no increase or even a decline in wages. In addition, the casualisation of a mass of rural workers without safety nets, the feminization of agricultural labour accompanied by low wages, and the persistence of child labour are worrying trends.

The index number of agricultural production (with triennium ending 1981-82 taken as 100) rose to 148.4 in 1990-91 and 175.7 in 1996-97, but since then has remained stagnant at this level, and may be around 172 in 2002-03. Similar is the trend for foodgrains (*Economic Survey*, 2003). The increase in agricultural GDP during the last five years has been because of higher relative prices, and not higher production.

The policy approach to agriculture, particularly in the 1990s, has been to secure an increased production through subsidies on inputs such as power, water, and fertilizer, and by increasing the minimum support price[2] rather than through building new capital assets in irrigation, power and rural infrastructure. This has shifted the production base from low-cost regions to high-cost, causing an increase in the cost of production, regional imbalance, and an increase in the burden of storage and transport of foodgrains. The equity,

2. The average excess of actual procurement prices announced for wheat over cost of production during the 1980s was 63 per cent, which increased to 96 per cent during the 1990s. A similar trend is observed in the case of rice.

efficiency, and sustainability of the current approach are questionable. The subsidies do not improve income distribution or the demand for labour. The boost in output from subsidy-stimulated use of fertilizer, pesticides and water has the potential to damage aquifers and soils – an environmentally unsustainable approach that may partly explain the rising costs and slowing growth and productivity in agriculture, notably in Punjab and Haryana. Moreover, deteriorating State finances have meant that subsidies have, in effect, (i) 'crowded-out' public agricultural investment in roads and irrigation and expenditure on technological upgradation, (ii) limited maintenance on canals and roads, and (iii) contributed to the low quality of rural power. These problems are particularly severe in the poorer States. Although private investment in agriculture has grown, this has often involved macroeconomic inefficiencies (such as private investment in diesel generating sets instead of public investment in electricity supply). Public investment in agriculture has fallen dramatically since the 1980s (Figure 1) and so has the share of agriculture in the total gross capital formation (GCF). Instead of promoting low-cost options that have a lower capital-output ratio, present policies have resulted in excessive use of capital on the farms, such as too many tubewells in water-scarce regions.

Figure 1

Public Capital Investment in Agriculture During 1974–75 to 1995–96 at 1980–81 Prices

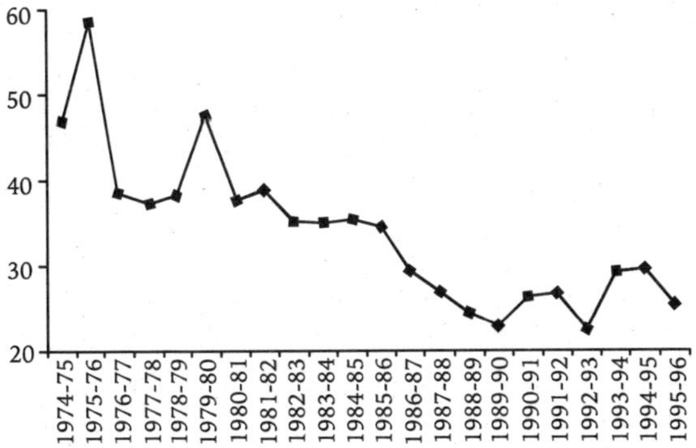

Source: Government of India (2000).

The intensity of private capital is in fact increasing for all classes of farmers, but at a faster pace in the Green Revolution areas and for large farmers. Thus, fertilizers, pesticides and diesel accounted for a mere 14.9 per cent of the total inputs in 1970–71, but 55.1 per cent in 1994–95. For large farmers in commercialized regions, their contribution could be as high as 70 per cent. But the proportion of output sold has increased at a much slower rate than the proportion of monetized inputs, including hired labour. The implication is a resource squeeze in agriculture. Whereas the need for resources to purchase these inputs has been increasing, the marketable surplus has been increasing at a slower rate to contribute to this, as the growth of non-farm employment has become very sluggish. It is not surprising that the repayment of loans is such a problem in Indian agriculture, and has even led to suicides in some cases.

Figure 2

Index of Terms of Trade Between Agricultural and Non-agricultural Sectors (triennium ending 1971-72 =100)

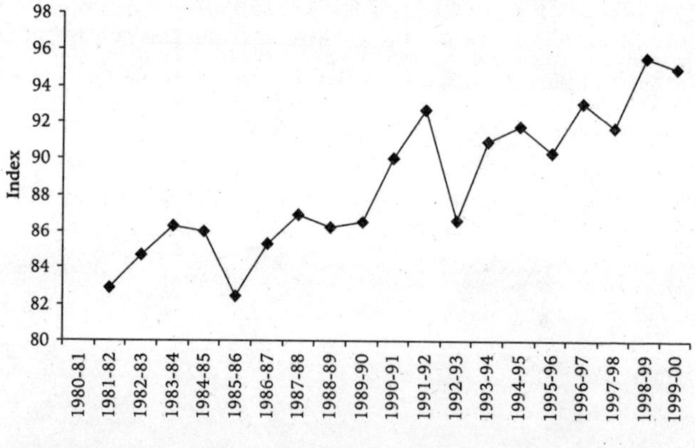

Source: MTA 2000, *Mid-term Review of the 9th Plan*, Planning Commission, New Delhi.

The need is for a better factor productivity in agriculture and for new technologies, which would be more labour intensive and would cut cash costs. One should also concentrate on small and marginal farmers, and on eastern and rainfed areas, where returns to both capital and labour are high. However, a major question is whether substantial and equitable productivity gains in agriculture can be made without a significant improvement in the quality of governance in these States.

Finally, the eastern and central regions should be the focus of attention during the next 10 years, as discussed below.

Agricultural Intervention and Regional Dimensions of Poverty

As far as spatial distribution is concerned, the poor in India can be broadly classified into two groups. Poverty in wet areas is generally associated with landlessness, because even a small farmer is able to rise above the poverty line due to high annual productivity through multiple cropping. The situation is different in dry areas, where a farmer with even four hectares of land may be quite poor, because of land hardly produces enough to sustain the family. In such areas, landed farmers often undertake wage labour, especially when the crop fails, to supplement their incomes. Poverty is linked with low productivity and its cyclic fluctuation, rather than with landlessness.

Figure 3

Percentage of People Below Poverty Line in 1999-2000

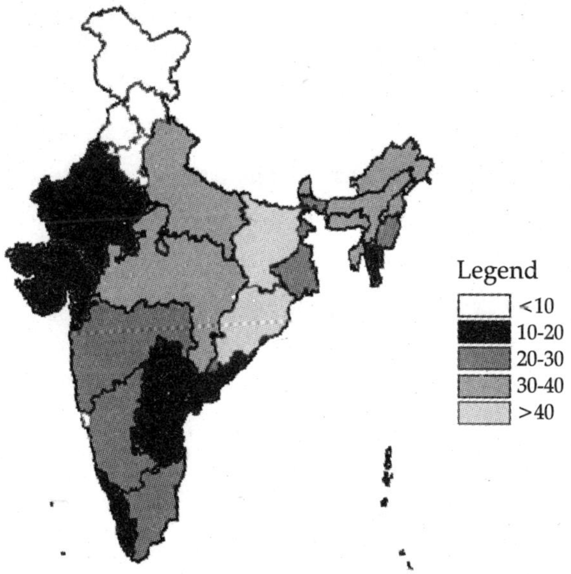

Source: Planning Commission (2000), *Poverty in India* (unpuLlished)

It can be seen from figure 3 that there are two regions of concentration of poverty:

- Eastern India – East UP, North Bihar, North Bengal, Coastal Orissa, Assam, and Tripura (all with plenty of groundwater);
- Central Tribal India – Bundelkhand, Jharkhand, Vidarbha, Madhya Pradesh, Chhattisgarh, Rajasthan, Western Orissa, and Telengana (regions of low agricultural productivity with plenty of degraded and forest lands).

The eastern region has fertile soils with plenty of groundwater, but is characterized by the following:

- smaller holdings
- heavy dependence on grain production
- less diversity of rural incomes
- less developed infrastructure
- less marketed surplus
- credit markets which are imperfect and inter-locked with output markets
- more dependence on the village merchant/big landowner for marketing small surpluses
- poor human capital as far as entrepreneurship is concerned.

On the other hand, the characteristics of peninsular India are:

- mono-cropped land of low productivity
- soil and water erosion
- vast areas of uncultivated and forest lands
- high levels of distress migration
- deteriorating road and rail network
- depleted groundwater levels
- cohesive rural population amenable to community participation.

Although these regions have different features, each in its own way requires improvements in water management as a basis for higher productivity.

Water and Agriculture

Despite large investments in irrigation in the past, only about 40 per cent of India's agricultural area is irrigated. The progress on this front has slowed down considerably in recent years, particularly in terms of major and medium irrigation projects, largely due to resource constraints faced by governments both at the Centre and in the States. However, resources are not the only problem. Most of the favourable locations for irrigation have already been developed, so that future irrigation may exhibit lower marginal returns and possibly greater environmental sensitivity. A major revival of public investment in irrigation capacity and water management is needed. The Accelerated Irrigation Benefit Programme is a potentially important instrument for providing resources to State governments in support of the ongoing irrigation schemes. Allocations under this programme need to be massively increased. Greater attention will also have to be paid to rain water harvesting, and increasing the irrigation potential through micro-watershed development. There is also considerable scope to improve the efficiency of existing irrigation infrastructure through better and more participatory management practices.

Much of the decline in poverty during the 1980s was due to an increase in paddy production in eastern India. However, a collapse in the supply of electric power in this region in the last ten years combined with no new breakthrough in seeds and technology has led to a plateauing of yields. Stimulating groundwater development is crucial to kick-start the Green Revolution in this region, as only around 20 per cent of groundwater resources are being utilized. Studies have revealed that diesel pump subsidy schemes operated by the State governments involve both higher capital costs than electric power, and have fared poorly due to lengthy, irksome, and complex procedures and heavy transaction costs, which leave little real subsidy for the farmers. East-Indian States should reform their pump subsidy scheme to ameliorate the pump capital scarcity that lies at the heart of the problem. It is also equally important to promote cost effective and improved manual irrigation technologies such as treadle pumps for sub-marginal farmers.

For dry-land areas, largely in peninsular India, watershed development programmes are being implemented by several departments of the Government of India, often with different and conflicting guidelines.

Even when approaches or guidelines are common, the allocation of funds is done by different departments and each does separate monitoring. The need for 'a Single National Initiative' has been felt for some time, and was also articulated in the 1999–2000 budget speech of the Union Finance Minister and the President's address for 2000-01.

Evaluation reports have shown that watershed projects cannot succeed without full participation of project beneficiaries and careful attention to issues of social organization. This is because success depends on consensus among a large number of users, whose livelihoods are affected differently by the range of resources (agricultural land, common grazing land, forest, *etc.*) being rehabilitated. Moreover, collective action is required for management of the commons as the costs and benefits of watershed interventions are unevenly distributed among the people affected. Unfortunately, most projects have failed to generate sustainability because of the failure of the government agencies to generate consensus among the people in the light of these differences. Field staff has no incentive to make the effort to pursue participatory approaches. Pressure to spend substantial resources by a fixed deadline is not conducive to developing people's capabilities, nor is strict orientation towards physical targets. There is continued insecurity about the availability of funding at the grassroots level, as there is no guarantee that the funds would be released in time by the Government of India or by other funding agencies. There is also no arrangement for handing over structures or for the maintenance of newly planted areas after a project is completed.

In summary, the following changes in agricultural policies are suggested:

- Agricultural output grew in the 1990s because of higher output support prices and input subsidies. Now, growth must come from higher investments in irrigation, seeds, power and roads. Therefore, public investment in irrigation, power, and roads should be stepped up by reducing subsidies on fertilizers, water, and power.
- Canal systems are in a poor shape owing to inadequate funding of operations and maintenance. These should be improved by stepping up plan allocations for maintenance, involving users' groups in management, and appropriate pricing of water to cover operation and maintenance costs.

- Water resources need to be developed in ways that will ensure year-round access by the poor to clean drinking water, since this is known to impact women's time allocations and certain non-income aspects of poverty.
- Demand issues that have remained neglected in preference to supply issues need urgent attention in view of (a) falling open market prices for various commodities even in deficit states, and (b) continuing high levels of malnutrition, especially among children.
- Finally, the eastern and central regions should be the focus of attention during and beyond the Tenth Plan.

Price Distortions and Minimum Support Price (MSP)

It is to be noted that all such suggestions will lead to cosmetic changes unless one confronts the basic issue of the MSP.

High procurement price and unloading of foodgrains in the market at a throw-away price has meant that foodgrains often meant for Sampoorna Gramin Rozgar Yojana (SGRY) or other such schemes are sold back illegally to government (*Outlook*, 26th August, 2002). To correct this price distortion, the market price should be higher than the Public Distribution System (PDS) price, which in turn should be higher than the support price for farmers. The reverse is the picture today; support price for wheat and common rice is Rs. 6.4 and Rs. 8.2 per kg, whereas the issue price for various schemes varies from Rs. 2 to 4 for wheat and Rs. 3 to 6 for rice, with market price ruling somewhere in between.

A recent study (Parikh *et al.* 2003) that examined the consequences of increasing the MSP of wheat and rice by 10 per cent, shows that it leads to a decline in overall GDP, increase in aggregate price index and reduction in investments. Even the increase in agricultural GDP resulting from higher MSP dwindles rapidly, and only a miniscule positive impact on agricultural GDP remains by the third year. More importantly, in terms of welfare, the bottom 80 per cent of the rural and the entire urban population are worse off.

Therefore, the MSP should be reduced to a level comparable with international prices. A low output price will result in more labour than capital being used as input in agriculture, thus leading to market-led land reforms. This is because economies of scale will operate in favour of those who have more labour, and, thus they will start buying land from those who are short of family labour, generally rich farmers.

This will also discourage black-marketing and reduce the burden of subsidies. Savings should then be encouraged in the poorest areas by doubling the number of old age pensioners, increasing the amount from rupees 75 to 200 per month. The fund allotment for one Mid Day Meal Scheme and ICDS (Integrated Child Development Scheme) should be doubled in those districts where 50 per cent or more people are below the poverty line. These measures will improve purchasing power and consumption of the poor, without much leakage.

Contrary to popular belief, there has been a significant jacking of MSP at the political level just in a few years. The price recommended by the CACP (Commission on Agricultural Costs and Prices) has generally been accepted with some marginal upward movement (especially for wheat) for the sake of publicity. Therefore, the formula for calculating the input costs should be changed, and be more realistic. Continued setting of MSP at C2 levels means that returns to family labour, land, and capital are determined by the government rather than the market. This is not compatible with market economy principles. It should aim for A2, which covers the cash costs incurred.

Moreover, the CACP should calculate the cost not only for high-cost regions such as Punjab and Haryana, but also for eastern UP and other such regions, where more labour and less capital are used to get the same output of grain.

As surpluses decline from States such as Punjab and Haryana due to reduction in the MSP, it is essential to realize the potential for production surpluses in Central and Eastern India, where presently, prices are below full costs of production. A basic focus of policy should, therefore, be to ensure effective price support in States and areas with future production potential. In January 2002, the author found that farmers in eastern UP were getting only Rs. 330 to 350 per quintal for paddy, whereas the farmers in Punjab were getting 540 for the same crop. In other words, the MSP should truly be a national level floor price, rather than remaining confined to established surplus regions.

In addition, we consider it vital to shift the Food Corporation of India's (FCI) focus to East and Central India. If decentralization has to proceed to its logical conclusion in the long-term, the entire subsidy in the PDS has to be devolved to the States (Sen 2002). This can be done by giving the states a subsidy in cash on their entire PDS distribution, in addition to the cash component already provided for the poor.

To persuade States such as Punjab and Haryana to move away from wheat and rice, the government would have to take three steps. First, to reduce the MSP, so that there is an economic incentive to move to other crops. Second, to give a part of food subsidy thus saved to farmers in these regions as compensation for the first few years. And finally, let the State governments take over procurement, and keep surplus grain in State government account, with a part of subsidy to be given to the state government for storage and other functions. The surplus States will be free to export, or sell in the deficit States, and thus make profits. The State governments will not face much of a problem exporting their surplus, because their overheads are much less than that of FCI, which is a highly inefficient and expensive organization. The surplus States will be able to make profits, a part of which can be used to augment rural welfare for farmers in the State. This will also act as an incentive to improve the quality of produce. At the same time, the FCI should be asked to extend its operations to eastern and central India, where the benefits of the MSP are hardly available to the farmers as of now.

The Sen Committee has worked out the economics of this package. The total compensation to both the farmers and State governments would at most be Rs. 6000 crore in the first year, and would decline subsequently. As against this, the savings on acquisition and carrying costs on the reduced procurement, envisaged at about 10 million tonnes, will be about Rs. 10,000 crore in the first year, Rs. 12,500 crore in the second year, Rs. 15,000 crore in the third year, and so on, assuming that the entire reduction in procurement will save on additional stockholding. There may be further savings in subsidies that would have been required to dispose of the additional stocks. Thus, reducing the MSP will be truly a win-win policy with environmental benefits thrown in as fallout.

Procurement of Foodgrains

New initiatives have been taken in India in the field of decentralized procurement of foodgrains. The decentralized procurement system, introduced in 1997, has been accepted so far by the State governments of West Bengal, Uttar Pradesh, Madhya Pradesh, and recently by Tamil Nadu. More such initiatives should be encouraged in the future. The deficit States should be encouraged to buy directly from the surplus States, and they should be compensated for transport, storage, *etc*. These States are bound to hire private agencies to do so, which will bring private expertise into this field.

Most storage godowns with the FCI are small-scale low quality structures, and foodgrains are stored in the open, called covered and plinth storage (CAP), leading to high storage losses. One should consider fiscal concessions to encourage new godown capacity in the private sector.

Private transporters get a low priority on railway movement forcing them to rely on more expensive truck transport. Similarly, selective credit controls by RBI restrict access to trade financing by the private sector. These problems deserve attention.

Regulated markets were supposed to improve efficiency, but many official market committees such as in UP, Punjab, and Haryana make it illegal for farmers to sell through alternative channels (*i.e.* selling directly to millers). The markets have thus emerged as taxing mechanisms, rather than facilitating farmers to get the best price.

The present extraction rates for both wheat and rice are about 10 to 30 per cent below the international standards, due to reservation of agro-processing units for the small-scale sector, which uses inefficient technologies. Therefore, remove licensing controls on Roller Flour Mills and other food processing industry. De-reserve food processing units, especially rapeseed and groundnut processing units, from the SSI list.

On the whole, laws and controls have repressed private foodgrain marketing, undercutting its potential contribution to long-term food security. However, recently GoI has made some progress in the liberalization of controls, and to facilitate the free trade and movement of foodgrains, the Government issued a Control Order tilted, 'Removal of (Licensing Requirements, Stock Limits and Movement Restrictions) on Specified Foodstuffs Order, 2002' on 15th February 2002. The Order allows any dealer to freely buy, stock, sell, transport, distribute, dispose, acquire, use, or consume any quantity of wheat, paddy/rice, coarse grains, sugar, edible oilseeds and edible oils, without a licence or permit. State governments would require the Centre's prior permission before issuing any order for regulating, by licences or permits, the storage, transport, and distribution of the specified commodities. This Order needs to be given wide publicity.

Land and Capital Markets

Another set of recommendations would be to look at increasing the concentration of land. The Gini coefficient for operational holdings has increased in the eighties, and this trend may have been further intensified in the last ten years. The distribution of operated area happens to be less unequal than owned area at all points of time, since smaller holdings predominate as lessees. Over time, however, the trends in the concentration in operated area have shown a pattern that is nearly similar to that of owned area. From 1971 onwards, the gap between the two Gini ratios has narrowed. At the all-India level, the Gini ratio for operational holdings declined during 1950s and remained stable during 1960s. However, during the 1970s and 1980s, there has been a significant and steady increase in the concentration ratio of operated area. The Gini ratio increased from 0.587 in 1971 to 0.624 in 1981 and further to 0.641 in 1991. The concentration in operated area thus has increased at a faster rate during the 1970s, followed by the 1980s, which coincided with technological change in agriculture in India. This rising inequality in the operation of land further dampens the demand for foodgrains.

Concentration Ratios of Owned and Operated Land in India

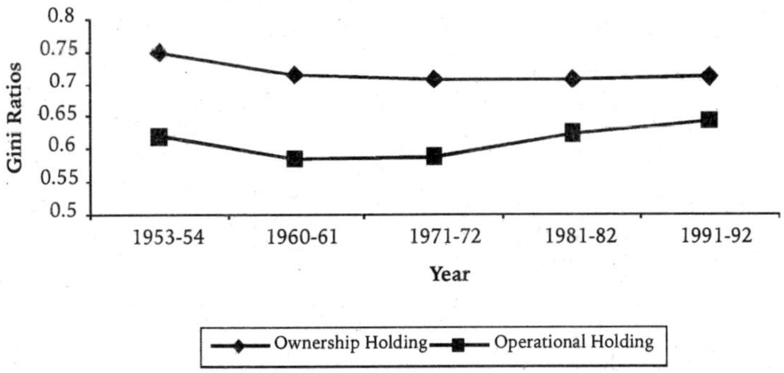

Source: Srivastava *et al.* 2003.

Land Ceiling and Tenancy Laws

In view of the continued pressure of population on land, it may not be advisable to remove, at the present juncture, the ceiling on the ownership of agricultural land. Ceiling on the ownership of land has in general made land market favourable to the small and marginal farmers, who can augment their ownership as well as operational holdings. However, tenancy laws guaranteeing security of tenure and prescribing the rental share have led to the growth of concealed tenancy, which discourages investment by the tenants and restricts the flow of credit provided to them. Since such tenants are in any case paying market rents, liberalization of tenancy laws can help to increase their employment and income by augmenting their operational holdings, stepping up investment, and getting better access to credit and inputs.

This argument is particularly valid in the Green Revolution areas, where market awareness is widespread even among the poor. Freeing the lease market for land in such regions may contribute to equity as well as efficiency of resource use. The nature of tenancies in these areas is very different from regions characterized by semi-feudal labour relations. The new forms of sharecropping arrangements in these regions involve high cost and output shares for the landowner, and a high degree of control by the landlord over the process of production. Like traditional leasing, the tenant participating in these arrangements is a small peasant, who is responsible for all manual tasks, but is not required to own any means of production, which are supplied by the landowner. The tenant is virtually a piece-rated labourer, but his/her involvement helps the landowner save on supervision. From leasing as a means of rental appropriation, landlords have moved to leasing as a means of control over labour power, the appropriation of its produce, and as a means of further accumulation.

In such cases, the pure tenants as well as the small and marginal farmers would be able to augment their operational holdings by leasing-in area, where there is pressure on land and where wages are low and poverty is high. This may also contribute to a more efficient use of land, labour and other resources. Similarly, in areas experiencing technological change and high growth, where population pressure on land is low and wages are high, the marginal farmers may gain by leasing out their area and taking up non-farm employment. Where wages and the rate of mechanization are high, the marginal and small farmers who are leasing-in area would be able to make a fuller use of their fixed equipment.

It is to be noted that the small farmer cultivates his/her land more intensely and puts in more labour per unit of land. The quality of supervision as well as of land and irrigation is also better on smaller holdings. Therefore, passing on the control of holdings of non-cultivating farmers over to the cultivating marginal and small farmers through an open leasing policy will improve overall production and labour absorption in agriculture.

Summing up

In this paper we have examined the growth performance and prospects of agriculture, the sector most directly relevant to the rural poor. Agriculture is characterized by slowing in rates of growth as yields level in Green Revolution areas and environmental problems increase, and there is growing competition arising from imports. Agriculture continues to be by far the most important source of employment and self-employment in rural areas, but is diminishing in importance, with a decline in the proportion of rural households receiving income from cultivation from 62.4 per cent in 1987-88 to 57.1 per cent in 1999-2000. Patterns of employment change are complex, and there is no doubt that there is much "distress" movement out of agriculture. The sector is also characterized by continuing heavy reliance on input subsidies and minimum support prices as ways of enhancing productivity, with negative effects in terms of crowding out productive investment in public irrigation, marketing infrastructure, and so on. Agricultural markets remain highly regulated, and the management of price support, subsidized food distribution, and restrictions on the movement of "essential commodities" have shown major weaknesses with wheat and rice stocks having reached about 60 million tonnes a year ago.

The use of scarce and costly irrigation water for highly water-demanding crops such as paddy and sugarcane, is mostly concentrated in areas having high local water availability. This needs to be redressed by appropriate fiscal measures. The low availability of low-cost sources of farm power (mainly for irrigation), such as electricity, has led to high investment in more costly sources, such as diesel engines, which is socially sub-optimal. It needs to be questioned whether, in future, agriculture can adapt to the opportunities and pressures resulting from globalization, given especially the low levels of literacy and weak product and factor markets in many rural areas. If it cannot, there is likely to be an agricultural "involution" back to subsistence crops in many areas, and what are the prospects for agricultural labour, already characterized by increasing casualization?

Growth in agriculture is likely to have major pro-poor employment effects (provided that operations such as harvesting and threshing are not mechanized with the help of subsidies). Growth in the future must rely less on regulated markets and subsidies on fertilizer, water and power, and more on higher investments in irrigation, seeds, power, and roads (all of which have suffered investment declines recently). The types of investment in wetter (east and northeast) versus drier areas (peninsular India) that are necessary are quite distinct, but improved management of water is essential in both. Among other things, perspectives on the conjunctive use of water needs to be reinforced, so that water is managed in ways that ensure year-round access to clean drinking water by the poor. This is known to impact women's time allocations and certain non-income aspects of poverty.

Finally, there are compelling grounds for paying at least as much attention in future to demand alongside supply issues, in view of (a) falling open market prices for various commodities even in deficit states, and (b) continuing high levels of malnutrition, especially amongst children. Pensions and feeding schemes are potentially among the more robust strategies in this case.

Policies on subsidized food distribution are politically popular, but have caused an enormous drain on public finances. The annual cost of food subsidies rose from Rs. 12,000 crore in 2000-01 to Rs. 26,000 crore in 2002-03. Guaranteed prices to farmers are also costly and poorly managed, having recently been well above free market prices. They need to be reduced to a level comparable with international prices, so as to promote the diversification of agriculture, environmental sustainability, and reduction in food subsidies. Other policy options in relation to agriculture and food include the removal of controls on the movement of "essential commodities" between

States, the phasing out of all arrangements in support of monopoly purchase, the encouragement of wheat and rice exports on private account, the decontrolling of sugar, and its removal from the Public Distribution System altogether, and the extension of price support scheme for foodgrains to poorer areas such as eastern UP and Bihar.

References

Deaton, A. and Drèze, J. (2002). "Poverty and Inequality in India: A Re-examination", *Economic and Political Weekly*, 7 September.

Dutt, G. and Ravaillon, M. (2002). "Is India's Economic Growth Leaving the Poor Behind?" *Economic and Political Weekly*, May.

GoI (2002). Chapter 5.1, Agriculture, *X^th^ Five Year Plan*, Planning Commission, New Delhi.

Parikh Kirit S., A. Ganesh-Kumar, Gangadhar Darbha (2003). "Growth and Welfare Consequences of Rise in MSP", *Economic and Political Weekly*, March.

Sen, Abhijit (2002). *Report On Long-Term Grain Policy*, Ministry of Agriculture and Cooperation, GoI, New Delhi.

Srivastava Ravi, N.C. Saxena and S.K. Thorat (2003). *Land Institutions, Policy and Reforms in India*, Paper for IFPRI, Washington.

Sundaram (2001). "Employment – Unemployment Situation in the Nineties: Some Results from NSS 55th Round Survey", *Economic and Political Weekly*, March 17.

3

What Ails Indian Agriculture?

SATYAPRAKASH, T.L.
ASHUTOSH APA TELI

Introduction

Indian agriculture can be looked at from two different perspectives. First, the institutional and second, the technological. The institutional approach was mainly characterized by land reforms and changing agrarian structures. Later, a whole array of institutional support mechanisms in credit, extension and marketing were provided. Simultaneously, new production technologies in the form of seeds and farming practices were provided to farmers. With the advent of the WTO, some agricultural commodities have started becoming uncompetitive. Pressure to find new niche areas in new crops, go in for value addition in crops and for higher productivity is building up. A major characteristic feature of Indian agriculture is its heterogeneity, also because of the large number of players in almost every activity. So, it is impossible to diagnose a single problem and to provide a strategy. Nevertheless, the lack of economies of scale remains the crux of the problem. Higher transaction costs of credit, scattered locations and higher cost for maintaining inventory make these forms unprofitable. This results in lesser and lesser capital formation and finally meager surplus production.

The second problem is that of credit. Over a period of time, consumer loans for cars and housing have become very popular, and interest rates are constantly falling. But agricultural credit is still lent at on an average 14-16 per cent rate of interest. In many farms, particularly for small farms, capital is the most serious constraint. This forces farmers to confine themselves to traditional agriculture with very less value addition. The most important imperative is to increase the total value of crop production. Wherever the institutional support was provided, farmers have diversified the crop produce and value of crop rose considerably. But in many cases efficient marketing systems are not available. Cotton farmers in Maharashtra couldn't get appropriate price for their produce. In Mysore, the Malemahadeswara sugar mill hasn't paid sugarcane farmers their due for five years. Dryland farmers usually resort to distress sale. Intervening credit support and delayed sale improved prices of pulses marginally. Marketing has been the weakest link in Indian agriculture.

Very low capital formation in agriculture has progressively deteriorated infrastructure conditions. This has been most severe in dryland agriculture. 29.02 per cent of area under agriculture is held by small and marginal farmers. This has an important implication on marketing. There is a need to open third marketing and credit channel in the form of NGOs or *panchayats* or co-operatives.

It is the extension agencies which popularize a technology and make farmers adopt a particular practice. Extension and research systems acting in tandem can revolutionize agriculture scenario in a locality. But, our institutional setup governing research and extension is characterised by low adoptive researches and low feedback in extension. Finally, political populism, large farmer lobbies, regulatory regime, price policy and a whole array of governance issues are involved while providing solutions to ailing Indian agriculture.

Not to forget, in the coming years 'water issues' will be the single biggest factor in determining pace of agricultural growth in India. Efficient governing of water bodies and introducing market principles may become inevitable. Rao (2003) gave a two pronged strategy to hasten up growth of agriculture. First, release initiative and enterprise of farmers and private sector by removing restrictions on agricultural trade and processing. Second, spur supply response to the incentives through infrastructure, agricultural research and credit. This once again takes us back to the same issues of credit-marketing, infrastructure and research and extension.

Issue of Small Farms

Normally in traditional agriculture there is an inverse relationship between size and productivity. Traditional agriculture is basically extensive. When modern approaches are followed, credit needs and infrastructure needs increase. It needs strong institutional support. The Malaysian Felda scheme and Kenyan tea gardens are the models to emulate. Huge infrastructure facilities, rapid access to processing industry through transportation chains and reach of extension agencies are needed. The fault lies more in supporting institutions rather than holding pattern.

The average size of smallholdings measuring less than 2 hectares is 0.6 hectares. Annual income required to support a family above the poverty level is now estimated to be Rs. 12,000. Can a farm size of 0.6 ha yield Rs. 12,000? Income from farming doesn't depend upon size of the farm alone, but capital invested in it. Hybrid seed production, vegetables, papaya, other fruits, dairy sericulture and so many other options are available.

Crops	*Net Return per ha (in Rs.)*
Potato	6165
Mustard	3296
Rabi rice	2879
HYV rice (Kharif)	1884
Wheat	766

This highlights the importance of credit in Indian agriculture. But, commercial banks generally view agriculture lending as a risky proposition, despite the fact that NPAs in farm sector are invariably lower than other sectors. Direct finance advanced by schedule commercial banks to marginal farmers declined steadily from 30.2 per cent in 1990-91 to 23.8 per cent in 1999-2000. Average lending rates of interest on farm loans still ranges from 14-16 per cent, which is much higher than the rate for housing, consumer durables and car loans at less than 9 per cent. Before mechanization in Japan, it used to take 1600-2000 man-hours to produce 4.7 tonnes of rice. Now it hardly takes one third of the previous time to produce 5.2 tonnes of rice. Energy surveys in Punjab have shown that human and bullock energy is costlier than diesel engine or electric engine.

Economies of scale don't allow small farms to operate on modern scale. This forces us to think of third institutional approach i.e., co-operatives or NGOs or *panchayats*. With substantial market imperfections, limited alternative choice for crops and incapability to confront input risk, co-operatives provide a policy option. Inadequate access to the markets for various complementary inputs like irrigation, credit, agro processing facilities, extensions and even information are other concerns in this regard. Thus, very high scope for co-operative action is required, considering unfavorable characteristics of input, production, agro processing and marketing subsystems.

When production is undertaken by a large number of scattered and small farm holdings, each having only small quantity of marketable surplus, a producers' co-operative can procure supplies at lower transaction cost through suitable backward linkages and can make such units viable through pooling. Farmers can be insulated from vagaries of market imperfections. Co-operatives provide a convenient delivery point for input, extension and technology. High perishability of raw material and seasonality require agro-processing, which supports the argument for co-operatives. Moreover, regular and enforceable contracts can be achieved through co-operatives. Huge mismanagement of funds has crippled co-operatives in recent times. So, there is a need for rehauling regulatory mechanisms and streamlining the 5Ms of co-operatives i.e. Mission, Membership, Manpower, Management and Money.

Today the need is to delink production and processing of high value crops. Processing should have elaborate net working. The failure of oil palm in Karnataka and strawberry in several areas across the country can be reasoned out on this basis. Processing industry should take care of crops like Chikku, where the market is not competitive, unlike mango. Marketing co-operatives are invariably needed if fruit crops are non-climatic, like grapes. The government should take up proactive policies to enable the building of such food-processing networks. Contract farming should be encouraged. Contract farming has shown remarkable results in Punjab and Haryana to make small farms competitive. But it is high time that we should allow the lease market to function. By putting restrictions, we have only imposed people to operate on unprofitable holdings. In case of Kerala, fragmentation has left many landholdings fallow.

Investment in Infrastructure

The RBI *Handbook of Statistics 2001* indicates that net area sown in mha has barely increased from 140.27 mha in 1970-71 to 142.07 mha in 1997-98. Acreage under irrigation has doubled from 38 mha to 72 mha. But, cultivation in arid lands hasn't been encouraging, although AIDIS (*All India Debt and Investment Survey*) indicates an increase in investment in orchards and plantation. According to RBI's *Report on Currency and Finance 2000-01*, gross domestic capital formation is 7.96 per cent in 2000. It is observed that inadequate public expenditure may lead to up to 25 per cent lesser private expenditure. Unless government takes a determined approach by making huge investments in the sector, private enterprise is hard to convince.

Keynesian logic says money spent, even if wasted, can have beneficial effects on growth of economy. Agencies like NABARD have specific roles to play in this regard. There is strong need to integrate marketing and credit linkages. Before that, NABARD should increase its equity capital to around Rs. 5000 crores and then to Rs. 50,000 crores over a period of 10 years. This should be facilitated by allowing NABARD to issue 30 years maturity bonds guaranteed by the government. Areas like watershed, horticulture *etc.*, need long term financing at a nominal rate of 10 per cent. Investment in dryland horticulture has profound rationale in water economics. Huge water use to an extent of 90 acre inches per crop in sugarcane and 360 acre inches in case of paddy is criminal wastage of water. Particularly considering the low rate of recharge in case of basaltic aquifers of South India, precious use of water should be regulated, preferably through institutions like water users associations. In the background of infancy of these institutions, it is rational to shift the policy towards dryland horticulture and agro-forestry. For example, the total demand for paper pulp itself is Rs. 6000 crores. Promoting tree crops like Mangium and other pulp yielding trees to establish pulp sheds on lines of milk sheds will easily find solutions to this demand.

Coming back to the issue of investment, rate of growth in GDP in agriculture during 1970-79 was only 1.74 per cent, but capital formation was highest with 9.5 per cent. But the 1980s experienced higher rate of GDP growth with 2.95 per cent in agriculture with a negative GCF. That is why NABARD should go for 30 years bonds. Gestation periods for watershed and dryland horticulture are too long to show conspicuous results. AIDIS survey doesn't find any visible deceleration in investment in minor irrigation, which is mainly in private household sector. But medium and major irrigations are not funded in a big way and suffer from time and cost overruns. The public accounts committee, while investigating cost efficiency of public sector projects, brought out the extent of cost and time overruns of irrigation projects ranging up to 500 per cent. Thus it is better to complement household investment with public investment.

The total investment in irrigation since independence comes to around Rs. 51,000 crores. Total estimated expenditure for river linking project comes to around Rs. 5,60,000 crores, which is 10 times the investment in irrigation since independence. But, it is argued that same expenditure can irrigate around 11.2 mha through minor irrigation. Nevertheless, the decision to invest in an irrigation project itself is a welcome step.

Price policies and public distribution system also have important ramifications on investment. Higher subsidies in this direction have a crowding out effect on resources. If PDS is wrapped up in Haryana, poverty levels may go up by only 2 per cent. Majority of poorest households in North East don't purchase any food grains from PDS. Actual per capita subsidy through PDS, as a difference between value of grains purchased and corresponding values at market price, comes out to be hardly Rs. 6. This is less than 1 per cent of the total household expenditure. In Maharashtra 30 per cent of poor don't use PDS because of lack of access. Majority of the population of Dharavi is not eligible to get PDS-BPL (below the poverty line) allocations.

Coming to administrative issue, decentralised services can never be delivered by centralised planning. Principles of provision of public goods and services clearly enunciate that if centralised service delivery won't result in cost reduction, it is preferable to decentralise the delivery. Transportation costs consume much of combined food subsidy of Rs. 12,000 crores. Thus we have to think of decentralizing procurement and involving PRIs (Panchayati Raj Institutions) in PDS delivery or introducing food stamps. Of course, delivery in far off places can cause hiccups. Only in those limited areas Government can retain its PDS operations or can form a separate grid in regions like North East. This will be useful in channelising financial resources. Ten per cent increase in minimum support prices of wheat and rice leads to decline in overall GDP by 0.33 per cent, increase in aggregate price index by 1.5 per cent, reduction in investment by 1.9 per cent and the bottom 80 per cent of rural and all urban population is worse off. Ten per cent increase in MSP will increase stocks by 16.5 mt after three years and reach 66.5 mt compared to a reference scenario. This reduces investment in irrigation, roads and other infrastructure, correspondingly lowering agricultural input over a period of time. The FAIDA report estimates an investment of Rs. 1,47,000 crores across food chain i.e., production point to consumption point, to have most beneficial value addition.

Value Addition

EXIM policy of 2002, announced formation of 41 agricultural export zones (AEZs) for produces like gherkins, flowers, Ratnagiri Alphonso *etc.* APEDA will act as the coordinating agency and initiative has to be taken by state governments. In the 1990s, total value of crop production increased considerably. The share of fruits and vegetable increased from 17.7 per cent (1990-91) to 22.7 per cent (1999-00) in value terms. Two most important things, which should be integrated into our strategy, are development of domestic market and diversification of farm production. Progressive diversification and domestic market development will lead to specialised food processing areas. FAIDA report brings out huge market potential in following areas.

Market Potential	*Rs. (in Crores)*
High size of market and less growth	
Sugar	24,000
Oil	5,00,000
High growth and large market	
Fresh poultry	27,000
Bakery	10,000
Packaged milk	36,000
Soft drinks	10,500
Processed meat	9,000
Coffee	7,400
High growth and small market	
Frozen vegetables	350
Fresh vegetables	1,200
Fruit drinks	2,000

Current estimates of income elasticity for food grains even in a poor country like India is placed at 0.2 to 0.3 or below. Thus, even if the growth rate is maintained at 4 per cent for next 20 years, income induced growth in demand for staple food grains will grow at less than 1 per cent per year. Thus, it will be more logical to grow non-food crops to achieve higher growth.

But scenarios are different in various states. Let us consider Punjab and Haryana. Given the input-output price structure, agriculture in Punjab and Haryana has become rice-wheat monoculture. In Punjab 43.20 per cent of the total gross cropped area is wheat and another 30.20 per cent is under rice. Similar conditions also exist in pockets like Tanjore delta. FAIDA report estimates the wheat market at Rs. 15,000 crores, in spite of hardly one per cent being in the hands of branded *atta* players. As consumers in India like distinct wheat flavour after grounding, branded *atta* is unlikely to take off.

Though five per cent agricultural growth rate is remarkable, the rice-wheat monoculture doesn't provide optimism, keeping the present price policy, unsustainable agriculture and the WTO regime in perspective. Economic cost of Punjab wheat through FCI is around Rs. 850 per quintal. But internationally it is available roughly at Rs. 475 per quintal. As our quality parameters and storage conditions are inferior, it is very difficult to compete in the global food market. Therefore, value addition holds the key in present context. Simultaneously, attempts to provide brand names to our geographic indicators will bring remarkable effect. Basmati rice, Coorg mandarins, Tejpur chillies are few to name. Administration has an important job to perform. Prescribing and disseminating quality standards, documenting geographic indicators undertaking cost accounting *etc* can be done.

Our failures in crops like coffee and areca show that our market intelligence is not strong enough to direct crop acreage planning. At the same time, we concentrated on global coffee market rather than internal commodity market. Unless we take advantage of strong home demand, the future of Indian coffee is bleak. Of course, emphasis on productivity is conspicuously missing. The elasticity of employment to GDP shows that for entire economy it was 0.53 in the period 1977 to 1983 and declined to 0.15 during 1993-2000. Similarly employment elasticity in agriculture dipped to zero during the same period. Specific efforts towards value addition coupled with higher investment in agriculture only can reverse this trend.

Let us come back to issues of value addition and investment. FAIDA report estimates around Rs. 50,000 crores as total loss due to wastage. Frictional cost in the chain between farm outputs to terminal consumption, huge number of players in the system and diseconomics of scale are responsible for this. Consolidators, commission agents, wholesale agents, retailers dominate the system and substitute for infrastructure. Less than 2.5 per cent of US population is dependent on agriculture. It is physically possible to tag each of them and to conduct a chain of operations. In the process, they have very less inventory costs and transaction costs. But, in India, the scenario is different. According to an estimate we need to invest around Rs. 1,47,000 crores across this chain. The breakup is as follows.

Activity	*Estimated Investment (Rs. in crores)*
Extension	12,000
Procurement	18,000
Production	75,000
Distribution	20,000
Retailing	22,000
Total	**1,47,000**

Issues in Research and Extension

The organised agricultural extension system came into operation only after independence. Since then, agricultural extension has played a major role in commercialising agriculture. Today's agriculture is progressively commercialising and hence, the number of players in agriculture is increasing. Hence the independent farmer of yesterday is dependent on more players today than ever before.

Today public extension system suffers from various limitations. The extension worker to farmer ratio is very wide, i.e., 1:1000. Educational background of village level extension worker is found to be less than adequate. At present, the role of village level worker is confined to providing advisory assistance to process of production. The important strategy to strengthen the public sector extension system is to make it autonomous and decentralized. Decentralization of management programmes through participatory involvement of farmers in decision-making and ultimately inducing farmers to take responsibility for extension programmes should be our strategy. Participatory involvement is doubtlessly effective in making services responsive to local conditions.

Public-private partnerships can be initiated to hasten up intensity of extension programmes. Consultative extension linkages between universities and private parties are one such mode. Contractual initiatives like contracts for development of technology, training of manpower and finding appropriate technological solutions can be signed. Collaborative efforts to utilise the available expertise and infrastructure of public extension is another option.

Promoting private initiatives like agri-clinics is a welcome idea. But success depends on sustained support to these clinics over a period of time. Strengthening co-operatives like AMUL and farmers' organisations will definitely pay dividends. Another notable initiative is E-Choupals introduced by ITC. These are commodity based service centres where unique internet kiosks cum one-stop shops for farmers are created. Although these are criticised as marketing channels for private companies, they are likely to fill up infrastructure gaps in marketing sector. Already 25 coffee kiosks have been introduced in Karnataka.

Another paradigm shift seen in research sector is concentration on frontier technologies like biotechnology, genetic engineering *etc*. This has led to neglect of classical researches like plant breeding, soil science *etc*. Higher productivity is not just a function of variety or genes introduced, but depends also on various agronomic practices, soil moisture regime *etc*. Therefore, the Indian farmer needs more of applied research. This brings us to an issue of objective evaluation of research outcomes, which may in turn help us to have a judicious mix of basic and applied research. How well does it prioritize biotechnology in the absence of well-established IPR regime? This is yet to be answered. Let us consider huge investment in gene banks like NBPGR, which has a germplasm collection of around 2,00,000. If the biological principle itself emphasises extinction, why should we invest so much on it? Much bio-piracy has already been done. So, it is nothing but closing the stables once the horse has fled. Even after so much of technological sophistication we are struggling hard to commercialise one transgenic variety of Bt Cotton. If substantial outcomes won't come over a period of time, such establishments are bound to lose political support. Thus, each investment should be continued based on objective evaluation and zero-based budgeting.

Emerging Issues in Regulation, Administration, Subsidies, etc.

Researches in UAS, Bangalore, indicate that investment in dryland areas through watershed development is hardly Rs. 6000 per hectare, as compared to around Rs. 60,000 for command areas. Roughly 65 per cent of area being dryland, there is a need to compensate dryland farmers by providing free electricity or electricity at nominal cost. But, such a subsidy should find a separate place separately in the state budget. The investible resources with government have to be raised by increasing tax-GDP ratio, as well as through better cost recovery for the input services provided.

In the atmosphere of political populism, change management becomes a crucial aspect. Farmers may not respond to sudden harder decisions. Transition from a regime where electricity is free or nominal at around 27 paise per unit to complete cost recovery will be really abrupt. Now, Karnataka has taken a middle path. Farmer has to pay a flat rate of Rs. 300 per HP or whatever the meter reads, whichever is low. As Howes and Murgai bring out:

"Seventy two per cent of the rural population doesn't cultivate any irrigated land. These are people who are landless (14 per cent) or landowners who do not cultivate any irrigated land (52 per cent). Majority (85 per cent) of SC and STs don't cultivate irrigated land. Out of those who cultivate irrigated land, 70 per cent are having less than 2 hectares of land. 83 per cent of poor have no access to irrigation of any form. Similarly, 70 per cent of large farmers and 60 per cent of medium farmers cultivating irrigated land own at least one electric pump set. By contrast 22 per cent of marginal farmers own these pumps. Over 80 per cent of benefits of subsidised electricity go to medium and large farmers. On an average, in case of Karnataka, large farmers who own pump sets receive Rs. 29,000 subsidy per year. This is roughly 10 times more the amount each household would receive if distributed equally, amongst all rural households. Higher and higher investments should be made in pump sets, bore wells, sprinklers, moving sprinklers, drip irrigation *etc* in those holdings, which are either marginal or small."

With respect to land management, the administration has two functions to perform. Firstly, proper land record maintenance and secondly, inculcating collective spirit while undertaking agricultural operations. In a study named "India: The Growth Imperatives Understanding the Barriers to Rapid Growth and Employment Creation" conducted by McKinsey, it is noted that unclear property rights and land market distortions account for close to 1.3 per cent of loss of growth an year. Proper record maintenance by digitizing and computerizing is the key to consolidation and other land management functions.

Secondly, it is important to educate people to operate on holdings of appropriate size. Usually around 10-12 acres of land is a profitable holding if economies of scale is considered as criteria. The detailed table pertaining to fig and pomegranate cultivation in Hiriyur *taluk* of Chitradurga presented in the following table clearly shows that pomegranate, fig and other horticultural crops have better returns. So, inculcating this mindset to diversify their cropping pattern and to operate on right size by co-operative or collective farming can be attempted by administration.

Government should progressively leave the agricultural sector for market principles to operate. Of course, equity interventions will still be relevant looking into agrarian structure. But, operations like monopsony cotton purchase in Maharashtra, food rationing in Calcutta *etc* definitely defy market principles. Statutory pricing and levying on sugar or rice milling will only increase malpractices. Removal of around 55 commodities from the Essential Commodities Act restrictions is a welcome step in this regard. Regulatory hurdles such as limits on storage, levy procurements, taxes like *mandi* fee, purchase tax, rural development cess *etc.*, need to be eliminated for the efficient functioning of market. World Bank analysis indicates that keeping groundnut crushing reserved under small scale industries has reduced total transaction to the tune of 30 per cent. A high level committee on Long Term Food Grains Policy has suggested removing restrictions on the interstate movements of food grains. Deregulation and decontrol are immediate imperatives.

Economics of Fig and Pomegranate Cultivation in Hiriyur taluk of Chitradurga in Karnataka

Particulars	*Per acre*	*Farm*
Average farm size (in acres)		15.44
Proportion of area under fig		30.00
Production of area under pomegranate		45.00
Area under fig in the farm (acres)		4.70
Area under pomegranate in the farm (acres)		5.47
Details of Fig Cultivation (in the third year of cultivation)		
Production (in kgs)	1413	6641
Gross income (in Rupees)	40844	191967
Net income (in rupees)	12788	60104
Discounted net income at 16% (Rs.)	8193	38508
Details of Pomegranate Cultivation (in the Vth year of cultivation)		
Production (in kgs)	4698	25698
Gross income (in rupees)	68658	375559
Net income (in rupees)	32483	177682
Discounted net income at 16% (Rs.)	15466	84597
Details of Cultivation of Ragi		
Production (in kgs)	800	8500
Gross income (in rupees)	3200	45305
Net income (in rupees)	1000	28460
Details of cultivation of Groundnut		
Production (in kgs)	300	5000
Gross income (in rupees)	4000	60000
Net income (in rupees)	2000	32925

Another example of the palm oil experiment in Karnataka can be worthwhile for discussion. Oil palm was promoted on large scale in 1990s in Karnataka. But it wasn't evaluated as to how the produce will be transported to processing point and what would be the economic feasibility of small farms. Palm nut has a strange constraint that it should be processed within 48 hours, if not it turns rancid. The palm oil experiment failed miserably. The most harm was done to the extension agency and its credibility amongst farmers. However this experiment has several learnings:

1. Target approach envisaged in various government agencies may turn out to be anomalous while executing projects.

2. Sound management principles, statistical approaches and logistics considerations are important for successful implementation.
3. Production and processing should be coordinated. Credit and processing should be linked, to remove distress sale and other market malfunctions.
4. Imperfection of scale can be managed only through huge investments in agricultural infrastructure, cold chains, roads, storage houses *etc.*

Strengthening the market system should be one of the major objectives. Introduction of market functions like future marketing/ forward marketing *etc.*, will help market to operate efficiently. At present forward marketing is conducted in commodities such as pepper, cotton, gur, hessian, potatoes, coffee, castor, palmolein *etc.* These are traded in 17 commodity exchanges. Commodity derivatives have a crucial role to play in price risk management process, especially in agriculture dominated economy. Derivatives like forwards, futures, options, swaps *etc.*, are used extensively in many developing and developed countries. The government has two important roles to play. Disciplining those who try to manipulate markets for their own benefit and enabling role by which the government provides the necessary legal and regulatory framework for smooth functioning of system. Constitution of commodity exchanges should be rehauled. All commodity exchanges in India are mutual organisations. They are promoted by traders, who carry out trading as well as keep management controls of exchanges. Many leading exchanges like New York Mercantile Exchange are demutualised organisations. Such demutualisation will definitely enhance the efficiency of commodity exchanges. The success of any project will depend upon extent of participation. Unless the project is demand driven, sustained participation can't be expected. Participation is the solution for various problems like corruption also. The extent of participation indicates the depth of interface that administration has achieved.

Willingness to participate can be indicated by extent of cost sharing that participants accept. Farmers pay around 20-30 per cent of costs of saplings supplied to them in the DANIDA projects in Karnataka. Cost sharing has profound impact in reducing corruption and enhancing efficiency. In case of DANIDA (Dharwar), number of saplings lifted was reduced and survival rate of saplings was increased. Other implication is that it makes the project collaborative and bureaucracy becomes accountable to stake holders separately. Practical execution of projects like watershed will depend upon realised benefits also. The MYRADA project of Kollegal, where farmers built bunds on field with 10-15 per cent slopes, is another example.

The NWDPRA guidelines extol participation and learning from farmers. The new guidelines of MoRD go to the extent of placing project funds under the control of communities. At the some time enabling atmosphere for workers is also important. VELUGU project for poverty alleviation in Andhra Pradesh is based on one such principle. As the public machinery has less time to devote for social organisation, the execution and supervision should be entrusted to NGOs and co-operatives and other agencies. Selective project funding should be made the rule. Funds may be with held until communities show evidence of being able to work without funds. This will not only have fiscal pressures on the community itself, but also on bureaucracy and force bureaucracy to work with communities with appropriate orientations. Higher transparency and accounting principles have reinvigorating effect on community participation. The collector of Kalahandi was proposing to publicise information on funds received by various agencies from the district organisation. Such steps will not only bring awareness but exudes confidence in community members.

Approaches like watershed development will provide convenient target groups through which various principles of crop diversification, marketing co-operatives and crop planning for dry lands and water sources situations can be disseminated effectively. Ultimately, it is very important to decide what should be our strategy to active higher agricultural growth. Should it be trade, terms of trade or technological change? If it is trade, should it be external trade or internal trade?

External trade as a strategy suffers from various constraints. For e.g.: Rice trade liberalization is bound to bring advantage to competitive countries where NPC (Nominal Protection Co-efficient) is less than one. Theoretically, it should improve prices in India through flow of rice from India towards potential markets outside. This will obviously improve terms of trade towards agriculture and will enhance public investment and hence, growth. But, the protectionist regime in US for rice is unlikely to allow this. Moreover, phyto sanitary measures and other considerations will help developed countries to use them as NTBs. For example, Japan is avoiding imports of Indian mangoes for more than 15 years. External trade may not yield the expected results. As farm sector dominates trade transactions in India, Ricardo's law of diminishing returns operate. Thus, the production possibility frontier of farm sector may not shift in correspondence with non-farm sector of developed countries. Thus external trade with distinct exchange regimes may not elicit desired growth in economy as a whole.

Thus, the most rational step would be to concentrate on internal market and finding new niches for production and marketing of crops in India. The huge domestic market is definitely likely to provide a large market to farm products. But different quality considerations for exports and imports, different packaging standards, *etc.*, go against such strategy. The predicament of shift differential in production possibility frontiers can be offset by proper technical and technological changes to some extent. This needs huge investment in R&D and an enhancement to 2 per cent of GDP. As over 90 per cent of farmers who own or operate over 65 per cent of land are marginal or small, we can't expect them to invest in these new technologies.

References

ASI Statistics (1993-94). McKinsey analysis.

Chadha, G.K. (2002). *Indian Agriculture in the New Millennium: Human Response to Technology Challenges*, 62nd Annual Conference of Indian Society of Agricultural Economics, New Delhi.

Chandrakanth, M.G. and Mengesha, B. (2001). *Economic Access to Ground Water Irrigation*, UAS, Bangalore, Ford Foundation.

Chandrashekara, P. (2001). *Private* Extension *in India: Myths, Relative Apprehensions and Approaches*. MANAGE, Hyderabad.

Correa, G.A. "Farm Size, Land Yield and the Agricultural Production Function: An Analysis for Fifteen Developing Countries", *World Development*, Vol. 13 (4).

Datta, K.S. (1996). "Sustainability of Small Producer Unit Strength through Co-operatives Lessons from Several Case Studies", in *Small Farms Diversification* edited by T. Haq, National Centre for Agricultural Economics and Policy Research.

Desai, M.B. (2002). "Terms of Trade, Trade and Technical Change", *Economic and Political Weekly*, Feb. 23, 2002.

Dev, S.M. (2003). "Agriculture, Employment and Social Sector Neglected", *Economic and Political Weekly*, April 5th 2003.

Dutta, B. and Ramaswami B. (2001a). "Targeting and Efficiency in PDS : A Case of Andhra and Maharashtra", May 5-11, *Economic and Political Weekly*, Vol. 35 (18).

GoI Report (2002). "Report of Special Group on Targeting Ten Million Employment Opportunities Per Year", Planning Commission.

Gulati, A. (2000). "Surplus Food: What's to be Done?", *Economic Times*, Sept. 21st 2000.

Gulati, A. and Bathla, S. (2001). "Capital Formation in Indian Agriculture", *Economic and Political Weekly*, May 19th 2001.

Gulati, A. and Narayanan, S. (2003). "Rice Trade Liberalisation and Poverty", *Economic and Political Weekly*, Jan 4th 2003.

Hiremath, B.N. and Ballabh, V. (1996). "Integrating Small Farmers with Market, Problems and Prospect", in *Small Farm Diversification* (ed.) T. Haq, National Centre for Agricultural Economics and Policy Research (NCAP).

Howes, S. and Murgai, R. (2003). "Incidence of Agricultural Subsidies", *Economic and Political Weekly*, April 19th 2003.

Iyer, R.R. (2001). "Water: Charting a Course for Future", *Economic and Political Weekly*, Mar. 31st 2001.

Kolavalli, L.S. and Kerr, J. (2002). "Mainstreaming Participatory Watershed Development", *Economic and Political Weekly*, Jan 19th 2002.

Maji, C.C., Haq, T. and Bhattacharya, A. (1995). "Small Farms and Surplus Generation – A Case of West Bengal", National Centre for Agricultural Economics and Policy Research.

McKinsey Report (1996). FAIDA

Mulji, J.S. (2003). "Agriculture and Unemployment", *Economic and Political Weekly*, April 12th, 2003.

Naik, G. and Jain, S.K. (2002). "Indian Agricultural Commodity Future Market, *Economic and Political Weekly*, July 27th 2002.

Parikh, K.S. (1994). "Who Gets How Much from PDS, How Effectively does it Reach Poor?", *Sarvekshana*, January to March 1994.

Parikh K.S., Kumar, A.G. and Darbha, G. (2003). "Growth and Welfare Consequence of Rise in MSP", *Economic and Political Weekly*, Mar 1st 2003.

Planning Commission, 9th Five-year Plan, midterm appraisal.

Prakashkumar (2002). Economics of Pomegranate and Fig Cultivation in Hiriyur *taluk* in Chitradurga, *Ph.D Thesis*, UAS, Bangalore.

Ramaswami, B. (2002). "Efficiency and Equity of Food Market Interventions", *Economic and Political Weekly*, Mar 23rd 2002.

Rao, C.H.H. (2003). "Reform Agenda for Agriculture", *Economic and Political Weekly*, Vol. 8 (7).

Shastry, T. (2003). In Seminar on "*Managing Large Developmental Projects*", LBSNAA, Mussoorie

Singh, B.P. (1996). "Backward Agriculture – Causes of Indian Poverty", in *Small Farms Diversification* (ed.) T. Haq, National Centre for Agricultural Economics and Policy Research.

Singh, K. and Kalra, S. (2002). "Rice Production in Punjab", *Economic and Political Weekly*, July 27th 2002.

Tarozzi, A. (2000). "A Birds Eye View of PDS Utilisation using 50th Round of the Indian National Sample Survey (July 1993-1994), Mimio.

The Hindu, Dec. 12, 2002: 13.

Varadarajan and Elangovan (1996). "Scope for Small Farm Agriculture", in *Small Farm Diversification* (ed.) Haq. T., National Centre for Agricultural Economics and Policy Research (NCAP).

Vyas, V.S. (2001). "Agriculture: Second Round of Economic Reforms", *Economic and Political Weekly*, March 10th 2001.

Vyas, V.S. (2002). "Our Agrarian Future", *Economic and Political Weekly*, Mar. 14th 2002.

Wadhwa, D.C. (2002). "Guaranteeing Title to Land", *Economic and Political Weekly*, Nov. 23rd 2002.

World Bank Report (1998). *Agriculture Scenario in Haryana.*

Zijp, W., Rivera, W.M. and Artholt (1996). "Decentralising Agricultural Extension", in *Decentralization of Fiscal System And Rural Development*, Binswanger, H. (ed.) Washington DC, The World Bank.

4

Growth and the Poor Farmer

Why is it so Important to Reform Agriculture?

AMIR ULLAH KHAN

Growth in Agriculture

There has been a phenomenal 16.9 per cent agriculture growth in the third quarter for 2003-2004. This is after a healthy 7.4 per cent in the previous quarter. More than 65 per cent of the population is directly affected by this growth, which meets the food requirements of a vastly populated nation. Food grain production will register an all-time high of 212.2 million tonnes this year. Exports of agriculture and processed food products have also risen by over 35 per cent to touch Rs. 13,828 crores. It is primarily because of this growth in agriculture that the overall GDP growth is set to reach new heights. This also shows how the economy is intrinsically agriculture based and will be so for a long time.

India's economic history over the last sixty years has been a mix of the good, bad and ugly. Growth rates have increased and per capita incomes have gone up. Liberalization and deregulation have yielded impressive results, and the economy is increasingly integrated to the world. However, agriculture continues to be the backbone. And all is not well in this sector. Productivity[1] gains were sustained in the 1990s after the liberalization process began, the yield rates for most of the agricultural products in India are far below a number of other countries. Except in the case of sugarcane, tea, coffee and jute, India's yields are lower than the world average. India is ranked second, both

---

1. Labor productivity in India's farm sector has grown by an average of 0.5 per cent over the past two decades, compared with productivity growth in East Asian farming of over 2 per cent a year (IMF, 2003).

in area and output, for sugarcane production and is the largest producer of tea and jute in the world. Even in the case of wheat, average yields in the Netherlands and Ireland are more than three times India's yield rates. In all other major crops, India's productivity is lower than world averages.

GDP and Agriculture Growth Rates

(Per cent)

Year	*GDP**	*GDP (Agriculture and Allied Sectors)*
1992-93	5.1	5.8
1993-94	5.9	4.1
1994-95	7.3	5.0
1995-96	7.3	–0.9
1996-97	7.8	9.6
1997-98	4.8	–2.4
1998-99	6.5	6.2
1999-00	6.1	0.3
2000-01	4.4	–0.4
2001-02	5.6	5.7
2002-03	4.4	–3.1
2003-04**	8.2	5.4

Source: *Economic Survey*

* At 1993-94 Prices

** Estimates

What are the Problems?

Out of 100 million holdings in India, more than 80 million have less than 1 hectare of land. By 2020, the number of such marginal holdings will increase to something like 100 million. Access to technology has been low and alternative distribution channels for marketing, seeds and technology have not evolved. Farmers organizations remain weak, as do rules and organizations. Irrigation has not been given due importance and utilization of irrigation resources, at 85 per cent, is below optimal.

However, input availability continues to be sub-optimal. Only 40 per cent of net sown area is irrigated and this constrains use of inputs or modern technology. Adequate seeds are not available. Adequate pesticides are also not available. Standards are not enforced. Reservations for the small-scale industry (SSI) sector have hindered development of farm machines and implements. Flow of institutional credit is also a constraint. Although 18 per cent of priority sector lending is supposed to be for agriculture, agriculture's share in net bank credit has been more like 12 per cent. States lack resources and this has adversely affected development of agricultural infrastructure. Public investments in irrigation, roads and technology upgradation have been affected.

In the 1990s, the quality of agricultural research, technology development and extension services has deteriorated. There are too many marketing controls on foodgrains and other crops. And the list of problems within agriculture goes on - preponderance of old and uneconomically sized orchards and poor management practices, perishable horticulture produce, high post-harvest losses, lack of modern and efficient infrastructure facilities and poor post-harvest management practices, underdevelopment of marketing infrastructures, absence of adequate standards, inadequate research and extension support, expensive imports[2], large-scale variations in credit support and tax structures for different commodities, instability of prices, poor risk management and inadequate information about sanitary and phyto sanitary (SPS) standards.

Given this context, the importance of freeing up Agriculture[3] and the need for markets, both domestic and foreign[4], cannot be neglected any more. The growth rate needs to be sustained and given the pervasive role of agriculture, it is axiomatic that reforms in the agriculture sector are imperative. Input subsidies leading to misuse

---

2. India has set a ceiling rate for its agricultural tariffs at very high levels, ranging from 100 per cent for food grains to 150 per cent for meat and fish. Some are as high as 300 per cent, such as for coconut and palm-oil products (*Gulati, 1998*).

3. The removal of export controls on rice and wheat is a landmark policy change clearly beneficial to farmers (World Bank, 1997). Given that rice alone accounts for 40 per cent of Indian agricultural production, it is a major step forward. However, several restrictions remain. For instance, the import duty on non essential goods such as almonds remains at 50 per cent. The grain sector is still regulated by canalizing agencies, to safeguard against food shortages.

4. Agricultural growth averaged 3.3 per cent per year in the last two decades of the twentieth century. India has achieved self sufficiency in food production; but it has yet to exploit its potential to export agricultural goods — today, only 1 per cent of world agricultural trade comes from India.

and over use, support prices causing market distortions and the absence of market information are some of the urgent issues that need to be tackled.

The Green Revolution Revisited

In the twentieth century, agricultural growth stagnated as a result of a series of droughts and famine. The Green Revolution in the 1960s raised productivity levels on the one hand, but was rather harshly criticized for widening income disparities between rich and poor farmers on the other. The late 1960s and early 1970s witnessed a modernized agriculture with new equipment and farm technology. New fertilizers led to high yielding varieties, tractors replaced cattle and the immediate result was that the production of crops such as wheat and rice increased remarkably. But growth was far from uniform.

States such as Haryana and Punjab, well endowed with irrigation and fertile soils, benefited. Secondly, large farmers were better placed to invest in new technology. Smaller farmers lacked capital. Many were displaced. Government policies reacted by compensating small farmers by heavily subsidizing inputs and credit in the agricultural sector. Free electricity and water was provided in some states. And in these fortunate states, farmers benefited from public spending on infrastructure and support services.

But subsidies breed inefficiency and capture, even by the non-agricultural user, for example in the case of diesel. In the case of the irrigation subsidy, "most of the actual expenses ended up financing the state's irrigation departments salary and wage payments to a bureaucracy with limited accountability for the operation and maintenance of government schemes." (World Bank, 1997). Subsidies also led to environmental and production distortions. The literature on fertilizer subsidy went to show that it caused serious nutrient imbalances in fertilizer application. Irrigation and rural power subsidies distorted cropping patterns and promoted crops that needed lots of water in dry regions.

In a price sensitive political economy, the government faced two conflicting priorities. The urban consumer wanted cheap food, and the farmer high prices. What ensued was a clear bias towards the more articulate and homogenous urban voter, and the farmer was surely getting penalized. Farm prices were kept below world market levels in order to ensure food supply at affordable rates to people in towns. On the other hand, industrial prices were high as tariff barriers protected domestic manufacturing. Between 1971 and 1988, the protection offered to agriculture was half of what went to industry.

This protection raised input prices for the farmer. Machinery imports were hurt as the rupee was over valued, increasing the costs of imports. In the 1980s agricultural prices fell by 25 per cent in relation to the industrial and services sectors, and investment in agriculture stagnated (World Bank, 1997; Rao, 1994). Agricultural trade was severely regulated. Exports were controlled by state owned enterprises called "canalizing agencies". The movement of produce was curtailed and controlled stocks and regulated distribution further reduced efficiency.

The Small Farmer

Who is a small farmer? For this it is important to look at land holding patterns in rural India. Data from the Department of Agriculture shows that

- Marginal land holdings (less than 1 hectare) were 50 per cent of the total in 1971 and in 1991 constituted 30 per cent of the total.
- The average size of marginal holdings works out to 0.40 hectares.
- Total number of holdings in India have gone up from 71 million in 1971 to 106 million in 1991.
- In the same period, area operated increased from 162 million hectares to 166 million hectares.
- Of the 71 million farm holdings, 36 million were held by small farmers in 1971.
- In 1991, of the 166 million, the number of small holdings went up to 62 million.
- The number of small holders (between 1 and 4 acres) in the same period went up from 24 million to 34 million.

- The average size of small holdings is roughly 2 hectares.
- The overall average size of holdings in India has dropped from 2.28 hectares in 1971 to 1.57 in 1991.
- In states like Jammu and Kashmir, Kerala, UP and West Bengal, the average is less than 1 hectare. Jammu and Kashmir's average is at 0.33 hectares.
- When compared to the developed world, the reality is stark.
- The average size of land holdings in the UK and US are 55 and 158 hectares respectively.

What does this mean to the policy maker or to the stake holder in Agriculture reform in India?

- Firstly, that small farm sizes will always keep farmers on the margin.
- Secondly, agriculture will continue to be un-remunerative if continued as it is.
- Some form of consolidation is urgently called for.
- This could be in the form of cooperative farming, contract farming or joint farming.
- The cluster approach could be one way out.
- Farmers in clusters attain better buying power and stronger negotiating stances.
- Extension services could be more easily reached.
- Information dissemination and availability becomes easier.
- Market access is smoother and distortions kept in check.
- Larger constituencies are developed and therefore greater lobbying power is ensured.
- Farming communities become less heterogeneous and could exercise their collective power in a democracy.

Serious Concerns

In this context, it is important to take a look at some of the critical areas of concern where the farmer and agriculture growth are concerned. Firstly, it is important to focus on the skewed nature of agriculture production in India. Despite oft repeated declarations of intent on the importance of crop diversification[5], the agriculture sector is heavily dependent on food grains. The relationship between foodgrains and food security is so strong that effectively nothing is done towards diversification. As food crops suffer because of monsoons and prices, the economy suffers. On the other hand, stocks pile up and lead to some embarrassment for the policy maker. Productivity levels continue to stagnate, putting greater pressure on land and other resources. Intensive agriculture gives way to an extensive route and yields do not show any growth.

Secondly, there is a need to look at the rural employment scenario, an issue much neglected so far. The pattern of employment as it has emerged is indeed a cause of concern. In 1951, 70 per cent of the total work force was engaged in agriculture and in 2001, this had dropped to 59 per cent. The proportion of labourers increased from 20 to 27 per cent and cultivators declined from 50 to 32 per cent. However these figures pale in comparison to the developed world. In Australia, 6 per cent and in France, only 7 per cent of the work force is engaged in agriculture. In the US and UK, the percentages are 3 and 2 per cent respectively. Even in Egypt, the work force in agriculture is less than 35 per cent. (FA Yearbook, 1997)

Thirdly, there is the disturbing trend in exports.[6] Indian Agriculture, according to Tenth Plan estimates, contributes only 14.7 per cent to total export earnings. What is worse is that almost all of this is due to export of primary goods and very little produce is processed. Even within this, there is a predominance of just five or six crops namely, tea, rice[7], oilseeds, tobacco, spices and sugar. If overall export growth rate should be taken to the target of 25 per cent a year, it is imperative that agriculture exports are increased and that processed food[8] replaces primary farm commodities in the export basket.

5. According to Hashim (1998), agriculture has developed a degree of immunity against monsoons; partly because of extended irrigation, but more so due to the diversification of agricultural activities.
6. The removal of export restrictions has led to an increase in cereal exports, which rose from 12 per cent to 27 per cent of total agricultural exports between 1991 and 1996 (WTO, 1998).
7. India accounts for 22 per cent of total world rice production and 4 per cent of world exports. (UNCTAD).
8. Although the country is the second largest producer of fruits and vegetables in the world, only 1 per cent of total production is commercially processed and exported to a limited number of markets in South Asia, the Middle East and Eastern Europe (World Bank, 2003).

However, these are but three of a large number of issues that confront any student of the agriculture sector. The number of problems is large and has been extensively discussed. Risk mitigation, credit availability, warehousing, infrastructure, marketing support, information issues, irrigation needs, extension services, quality of seeds, rural industrialization, harsh regulation, movement controls and many others continue to haunt the farmer. What is important here is to realize that growth in agriculture and access to markets for the small farmer is critical if the agriculture sector is to grow. Further, this is crucial if the overall growth rate of 8 to 10 per cent is to be sustained. That is why the importance of looking at growth rates and the small farmer.

References

Gulati, A. and Rao, H. (1992). "Indian Agriculture: Emerging Perspectives and Policy Issues", *Economic and Political Weekly*, December.

Gulati, A. and Sharma, A. (1997). "Freeing Trade in Agriculture", *Economic and Political Weekly*, December.

Hashim, S.R. (1998). "Economic Growth and Income Distribution", *Economic and Political Weekly*, 21 March 1998.

IMF (1995). *India: Economic Reform and Growth*, Occasional paper 134, Washington: International Monetary Fund.

Keshari, K. *et al* (1995). "Implications of GATT-94 on Exports of Indian Agro-processing Firms", *World Trade Research and Information Report*, Vol. 1, No. 3.

Patnaik, P. (1997). "The Context and Consequences of Economic Liberalization in India", *Journal of International Trade and Development*, Vol.6, No.2, July 1997.

Pursel, G. (1996). *"Some Aspects of the Liberalization of South Asian Agricultural Policies: How can the WTO Help?"*, Draft paper for the Food and Agricultural Organization.

Storm, S. (1997). "The Unfinished Agenda: Indian Agriculture under the Structural Reforms", *Journal of International Trade and Development*, Vol.6, No.2, July 1997.

Thomas, P. *et al* (1994). "Dunkel Text: Implications for Rural Sector", *Economic and Political Weekly*. March.

UNCTAD (1996). *Strengthening the Participation of Developing Countries in World Trade and the Multilateral Trading System*, Geneva: United Nations Conference on Trade and Development.

World Bank (1996). *India: Recent Economic Developments and Prospects*, Washington: World Bank.

———. (1997). *India: Five Years of Stabilization and Reform and the Challenges Ahead*, Washington: World Bank.

5

Challenges of Integrating Small Holders in Markets

S.J. PHANSALKAR[1]

Introduction

A distinct value preference is inherent in the title of the paper. Small holders are in fact participants in the market exchange even as of now, as they have been for centuries. Arguably, the question of integrating them in the markets does not therefore arise. But there is a widely shared perception that small holder farmers, particularly those who have little bargaining power, those who are located in far flung areas and those who depend entirely on their farm produce to buy them their simple needs, are essentially unequal participants in the exchange. Producer share in the consumer rupee is taken as a measure of how good is the market for the producer. This may be a bit naïve, but is widely done. This widely shared view holds that not only are the existing terms of this exchange unfair and exploitative for the small holders, they also inhibit greater investment and entrepreneurship.

Yet the theory of perfectly competitive markets and market efficiencies would hold otherwise. If a very large number of such small holders were being unfairly treated by the market for extended periods of time, then obviously someone would make supernormal profits and that would attract new actors to enter the markets, reducing the monopolistic sway of the extant players. Strangely enough, there is enough scholastic evidence and argument that claim that markets for most agricultural commodities are reasonably efficient. A study of the

1. I wish to thank IDE for permitting me to use the materials developed during the course of work with them for this purpose. I also thank Sarvashri S. Shivkumar, Trilochan Shastry, S.C. Rajsekhar, Sanjeev Gupta, and Hemant Nayak for directly or indirectly helping me evolve the arguments in this paper.

oilseeds sector in which I participated, showed that the market imperfections were a result of fragmented and incoherent regulation, policy induced instability and infrastructure bottlenecks. A more recent survey in the vegetable market reveals that other than the pure broker (*adati*, who is a commission agent and works on a fixed percentage basis), virtually none of the market players makes any substantial profits. Some barely manage to exist. Yet producer share of the consumer rupee seldom exceeds 20-25 per cent.

The key to resolve this paradox is to recognize that there are strong institutional influences, infrastructural bottlenecks and regulatory and other constraints that on the one hand define the rules of transactions, and on the other, simultaneously make the agricultural markets inefficient and one-sided. Thus I would like to pose this paper as one that describes the challenges of institutional reforms and in creating fair and equal market exchange opportunities for the small holders for them to prosper from improved market performance.

The main premise of this paper is that small holders stand to gain if they can access markets in such a manner that they receive prices that are fair and consistent with the systemic risks and returns features of the national market. An empowered and informed integration of small holders into markets can lead to significant poverty impacts and lead to enabling them to realize the full economic potential of their assets and put them on an upward ratchet. Hence it is desirable to explore and evolve ways of moving towards such an empowered and informed integration into markets, at least for producers of those commodities where the gains promise to be particularly large.

This paper is informed by my current engagement on this subject on behalf of IDE, my past association with studies of agricultural markets and my discussions with some noteworthy individuals. The views in this paper are mine. I try to present them in a direct and informal manner. I extensively use the illustration of vegetable markets, though I believe that the arguments have a general application.

Conceptual Framework

The essential condition for benefiting from the market is the possession of or access to assets required to produce goods and services that are demanded. Small holders do have at least small patches of land on which to grow horticultural crops. They have family labour, which can be applied to the diverse tasks in the production process. Agencies such as the IDEI provide them technology for efficient water delivery to the crops, if and where they have access to water. The essential condition can thus be met for all small holders with access to a base level of water.

Effective participation in the market requires:

- Access to information: The small holder must know what product is required when and where. It is perhaps even better if s/he were to know the information about arrivals during specified time slots of a year so s/he can decide that her produce is harvested just after or just before periods of peak harvest. That will enable her to gain better realization. A finer point is about the sub-type or variety of a vegetable required or preferred in a market.[2] Specific varieties are in high demand in narrow time windows about which the producers need to know ahead. They can then plan planting and nurturing the crops so as to make the crop ready for harvest just at the right time. Prior information on arrivals as well as prices prevailing in proximate *mandis* may save the producer from incurring prohibitive sunk costs that force him to sell at a loss in unfavourable circumstances.
- Access to logistics of packing, transport, intermediate and final storage etc. For instance shortage of Railway wagons can cause banana realizations to plummet in South Gujarat and Khandesh. Truckers strike causes doom for mandarin orange growers of Nagpur. The dependence of potato growers on cold storage owners is proverbially known in North India.
- Access to working capital is important at almost all stages of cultivation, but its importance at the time of marketing is crucial. Producers are tempted to sell their produce for a price discounted by as much as 30 per cent for spot payment and at these points in time, access to working capital would increase their incomes.

---

2. For instance, *katargam papdi* (a special small and sweetish variety of French beans) is extremely popular around *Sankranti* in Gujarat. All manners of leafy vegetables are required around the festival of *mahalaksmi* in September in Vidarbha. The yellow *genda* flowers are in huge demand on *Dassera* and on *Diwali* all over India.

- Assurances are needed to enable the small holders to take necessary risks. Mere information is not enough. She needs to know the agents and market players and also needs to have assurances about their behaviour.

Yet it must be recognized that markets are large and cruel. They behave in their own uncontrollable manner. Virtually no amount of prior information, access to logistics, working capital and assurances can ensure profitable deals for a producer all the time. For a market player, the total loss function (a sum of actual and opportunity loss) is proverbially non-zero. Each player must face a combination of a systemic risk and an idiosyncratic risk. The former is common to all the market players: small and big. Sources of such risks can be Acts of God, strikes, riots, sudden shifts in market tastes caused by outbreak of diseases, rumour induced shifts in market preferences etc. Idiosyncratic risks are unique to each producer and depend on the quality of her produce, timing of her harvest, her own logistics arrangement, her contract with a market agent and so on. The above access and assurances can reduce the idiosyncratic risks to a minimum and allow her to make intelligent guess on the systemic market risk.

The access and assurances listed above are of course factors that improve effectiveness of market access for all types of producers of agricultural commodities. The diverse attributes of the product/market about which symmetric and reliable information can help build more evolved and mature markets and hence help efficient and transparent markets for producers are given below.

- Diversity in product type: Wheat as a commodity is just one grain. There may be types of wheat, but the difference between them is not as much as between say bottle gourd and okra. This diversity is the highest in vegetables, then perhaps in fish then in fruit *etc*. Each vegetable has different attributes in terms of keeping quality, resistance to thermal shock, tolerance to differing moisture and temperature regime *etc*. Different visual, organoleptic or chemical attributes may be used for assessing the quality for different vegetables. Thus the greater the diversity, the greater the complexity in managing quality, packaging, transport, storage *etc*. *Ceteris paribus*, the greater the diversity of a produce type, the shallower is the market for each species in the group.

The market for sweet peas is perhaps much smaller than market for lentils.

- Heterogeneity: Some products are homogeneous and variation in them is not valued. For instance, for a manufacturer of French fries, variation in potato quality may be a pain. On the other hand, in several ordinary vegetable products, diversity is large and the preferences for each type sharply defined. In brinjal, small shiny black ones may be preferred for making *bharela baingan*, long and tapering ones may be demanded for a similar purpose in hotels, medium size fruit may be required by low and medium grade restaurants for making the ordinary curry and bumper fruit may be wanted for making *bharta*. Small tomato may be fine for manufacturers of sauce and makers of *sambhar* or *rasam*, but salad purpose needs nice shiny and large fruit.
- Identity preservation: Given the heterogeneity of produce, it may be important to undertake the post harvest and marketing of the produce in such a manner that the identity of the produce is preserved. Who would want to pay for spinach inextricably mixed with some other leafy vegetable? Should such loss of identity at all happen because of foolish handling? Surely I would want to pay more for *katargam papdi* if no other type of French beans were mixed in it. At times, this could be a finer issue. Demand may be for a commodity with the same phyto-chemical property and not mere physical properties. This happens for instance in medicinal herbs. The question is to what extent is the marketing system able to preserve the identity and whether the market is willing to pay for this.
- Traceability: This refers to the difficult yet possible mechanism of tracing a final consumer lot of a product to the farm on which it was grown. This kind of traceability is of crucial importance in marketing of organic produce. Surely the credibility of an organic marketer would rise tremendously if he guaranteed traceability and could adduce evidence of his logistical tracking system.
- Price discovery: This of course is the most important thing from the point of view of producers. For a produce that is

assessed by producers on its visual and physical attributes, by the processors on its chemical or phyto-chemical attributes and by the buyers on its organoleptic attributes, it is well nigh impossible to devise mechanisms that will make the process of price discovery objective and fair to all. In horticultural produce, the possibility of a benchmark price is perhaps bleak. Yet, it is important to recognize that the price discovery process must be reasonably objective and transparent. It must be objective in the sense of its independence from the specific personality of the seller or the buyer. Transparent in the sense that fair or otherwise, it is known to both the parties that a specific attribute is being awarded or discounted. For example, illustratively, both farmers and buyers must know it up front that tomato must be oblate spheroids with the longer axis not longer than 4 cm and that penalties will accrue for both over and undersized fruit. Whether a tomato of this size necessarily produces good ketchup in the factory or gives nice fresh salad to the buyer is beside the point. Optimally, price discovery must occur without too much pain - for instance, not after the producers have brought the produce to the market after trudging twenty miles in freezing cold. The price discovery must be an open process: closed hand deals are inferior in this regard compared to open auctions, however fixed they may be.

- Fragmentation: The number of producers in a unit area involved in producing the commodity or the number of producers required to get one unit of the product defines the extent of concentration. Fragmentation results when the concentration is very low. For instance, every one in Patiala grows wheat in winter and hence the fragmentation in the wheat market there is extremely low. On the other hand, to get say ten tonnes of sweet peas in East Nimar district (one of the pea producing districts) one may have to transact with fifty producers. The production is thus very fragmented. Fragmentation can also be understood as an obverse of the extent of integration of different markets. If prices prevailing in Kalmeswar, 24 km from Nagpur, are widely different from those in Nagpur, we would say that markets are fragmented.

These two concepts are logically dependent on each other (except in very special cases such as opium). If producers are scattered over a wide area and if each one of them produces only a small volume of a produce, then the chances are that the concerned markets would be fragmented as well. This is because integration of markets needs coordination and that in turn needs investment either in infrastructure or in social capital or both. With widely scattered miniscule production volumes, no one finds this investment worth making.

- Transaction velocity: This is the number of times a product is physically handled (loaded, bagged, unloaded, opened, loaded again *etc.*) between the producer and the end user before the product loses its current form and identity. When a farmer harvests his vegetables from his farm and gives it to his wife for making dinner, the velocity is the minimum. Sometimes, this velocity may be as large as ten. Each handling means handling labour, possible contamination, handling losses, wastages and delays.
- Non-value adding transactions costs: In general, the important functions performed by market intermediaries include pooling, assembly, sorting, quality assurance, risk buffering, weighment, price discovery, negotiation and payment routing. These functions need to be performed if the commodity is to reach from the producer to the ultimate user while the two remain unknown to each other. Market intermediaries add time and space value to a produce, for which, they charge service fees as institutionalized in the market. Such fees are involved every time the commodity is transacted. When the transactions velocity is high, the gross transactions costs are very high. But unless the intermediaries are in a position to add values other than mere time and space values, or perform other functions as noted above, the cumulative transactions costs may be essentially non-value adding. This would happen all the more if there is no real need for the buyer and the seller to remain unknown to each other. As one can guess, highly fragmented markets for diversified, heterogeneous and perishable commodities are likely to have very high non-value adding transactions costs.

Gross inefficiencies of the market can result from poor communication infrastructure and high fragmentation. Traditionally, monopolistic power of the market traders arising out of institutional factors such as indebtedness of small producers, interlocking of markets and familial link between market players is associated with gross inefficiencies. It has been observed that high incidence of market cess and taxes can cause a great deal of distortion in the market, as much of the commodity gets transacted outside the formal market with very little institutional checks on contract enforcement. This too causes inefficiencies.

Thus credible information on the above factors backed by willingness to act according to the information, if available to the small producers, will make market interactions beneficial for the small holders. Specifically this information will have to be available on:

- Locating markets;
- Identification of market players;
- Current market institutions;
- Availability of safeguards from monopolistic power;
- Ways of managing transactions costs: search, monitoring and enforcement;
- Price discovery;
- Trends in demand pattern.

In addition to the above information, actual services may need to be provided regarding

- Sorting, pooling, packaging, storage, transport logistics;
- Choice of market for a given lot at a given point in time;
- Quality assurance;
- Payment recovery;
- Generating information on markets, season and segment-wise demand pattern *etc.*

In general, the subject of how to ensure small holders get the right type of technology, agronomic practices and materials for putting these in practice is better studied and understood. There are problems due to fragmentation and geographic scatter that make the provision of related services expensive. Demand of small holders is often below the antennae of existing market players who are used to dealing with large producers.

We list the factors that will make technology interface beneficial for small holders.

- Content management of the field of taking technology from the scientist to the farm, using whichever medium is critical. Scientists are prone to speak and write in researchese that is little understood by farmers, particularly small holders. Scientists are also prone to making assumptions about resources and skills that may not be realistic for small holders. Converting the essential message from the scientist, retrofitting it in the context of the small holder and then ensuring that it is disseminated at manageable costs is a challenge.
- Content management is about existing knowledge. Some knowledge will have to be generated all the time. This is the overall field of R&D of an appropriate type, including adaptation trials.
- Localizing a technology or an agronomic practice involves specific adaptation of a standard practice to the specific resource conditions of a farmer. For instance, a practice may be known for light *domath* soils, while a farmer has sloppy and blackish soil. He naturally wants to know how to modify the standard practice.
- Value engineering: IDEI is of course very good at it and knows what this means. We need to generalize this concept to the process of replacing components, materials and processes with others that serve the same purpose, but at lower costs. This is really necessary for enabling the small holders use the technology for increasing their incomes.
- Problem solving: With the best laid and executed R&D, adaptation trials and localizing, problems are bound to arise during the crop cycle. Thus there is a need for practical problem solving for the small holders in a manner consistent with their resource conditions.
- Product choice: This links up with assistance in marketing. In the relatively wide range of choice, the small holder needs

to be assisted in choosing a product and its specific variety/sub-type so as to maximize the likelihood of her fetching the best price.

- Technology choice: When alternate choice of technique is available, as it usually would be, the small holder needs considered suggestions about what is best for her. This includes, for instance, advice about choice of time at which the crop should be sown.
- Sourcing and supplying materials: Since the demand of small holders for materials such as seeds, manures and fertilizers is in very small lots, they are often below the antennae of the usual supply chain of the concerned commodity. Hence assistance in terms of choosing good quality materials and repacking them in lots of sizes that make sense to the small holders would be a welcome service and one that will reduce the hassles of the small holders.
- Handholding and training of the small holders may become relevant, particularly when new crops are chosen, new technologies including new irrigation technology is chosen or new ways of post-harvest processing or marketing are chosen for and by them.

Defining the Problem of Creating Market Based Systems for Enhancing Small Holder Participation

The discussion above indicates the diverse services that are needed by small holders and the problems that are faced. We do not think that there are enough service providers who are providing these services and there certainly are no providers who provide all the services. Either there are no service providers in the market for small holders, or such service providers who exist charge fees that small holders cannot afford. One can hypothesize many reasons for absence of service providers for the services indicated earlier. Some of these reasons could be:

- Services for some of the areas essentially create public goods. Examples of these are R&D, adaptation trials, localization of technology, content management for extension are some such services. Since they create public goods, no single private producer is willing to pay for the services. In any case, the costs involved in creating necessary infrastructure and human resources for this purpose are high. Thus we find that Universities and State Departments of Agriculture are the only "service providers" of this type.

- From my earlier research in BDS[3], I had found that small enterprises are unwilling to provide for "strategic" services that can contribute to the general improvement in their performance. Rather, they are willing to pay for "transaction" oriented services that can be seen to result immediately in some concrete gain to the enterprise. A similar tendency is to be expected in small holders. A small holder is likely to be willing to pay a portion of extra realization to a service provider rather than upfront fee for information, which could but may not, result in any concrete incremental profit. In other words, information *qua* information is not considered at all valuable unless it is backed by machinery that can show its money value there and then. This is perhaps a strong hypothesis and one that can become a powerful guide to action.
- Geographical scatter and fragmentation of production makes any compact business of providing services very cost ineffective. We can hypothesize that if compact clusters of producers of the same products were to emerge, service providers would also come up to cater to them. (From personal observations, I can say that this is true: even in remote Lohardaga in Jharkhand, there are service providers for agronomy, materials and related services since there is a vibrant vegetable cluster in that region.) Some mechanism of "aggregating" the latent demand for services needs to be discovered.
- Since neither limited services (meeting say only one or two of these functions) for a range of crops nor the whole range of services for just the horticultural crops seem to have economic potential that justifies existence of service providers dedicated to horticulture, what we have is a class of service providers and market players who seem to

3. *Business Development Services for Small Enterprises: A case study of A.P.* Paper presented in Hanoi Conference on BDS, April 2001.

undertake a wide array of activity for an undifferentiated client group that includes, but is not limited to, small holder horticulturists. This class has limited willingness or interest in learning about the special problems of the small holders and solving them.

Thus the problem may be formulated as follows:

We need to create a new class of market actors who will be willing to focus on small holder horticulturists and provide services to them. We would like to see this happening in a phased manner, such that both the horticulturists and the service providers find incentives in the new economic exchange that are profitable enough to spur an increasing range of services on both the technology/input side as well as on the market access side. Eventually we would like these new market actors to be fully sustainable, based on the service charges they can levy on the producers.

What is Involved in Managing the Market Related Features?

Diversity in the range of products is a matter of pride for the region and hence there is no need to artificially reduce the level of diversity. Diversity offers a scope to vary product mix across seasons, as well as define the focus of operations given the chosen customer profile. The only caveat is that diversity reduces the potential volume of any one of the products and to that extent poses logistic, management and accounting problems. This management needs very sound systems. Thus any organization or interventions that can successfully manage these issues may continue with as much diversity as there is.

Heterogeneity refers to variation in visual, physical, organoleptic and phytochemical variations in the same product category (*e.g.* green *vs* deep purple brinjal, sour *vs* sweet pineapple *etc.*) Some products such as milk may be such that bulking will not damage the basic product and the resultant average quality attributes such as fat content may be within acceptable level. Some products (*e.g.* fish) simply cannot be homogenized through bulking. The problem with heterogeneity is that while the market expects consistent and uniform quality of the product they buy, the heterogeneous supply makes it difficult. Maintaining such consistent and uniform quality may be impossible in unprocessed products and very difficult in processed ones. Systems have to be evolved where the processed or unprocessed products of a type go to a select market segment where that type is acceptable, so that acceptance, consistency and uniformity may be achieved. Alternately, efforts need to be made to reduce heterogeneity at source through incentives.

Identity preservation and traceability are both important in more evolved and perhaps specialized marketing systems. The former is important in products where the specific agro-climatic features of a place make the important product attribute unique and special. Admixture of the requisite specific product with others ruins this unique attribute. For example, for whatever reasons, people prefer *sharbati* wheat and admixture of this wheat with others ruins its special flavour. Traceability is important for verification of some promised specifics. A buyer paying for organically grown fruit would like some guarantee that he is in fact given organic produce and hence tracing the product back to the producer becomes important. To achieve both these, tracking systems have to be evolved during transport, storage, processing and subsequent flow and these coupled with IT can generate the necessary identity preservation or traceability. The organization managing this has to evolve these systems and hence it must find it worthwhile to do that.

Price discovery refers to obtaining information and then through bargaining, a commitment on price at which the farm produce can be sold. Information on price prevailing, by itself, is helpful but never enough. It helps no one if a small holder were told that the rates even in the proximate market are in a certain range, unless he has some guarantee that he will receive the rate in that range. In the absence of this guarantee, he will remain subject to the mercy of the trader or broker and can at best know the extent to which he has been cheated! Effective price is the core of any transaction. Farmers relate the price they get to the price paid by urban consumers and complain of exploitation. Traders recognize that the market does not know the meaning of equity and fairness, but simply operates on short term demand and supply. In fact, short term and highly localized demand - actually demand as manifest by calls in the *mandi* - and the short term localized supply around the time the deal occurs, more or less rule the price of any lot. In an instance I studied some years back, price of bananas in the *mandi* varied between Rs. 0.05 to Rs. 5.00 per kilogram in a span of one month! This price has virtually no direct bearing on consumer price, price prevailing in a town five hundred kilometers away or the cost of production. This kind of relation depends on a host of factors: substitutes and their price and supply, perishability, transportation bottlenecks, expectations and so on. What is involved in effective and pro-poor price discovery is first to recognize that there is nothing like a pro-poor price! But more importantly, it may involve the ability to obtain fairly dependable assessment of prevailing prices in all the *mandi*s that can be reached in the next few hours, knowledge of fairly dependable transportation arrangements and costs of handling, commissions and cess, the damage to product life due to transport and most importantly chance of default on payment by the distant party. It may also involve the ability to understand the processing economics of commodities that can be processed and the knowledge about the situation in the markets of all the downstream products. This too would help only if the intervener had standing arrangements of a backup nature to get his poor farmers' produce processed. Clearly, the task of effective price discovery is to be done by some one who is in the market and can stand its heat.

Fragmentation may be understood informally in the sense of what fraction of a normally transportable full truckload can come from one single producer on an average day. More generally and at a macro level, if the top producing district accounts for only a small portion of the national production of a commodity, then its production is fragmented. In this macro sense, tomato production is far more fragmented than say apple production, but perhaps less fragmented than that of brinjal, which is produced practically everywhere.

Operational meaning is more important for a practical intervener. If it takes thirty producers to fill one truck of tomatoes on one day, the production is highly fragmented. If a single producer can give you five truckloads the same day, the fragmentation is less. Fragmentation in production results essentially from the fact of highly fragmented landholdings. Further, as landholdings fall, at least up to a point, the tendency to achieve risk reduction through crop diversification will mean that fragmentation in production will still be on the rise. An intervener can reduce real fragmentation only if he is able to persuade a large group of producers to coordinate their crop choice, planting and harvesting activities so as to result in reduced fragmentation at the time of sale. This can happen if the situation is like a tight member-processor coupling, as in a sugar co-operative, or in contract farming situations. Such aggregation can result only if the benefit of producing the commodity in question is demonstrated in terms of higher income, less risk of virulent diseases and pests and low risk of market collapse. These are difficult conditions to achieve for a small intervener. He may therefore focus on either achieving virtual aggregation or devise systems of coping with fragmentation that yield the benefits of shared costs of aggregation. This may mean bringing about arrangements of shared transportation, shared packing or a multiple sale.

Transaction velocity, that is, the number of times a commodity is physically handled before it gets to the final user from the producer, can be reduced either by way of vertical integration by a processor or by an intervener reaching out to actors as far from the producer in the value chain as possible. If a tomato ketchup company directly fetches tomatoes from large growers in a compact area, the velocity is at the minimum. If it fetches through just one transit *mandi* like say Pune, the velocity is already at least doubled. But if it procures tomatoes from whosoever will sell it, then the velocity could be quite high, may be four or five, since presumably produce could eventually reach the processors through village markets, primary *tehsil* markets, transit *mandis* and brokers. The transaction velocity for fresh produce can be reduced if a produce aggregator, in co-operative or whichever fold, took the produce directly from farmers, sorted and repacked it and sold through his shops in the city. This is done for instance by Mother Dairy or FRESH, and here the velocity is at least 2.

Non-value adding transactions costs usually get added up when transactions velocity is high or when wholly unwarranted reasons tend to increase the number of players in the value chain. Sometimes these could be regulatory or tax reasons. An example of these costs can come from the brokerage in the trade of a commodity where the buyer is known and sellers can be clearly enumerated by the buyer. A transparent system would do away with the broker entirely, but reasons for preferring them could vary from the desire to buffer the buyer from the sellers, financing a bit of working capital, managing cash expenses of the unproductive type or plain draining the cash of the company to suit the promoter. An intervener can reduce these only by reducing the transactions velocity or by devising operating systems that can maintain competitiveness despite the regulatory or tax regimes and are not inhibited in becoming accessible and transparent to the farmers.

What is Involved in Managing Production Related Inputs?

Content management for giving continuous, relevant and meaningful messages is indeed a difficult task. The field situations are both diverse and also evolving. The intervener can at best be an interlocutor between the field and the laboratory or the scientists. The problems are of stretching the known solutions to slightly changing ground reality, changing the language to suit what is understood and changing the materials to suit the farmers' pocket. Most interveners address these issues by incorporating some scientific abilities in themselves. Content management is about existing knowledge. Some knowledge will have to be generated all the time. This is the overall field of R&D of an appropriate type, including adaptation trials. When the intervening organizations discover that some problems come up all the time, they often design and conduct field R&D and trials for them. This they can do only if they have some scientific ability incorporated within themselves. The same team also tries to localize the technology. The intervener also needs to work and try out things for replacing components, materials and processes with others that serve the same purpose but at lower costs. This is really necessary for enabling the small holders to use the technology for increasing their incomes. This can be done by extensive field interaction and experimentation. Few interveners are doing this. IDEI is among the experts in this field.

Problem solving: With the best-laid and executed R&D, adaptation trials and localizing, problems are bound to arise during the crop cycle. Thus the intervener needs to work with the small holders, to learn about their problems and to find solutions consistent with their resource conditions. Handholding and training of the small holders may become relevant, particularly when new crops are chosen, new technologies, including new irrigation technology, is chosen or new ways of post-harvest processing or marketing are chosen for and by them. While some interveners do the latter, problem solving is usually an unattended area.

Choice of products and technologies: This can be done only by an intervener who is also working with small holders in marketing field, since this links up with the assistance in marketing. In the relatively wide range of choice, the small holder needs to be assisted in choosing a product and its specific variety/sub-type so as to maximize the likelihood of her fetching the best price. Similarly, the small holders need attention, at least initially, in technology matters: when to plant, how to plant, what inputs to give, how to do the specific operations *etc*. Interveners seldom attend to this matter.

Interveners often involve themselves in sourcing and supplying materials. This they do as the organized intervener has both the manpower and often the money resources to engage in it. More importantly, the suppliers of these things see the intervener as an important link to ultimate users and hence try to co-opt the intervener. Since the demand of small holders for materials such as seeds, manures and fertilizers is in very small lots, they are often below the antennae of the usual supply chain of the concerned commodity, the intervener has to work with the suppliers to design special packages meant for small holders. This assistance in terms of choosing good quality materials and repacking them in lots of sizes that make sense to the small holders is seen to be a welcome service and one that will reduce the hassles of small holders. This can fetch some margins for the intervener to enable him to run the show.

Organization and Incentive Question

Contours of the task of providing services to small holders for their better integration into markets have been discussed above. The central questions are

- who are best suited to render these services, and even more importantly,
- what is their incentive in doing so.

In the first place, I draw upon my recent engagement in this subject on behalf of IDE India to suggest what type of an actor finds it natural to engage in what kind of a service. Then I turn to the incentive question.

While engaged in this work, I came across

- Corporate sector interventions in reaching out to farmers (though not necessarily small holders) and providing them services;
- NGOs reaching out to small producers and providing them a range of services;
- Producers' co-operatives working on behalf of producers and rendering them a number of services;
- Informal groups of producers themselves springing up and making the services happen;
- Individual service providers working in chosen thematic areas and providing services.

I must make it clear that I did not have the mandate, nor the intention, of undertaking a comprehensive evaluation of these interventions. Rather, I investigated with a sense of curiosity about what they do, why and how. Neither the above list nor my own study is exhaustive. It is not as if I have studied all the possible actors of each type. Table 1 is based on observations from the exposure to these actors. Blank entries in a cell indicate that the particular type of intervener does not provide that service. An entry attempts to describe the nature of service offered.

From the Table, we find thus that corporate intervention and producer co-operatives are good at price discovery and effective market linkage. The latter are also good in price risk mitigation and organizing financing for production, though usually on a modest scale. We find that NGOs are usually good in inducing new growers by arranging for training and skill building, problem solving and handholding, supply of materials and technology *etc*. But they are weak in market linkages and price discovery. Also they cannot absorb risks. Informal, spontaneous groups of producers are usually very powerful "interventions" that offer a range of services addressing the most acutely felt demand. What is clear is that none of the interventions are able to significantly absorb risks for the farmers, nor are many able to do adaptive R&D. Small informal groups who work for themselves are best at this. What is also perhaps true is that fragmentation makes aggregation difficult and the more fragmented a particular sub-system, the more difficult it is to service small holders.

Table 1

What Do Current Interveners Do?

Attribute	*Corporate interventions*	*NGO*	*Producers Corporative*	*Informal Groups of Producers*	*Individual Service Providers*
Primary motivation	Expanding and stabilizing supply or market base	Livelihoods promotion among small and marginal holders	Obtaining better value for members produce and increasing returns to their efforts	Individual economic gain through collective action	Own livelihood
Market links	In some cases, yes	In some cases yes but generally weak	Yes, strong links	Yes	Usually not
Credible Price discovery	Yes	No	Yes, this is the basic purpose of the group coming together	No	No
Logistics of marketing	Yes	Pooled transport, some times storage and rarely some processing	Variable, as per need	Pooling and cost sharing arrangements	May do for a fee, but rarely
Managing diversity and heterogeneity	Seldom	Look at it proactively but difficulty in managing	Try to reduce	Try to reduce	
Identity preser-vation and traceability	Yes, in case of specialized produce	No	No		Usually yes
Content manag-ement of agronomy issues	Rarely	Usually	Facilitation at members behest	Emergent depending on felt needs	Yes

Contd. ...

...Contd. ...

Attribute	*Corporate interventions*	*NGO*	*Producers Corporative*	*Informal Groups of Producers*	*Individual Service Providers*
Adaptive, practical R&D	Rarely	Rarely	Rarely	Yes	No
Platform for info exchange	Yes	Yes	Yes	Yes	No
Problem solving	No	Weak	Weak	Yes	Yes
Training and Handholding	No	Yes	No	No	Yes
Sourcing materials and technology	Yes	Yes	Facilitation	Facilitation	Yes
Providing finance	No	Yes, usually	Yes, as loans recoverable through produce sales	No	As money lenders or for encouraging acceptance of sales/services
Aggregation	Yes	Yes but in target group	Yes	Yes	No
Risk absorption and mitigation	Risk mitigation only through information	Yes, but usually so long as donor support lasts	Yes	No	No

Source: Self compiled, based on observations

Concluding Comments

Based on the above discussion, we answer three key questions in this section and offers some suggestions.

Is it Worth Attempting to Achieve an Empowered and an Informed Integration of Small Holders into Markets?

I have made our own value position clear. Hence, purely from the point of view of social value, this is certainly desirable. But is it possible that the poverty impacts achieved by achieving an empowered and informed access for small holders can be achieved much more easily and cheaply through other means? Is the trouble worth taking in that sense? We have both a general and a specific answer for this question. The general answer is to the extent the small holders get a fair access to the market and market efficiency improves, the society as a whole stands to gain from improved efficiency in flow of goods, services, capital and information. The specific answer is that the poverty impacts achieved through improvement of the quality of access for small holders will produce gains that are sustainable. When interveners' efforts nudge market evolution towards greater maturity, it is unlikely they will recede into the old constrained, institutionally bogged down and informationally handicapped stages. Also similar gains produced from other means are likely to last as long as the investments keep coming in those efforts.

Is there an Optimal Organization form for Interventions?

I believe that insistence on a specific form of organization for intervention is likely to have merely ideological justification. I have seen live examples of each of the five organizational forms. I have also seen the sixth form - that of State sector agencies attempting to provide services of different kind, but have not reported that here. The following table attempts to sum up the widely held perceptions about the six organization forms on diverse relevant attributes. These are stereotypes, but often stereotypes are based on a substantial element of truth. Also, our observations corroborate the table. We do not think any single form will meet the case of answering all the needs discussed above. Considering high costs and investments in R&D, it is natural that they would be in the public sector. To get the very small and marginalized unattended families on board, NGOs would be the optimal agencies. Small groups of producers themselves contribute vibrancy and dynamism to the group. The corporate sector brings in the much-needed hard-headed approach to the management of exchanges. Individuals bring in the flexibility and speed of response. Besides, the intervention is always motivated by a specific interest group, and this group defines the organizational form that suits its purpose.

Table 2

Typical Behaviour of Different Forms of Interventions

Format	*Responsiveness to Market*	*Responsiveness to Producers*	*Transparency in Exchanges with Small Holders*	*Speed of Response and Flexibility*	*Cost of Maintaining*
Corporate sector	High	Low	Medium	High	Medium
NGO	Poor	High	Variable	Low	Medium
Producer co-op	Medium	High	High	Low	High
Informal group	High	High	High	High	Low
Individual service providers	Medium	High	Low	Medium	Low
Public sector	Medium	Poor	High	Poor	High

How does the BDS Model Fit the Need?

It should be clear now that the Business Development Services model fits the case optimally. Small holders are seen as entrepreneurs who need to survive and thrive in existing markets. They need a plethora of services, including those listed above for achieving a greater fit. Unless the small holders themselves realize their need and translate it into demand, no organizational form can provide appropriate services properly, efficiently and effectively. There is of course a phasing involved here. Small holders may passively accept their unequal participation in markets as an immutable reality. They need to be made aware that this can change and that changed relationships with the market will benefit them. This kind of a task involves community or group building work. However, once this is achieved, then the rest of the task is to facilitate emergence of appropriate service providers. Consistent with the BDS philosophy, we may suggest that both sectoral and cluster development foci are essential for any facilitator to transform the relationship of small holders to markets. Sectoral focus can yield cohesion and consistency. A cluster approach can more easily achieve a much-needed aggregation.

How can One Address the Challenge of Enabling Empowered Integration of Small Holders in Markets?

I suggest that any national or international facilitator who is interested in enabling empowered and informed market access to small holders for its potential for poverty impacts, may do well to start with a sectoral focus. Within a sector, it would be perhaps more efficient to adopt an approach of "sharpening the tools" with existing clusters, while simultaneously engaging in strategies to encourage emergence of new clusters. Within such clusters, aggregation for some purposes is automatic, while for others, one may induce it more easily. It is best to work with a consortium of different service providers without being inhibited by their organizational format. However, it is indeed fruitful to encourage emergence of groups of self-motivated farmers and nurture such groups. Strategically, one may experiment with the idea of "clubs" of small holders (vegetable or fruit or medicinal herb growers). Supporting such clubs with interactions with a range of service providers will perhaps fire their imagination and transform them from passive takers of existing conditions to vibrant demanders of better access and participation. The rest of the steps can follow a conventional BDS approach. Attempts to create super-structures in NGO or producer co-operative modes, when the grass-root small holders have not acquired the fire in the belly, may be expensive and counterproductive. The organization can emerge in response to felt needs and economic rationale.

The steps could then be:

- Decide on sectoral focus;
- Identify existing clusters which permit aggregation for sharpening the tools;
- Encourage emergence of clubs or other forms of informal groups of small holders;

- Work with them to evolve a priority list of issues that concern them and hinder their integration with markets;
- Identify service providers who can bring in the necessary input/link/service;
- Work with the service providers to interest them in small holders, perhaps subsidizing their logistics initially help them to evolve product forms, packages and pricing models that suit the small holders;
- Encourage gradually increasing interaction of small holders and the service providers to eventually withdraw from the clusters to focus on newly emerging clusters.

6

Managing Risk: Insurance for the Rural Poor?

SALEEMA RAZVI

Introduction

Vulnerability is both a cause and a symptom of poverty. It resides in the many shocks that pervade the lives of the poor. The frequent occurrence of these shocks can easily erode hard won gains and force households quickly back into poverty.[1] Over the past few years, a growing body of evidence[2] shows that microfinance has had a positive impact on the poor. Growth of enterprise revenues and, in turn, increased household incomes have brought important benefits to many households. However, focusing only on static measures of household earnings and income tends to mask the more dynamic side of poverty — the vulnerability of the poor to risk.

Risk comes in many forms, for example, illness, death, fire or theft. These risks could occur frequently and create financial pressures that exacerbate the ever-present stress of meeting regular needs such as food, rent and school fees. To cope with risk the poor use a diversity of strategies. These include borrowing, saving, selling productive and non-productive assets, and other forms of 'self-insurance', informal group-based risk sharing systems, and, occasionally, formal insurance. Yet, the effectiveness of these strategies is limited. Factors such as lack of timeliness, limited coverage and high costs suggest an insurance landscape that is far from perfect. In addition, poverty impedes many from taking risks and gaining access to what is on offer.

---

1. World Bank; *Investing in Health. World Development Report 1993*, New York: Oxford University Press for the World Bank.
2. Miller, M; Northrip, Z; Bamako 2000: *Innovations in Microfinance*, 2001.

In the absence of insurance, the poor often avoid risky but potentially profitable economic activities and enter into informal insurance arrangements or rely on precautionary savings. It has been found that the largest gap between demand and access for the rural people is for insurance. This paper examines the vulnerability of the poor farmer with regard to risks faced especially of health and illness. It also examines the health insurance schemes available for the poor in India.

Risk Assessment

It was once assumed that poor people had no need for financial services, and perhaps needed only credit. Yet the conditions under which the poor live suggest otherwise. For poor people, risk is familiar and high. Strategies for managing and coping with risk are part of everyday life. Research[3] and experience have shown that the poverty and uncertainty poor people face require diverse financial services. Borrowing helps households achieve food security and alleviate poverty. In times of stress, the poor need to borrow to pay for essential consumption. But borrowing alone is not enough to pull households out of poverty. Poor people also require savings services to help them manage better their resources over time and to enable them to plan and finance their investments. And most importantly, the poor need access to insurance to lessen the blow when, for instance, a breadwinner falls ill, crops fail, or prices for their products plummet.

Types of Risks

Life Cycle Needs

Low-income households are most commonly exposed to expenditure requirements for life cycle needs, such as paying for a child's education, re-stocking household supplies, paying a sufficient dowry, or saving for retirement. These needs arise when flows of income do not coincide with required expenditures. While households are generally aware whether and when these events will occur, the high likelihood and frequency of their occurrence create an on-going uncertainty as to whether the household will have sufficient income

---

3. Freiberg, J; *Social Security for the Poor – Options and Experiences*, 1999.

or assets to cover the cost associated with these events. While individually these events have the least severe impact, their frequency makes managing them a pressing need for many low-income households.

Death Risks

Death risks include the costs that result from the death of a family member. The degree of uncertainty regarding death is greater than that caused by life cycle events, but less than that caused by most other risks faced by low-income households. The loss a household experiences when a death occurs (apart from the emotional loss) includes both a one-time component (*e.g.*, cost of proper burial, cost of settling the deceased's accounts, etc.) and, potentially, an ongoing component to replace income that the deceased formerly provided to the family.

Property Risks

Property risks include events leading to theft, damage, loss, or destruction of a household asset. Crop losses, livestock illness or death, and fire, are all examples of the types of asset losses that low-income households may need to protect against. Given the range in value of these assets and the situation specific nature of property risks (*i.e.*, the likelihood of theft varies substantially by community), the impact of property risks will vary by family and locality. In general, property risks are likely to cause households greater uncertainty than death risks or lifecycle needs because they cannot be sure whether, when, or how often a fire or theft might occur. The relative value of a household's loss due to a property risk will depend on the asset at risk.

Health Risks

Besides life cycle needs, health risks—accidents, illnesses, and injuries that require households to pay for medical treatment—are among the most common concerns of low-income households. The cost to a household of each accident, illness or injury is generally one-time and, like property risks, can vary from relatively small, such as purchasing aspirin, to relatively large, such as major surgeries. The frequency with which health risks can occur, and the household's limited ability to predict whether or when they will be affected, suggest that health risks generate a greater degree of uncertainty than other risks.

Disability Risks

The causes of disability risks are essentially the same as those for health risks (accidents, illnesses, and injuries), however there is a greater relative cost to a household of having a family member disabled than injured or sick. A disabled family member may require ongoing treatment expenses besides the cost of the initial medical attention. Households may also incur additional costs in replacing lost income if the family member is no longer able to work. This is especially problematic if the disabled family member is young. Instead of becoming a future source of income for the family, their disability requires an on-going expense. Consequently, when these risks occur, low-income households have greater difficulty overcoming disability risks than health risks.

Mass, Covariant Risks

Mass, covariant risks are the threat that an event, such as an epidemic, a natural disaster, and war, could cause substantial losses for a large portion of a population at the same time. These risks could fit into the categories described above based on the impact they have on households. Death, property damage, illness, and disability are all associated with mass, covariant risks.

Mass, covariant risks are considered separately[4] because:

(1) They tend to be difficult or impossible to predict;

(2) They affect many people at the same time, thus hampering the ability of risk-pooling mechanisms to protect against these risks; and

(3) The cost associated with mass, covariant risks tends to be significantly greater than that resulting from other risks. This is because households are forced to deal with multiple losses at the same time (*e.g.*, severe flooding leading to death of a family member, destruction of the family's home and several injuries to remaining family members); and a

4. Miller, M; Northrip, Z; *Bamako 2000: Innovations in Microfinance, 2001.*

households' traditional risk coping strategies, such as intra-family gift giving, reciprocal exchange and non-financial savings tend to be weakened or destroyed because neighbors and local family members are suffering the similar losses at the same time.

Why Health Insurance?

Insurance protects against unexpected losses by pooling the resources of the many to compensate for the losses of the few. The greater the uncertainty of the event, the more insurance becomes the economical form of protection. Insurance replaces the uncertain prospect of large losses with the certainty of making small, regular, affordable premium payments. The primary function of insurance is to act as a risk transfer mechanism, to provide peace of mind and protect against losses.

Insurance is not the only way of dealing with risks, and not all risks are insurable.[5] However, health risks such as those relating to illness, injury, disability, maternity and the like are considered to be eminently insurable as these risks are mostly independent or idiosyncratic, that is, not correlated among community members.[6] Moreover, among several risks facing poor households, health risk is considered to be crucial as it has a destabilizing effect on household finances: directly, by thrusting health expenditure in the event of illness and indirectly, by affecting the income earning capacity of households.[7]

Health insurance enables access to better medical services and a longer and better quality of life. Thus, access to adequate insurance protection can assist the poor to achieve sustainable growth and provide them with the capability to attain a better standard of living. It can mitigate the impact of personal and environmental calamities on the build-up of assets and provide escape from the vicious circle of poverty. Insurance can also protect those that have risen above the

5. Brown, W; Churchill, C; *Providing Insurance to Low-Income Households*, USAID, 1999.
6. Alderman and Paxson, (1994). *"Do the Poor Insure? A Synthesis of Literature on Risk and Consumption in Developing Countries,"* in Bacha (ed.) *Economics in a Changing World: Vol. 4: Development, Trade and the Environment*, Macmillan Press, London, England.
7. Asfaw, A., von Braun, J., Assefa Admassie, A., & Jütting, J; The *Economic Costs of Illness in Low Income Countries: The Case of Rural Ethiopia."* Mimeo.

poverty level against unforeseen events that may cause them to fall back into poverty.

For most people living in developing countries "health insurance" is however an unknown word. It is generally assumed that, with the exception of the upper classes, people cannot afford such type of social protection. This is unfortunate, as poor people need as much protection against the financial consequences of illnesses. Illness still represents a permanent threat to their income earning capacity. Beside the direct costs for treatment and drugs, indirect costs for the missing labour force of the ill person have to be shouldered by the household.

Health insurance schemes are an increasingly recognized factor as a tool to finance health care provision in low-income countries. Given the high latent demand from people for health care services of a good quality and the extreme under-utilization of health services in several countries, it has been argued that social health insurance may improve the access to health care of acceptable quality. Whereas alternative forms of health care financing and cost recovery strategies like user fees have been heavily criticized, the option of insurance seems to be a promising alternative as it is a possibility to pool risk transferring, unforeseeable health care costs to fixed premiums. Recently, mainly in Sub-Saharan Africa but also in a variety of other countries, non-profit, mutual, community-based health insurance schemes have emerged. These schemes are characterized by an ethic of mutual aid, solidarity and the collective pooling of health risks. In several countries these schemes operate in conjunction with health care providers, mainly hospitals in the area.

This study focuses on rural areas because here the need for insurance is especially high, but private insurance markets do not exist and public measures often fail to reach their target population. It looks at community-based health insurance as a means of financing health care for the rural poor.

Community Based Health Insurance (CBHI)

Community based health insurance is seen as an effective way in financing health care costs. Health insurance by pooling of risks across members who participate in health insurance lessens the financial burden of members affected by illness. Indeed, several types of community based health insurance schemes have emerged in Sub-Saharan Africa[8], Asia and in other regions.[9]

Community health care financing schemes are usually based on the following characteristics: voluntary membership, non-profit objective, link to a health care provider (often hospital in the area), risk pooling and relying on an ethic of mutual aid/solidarity.

Benefits

The real benefit of CBHI lies in keeping the transaction costs low, in the design of schemes suited to the community needs, in influencing health behaviour through health education, and in influencing the supply of health care. Its advantage lies in being able to reach low-income people in rural areas and working in the informal sector who are otherwise difficult to reach, to exploit social capital in bringing about greater awareness, correct adverse selection and moral hazard problems, encourage preventive measures and increase access to health care. Popularizing insurance among low-income people requires conveying the idea, canvassing for it, collecting premium, and verifying claims and then reimbursing these claims, thus incurring high costs. In case of formal providers, all these functions typically take up a significant part (at least 20 per cent) of the premium amount. In CBHI schemes such costs can be kept low, say to 5-6 per cent. This is because many of these tasks can be performed by the community members themselves.

Besides, in poor communities, the financial barrier is only one of the barriers to accessing health care. Often, there are many non-financial barriers that must also be overcome through the design of schemes, which ought to take into account characteristics of the community. All these aspects can best be handled if the scheme is community based. Additionally, the problems of adverse selection and moral hazard that arise due to informational asymmetries too can be reduced by making use of local knowledge that is readily available among people living in close communities.

---

8. Wiesmann, D., & Jütting, J. (2000). The Emerging Movement of Community Based Health Insurance in Sub-Saharan Africa: Experiences and Lessons Learned, Afrika Spectrum, 2/2000, pp. 193-210.

9. Bennett, S., Creese, A., & Monash, R. (1998). *Health Insurance Schemes for People Outside Formal Sector Employment*, ARA Paper No. 16, WHO, Geneva.

Limitations

But community based schemes also have certain weaknesses such as low capital base, low level of revenue mobilization, frequent exclusion of the poorest of the poor, small size of risk pool, limited management capacity, and isolation from more comprehensive benefits. Some forms of CBHI also have important limitations.[10] For example, where an NGO itself provides insurance (acts like an insurer) the ability of the NGO to have a pool of well diversified risk is limited. This in turn restricts the ability of NGO to cover or insure variety of risks facing the target population. Moreover, where CBHI schemes are critically dependent on external funding, extending the reach of these schemes then depends on the amount of such funding available. Furthermore, the insurance schemes launched either by national or state-level governments when elections are in sight tend to be populist or vote-catching ploy. Since such schemes have to be renewed every year, these tend to be dropped once the elections are over. It is to be seen if the universal health insurance scheme belongs to this category.

A few micro-level studies that have tried to estimate demand for health insurance based on the willingness-and- ability-to-pay for health insurance have come out with positive findings. A survey-based study[11] on the willingness to pay even in case of Ethiopia - one of the poorest countries in the Sub-Sahara Africa - shows that the poor are willing to pay up to 5 per cent of their monthly income for a scheme that can take care of their costs of illness.

Health Insurance for the Poor in India

Health insurance for the poor in India is still very much in the nascent stage. It takes different forms, being either community-based (CBHI) or non community-based (like *Jan Arogya* policy of the government). The Community Based Health Insurance (CBHI) can itself take several forms.[12]

---

10. Gumber, A; *"Hedging the Health of the Poor – The Case for Community Financing in India"*, 2001.
11. Asfaw, A., von Braun, J., Assefa Admassie, A., & Jütting, J. *"The Economic Costs of Illness in Low Income Countries: The Case of Rural Ethiopia"*. Mimeo.
12. Gumber, A; *"Hedging the Health of the Poor – The Case for Community Financing in India"*, 2001.

Community and self-generated financing programmes are those usually run by non-governmental organizations (NGOs) or non-profit making organisations.[13] These organisations rely on finances from various sources, including government, donor agencies, and community and self-generated sources. Also many innovative methods of financing health care services have been used, like progressive premium scales, community-based pre-payment/insurance schemes, and income-generating schemes. The target population for provision of health care services by such organisations is primarily workers and families outside the formal sector. The sources of revenue for the programmes can be categorized as:

(a) User fees defined as the payment made by the beneficiaries directly to the health care provider, such as fees for services or prices paid for drugs/immunization. This mode of financing is not common.

(b) Prepayment/insurance schemes, including payment by members for drugs either at subsidized rate or at cost price.

(c) Commercial schemes for-profit actively run by organisations to finance health care.

(d) Fund raising activities by organisations for financing health care services. In some cases the revenue raised in this manner constitutes more than 5 per cent of the total funds of the organisations.

(e) System of making contributions in kind (such as rice, sorghum, community labour, *etc.*). This method is not very popular due to difficulty in management.

(f) Other sources of community-based and self-financing include instances like Tribhovandas Foundation providing health care through village milk cooperatives and Amul Union (the milk cooperative organization) contributing significantly towards health services through putting a cess on milk collection.

All these forms currently exist in the country, but only in small pockets, depending on the local conditions that vary considerably

---

13. Dave, Priti; "*Community and Self-Financing in Voluntary Health Programs in India*", Health Policy and Planning, Vol.6 (1).

across regions. The most pertinent point about these schemes is their rural orientation and ability to mobilize resources in a village community. However, most of these schemes have catered to a small section of population with limited health coverage restricted to elementary, preventive, and maternal and child health (MCH) care.

CBHI schemes are designed in a number of ways, depending on the socio-economic characteristics of the target population, health profile of the population, and the health risks prevalent in the region. The decentralization process initiated in the country with the 73rd and 74th Constitutional Amendment aimed at promoting local bodies (*Panchayati Raj* Institutions (PRIs) in the rural areas and *Nagar Palikas* in the urban areas) has raised hopes of being able to reach the poor through community based initiatives with some subsidy to those who cannot afford the costs.[14]

Community Based Universal Health Insurance Scheme

Prior to the announcement of the proposed community based universal health insurance scheme by the finance minister of India, various states governments were contemplating launching a health insurance scheme for their poor population. State governments intensified their efforts when a similar announcement by the central government in the budget 2002-03, didn't take off. Without sufficient knowledge base, the state governments were trying to enter into an arrangement with the providers of medical services, public insurance companies and the target community, whereby insurance companies would reimburse treatment costs of the target community and the governments would subsidize the premium to the insurance company for the insurance sold to the target community. Some state governments had thought of paying the premium through their general revenues, while others had planned to cross-subsidize premium by bringing state government employees also under Mediclaim policy (Punjab and West Bengal governments were thinking alone these lines).[15]

---

14. Gumber, A. and V. Kulkarni. Paper presented in the National Consultation on Health Security in India Organized by Institute for Human Development and UNDP with support from Ministry of Health and Family Welfare, Government of India, July 26-27, 2001.

15. Ahuja, R; *Health Insurance for the Poor in* India, ICRIER, 2004.

Features

The scheme comes in three different categories:

(i) Re 1 per day per year for an individual,

(ii) Rs. 1.5 per day per year for a family of up to five members, and

(iii) Rs. 2 per day per year for a family of up to seven members.

Benefits include providing medical expenses upto Rs. 30,000 per family in case of hospitalization. If an earning member falls sick, the scheme also provides for the loss of livelihood at the rate of Rs. 50 per day up to maximum of 15 days, and in case of death of the earning head of the family due to personal accident, Rs. 25,000 is to be given to the nominee.

In all these categories, the government provides a subsidy of Rs. 100, which remains fixed whether it is an individual who buys insurance or a family of five or of seven. While the scheme is open to anybody who wants to participate in it, the subsidy is given only to families below the poverty line. Moreover, the scheme is designed to cover not a poor individual/family on Indian streets, but those who are members of some group or the other, such as cooperative societies, *bidi* workers, handloom weavers *etc*. In other words, the proposed scheme is a group insurance scheme with membership of at least 100 families.

The scheme is not designed to cover the entire population below the poverty line (BPL), at least not in the initial phase. If the scheme survives and does not get extended to include other BPL families, state governments would then need to think of reaching those poor who are not a part of any occupation-based or any self-help group for which the scheme is currently intended.

Some other salient features of the scheme are (i) individuals between the age of 3 months and 65 years can join the scheme (ii) total hospital expense that can be reimbursed under the scheme for any one illness can be up to Rs. 15,000, with a cap on the amount payable for different types of hospital expenses (iii) a number of illnesses/situations are excluded, for example maternity insurance is not included, and (iv) claims will be settled either by an intermediary called third party administrators (TPAs) or by the insurance companies themselves.

In principle, both public and private insurance companies can participate in the scheme. In reality, participation of private insurance companies seems unlikely, especially when there are other more lucrative areas still to be tapped.

Health insurance schemes for the poor should take care of not just the in-patient or hospital care, but also of the out-patient care. It is often suggested that insurance be provided only for in-patient care and that out-patient care be left outside the ambit of insurance. The reasons given are: that people can, by and large, afford out-patient care because it is relatively inexpensive; it is the in-patient care that pushes them into poverty trap; that administratively it is difficult to include out-patient care; and, that out-patient care would lead to cost escalation. Ideally, both in-patient care and out-patient care should be covered, and the decision of whether or not a patient needs hospitalization should be professionally made and should not be a function of whether or not the patient has health insurance cover.

The UNDP has sponsored at least three different kinds of community based health insurance experiments in the country, two of which are in Karnataka and one in W. Bengal. One common feature in all three experiments is that the issue of outpatient care too has been addressed – basically through (soft) credit. The second common feature is that health insurance arrangement is with the formal (public) insurance provider. The main difference between the two experiments in Karnataka is in the mediator. In one case an NGO is the mediator, and in the other case it is the local government that mediates between the people and the insurer. In both these experiments, public health facilities are used. At present only people below poverty line are covered in these experiments. All ailments are covered, but there is a cap on the maximum number of days a person can be hospitalized. In case of illness the person is given wage loss. In the West Bengal experiment, because of the absence or dysfunctional public health facilities, private health care providers are used. In this scheme members have to pay only part of the costs (make co-payments) instead of full costs paid by non-members for most treatments.

The Karnataka Government has launched a health insurance scheme for farmers' cooperatives, which will for the first time extend a healthcare benefit to the community.

With 90 per cent of the members of the over 30,000 cooperatives societies in the States being farmers, the scheme comes as a welcome step and aims to provide the best medical care and services to 25 lakh farmers co-operators in Karnataka.

The scheme will be implemented in close association with Narayana Hrudayalaya. A random survey of the health profile of 50 lakh farmers showed they suffered from heart diseases, bleeding stomach ulcers, burst appendix, gall stones, enlarged prostrate and cataract. The health insurance scheme would ensure that a nominal monthly payment of Rs. 5 would help them access the best health care.

Conclusion

In the current debate on health security for the poor, health insurance is made out to be panacea for all the ills facing the poor. Health insurance, no doubt, has emerged as an important financing tool as it promises to mobilize some resources from the people themselves *i.e.*, those who buy insurance. But health insurance, which strengthens the demand side, makes sense only when the supply of health care is reasonably well developed. Where this is not so, health insurance is meaningless. The supply of health care in the rural and remote areas of country is far from satisfactory. Although public health care centres are pervasive, these centres have degraded over time in most states due to lack of funds, accountability and so forth. Any attempt at introducing health insurance for the poor must also be accompanied by revival of health care facilities at these centres. Finally, both the provision and access to health care services should be a part of a bigger health strategy which includes other public health programs such as safe drinking water, sanitation, family planning *etc*. as each of these are important determinants of health outcomes.

7

The Indian Microfinance Experience

Accomplishments and Challenges[1]

RAJESH CHAKRABARTI

Introduction

Home to the largest population of poor in the world, India has been a natural candidate for experimenting with microfinance as a tool for poverty alleviation. With a nationalized formal banking sector that has emphasized rural and developmental banking for several decades now, India's involvement with small credit, targeted primarily at the rural poor, is hardly new. However, recent years have generated unprecedented interest in microcredit and microfinance in the form of group-lending without collateral; thanks in part to the remarkable success of institutions like the Grameen Bank in neighbouring Bangladesh and BRI, BancoSol, and others in more distant lands. The performance of organizations like SEWA in Western India and SHARE and BASIX in Southern India have convinced many a sceptic that microfinance can indeed make a difference in India as well. Over the past decade, NABARD's "SHG-Bank Linkage Programme" aimed at connecting self-help groups of poor people with banks, has, in fact, created the *largest microfinance network in the world.* The self-help group approach has won enthusiastic supporters among influential policymakers like the former Andhra Pradesh CM, Chandrababu Naidu. Even the central government has recognized the advantages of group lending and has adopted the approach in its battle against poverty.

---

1. I would like to thank India Development Foundation, Gurgaon, where most of the paper was written, for its warm hospitality. The views expressed here, however, are those of the author alone, who is also entirely responsible for all remaining blemishes and shortcomings.

Microcredit, in the sense of small loans to the poor, is of ancient origins in India. Traders and moneylenders have traditionally provided credit to the rural poor, usually at exorbitant rates of interest, leading to considerable hardship and impoverishment of borrowers, including undesirable and illegal practices like bonded labour. What we refer to as microfinance today does not include such exploitative practices, but rather lending to the poor at reasonable but sustainable rates.

Within India, the microfinance movement in Western and Southern India have received most attention, both in the media as well as in academic research.[2] The poster boys among the Indian microfinance NGOs – SHARE, BASIX, SEWA, MYRADA, and PRADAN, for instance, have deservingly received attention from academicians, media-persons as well as the government. Andhra Pradesh, in particular, has witnessed a remarkable growth in microfinance activities and its success stories have been widely reported as well.

However, Self-Help Groups (SHGs), usually at the behest of certain developmental non-government organizations (NGOs), have quietly mushroomed in most districts of India over the last few years. Millions of poor, predominantly women, are now members of thousands of SHGs. Given the lack of an easily accessible data source covering the operation and performance of multiple microfinance institutions (MFIs) and SHGs spread out over a region, it is hardly surprising that much of the extant research on microfinance in India, as in most other countries, has focused on developing case studies, often covering the well-known success stories. In this paper, we seek to follow a slightly different approach.

The paper is organized in the following manner. The next section provides a brief background of lending to the rural poor by the rural banking sector in India. The following section takes a look at the different aspects of Self-Help Groups as the emerging entity in microfinance. The fourth section studies the performance of the rural banking system in the microfinance area. The fifth and final section concludes with a pointer towards the future.

---

2. See, for instance, Fisher and Sriram (2002).

The Banking Sector and Lending to the Rural Poor: A Background

With directed priority-sector lending as an explicit feature of the formal banking sector, India has built up a network of rural banks that is rare, if not unparalleled, in the world. In 1999, 196 Regional Rural Banks (RRBs) had over 14,000 branches in 375 districts nation-wide, covering, on an average, about three villages per branch. The rural banking system, in its entirety, has an even more impressive coverage. Together, the RRBs, the nationalized commercial banks and the credit cooperatives — comprising Primary Agricultural Credit Societies (PACS) and Primary/State Land Development Banks (P/SLDS) — have one branch for every 4,000 rural residents (Bhatt and Thorat, 2001).

In spite of such an impressive coverage, the formal banking sector has had a limited impact on microfinance or lending to the poor. The RRBs were set up in the mid-70's with a clear mandate for lending to the poor, as it was felt that the cooperative banks were being dominated by the rural wealthy and that the commercial banks had an urban bias. For the first two decades of their existence, political pressure and focus on outreach at the expense of prudent lending practices, led to very high default rates with accumulated losses exceeding Rs. 3,000 crores in 1999. The reforms in the mid-90's, following the recommendations of the Narasimhan Committee Report, removed some of the constraints on the functioning of RRBs, easing their interest ceiling and allowing them to invest in the money market. The financial situation of the RRBs has improved since then, with declining losses, and over 80 per cent of the RRBs are now profitable. However, much of this turnaround has resulted from a shift to investment in government bonds (that have gained with falling interest rates) and loans to the non-poor in rural areas.

The focus on financial sustainability has cost outreach dearly. Recent years have witnessed – perhaps predictably – a sharp decline in the share of rural and small loans in the portfolio of the banks. The locational distribution of bank branches has also undergone a considerable shift away from the rural areas (see Figure 1).

Over its entire lifetime, the formal rural banking system in India has struggled to balance the dual objectives of outreach and financial performance. A post-reform shift in focus has benefited the latter only at the expense of the former.

Figure 1

Reorganization of the Banking Sector

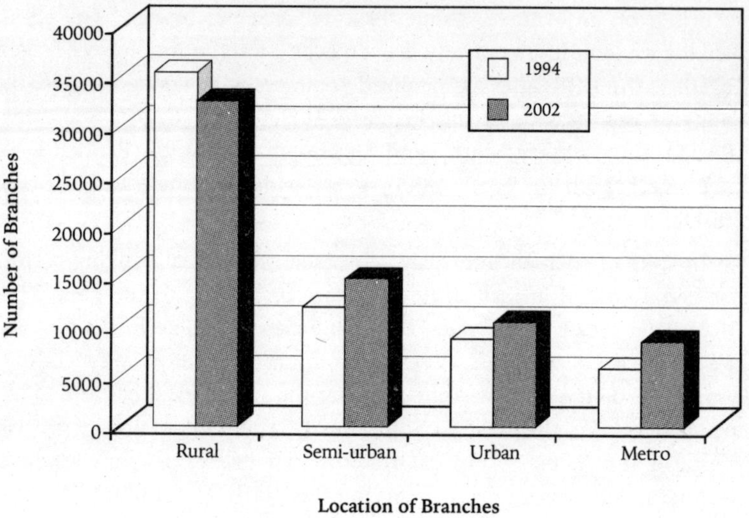

The lending portfolio of scheduled commercial banks also reflects this shift away from rural areas. At the end of 2001-2002, the share of agriculture in the outstanding credit of scheduled commercial banks was less than 10 per cent, which is even less than the share of personal loans (housing loans and loans for consumer durables).

Small loans have also declined in importance in recent years. Since over 98 per cent of rural loans are below Rs. 2 lakh, this implies a concomitant shift out of rural areas. The logic of this shift is easy to understand. In 2002, 45 per cent of the borrowers of scheduled commercial banks were from rural areas, but they accounted for only 13.4 per cent of their outstanding loans. For metros, the corresponding numbers were 15 per cent and 54 per cent respectively. With their focus shifted to financial performance, the banks are naturally shifting their portfolio to the low cost segment.

Microfinance provides an important way to balance the outreach among the rural poor while keep the cost of lending low. To the extent that the costs of credit risk assessment and monitoring can be reduced with the help of NGOs, banks can actually reach out to a large number of truly poor households without incurring heavy transactional expenses.

Self Help Groups (SHGs) as Borrowing Units

Self Help Groups (SHGs) form the basic constituent unit of the microfinance movement in India. An SHG is a group of a few individuals – usually poor and often women – who pool their savings into a fund from which they can borrow as and when necessary. Such a group is linked with a bank – a rural, co-operative or commercial bank – where they maintain a group account. Over time, the bank begins to lend to the group as a unit, without collateral, relying on self-monitoring and peer pressure within the group for repayment of these loans.

A SHG consists of five to twenty persons, usually all from different families. Often a group like this is given a name. Each such group has a leader and a deputy leader, elected by the group members. The members decide among themselves the amount of deposit they have to make individually to the group account. The starting monthly individual deposit level is usually low – Rs. 10 or Rs. 20 (about 20-40 US cents). For a group of size 10, this translates to Rs. 100 to 200 (about $2 to $ 4) of group savings per month. On the basis of the resolutions adopted and signed by all members of the group, the manager of a local rural or commercial bank opens a savings bank account. The savings are collected by a certain date (often the 10th of the month) from individual members and deposited in the bank account.

However, joining an existing SHG is often a costly affair for an aspiring villager. In order to maintain parity among the members, a new member has to join by depositing the total accumulated individual savings and interest of the group. Besides, the new member has to be accepted by every member of the existing group. Thus, it is often easier for a person not affiliated with an SHG to start a new SHG than joining a pre-existing one.

Loans are then given out to individual members from these funds upon application and unanimous resolution drawn at a group meeting. The bank permits withdrawal from the group account on the basis of such resolutions. Such loans, fully funded out of the savings generated by the group members themselves, are called "inter-loans". The repayment periods of loans are usually short, about 3-6 months. After regular loan issuance and repayment for six months, the bank considers making a bank loan to the SHG. The maximum loan amount is a multiple (usually 4:1) of the total funds in the group account. This limit is also reached gradually starting from a lower (2:1 or 1:1) figure. Thus, a 10 member SHG with individual monthly deposit level of Rs. 20, completing a six-month successful "inter-loaning", accumulates total savings of Rs. 1,200 (part of which may be lent out to individual members) and is eligible for a maximum bank loan of Rs. 4800.

Role of NGOs in Microfinance

Self Help Groups are almost always formed with outside assistance. Developmental NGOs, often with considerable history of working in a particular area for projects like literacy, sanitation, *etc.*, take to organizing SHGs, bringing together people, explaining to them the concepts, attending and help coordinate a few of the initial group meetings, helping them maintain accounts, and linking them with the banks. Of late, some of the rural banks themselves are being designated as Self Help Promoting Institutions (SHPIs), and they help in the formation and 'nursing' of SHGs. Figure 2 gives the country-level breakdown of SHGs according to their promoting institution. While Figure 2 shows that over half of the SHGs are formed by government agencies, it should be remembered that about 60 per cent of government-formed SHGs come from a single state, Andhra Pradesh, where the state government has played a very pro-active role in SHG financing.

Over the last quarter century, a few organizations, outside the purview of the public sector, have succeeded in effective poverty alleviation by providing microcredit. Self Employed Women's Association (SEWA) in the Western Indian state of Gujarat and Working Women's Forum in the Southern state of Tamil Nadu were among the pioneers in this effort. The sector received a major boost in the 1990s with the entry of several non-government organizations (NGOs). Many of these NGOs have been previously functioning in different developmental roles among the poor, and later added microcredit provision to their list of services. A few others, impressed by the success of microfinance elsewhere, started off as MFIs. Self-Help Groups (SHGs) among the poor, mostly women, have rapidly become a common rural phenomenon in many Indian states. NGOs provide the leadership and management necessary to form and run such groups in most cases. They also act as the crucial link between these groups and the formal banking system. Presently, well over 500 NGO-MFIs are actively engaged in microfinance intermediation across the country.

Figure 2

Distribution of SHGs Among Different Promoting Institutions

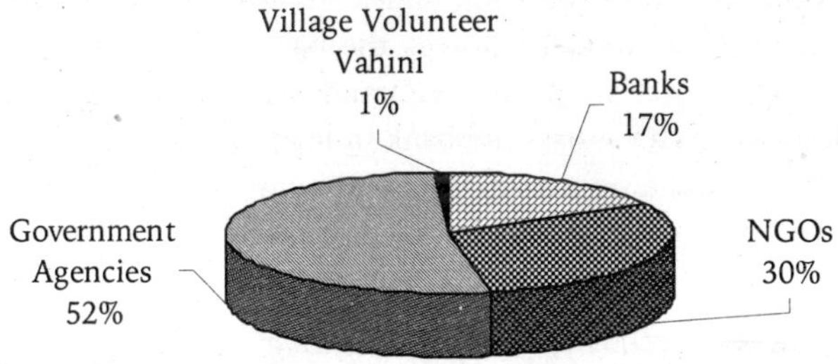

Source: Harper (2002)

There are several major legal, regulatory and financial challenges for NGOs involved in microfinance activities. Legally, they are usually registered as societies and trusts with no equity capital and, consequently, can never be "capital adequate" in leveraging debt. Also, these NGOs do not come under any specific control by any regulatory body and their only responsibility is to submit annual accounts to the Registrar of Societies. This lack of specific regulatory provisions has acted as a mixed blessing in the area – it has allowed for organic growth and spread of NGO—MFIs, and, at the same time, led to lack of financial sustainability for most of these organizations, sometimes with disastrous effects on the goodwill of microfinance at large.

Linking SHGs to the Formal Rural Banking Sector

The main advantage of Self-Help Groups lies in their joint liability and consequent "peer monitoring" of member borrowers. In association with sponsoring NGOs, they serve to reduce the transaction and monitoring costs of small lending for the banks as well as reach credit to the absolute poor. It is, therefore, hardly a surprise that they have attracted considerable attention in the rural banking sector, as well as from the government in recent years.

Several alternative models of SHG-NGO-bank relationship have emerged in recent years. One such model is where the bank lends directly to the SHG and the latter further lends it to individual members. As a variant of this model, an NGO may provide training and guidance to the SHG, still dealing directly with the bank. This has been the most popular model in the Indian context. Alternatively, the NGO itself may act as an intermediary between the bank and the SHG, borrowing from the bank and lending it to (usually multiple) SHGs. Yet another model involves the bank lending directly to the individual borrower with the NGO and SHG acquiring an advisory role. Here, the NGO assists the bank in loan monitoring and recovery. Figure 3 gives the approximate nationwide distribution of SHGs among the different bank financing models.

Government Support for SHG-based Financing

While most of the SHG formation/nursing process has initially been in non-government hands, the developmental potential of the SHG-based microfinance process has not gone unnoticed by the government. In recent years, government developmental programs have also sought to target the poor through the SHGs. Starting with the *Rashtriya Mahila Kosh* and the *Indira Mahila Yojana*, the government has used the SHG approach in many of its anti-poverty projects. The most important of the government programs using the SHG approach is the *Swarnajayanti Gram Swarojgar Yojana* (SGSY) launched in 1999. With increasing acceptance of the SHG based developmental approach, there is pressure on village and block-level administrators to achieve targets of forming a certain number of SHGs by a specified date. Thus, *Panchayat*s are also promoting SHGs in many areas.

Non-banking Financial Corporations (NBFCs) and other non-government organizations (NGOs) typically connect these SHGs to local banks or to the funds provided by wholesale credit suppliers like NABARD or SIDBI (Small Industries Development Bank of India). The SHGs develop a habit of saving among its members for a period of time, and then begin making loans to applying members from the collective savings of the group. After a few rounds of successfully re-paid loans, an SHG begins borrowing from an outside source, that is, a bank. Banks usually consider SHGs "bankable" after six months of their existence.

Figure 3

Distribution of SHGs Among Different Bank Financing Models

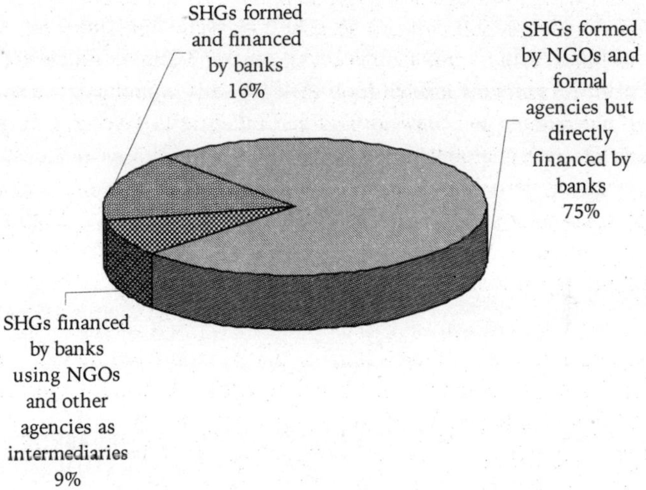

Source: Kropp and Suran (2002)

Government involvement in microfinance has, however, not been an unmixed blessing. Politicizing of the subsidy allotment among SHGs has become a big problem. Qualification for government subsidy is easily influenced by *Panchayat* members. Thus, *Panchayats* are now competing with NGOs and rural banks in forming SHGs. While the *Panchayat*-formed SHGs have the lure of government grants, they are often open to political pressure and misuse of funds by the recommending *Panchayats* and/or political parties. Besides, the NGO-formed SHGs have the benefit of honest and expert counseling from the nursing NGOs. Thus, the quality of NGO-formed groups are usually superior to those formed by the local government (*Panchayats*), and villagers are often keen to join the former. These age-old problems of government initiatives in poverty reduction, unless stemmed quickly, can actually harm the movement by eroding the fundamental precepts of self-help and empowerment of the poor.

The Swarnjayanti Gram Swarojgar Yojana

Swarnjayanti Gram Swarojgar Yojana (SGSY) has emerged as a main anti-poverty programme instituted by the government in recent years. Started in April 1999, it seeks to lift the rural poor out of poverty in three years by generating significant sustainable income. Organizing the poor into self-help groups (SHGs) lies at the heart of this approach. The goal of the programme is to enable the poor attain income generating assets. According to the SGSY Guidelines, "*The SHG approach helps the poor to build their self-confidence through community action. Interactions in group meetings and collective decision making enable them in identification and prioritization of their needs and resources. This process would ultimately lead to the strengthening and socio-economic empowerment of the rural poor as well as improve their collective bargaining power.*"[3]

The SGSY strategy includes identifying a cluster of activities at the block level and funding SHGs to perform these activities. The programme is implemented countrywide through a hierarchy of SGSY committees, at the central, state, district, and block levels. The actual implementation requires close interaction between the government officials at various levels, particularly the DRDAs (District Rural Development Agencies), managers from the participating banks, NABARD, as well as NGOs. The actual disbursement of government funds is through the DRDAs, who distribute the subsidy to the banks. The programme recognizes the important role that NGOs play in the formation and nurturing of Self-Help Groups, and seeks to include them in the exercise.

---

3. *Swarnjayanti Gram Swarozgar Yojana* Guidelines, Government of India, Ministry of Rural Development, New Delhi.

From the point of view of SHGs, SGSY is an excellent source of subsidized credit. If a group survives for 6 months, it becomes eligible for a revolving fund of Rs. 25,000 from a participating bank. Out of this loan, Rs. 10,000 is in the form of government subsidy, and the banks may charge interest only on the amount exceeding Rs. 10,000. The Rs. 25,000 fund injection becomes a part of the group corpus. With some exceptions, six months after the receipt of the revolving fund, the groups are tested for their preparedness to take up economic activities. If they pass the test, they are eligible for loan-and-subsidy for economic activity up to a maximum of Rs. 10,000 per group member or Rs. 1.25 lakh per group, whichever is lesser. There are also incentives, payable in several stages, to NGOs or "animators" incubating and nurturing SHGs.

Though financing is a very important part of SGSY, it is not the only element. Identification of activity clusters, recognizing training needs of *swarozgaris*, imparting proper training, and building capacity of the groups and group members in the selected activities are all essential elements of the programme. Also, SGSY is not the first or only government programme to try the SHG approach. DWCRA (Development of Women and Children in Rural Areas), for instance, is also based on the same approach.

Banking Sector and Microfinance

The formal banking sector has played an important role in providing microfinance in India. Much of the microfinance initiative in India has involved the Self-Help Groups (SHGs), predominantly of poor women. NABARD's Bank Linkage Programme, pilot-tested in 1991-92 and launched in full vigor in 1996, has been a major effort to connect thousands of such SHGs across the country with the formal banking system. By late 2002, it connected about *half a million* SHGs to the banking system with total loan disbursement of about Rs. 1,026 crore. Efforts of other organizations supplement that of NABARD. By March 2001, SIDBI, for instance, had disbursed over Rs. 30 crore to SHGs through 142 MFI-NGOs.

The emphasis on linking the SHGs of the rural poor to the formal banking system was made in the mid-80s in the Asia and Pacific Regional Agricultural Credit Association. As a result, the SHG-Bank linkage emerged. RBI included the programme in its "priority sector lending" and in 1999, the Government of India recognized it in its budget. A few studies commissioned by NABARD on the tenth anniversary of the launching of the programme in 2002 attempted an assessment of the programme. The findings indicate that the programme has emerged as the largest microfinance network in the world with some impressive statistics.

As of March 2002, the programme covered 461,478 SHGs with total cumulative lending of Rs. 1,026 cores (US $ 218.27 million). The accumulated savings in SHGs exceeds Rs. 875 crores (US $ 186.31 million) by unofficial estimates. 90 per cent of SHGs financed were exclusive women groups. 444 banks (121 RRBs, 209 cooperatives banks, all 27 public sector banks, and 17 private banks) with a total of 17,085 branches participated in the programme providing credit to about 7.8 million poor households in 488 districts. Average loan sizes were Rs. 22,240 (US $ 463) per SHG and Rs. 1,300 (US $ 27) per member. Over time, the programme is estimated to cover well over 500,000 SHGs with cumulative loans exceeding Rs. 1200 crore reaching over 8 million households. (Kropp and Suran, 2002 and Seibel and Dave, 2002).

The State-wise distribution of SHGs linked with banks shows a considerable variation in the share of total SHGs (see Figure 4). Andhra Pradesh has a disproportionately large share of over 42 per cent of all linked SHGs. Tamil Nadu and Uttar Pradesh (including Uttaranchal) follow with about 12 per cent and 11 per cent shares respectively. Karnataka comes next with about 9 per cent. The rest of the country, thus, accounts for about a quarter of the total SHGs combined. From an all-India perspective, therefore, the SHG-bank linkage experience has been very strongly biased towards the South and has not provided a balanced access to credit for the poor in India.

In spite of the impressive rise of microfinance institutions, the scope of further microfinance efforts in India is almost unlimited. Indeed, poverty alleviation in India is a Herculean task. India has roughly about 60 million poor households, accounting for over 350 million people, about 35 per cent of the entire population. Even NABARD aims at reaching only 100 million of the poor (less than a third) by 2008. Clearly, a quantum leap in microfinance activities is necessary if it is expected to make a serious impact on the poverty situation in India. There are, of course, other issues connected with microfinance and poverty alleviation. As elsewhere in the world, it is contended that in India too microfinance often eludes the "poorest of the poor," and it is the people above poverty line – barely or comfortably – who can benefit from such micro-financial services.

Figure 4

State-wise Distribution of Linked SHGs

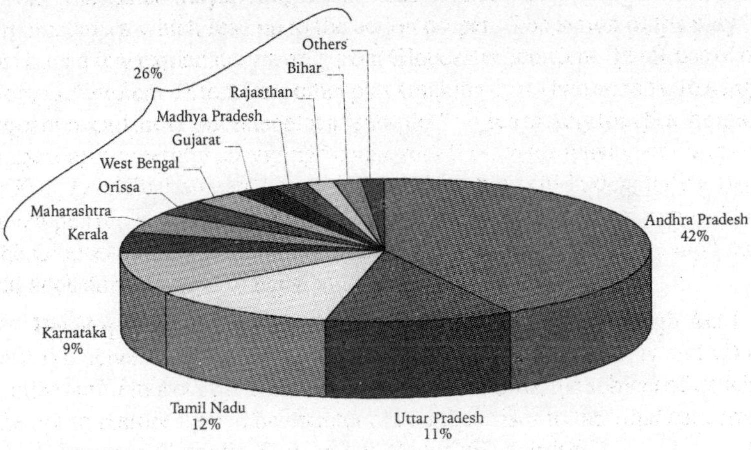

Source: Created from data in Bansal (2003). The state names refer to the pre-reorganization States. "Others" include Himachal Pradesh, Haryana, Punjab, Jammu & Kashmir, Assam, Meghalaya, Tripura, Sikkim, Manipur, UT of Andaman and Nicobar Islands, Goa, and Pondichery.

The Road Ahead – Prospects and Challenges

In this paper, we have sought to provide a bird's-eye view of the microfinance sector in India. There have definitely been significant advances in recent years and the concept and practice of SHG-based microfinance has now developed deep roots in many parts of the country. Impact assessment being rather limited so far, it is hard to measure and quantify the effect that this Indian microcredit experience so far has had on the poverty situation in India. Doubtlessly, a lot needs to be accomplished in terms of outreach to make a serious dent on poverty. However, the logic and rationale of SHG-based microfinance have been established firmly enough in that microcredit has effectively graduated from an "experiment" to a widely-accepted paradigm of rural and developmental financing in

India. This is no mean achievement. In fact, to the extent that people's mindsets are the biggest roadblock in the success of an innovation, it may well be one of the most important steps in the saga of microfinance.

The path ahead is obviously strewn with challenges. Scaling up of projects and bringing millions of people within the fold of microfinance is no mean task. The most convincing feature of this form of financing, which justifies its admittedly higher costs, is the near-perfect repayment rates. The expansionary zeal of microcredit practitioners should be balanced with the quality of loans – indeed a momentous challenge. Government involvement in SHG-based microfinance is a welcome development but it is not free from ills. Government aid almost always brings in its wake political favoritism and corruption. Therefore, it is important to ensure that the government microfinance initiatives do not go the same way as their several well-intentioned predecessors.

The biggest challenge in development, however, is the simultaneous development of investment potential and improvement of skill levels of the borrowers. A glut of low-skilled services is an unwelcome substitute for scarcity of credit. As microcredit alleviates the credit availability problem, the need for micro-consulting, business planning, and services like marketing, are being felt with greater acuteness. Microcredit cannot be expected to be a panacea to rural developmental problems. In some sense, its role is similar to that of credit in the general economy. It is a string that can hold back progress, but it is almost impossible to push on a string. There is a very real need investments that yield higher returns than the sustainable microcredit interest rates for the microcredit initiative to be truly successful.

However, so far the evidence – largely anecdotal – points to the several beneficial side-effects of microcredit. In particular, empowerment of women and the inculcation of financial training and discipline amongst the poor will undoubtedly have long-term socio-economic benefits. The principles of self-help and microcredit, thus, hold the key to economic and socio-cultural freedom for India's millions of poor, opening the gates of a hitherto untapped reservoir of human enterprise.

References

Bansal, Hema (2003). "SHG-Bank Linkage Programme in India: An Overview", *Journal of Microfinance*, Vol. 5, Number 1.

Bhatt, Nitin and Y.S.P. Thorat (2001). "India's Regional Rural Banks: The Institutional Dimension of Reforms", *Journal of Microfinance*, Vol. 3, Number 1.

Damodaran, Harish (2003). "Banks More Shy of Rural Lending", *The Hindu*, July 12, 2003.

Fisher, Thomas and M.S. Sriram (ed.) (2002). *Beyond Micro-credit: Putting Development Back into Microfinance*, New Delhi: Vistaar Publications; Oxford: Oxfam.

Harper, Malcolm (2002). "Promotion of Self Help Groups under the SHG Bank Linkage Programme in India", paper presented at the seminar on SHG-bank Linkage Programme at New Delhi, November 25-26.

Kropp, Erhard, W. and B.S. Suran (2002). "Linking Banks and (Financial) Self Help Groups in India -An Assessment", paper presented at the seminar on SHG-bank Linkage Programme at New Delhi, November 25-26.

Seibel, Hans D. and H.R. Dave (2002). "Commercial Aspects of SHG Banking in India", paper presented at the seminar on SHG-bank Linkage Programme at New Delhi, November 25-26.

8

Soil Degradation in India

An Environmental and Socioeconomic Hazard

S. BHATTACHARYA
M.Q.I KHAN
S. RIYAZUDDIN

Introduction

Soil is a vital natural resource and acts as a life supporting system. Existence of all living things on earth is linked, directly or indirectly, to soil. It is a strong parameter to judge a country's sustainable wealth. Other parameters like oil, minerals, etc., might exhaust at some point of time, and therefore, do not guarantee the continuity of wealth for long term. Soil is a fragile mass, which deteriorates physically and chemically due to environmental pressures or gets washed away from the land, through the streams and rivers, to the ocean. Maintaining quality of soil resource base is a key issue in ensuring sustainability of agriculture. Although in the past few decades, India has successfully emerged as a self-sufficient nation in food production due to Green Revolution, a stage has come now to evaluate the sustainability of food production in proportion to the future demand. To meet the demand of the increasing population in India, the food grain production must be increased from the present 200 Mt to 300 Mt by the year 2020 (Bhalla *et al,* 1999).

The stagnation in crop yields during the past few years is a matter of concern in the context of the forthcoming requirements. As the potential of Green Revolution has been utilized to a large extent, it is now the turn of the soil, which should deliver the goods. This precious and finite resource is declining in quality and quantity, resulting in decreased productivity. At the same time, many areas are being abandoned due to severe degradation in soil. Although, the land degradation process is as old as agriculture itself, the situation has worsened in the recent times due to population pressure, industrialization and urbanization. Ecologists and environmentalists believe that accelerated soil degradation is a cancer on the land that rapidly depletes the soil productive capacity, causing major concern for at least two reasons. First, soil degradation undermines the productive capacity of an ecosystem and worsens the socioeconomic conditions of the farmers. Second, it affects the global climate through alterations in water and energy balances, disruptions in the cycles of carbon, nitrogen, sulphur and other elements, pollution of natural water, and enhanced rate of forest degradation. The decrease in the vegetative cover ultimately enhances the emission of greenhouse gases into the atmosphere and leads to global warming. Archaeological evidences have shown that soil degradation was responsible for the extinction of the Harappan civilization in Western India, Mesopotamian Civilization in Western Asia, and Mayan Culture in Central America (Oslon, 1981).

According to United Nations Environmental Programme (UNEP) (1982), one of the three most pervasive threats to sustainable agriculture is soil degradation, which, by definition, is the decline in the soil quality caused through its misuse by humans. (The other two are the narrowing of the genetic base in agriculture and the incidence of pest and diseases). This paper presents a scenario of the degradation of Indian soils and its impact on the environment and socioeconomic conditions. Smaller land holdings have been shown as a major setback to the management of the degrading soils. A couple of measures have been suggested to sustain the soil health, which may improve the productivity, socioeconomic conditions and overall environment.

Magnitude of Soil Degradation in India and the World

Soil degradation is a universal problem, but is more pronounced in the warmer regions. Population pressure is another cause of degradation, because of overexploitation of the resources for meeting the pressing demand of food, fibre, and fuel. In India, arid, semi-arid and dry sub humid areas represent 78 per cent of the geographical extent. The net pedo-demographic situation can be judged by the fact that it covers 2.4 per cent of the global land area and supports 18 per cent of the world population with 9.5 per cent share of the world's degraded lands.

Assessment of Soil Degradation

Several agencies and researchers have assessed the extent of soil degradation in India. For example, the National Commission on Agriculture (1976) estimated that against a geographic area of 329 million hectares (Mha), 181 Mha (55.1 per cent) falls under degraded soils. The Food and Agricultural Organization (FAO, 1981) reported that 162.5 Mha (49.4 per cent) of Indian soils were degraded. Sehgal *et al* (1994) carried out mapping of degraded soils and discovered that an area of 187.7 Mha (57.1 per cent) was under various kinds and degrees of degradation. The Ministry of Agriculture and Cooperation (1982) estimated that 175 Mha (53.2 per cent) of land was subjected to varying kinds and degrees of degradation (Table 1). The reports of FAO (1981) and that of Sehgal *et al* (1994) are based on the spatial data collected by mapping the degraded soils at a scale of 1:5 M and 1:4.4 M, respectively. The rest of the data is based on the no spatial information compiled from various sources.

Table 1

Extent under Soil Degradation in India

Sl. No	*Source*	*Area in (Mha)*	*Per cent*
1.	National Commission on Agriculture (1976)	181.3	55.1
2.	FAO (1981)	162.5	49.4
3.	Ministry of Agriculture & Cooperation (1982)	175.0	53.2
4.	Sehgal *et al* (1994)	187.7	57.1

The spatial assessment made by Sehgal *et al* (1994) is a recent information generated following the criteria developed by an International Group on Global Assessment of Degraded Soils (GLASOD), which is presented in Table 2. It may be observed that about 57 per cent of the total geographical area of the country has been affected by various soil degradation problems, induced largely by human intervention. The rest of the area is either stable or free of degradation, and is contained in different mapped units showing degradation problems. In case the slight severity of problem, being nominal, is excluded from the calculations, the total affected area works out to be 151 Mha, representing 45.9 per cent of the total geographical area.

Table 2

Extent of Soil Degradation (Human Induced) in India

S.No.	Degradation Type	Degree of Degradation						Area Affected (Mha) without Slight Degree of Degradation	%
		Slight	Moderate	Strong	Extreme	Total Area (M ha)	%		
1.	**Water erosion**					**148.9**	**45.30**	**121.6**	**37.0**
	a) Loss of top soil (Wt)	27.3	99.8	5.4		132.5	40.30	105.2	32.0
	b) Terrain deformation (Wd)		11.8		4.6	16.4	5.00	16.4	5.0
2.	**Wind erosion**					**13.5**	**4.10**	**13.2**	**4.0**
	a) Loss of top soil (Et)	0.3	5.5	0.4		6.2	1.90	5.9	1.8
	b) Loss of top soil/terrain deformation (Et/Ed)		4.6			4.6	1.40	4.6	1.4
	c) Terrain deformation/ over blowing (Ed/Eo)			2.7		2.7	0.80	2.8	0.8
3.	**Chemical deterioration**					**13.8**	**4.20**	**11.0**	**3.3**
	a) Loss of nutrients (Cn)		3.7			3.7	1.10	3.7	1.1
	b) Salinization (Cs)	2.8	7.3			10.1	3.10	7.3	2.2
4.	**Physical deterioration**					**11.6**	**3.50**	**5.2**	**1.6**
	a) Waterlogging (w)	6.4	5.2			11.6	3.50	5.2	1.6
	Total affected area	**36.4**	**137.9**	**8.5**	**4.6**	**187.7**	**57.10**	**151.0**	**45.9**
5.	**Land not fit for agriculture**					18.2	5.50		
	a) Ice-caps (I)					4.1	1.20		
	b) Salt flats (Z)					2.2	0.70		
	c) Arid mountains (M)					11.2	3.40		
	d) Rock outcrops (R)					0.7	0.20		
	Soils with little/no degradation problem					**90.5**	**27.50**		
	Stable terrain (Under natural condition - Sn)					**32.2**	**9.80**		
	Total geographical area					**328.7**	**100.00**		

Source: Sehgal *et al* (1994)

It may be seen in the Table 2, that the water erosion is a major problem causing loss of topsoil and/or terrain deformation in about 148 Mha of the land area (representing 45 per cent). Wind erosion is dominant in the western regions, covering 13.5 Mha (representing 4.1 per cent) of the total area. It causes loss of the topsoil in 1.9 per cent, terrain deformation in 1.2 per cent, and over blowing and shifting of sand dunes in 0.5 per cent of the affected areas. The influence of human-induced chemical deterioration is observed in 13.6 Mha (representing 4.1 per cent of the total area), causing salinization in 10.1 Mha and loss of nutrients and/or organic matter in 3.7 Mha of the area. Water logging and/or areas affected by submergence or flooding cover about 11.6 Mha. The land that is not fit for agriculture including active dunes, salt flats, rock outcrops, ice-caps, etc. covers almost 18.2 Mha. Another area of about 5.0 Mha is under roads, water bodies, buildings, etc., which could not be separated in the present study. An estimated area of 32.2 Mha (representing 9.8 per cent), supporting dense forests on geological stable land, is considered under stable terrain, where human-induced degradation problems are relatively insignificant.

The severity of the soil degradation has been assessed based on the degree of the problem and the relative extent covered by the problem within a mapping unit. Four severity classes have been grouped, viz., low, medium, high and very high. Table 3 represents the areas under different severity classes for each of the land degradation type.

The assessment made by the Ministry of Agriculture (1996) is presented in Table 4, which shows the earlier assessment (1982) in comparison with the present assessment (1996) of the degraded soils. During the earlier assessment, it was found that 173 Mha of land was degraded, whereas the present assessment revealed only 107.4 Mha. The decrease in the problem area has been attributed to the soil conservation measures organized by the government. The areas under different types of degradation are shown in Table 5. The highest extent of degradation has been reported through water erosion followed by wind erosion, salinity, water logging, ravines and shifting cultivation.

Table 3

Severity of Soil Degradation and its Extent (Mha)

S.No.	Degradation Type	Severity of Degradation				
		Low	Medium	High	Very High	Total Area
1.	Water Erosion (W)	5.01	24.30	107.2	12.4	148.9
2.	Wind Erosion (E)					
	a. Loss of top soil (Et)			6.2		6.2
	b. Loss of top soil or terrain deforestation (Et/Ed)			4.6		4.6
	c. Loss of soil due to terrain deformation or due to over blowing (Ed/Eo)				2.7	2.7
3.	Chemical Deterioration (C)					
	a. Salinization (Cs)	2.8	2.00	5.3		10.1
	b. Loss of nutrients (Cn)			3.7		3.7
4.	Physical Deterioration (P)					
	a. Water logging (Pw)	6.4	5.20			11.6
	Total area	**14.2**	**33.20**	**124.3**	**16.1**	**187.7**

Source: Sehgal *et al* (1994).

Table 4

Present status of land degradation (Area in lakh ha)

Sl no.	State	Geographical Area	Earlier Assessment (1982)		Present Assessment (1996)	
			Area	% of Geo Area	Area	% of Geo Area
1.	Andhra Pradesh	275.07	122.31	44.5	96.65	35.1
2.	Arunachal Pradesh	83.74	26.54	31.7	11.95	14.3
3.	Assam	78.44	29.99	38.2	19.63	25
4.	Bihar	173.88	65.52	37.9	47.51	27.4
5.	Goa	3.70	2.00	54.1	2.14	57.8
6.	Gujarat	196.02	125.86	64.2	85.53	43.6
7.	Haryana	44.21	41.62	94.1	14.43	32.6
8.	Himachal Pradesh	55.67	19.14	34.3	12.06	21.6
9.	Jammu & Kashmir	222.24	8.93	21.2	12.25	29.1
10.	Karnataka	191.79	114.03	59.5	82.77	43.2
11.	Kerala	38.86	19.35	49.8	12.28	31.6
12.	Madhya Pradesh	443.45	207.17	46.7	127.15	28.7
13.	Maharashtra	307.69	198.46	64.5	74.53	24.2

Contd. ...

...Contd. ...

Sl no.	*State*	*Geographical Area*	*Earlier Assessment (1982)*		*Present Assessment (1996)*	
			Area	*% of Geo Area*	*Area*	*% of Geo Area*
14.	Manipur	22.33	7.34	32.9	13.26	59.4
15.	Meghalaya	22.43	11.02	49.1	11.02	49.1
16.	Mizoram	21.08	6.10	29.4	10.02	47.5
17.	Nagaland	16.58	10.38	62.6	8.21	49.3
18.	Orissa	155.71	78.03	50.1	58.02	37.3
19.	Punjab	50.38	32.30	64.1	10.7	21.2
20.	Rajasthan	342.24	373.94	109.2	190.01	55.5
21.	Sikkim	7.10	3.03	42.6	3.67	51.7
22.	Tamil Nadu	130.06	38.22	29.4	41.11	31.6
23.	Tripura	10.49	2.79	26.6	2.95	28.1
24.	Uttar Pradesh	294.41	131.15	44.5	101.05	34.3
25.	West Bengal	88.75	43.03	48.5	24.55	27.7
26.	Union Teritorries	10.96	3.50	31.9	0.85	7.8
	Coastal land: No state wise data		14.65			
	Total	**3287.26**	**1736.4**	**52.8**	**1074.3**	**32.7**

Source: Ministry of Agriculture, 1996.

Table 5

Land degradation status in India (Area in Lakh ha)

Sl no.	*Type of Degradation*	*Earlier Assessment (1982)*	*Present Assessment (1996)*
1.	Water Erosion	1071.26	571.55
2.	Wind Erosion	177.96	104.60
3.	Ravines	39.75	26.78
4.	Salt Affected	76.16	63.23
5.	Water Logging	85.26	31.97
6.	Mines & Quarry Wastes	—	2.53
7.	Shifting Cultivation	49.12	23.78
8.	Degraded Forests	194.94	248.97
9.	Spl. Problems	27.3	0.89
	Coastal Sandy Areas	14.65	—
	Total	**1736.4**	**1074.3**

Source: Ministry of Agriculture, 1996.

With a view to study further details, the National Bureau of Soil Survey and Land Use Planning has conducted soil survey for different states at 1:2,50,000 scale (NBSS & LUP, 1990) and published reports for a few states. The compiled data on land degradation for the entire country is yet to be published. A greater intensity survey has been carried out in the selected areas at 1:50,000 scale by numerous agencies and individuals (Dwivedi and Srinivas, 1998, Rao and Venkataratnam, 1991, Khan *et al*, 1997, etc.) However, there is a need to conduct countrywide surveys at the 1:50,000 scale and larger for better appreciation of the problem.

Wastelands

Wastelands are described as degraded lands, which can be brought under the vegetation cover with reasonable effort. These lands are currently underutilized and deteriorating for lack of appropriate water and soil management or on account of natural causes (National Remote Sensing Agency and Ministry of Rural Development, 2000). The National Wasteland Development Board (NWDB), Ministry of Rural Development and a task force group constituted by the Planning Commission jointly classified the wastelands into 13 categories. National Remote Sensing Agency (NRSA) (1985) earlier carried out a mapping of wastelands, wherein, 53.3 Mha of land in India was identified as wasteland. Further, this exercise led to a major national mission, at the behest of the Ministry of Rural Development towards a district wise wasteland mapping at a scale of 1:50,000. This was done using satellite data with the active participation of the Department of Space and other departments/agencies of state and central governments. It was found that 63.85 Mha (20.17 per cent, excluding Jammu and Kashmir) of area was under wastelands **(Table 6)**. Different categories of wastelands in India and their extent are presented in **Table 7**. However, the data on wastelands does not indicate the severity of the degradation type. For example, erosion, which covers a large extent of the country, cannot be assessed from the wasteland data, as the only indication of erosion is observed in the gullied/ravenous category, which is less than one per cent of the area. Attributing gullied/ravenous lands to the *very severely eroded* class, the areas under the rest of the classes, i.e., slight, moderate, and severe cannot be assessed from the wasteland data. Soil erosion is the most severe problem plaguing the soils, which has been reported to

Table 6

State-wise Wastelands of India

(Area in 00 ha)

S.No.	State	No. of District Covered	Total Geog. Area of District Covered	Total W.L. Area in District Covered	% of Total Geog. Area
1.	Andhra Pradesh	23	275068	51750	18.81
2.	Arunachal Pradesh	13	83743	18326	21.88
3.	Assam	23	78438	20019	25.52
4.	Bihar	55	173877	20998	12.08
5.	Goa	2	3702	613	16.57
6.	Gujarat	25	196024	43021	21.95
7.	Haryana	19	44212	3734	8.45
8.	Himachal Pradesh	12	55673	31659	56.87
9.	Jammu & Kashmir	14	101387	65444	64.55
10.	Karnataka	27	191791	20839	10.87
11.	Kerala	14	38863	1448	3.73
12.	Madhya Pradesh	62	443446	69714	15.72
13.	Maharashtra	32	307690	53489	17.38
14.	Manipur	9	22327	12949	58.01
15.	Meghalaya	7	22429	9904	44.16
16.	Mizoram	3	21081	4072	19.13
17.	Nagaland	7	16579	8404	50.69
18.	Orissa	30	155707	21342	13.71
19.	Punjab	17	50362	3339	4.42
20.	Rajasthan	32	342239	105639	30.87
21.	Sikkim	4	7096	3570	50.31
22.	Tripura	4	10486	1276	12.17
23.	Tamil Nadu	29	130058	23014	17.71
24.	Uttar Pradesh	83	294411	38773	13.17
25.	West Bengal	18	88752	5718	6.44
26.	Union Territory	20	10973	574	5.23
	TOTAL	**584**	**3166414**	**638518**	**20.17**
	***Un-Surveyed Area (J&K)**		**120849**		
	Total Geo. Area		**3287263**		

Source: National Remote Sensing Agency & Ministry of Rural Development (2000).

be 48 per cent of the geographical area by Sehgal, *et al* (1994), 45 per cent by the National Commission on Agriculture (1976), 47 per cent by the FAO (1981), and 21 per cent by the Ministry of Agriculture (1996). Even if the categories like the *land with or without scrub, shifting cultivation, degraded forests, pastures and plantations, mining/Industrial wastelands, barren rocky/stony/sheet rock, and steep sloping* are assumed to be causing soil erosion, the total extent under these categories cover only 15 per cent of the geographical area, and hence, there is no scope of assessing the extent and degree of soil erosion. It is necessary that a degradation map must contain the areas under different degrees/ severity of a given problem for prioritization of the degraded areas. Perhaps for these reasons, a general opinion is being build up among the soil scientists that a fresh land degradation inventory is inevitable at 1:50,000 scale for a proper assessment of the location and the extent of the degraded soils with clear cut type and severity of degradation and relatively accurate assessment of the extent.

Table 7

Category-wise Wastelands of India

S.No.	*Category*	*Total wastelands (Area in sq km)*	*% to Total Geographical Area Covered*
1	Gullied and/or Ravinous land	20553.35	0.65
2	Land with or without scrub	194014.30	6.13
3	Waterlogged and Marshy land	16568.45	0.52
4	Land affected by salinity/ alkalinity- coastal/inland	20477.38	0.65
5	Shifting Cultivation Area	35142.20	
6	Under utilised/degraded notified forest land	140652.30	4.44
7	Degraded pastures/grazing land	25978.91	0.82
8	Degraded land under plantation crop	5828.09	0.18
10	Mining/Industrial wastelands	1252.13	
11	Barren rocky/stony waste/sheet rock area	64584.77	2.04
12	Steep sloping area	7656.29	0.24
13	Snow covered and/or glacial area	55788.49	
	Total wasteland area	**638518.3**	**20.17**

Source: National Remote Sensing Agency & Ministry of Rural Development (2000).

Human-induced Soil Degradation

Soil is a dynamic entity, which is evidenced by continuous formative, and evolutionary changes until a dynamic equilibrium is achieved. Anthropogenic perturbations alter this state of equilibrium and may change the rate and direction or the principal processes (Rozanov,1990). The accelerated degradation is therefore attributed to human interventions to meet the competing demands of the rapidly growing population. Some of the actions affecting the soil quality are discussed below.

Rainfed Agriculture: Soils in their natural setup are undulating or rolling. Generally, the farmers resort to land shaping and leveling, and develop their lands if there is an irrigation source. In rainfed farming, accounting to 60 per cent of the cultivated area, they till the soil in a haphazard way without consideration of the direction of the slope. Tillage along the soil slope makes the soil extremely vulnerable to erosion on the receipt of very first shower. As the soil loss cannot be perceived in a short time span, the farmers of the soil are left ignorant of the consistent degradation.

Among the earlier studies, a survey of the soils of Sholapur district of Maharashtra in 1870, and again in 1945, showed that in a period of 75 years, nearly 17 per cent of the land with a soil depth of more than 50 cm was converted into shallow soils (with less then 50 cm depth) (Basu *et al,* 1960). Dhruvanarayana and Rambabu (1983) estimated that soil erosion by water takes place at an average rate of 16.35 tons per ha per year totalling for 5334 million tons per year for the entire country. Nearly 29 per cent of this total eroded soil is permanently deposited in the sea and nearly 10 per cent in reservoirs, resulting in the reduction of storage capacity by 1 to 2 per cent annually. The remaining 61 per cent of the eroded soil gets deposited in the valleys. Table 8 shows the assumed and observed siltation rate of a few reservoirs causing threat to the designed command area.

It is estimated that soils supporting rainfed agriculture are subject to severe sheet and rill erosion with an annual soil loss of 20 to 100 tons per ha per year (Dhruvanarayana and Rambabu, 1983). Even the soils under normal cultivation (such as for rainfed sorghum and cotton) with a land slope of 1 to 3 per cent have been observed to erode annually at a rate of 13.6 tons per ha per year (NBSS staff, 1987). Whereas, it takes 300 to 1000 years for formation of a new soil layer of 2.5 cm (Lal, 1993).

Table 8

Siltation Rate of Selected Reservoirs

(m/ha 100 sq km/year)

Reservoir	*Year of Impounding*	*Year of Observation*	*Siltation Rate*	
			Assumed	*Observed*
Beas	1974	1981	4.29	23.59
Chambal	1960	1976	3.61	5.29
Maithan	1956	1979	1.62	12.15
Nizamsagar	1931	1973	0.29	6.34
Panchet	1956	1974	2.47	9.92
Ramganga	1974	1974	4.29	17.30
Tungabhadra	1953	1972	4.29	6.11

Source: Dhruvanarayana and Ram Babu, (1983)

Removal of natural vegetation: Natural vegetation is a source of soil conservation by checking the soil loss through surface runoff. It also maintains the carbon-dioxide proportion in the atmosphere and prevents climatic changes. The removal of trees and bushes for fuel wood from forestlands and the Common Property Rights (CPR) causes a heavy damage to the soil because of soil erosion. Uncontrolled grazing far in excess of the sustainable capacity is another cause of soil erosion.

Singh *et al* (1994) reported a soil loss of more than 80 tons per ha per year in the Shivalik hills and 40 tons per ha per year in the shifting cultivation of Orissa and the northeastern forests. Dent (1984) observed that the Himalayas are the most severely degraded region of the world. Of the 75.35 Mha under forest cover, 40 Mha faces severe degradation. The remaining area with a crown density (11 per cent) against the recommended 33 per cent is far less to meet the growing demand of various tree products, including fuel, fodder, grazing and environmental balance (Singh, 2000).

Irrigation: India has made a significant development in irrigation by increasing the irrigated area from 21 Mha during 1951 to 57 Mha in recent times. While it has contributed significantly in increasing the foodgrain production, there has been a gradual drop in the groundwater table, and increase in water logging, and soil salinization.

It hardly needs to be emphasized that one-third to half of the irrigated land is getting degraded through salinization, alkalization, and water logging because of canal irrigation (Kanwar, 2000). These problems are common in many tank-fed areas, though the rate and magnitude of the problem is low when compared to the canal irrigated areas. In the Nagarjunasagar project, nearly 25,000 ha of the 1,40,000 ha under irrigation have been affected by salinity and water logging in a period of 14 years (Sehgal *et al*, 1994). Similarly, the left bank canal of the Tungabhadra Irrigation project in the Karnataka state suffered salinity and water logging in 30,000 ha within 30 years of commissioning of the project (Bowonder and Ravi, 1984). Added to these problems, irrigation from uncontrolled sources, such as canals and large tanks, floods the fields beyond the threshold and removes the applied nutrients by seepage, leaching, or flooding, causing nutrient deficiency.

Overexploitation of soil nutrients: Increased productivity implies an increased removal of the soil nutrients. The fertilizer application has not been in accordance with the increasing food production in the past few decades, resulting in the overexploitation of the nutrients. By harvesting about 200M tons of food grains every year, India is removing 25M tons of plant nutrients, whereas the annual input of fertilizers and manures is hardly 17.5 M tonnes (Kanwar, 2000). It is not only the micronutrients, but also the secondary nutrients are assuming an alarming status. In a study conducted in Andhra Pradesh (A.P.), it was revealed that 56 per cent of soils are low in nitrogen, 79 per cent in phosphorus, 3 per cent in potassium, 51 per cent in zinc, 22 per cent in iron (NBSS & LUP, 1996). Similarly, sulphur deficiency has been reported in the red soils of A.P. (Saharan *et al*, 1989).

Pollution: Fast urbanization and industrialization has led to the release of sewage, sludge, and industrial effluents through the streams, which result in toxification of the surrounding soils. In some intensively cultivated soils, the Punjab farmers, for example, have resorted to the indiscriminate use of fertilizers (400 kg per ha), which has resulted in groundwater pollution, mainly enriched with nitrates (Sehgal et *al*, 1994).

Poor attention on organic matter: The importance of soil organic matter in sustaining soil productivity has been appreciated since the dawn of human civilization. It is known to serve as a soil conditioner, nutrient source, conducive for microbial activity, preserver of soil environment, and determinant of sustained soil productivity. The accelerated vegetative growth witnessed by the application of chemical fertilizers has kept the farmer in the dark from the consistent depletion of the soil organic matter. Additionally, the unfavorable climatic conditions in the Indian peninsula have further enhanced the rate of decomposition of the soil organic matter, and its consequent depletion. A stage has reached where the soils are not showing a significant response to the added chemical fertilizers due to insufficient organic carbon content in the soil. Seventy per cent of the Indian soils, which are located in the arid, semi-arid and sub humid climatic regions, are deficient in organic matter, while it is adequate in humid and per-humid regions (Goswami *et al*, 2000). Unfavourable climatic condition for the Indian farmers and limited potential for farmyard manure production has lead to the deficiency of organic carbon content. It can however improved through crop residues, green manures, bio-fertilisers, etc.

Impact of Land Degradation on Soil Productivity

The change in physical condition and chemical composition of soil due to the degradation processes is bound to reflect on agricultural productivity. A few examples of the decrease in agricultural production due to soil degradation processes are presented below.

Loss of soil productivity due to soil erosion: Soil erosion implies loss of soil resulting in decreased soil depth, particularly removal of the top fertile soil. It affects not only the nutrient content but also the water holding capacity, thereby reducing the crop yield. Yadav *et al.* (1983) conducted experiments for three successive years by raising different crops in black soils with different degrees of soil erosion and depth. They reported that the loss of productivity in sorghum, soyabean, pigeon-pea, and cotton because of slight, moderate, and strong erosion was up to 10, 10-35 and 50-75 per cent, respectively, as compared to the model yield. The yield of the same crops in the soils with <50cm, 50-100 cm and >100 cm depth showed a decline of 63-73, 15-46 and 12-13 per cent, respectively. The declining crop yield in deep soils could be due to other factors such as texture, drainage, *etc*. (Table 9).

Table 9

Loss in Crop Productivity at Different Degrees of Erosion and Soil Depth

Soil Parameter	*Class Range*	*Loss in Productivity/Actual Yield, Q/ha and (per cent loss)*				
		Sorghum	*Cotton*	*Pigeon pea*	*Groundnut*	*Soybean*
Erosion	e1: Slight (5-10 ha yr)	0.8 (2.5)	—	—	1.0 (5.8)	—
	e2: Moderate (10-20t ha yr)	5.9 (18.5)	1.4 (7.8)	4.1 (21.5)	5.9 (34.5)	6.0 (29.8)
	e3: Strong (20-40t ha yr)	21.7 (68.0)	11.0 (61.1)	11.1 (58.1)	11.7 (68.0)	12.7 (62.9)
Depth	Deep (>100cm)	—	—	—	2.1 (12.2)	2.7 (13.4)
	Medium (50-100 cm)	14.1 (44.2)	8.4 (46.6)	5.0 (26.2)	0.6 (3.5)	3.0 (14.9)
	Shallow (<50cm)	23.4 (73.4)	6.7 (37.2)	11.2 (58.6)	9.2 (53.5)	12.7 (62.9)
Model yield		31.9	18.0	19.1	17.2	20.2

Source: Yadav *et al* (1983).

Loss of soil productivity due to alkalinity: Uncontrolled irrigation is gradually leading to alkalization of soil, which is indicated by the Exchangeable Sodium Per cent (ESP) values rising above 15 per cent. The loss of soil productivity in the soils with 15-40 and >40 per cent ESP has been estimated to be 25-50 and >50 per cent respectively as shown in **Table 10** (NBSS staff, 1992).

Table 10

Expected Loss of Soil Productivity due to High Exchangeable Sodium Percentage in Different Soils

Exchangeable Sodium Percentage	*Loss in Productivity (%)*	
	Alluvium-derived Soils (Inceptisols/ Alfisols)	*Black Soils (Vertisols)*
Up to 5	Nil	Up to 10
5-15	<10	10-25
15-40	10-25	25-50
>40	25-40	>50

Source: NBSS Staff (1992).

Loss of soil productivity due to imbalanced fertilizer application: Imbalance in fertilizer application is another cause of low productivity. The need of a balanced fertilizer application including macro, micro, and secondary nutrients and organic matter can be well understood by the decline in crop yield due to imbalanced application of one nutrient or the other. Swarup (1998) experimented the crop response in different soil types under varying combination of fertilizers, such as (i) Nitrogen (N) + Phosphorous (P) + Potassium (K) + Farm Yard Manure (FYM), (ii) N+P+K+ Zinc (Zn), (iii) N+P+K, (iv) N+P and (v) only N. It was discovered that crop productivity was highest under the combination of FYM (organic matter) with N, P & K at all the centers expect Hyderabad, where the micronutrient placed an important role. The crop productivity was the second best under the combination of micronutrient (Zn) with N, P & K. The yield gradually decreased when one or more nutrients were eliminated in rest of the treatments **(Table 11)**. The data highlights the importance of organic matter content in soil as also the role of micronutrients for optimum productivity. The above experiment cautions against the gradual reduction of biomass and the depletion of micronutrients in Indian soils due to various degradation processes.

Table 11

Loss of Soil Productivity due to Imbalanced Nutrient Supply (t/ha)

Centre	*Crop*	*Control*	*N*	*N & P*	*N,P & K*	*N,P,K & FYM*	*N,P,K & Zn*
Inceptisols							
Delhi 1972-95	Maize-wheat	1.4	4.1	5.9	7.1	8.1	7.6
Hyderabad 1972-95	Rice-rice	2.2	4.4	5.6	6.2	6.7	7.0
Vertisols							
Coimbatore 1972-95	Fingermillet-ragi	1.3	1.8	5.5	5.7	6.7	5.8
Jabalpur 1972-96	Soyabean-wheat	2.1	2.6	6.0	7.1	8.1	7.6
Alfisols							
Bhubaneshwar 1973-94	Rice-rice	3.0	4.1	5.0	5.8	7.2	5.8
Palampur 1973-97	Maize-wheat	0.6	1.0	3.8	5.7	7.9	6.1
Ranchi 1973-97	Soyabean-wheat	1.7	0.9	3.4	4.4	5.0	NA

Source: Extract from Swarup, 1998.

Stagnation in Foodgrain Production

The foodgrain production in India increased four fold from 50 M tons to 200 M tons during the second half of the 20th century, obviously due to green revolution, increased irrigated area, higher dose of fertilizers and pesticides, and other technological advancements. The complacence of giant strides into these developments has slowed down in the last few years, which is evident from the yield trend plateauing around 160 kg/ha between 1996-97 to 2000-01 despite consistent increase in the irrigated area and fertilizer application in the country (Table 12). The reason for stagnation of the yields could be attributed to loss of soil productivity due to its degradation.

Table 12

Food grain Productivity Trends from 1967-68 to 2000-01

Sl. No	*Year*	*Gross area under food grain production (M ha)*	*Gross area under irrigation (M ha)*	*Fertilizer consumption on per unit of gross cropped area (Kg/ha)*	*Food grain Yield (Kg/ha)*
1.	1967-68 to 1996-97	121.4 to 123.5	33.2 to 73.2	9.4 to 75.4	783.0 to 1614.0
2.	1997-98	123.8	73.1	84.8	1552.0
3.	1998-99	125.1	75.5	88.1	1627.0
4.	1999-2000	123.1	76.0	94.7	1697.0
5.	2000-2001	119.7	76.0*	86.3	1636.0

* Provisional

Source: Fertiliser Statistics (2001-02)

It is no wonder that the productivity could attain a declining trend in the near future, as the scope of increasing arable land or bringing new areas under irrigation is limited. It is, therefore, inevitable that the food production demand of 300 M tons by 2020 is met through sustainable soil health management.

Role of the Farmers in Soil Management

The farmers in India live in a precarious condition, facing the vagaries of the monsoon, incidence of pests and diseases, fluctuation in market rates, difficulties in storage and transport, and last, but not the least, the financial crunch. The uneconomic cultivation owing to low productivity trends is a further blow to their existing problems. The farmers, especially from the marginal, small and even semi-medium groups are too resource poor to meet the cost of inputs like seeds, fertilizer, pesticides, etc., and soil development. The degradation of soils due to lack of management by the small and marginal farmers is a dangerous signal for the future, as large number of farmers will be turning to small and marginal categories. The data shows that 69.7 per cent of the farmers belonged to the small and marginal size group during 1970-71, which has gone up to 78.2 per cent during 1990-91(Fertilizer statistics, 2001-02). It is therefore to be ensured that the small-size holdings are protected against soil degradation through sufficient financial and technical support of the government.

The soil problems are also observed in the fields of many large farmers, as they leave their lands fallow and unmanaged for the tenancy complications, resulting in soil degradation. Even if they lease out the land, the tenant or the sharecropper of a short term does not invest on soil management, as it pays in a long run. Thus the lands need to be considered as national asset and concerted efforts may be bestowed for protection of this non-renewable resource.

Mapping Degraded Soils

From the discussion in the preceding paragraph, it is has been logically understood that the lands of small and marginal farmers are relatively more degraded than those belonging to large farmers. Currently about 78.2 per cent of the farmers in India belong to the small- and marginal-size groups, cultivating 27.4 per cent of the agricultural lands. It can't be precisely said as to what percentage of degraded soils belongs to these groups, since there is no spatial information available on degraded lands and the ownership boundaries of small and marginal farmers.

For the first time in history, soil mapping has been conducted for the entire country at a scale of 1:2,50,000 (1cm=2.5km) (NBSS & LUP, 1990), which is too small a scale to be superimposed over the cadastral maps duly represented with small and marginal holdings. This objective can be achieved, when soil maps of the country are prepared on 1:12,500 scale and at the same time the cadastral maps are updated and digitized to superimpose over the soil maps in a GIS environment to identify the location extent and ownership or degraded soils, which is a long-term exercise.

Government-initiated Programmes

The Ministry of Agriculture is tackling the problem of soil degradation through several programmes like National Watershed Development Project for Rainfed Agriculture (NWDPRA), and River Valley Project (RVP), Watershed Development in the Shifting Cultivation Areas (WDSCA) and Reclamation of Alkali Soils (RAS). Similarly, Ministry of Rural Development is organizing Drought Prone Area Programme (DPAP), Desert Development Programme (DDP), and Integrated Wasteland Development Programme (IWDP). All these programmes are aimed at conservation of soil and water for improving the productivity and socioeconomic conditions and attain ecological balance. Besides these programmes, there is a focus on soil health management by providing facilities for soil testing and creating a network of soil testing laboratories, such that every farmer has an access to soil testing. The government is encouraging the use of bio-fertilizers, vermicompost, fly ash, gypsum, and green manure seed by providing a subsidy for the upkeep of soil fertility.

All these programmes have helped in reclaiming a considerable area, which can be seen from the comparison of earlier assessment of 174 Mha (1982) and the recent assessment of 107 Mha (1996) **(Table 4)**. However, Sehgal *et al* (1994) reported an area of 187 M ha under soil degradation. This might be due to different approaches to the assessment. Acknowledging the efforts taken by the government in a large scale, it is to be remembered that soil degradation is a recurring phenomenon, which needs a continuous monitoring and management for sustaining the soil health.

Constraints in Soil Management

Major soil degradation processes in India are soil erosion, salinization, water logging, and nutrient deficiency. Soil erosion is mostly a hazard in rainfed agriculture, which can be checked by adopting soil conservation measures such as bunding, leveling, gully control structures, etc. These measures are too expensive to be incurred by a majority of Indian farmers. But for the government-initiated activities, the farmers themselves do not come forward to mitigate this hazard. Non-affordability of farm machinery by most of the farmers is another constraint to attempt the task of bunding and leveling.

Soil salinization and alkalization are the recurring problems, which require a perfect land shaping, leveling, and drainage network. The alkali soil needs a chemical treatment with gypsum at a rate of 5 to 15 t/ha at 3 to 5 year interval. These costly operations are beyond the capacity of resource poor farmers.

Water logging is another problem prevalent mostly in command areas, which is a difficult task to manage, as the waterlogged soils are situated in concave relief topography, and need heavy investment for creating and maintaining drainage network and pumping out the groundwater from the root zone.

Soil nutrient management is relatively an easier task compared to the engineering works discussed above. Farmers are found to be crazy for fertilizer application and they do invest a considerable amount for this input. The only problem is the imbalanced fertilizer application and ignorance about the micronutrient deficiency. The farmers are lagging behind in organic matter application due to lack of physical resources for preparing FYM or Compost.

Recommendations

Keeping in view the magnitude of the soil degradation hazard and its impact on the crop production, socioeconomic conditions and ecological balance, a few necessary measures are suggested.

- Conduct a detailed inventory of soil resources at a scale of 1:12,500 to determine the precise locations and extent of degraded soils, indicating the magnitude of the problem.
- Integrate the land resource/degradation data with the cadastral maps in GIS environment to identify the farm holdings/farmers affected with the soil degradation hazard.
- Plan updation of cadastral maps or a fresh cadastral survey, for an effective developmental planning, as the existing village maps do not contain the recent land fragmentation.

- Make use of the high-resolution satellite data of IRS-PAN/SPOT/IKONOS or the forthcoming CARTOSAT data, which would depict all the physical features and land parcels.
- Prepare an optimal land use plan according to the soil suitability.
- Prepare soil fertility maps showing the nutrient availability/deficiency including macro- and micronutrients.
- Arrange to display the soil resource database and soil test data on the Internet.
- Prepare soil and water conservation plan on a watershed basis duly showing the contours at 50 cm interval.
- Provide liberal long-term credit to the farmers, especially to the small- and marginal-size groups for soil and water conservation works.
- Exploit the ground water potential by locating the borewell points free of cost. It may be a boon to the farmers if they are charged for digging borewell, only if there is optimum yield of the water.
- Create awareness among the farmers for soil testing and soil conservation measures.
- Promote the use of green manure, vermicompost, and bio-fertilizer for enrichment of the soils with organic matter content.
- Guide the farmers to plough the land across the slope for *in situ* moisture conservation.
- Develop a watershed culture in the farming community for a holistic approach to land development.
- Train the farmers in soil health management through TV, radio, teleagriculture, group meetings in farmer clubs, melas, exhibitions, etc.
- Use the commercial breaks in the TV programmes for educating the farmers on the benefits of soil management, and also show the impact of the soil hazard for awareness among the farmers to sustain the soil productivity.
- Monitor the soil health/soil degradation status using remote sensing and G.I.S. techniques.

- Learn lessons through the success stories in soil health management of adjoining farms, villages, mandals/tahseels, districts, states, and countries.

Conclusion

Soil is a nonrenewable resource, which needs to be sustained by regular management and monitoring of various degradation processes that may affect the productivity. Every effort has to be taken to involve the farmers in protecting their soils from any kind of degradation. A helping hand, especially to the small and marginal farmers, is essential to enable them to purchase farm machinery for land shaping and leveling and other inputs through liberalized financial assistance. A proper care of the soil would result in enjoying the fruits of life and leaving the soil in a healthy state for the future generations. Any ignorance in this aspect would leave our generations in a miserable state of food scarcity and social insecurity.

References

Basu, J.K, D.C Kaith and M.S.U. Rama Rao (1960). Soil Conservation of India, Farm Bulletin 58, Farm Information Unit, Directorate of Extension, Ministry of Food and Agriculture, New Delhi. 64.

Bhalla, G.S., Peter Hazell and John Kerr (1999). *Prospect for India's Cereal Supply and Demand to 2020*, International Food Policy Research Institute, Washington DC. Discussion Paper 29, 24.

Bowonder, B and C. Ravi (1984). *Waterlogging from Irrigation Projects*. Administrative Staff College of India, Hyderabad, 41.

Dent, F.J. (1984). *Land Degradation: FAO Investigations on Environmental Education and Training in Asia and the Pacific*, FAO Regional office, Bangkok.

Dhruvanarayana, V.V. and Ram Babu (1983). *Estimation of Soil Erosion in India*, J. Irrig. Drain. Engg., ASCE, 109(4); 419-34.

Dwivedi, R.S. and Sreenivas, K. (1998). Delineation of Salt affected Soils and Waterlogged Areas in the Indo-Gangetic Plain using IRS-IC LISS III data, *International Journal of Remote Sensing* 19:2739-2751.

FAO (1981). *Soil and water conservation COAG/81/8*, Presented to the 6th session of the Committee of Agriculture, Rome, Italy.

Fertiliser Statistics (2001-02). Fertiliser Association of India, New Delhi.

Goswami, N.N., D.K. Pal, G. Narayanaswamy and T. Bhattacharya (2000). Soil Organic Matter-Management Issues, Int. Conf. on Managing Natural Resources for Sustainable Agriculture Production in the 21st Century, Feb 14-18, 2000, IARI, New Delhi.

Kanwar, J.S. (2000). Soil and Water Resource Management for Sustainable Agriculture – Imperatives for India. Int. Conf. on Managing Natural Resources for Sustainable Agriculture Production in the 21st Century, Feb 14-18, 2000, IARI, New Delhi.

Khan, Q.I., B.R.M Rao, L. Venkataratnam, S.S. Thammappa, M.A. Fyzee, V. Krishna Rao, A.S. Raju, and G. Sujatha, (1997). *Salt Affected Soils in South Coastal Districts of Andhra Pradesh – A Remote Sensing based Inventory*, Geographical Information Systems and Remote Sensing Applications Ed. I.V. Murali Krishna, Allied Publishers Ltd, Hyderabad.

Lal, R. (1993). Agriculture Sustainability and Soil Resilience, *Desertification Control Bulletin*, UNEP, ISSN. 0379-2455.

Ministry of Agriculture (1996). *Draft Report on Status of Land Degradation in India*, Govt. of India, New Delhi.

Ministry of Agriculture & Co-Op (1982). *In the Draft Report on Status of Land Degradation in India*, Govt. of India, New Delhi.

National Commission on Agriculture (1976). Report III, Govt. of India, New Delhi.

National Remote Sensing Agency, (NRSA) (1985). *Wasteland Map of India*.

National Remote Sensing Agency & Ministry of Rural Development (2000). *Wastelands Atlas of India*, 81.

NBSS & LUP (1990). *Soil Resource Mapping of Different States of India – Why and How?*, Soil Bull. 23. NBSS & LUP, (ICAR), Nagpur, 49.

NBSS & LUP (1996). *Soils of Andhra Pradesh*, National Bureau of Soil Survey and Land Use Planning (NBSS) Publ. 69. 94.

NBSS Staff (1987). *Benchmark Soils of India*. Bull 15 NBSS & LUP Publ., Nagpur, India, 24.

NBSS Staff (1992). *Annual Report*, 1990-91. NBSS & LUP, Nagpur, 176.

Oslon, G.W. (1981). *Archaeology: Lesson on Future Soil Use. Journal of Soil & water conservation* 36:1-18.

Rao, B.R.M., and Venkataratnam, L. (1991). *Monitoring of Salt-affected Soils—A Case Study Using Aerial Photographs and LANDSAT-TM Data*, Geocarto International, 6, 5-11.

Rozanov, B.G. (1990). Human Impacts on Evolution of Soils under Various Ecological Conditions of the world, 14th International Congress of Soil Science, Plenary Papers, 12-18 August 1990. Kyoto, Japan, 53-62.

Saharan, N., K.L. Sharma, S.K. Das and P. Srinivasa Rao (1989). Importance of Sulphur Fertilization in Sunflower in Dry Land Alfisols, National Seminar on Sulphur in Agriculture 7-8 Sept. 1989, UAS, Bangalore.

Sehgal, J.L. and I.P. Abrol, R.K. Saxena, and R.M. Profali (1994). *Soil Degradation in India: Status and Impact*, Oxford and IBH Publ. Co. Pvt. Ltd., New Delhi.

Singh G.B (2000). Overview of Natural Resources in India, Int. Conf. On Managing Natural Resources for Sustainable Agriculture Production in the 21st Century, Feb 14-18, 2000, IARI, New Delhi.

Swarup, A. (1998). *Long term fertilizer experiments in 50 years of Natural Resources Management Research* (Singh G.B. and B.R. Sharma, Eds) ICAR, New Delhi, 221.

UNEP (1982). World Soil Policy, United Nation Environment Programme, Nairobi, Kenya.

Yadav S.C., J. Sehgal and S. Vadivelu (1993). UNDP Terminal Tech. Paper on study of factor of Land Evaluation System. NBSS Publ. 73-100.

9

Is Drip Irrigation an Answer to the Water Problems of Small Farmers?

SHAGUN KRISHNAN

Introduction

"Water is the petroleum of the 21st century"

— *Yao Graham*

Water paucity is becoming the cause of worry everywhere. Worldwide, agricultural sector uses two-thirds of all fresh water. The ever-increasing demand for water from all sectors is making it difficult to sustain the available resources. In India, the demand of water for drinking and industries is expected to increase from 7,957 cubic millions to 63,351 by 2050.[1] The agricultural sector consumes more than 80 per cent of available water for irrigation in India. Half of the irrigation water is lost through evaporation. With the growing demand for water and insufficient water resources, technologies like drip and sprinkler system were introduced in the early sixties. Today, these technologies are used worldwide, especially in the countries where water is scarce. USA holds the first place in having maximum area under drip irrigation. India has the seventh place in the world with more than 17.53 million acres of land under the drip irrigation system. The area under drip irrigation has increased from 3,706 acres in 1985 to more than 17 million acres now, and is expected to grow more. Maharashtra has the maximum area under drip irrigation, with more than 98,000 acres, followed by Andhra Pradesh with more than 31,000 acres. Karnataka comes third in the country, with more than 30,000 acres under drip irrigation.

Karnataka, being one of the drought prone regions of India, has many districts that do not have perennial resources of water, like

1. *Market Assessment – Drip and Micro Irrigation System.*

rivers or canals. These districts are totally dependent on the underground resources. One such district is Kolar, where ground water is the only source of water. Owing to consecutive droughts in the region, the ground level has gone down alarmingly. There are tanks, but due to silt and drought, water storage is inadequate. Kolar district is famous for sericulture. Mulberry is the main crop, whose leaves are used for rearing silk cocoon. Acute water shortage had forced farmers to stop cultivating mulberry. In the last few years, with the support of the International Development Enterprise - India (IDEI), farmers have started using the drip system of irrigation for mulberry cultivation. To estimate the effectiveness of the drip irrigation system for mulberry, a survey was undertaken in the Kolar district of Karnataka and the study presented here is based on that survey.

IDEI believes that, water is the source of life, and hence, one should utilize every drop of it carefully. This approach is of crucial significance for the small farmers, with less than an acre of land and no access to any mode of irrigation. Using the low cost IDEI irrigation technologies, the small farmers have been cultivating vegetables or flowers, which are high yielding and earn a good amount of money. IDEI's objective is to improve the living standard of small farmers of India and other Asian countries.

IDEI's drip irrigation kits are designed according to the requirements of the farmers in different regions of India. The smallest kit called a *bucket kit* consists of a 20-liter bucket connected with tubes to irrigate $25m^2$ of land. The total cost of this kit is about Rs. 250, slightly more than USD 5. A 200-liter *drum kit* with pipes that irrigates $125m^2$ of land costs Rs 750, *i.e.*, around USD 15. These low cost kits are very popular amongst poor farmers owing to their economic affordability. However, these kits have high labour requirement as compared to the automatic drip system. The IDEI designed fully automatic drip system for big and middle range farmers, also works out to be cheaper than the other drip kits available in the market. The drum and bucket kits are used in regions where rain harvesting is practiced. In some parts of Karnataka farmers are using low cost drip system kits for stored rainwater.

In Karnataka's Kolar district, the farmers had stopped cultivating the traditional mulberry crop because of water scarcity. Only after IDEI's presence in that region and the affordability of the drip system designed by IDEI called KB - *Kushi Ka Bandhu* (the one who brings happiness) farmers have not only re-started the cultivation, but also extended the area under mulberry. The mechanism marketed by IDEI is more durable and cheaper than the competiting products. The table below shows the comparative price per acre of land, for mulberry production.

Mulberry	*IDEI's Price*	*Market Price**	*% Difference*
3 Feet by 3 Feet	14,235	19,600	37.69
2 Feet by 2 Feet	18,220	25,700	41.05

* Market Price is taken from the study by NABARD 2001

This is one of the many contributions of IDEI in Kolar district. They have helped farmers in choosing the type of crop, in order to improve the yield of the crop. It was IDEI's initiative that encouraged farmers to use the drip system and also avail of the subsidy from the sericulture department of Karnataka.

Reaching this stage was not easy for IDEI, as initially they did not get a very positive response from the farmers. Fortunately, a few progressive farmers came forward for installing the drip system. Their plots were used as model plots for other farmers to demonstrate the change in yield, quality of leaf and water saving due to the drip system. The IDEI staff used documentary films depicting the change in the quality of life of the farmers who had installed the drip irrigation system in their land. The audiovisuals helped in increasing awareness about the drip system amongst the farmers. Today, more than 35 per cent of irrigated land is under drip irrigation in Kolar.

A farmer from Thondala village says "It's IDEI who has made us aware of the drip system; there was no proposal from the Government". Another farmer from Nayakar Halli wants IDEI's help in other low cost agricultural machinery. Indeed, the farmers in Kolar district trust an IDEI staff more than any Government representative.

The details of the area under drip irrigation, in Kolar district, are given in the Appendix. The implementation of technology at such a major scale would not have been possible without IDEI's dedication.

Kolar – District Surveyed

Kolar[2] district is located in the eastern dry zone of Karnataka. Net irrigation area is 19.57 lakh acres, out of which 17.27 lakh is irrigated by ground water and the rest is irrigated by other sources, like irrigation tanks. Annual rainfall is around 744 mm but erratic, resulting often in a shortage of water. Given the absence of any perennial river, groundwater assumes tremendous importance, as it is the only source of water. There are 4500 irrigation tanks, but all of them have desiccated due to continuous droughts. The water table is gradually receding and in many places is at 600 ft – 800 ft below ground level. A study by NABARD in the 11 *taluks* of the district reveals, that out of 11 *taluks*, 4 *taluks* fall under 'Grey', 5 fall under 'Dark' and only 2 fall under the 'White' Category.[3] The white category *taluks* of Gouribidanur and Bangarpet have sufficient water resources. For our survey, *taluks* falling under the dark category were selected.

The acute scarcity of water in the region is motivating farmers to install the drip system. The area under drip irrigation in Kolar district is approximately 5,690 acres. Being one of the dark regions of Karnataka, the potential for drip irrigation is very high, as it facilitates judicious use of existing groundwater reserves. Sericulture[4] is the main source of livelihood in this district, though the water shortage has led many farmers to shift to rain-fed crops, like ragi, mango, jowar, cashew nuts and eucalyptus.

Cropping Pattern

Mulberry is the main crop cultivated in Kolar district, grown in over 78,127 acre. Mulberry is a forest tree used in sericulture. Mulberry leaves are used for rearing silk cocoons. The leaf protein is the main source for silkworms to biosynthesise silk. The leaf protein is made up of fibroin and sericin. Annually five crops of mulberry are grown.

There are two patterns of growing mulberry. The more traditional pattern is one where the crop spacing is 2 feet by 2 feet. The second

---

2. Details of Kolar district are given in Appendix.
3. Finding of NABARD study given in Appendix.
4. Details of sericulture activity given in Appendix.

pattern of 3 feet by 3 feet crop spacing is new. Most of the farmers adopt the new pattern after installing drip irrigation as it gives better quality of leaf, less leaf wastage and more yield.

Drip Irrigation and its Advantages

Drip irrigation was started in Israel, to optimise the use of available water. In drip irrigation, water is supplied slowly to a specific area of the plant, in a very steady manner. Linear Low-Density Polyethylene (LLDPe) tubes used for the system are an ideal choice, as they are durable and flexible, leading to uniform water application and longer life of the system. Drip system conserves water while providing the required moisture for the roots.

Drip irrigation system is the best water saving technology as water is directly applied to the root zone of the plant. Evaporation of water is reduced drastically and, the soil does not get satiated, as the water application is very slow compared to the conventional furrow system. In addition to these, there are other hidden benefits from drip irrigation. It saves labour cost by up to 80 per cent, since everything, from pumping water to directing the exact quantity of water supply, is automatic. There is no need to inspect the direction of the flow of water, whereas in the furrow system of irrigation 3 man-days are required to inspect and irrigate one acre of land. It reduces 70 per cent of the weed problem. Water is applied to the specific area; hence the growth of weeds is checked, resulting in less inter-cultivation activities. Also, drip irrigated plants generally have shorter growing season and bear fruits earlier, with less pest damage. All of these are advantages of this irrigation system over that of the furrow system.

Furthermore, the drip system contributes to greater efficiencies in the use of fertilizers, by about 30 per cent. This is because water containing fertilizers and pesticides is applied directly to the plant roots in the quantities necessary for optimal plant growth.[5] The efficient use of fertilizer not only saves the cost of fertilizer but also minimizes the groundwater pollution, which results from the excess fertilizer (especially the nitrates) getting mixed with the groundwater.

5. R.S. Saksena, Consultant Planning Commission and Chief Engineer, Ministry of Water Resources.

Historically, the drip irrigation system's major drawback for small farmers has been the very high installation cost.[6] With IDEI's low cost model, it is actually cheaper than the spray or sprinkler irrigation systems. Indeed, it is the most cost efficient system in the present scenario. Drip systems can be designed for use in all types of land and soil conditions, including the hilly regions. It works well, even with the red loamy soil where the moisture holding capacity is not as much as in other soils. Soil moisture does not vary from plant to plant. The Cost-Benefit (CB) ratio for the drip system for almost all the crops is lower than unity.

In Meghalaya, tribal farmers use the drip irrigation system in a different way. Instead of plastic pipes they use bamboo, due to the abundance of bamboo in the region, to irrigate pepper and areca-nut (betel) crops. Water from a natural stream is diverted to a point of higher elevation than the plot to be irrigated, and is conveyed by gravity through bamboo channels.

Installation of Drip System: The main PVC pipe is laid along the length of the plot. Sub-main PVC pipes run perpendicular to the main PVC pipes. LLDPe lateral tubes are connected to the sub-main pipes. The spreads of these lateral pipes are determined by the spacing of the crops. E.g., if mulberry, with a spacing of 3 feet by 3 feet, is grown in an acre of land, one can put in 74 rows, requiring 37 lateral pipes. The system has various designs based on the requirement and affordability, like inline drip, micro-tube system, pressure compensating drip system etc. but it does not have much effect on the water use efficiency. The diagram below shows a typical drip system layout.

Literature Review

Most of the studies on drip irrigation strongly recommend the use of the system. It is economical, especially, in areas with scant, water resources. Use of the drip system with mulch reduces evaporation. Up to 66 per cent of water can be saved with drip irrigation; combined with mulch the saving goes up to 77 per cent. In India, states that have a water shortage, like Rajasthan, Madhya Pradesh and Karnataka, are slowly adopting drip technology. During the last five years, both states and central government have announced subsidies for installing

6. Detailed Installation Cost of Drip Irrigation System is given in Table 3.

the system under various schemes like use of plastic in agriculture, national pulses development project, intensive cotton development programme, oilseeds development programme. The state government of Karnataka offers subsidy under the scheme of Sericulture development in state.

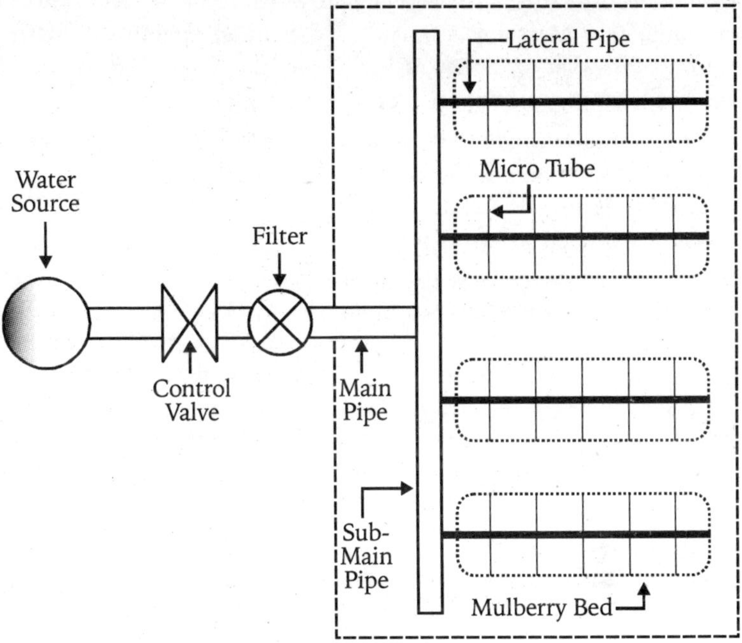

In India, however, this form of irrigation is still not as popular, as it should have been.

One of the major reasons behind this is the poor awareness and inadequate knowledge about its utilities and efficiency. Only 16 per cent of the farmers use this method. Another reason could be that the cost of installation is too high for a small farmer, who has difficulty in accessing loans.

Often, the lack of technical training to the farmers have led to various maintenance problems, discouraging other farmers from adopting the technology. The drip irrigation system is a network of pipes, and clogging at one point can affect water flows in the entire system. Improper training and the lack of after sales services from the dealers aggravate this problem.

The drip irrigation system has not been a successful investment in an orchard, as the results (fruits) have a long gestation period of 4 to 5 years and sometimes even more than that. Farmers are unable to block their investment for such a long time. Studies on the drip system in orchards have revealed that the cost-benefit ratio of installing such a system is actually higher in an established orchard is lower than that for a new orchard. Also, the drip irrigation system has not been very useful for crops like rice and wheat.

Other studies argue that in most regions in India this is a good system for water and power conservation and, it improves the crop-yield. It is very good for horticulture crops like tomato, cucumber, flowers, *etc*. It performs especially well for fruit crops like guava, mango and pomegranate. Universally, the use of drip irrigation in the growing of tomatoes has shown an increase of 54 per cent in yield. The technology is promising for high water demand crops like sugarcane and cotton. The benefit-cost ratio for sugarcane in Maharashtra is to 3.42 as calculated in the NICID report; however, only 3 per cent of the total Maharashtra sugarcane is cultivated under drip irrigation.

Malik *et. al*, (2002) confirm that not only the benefit-cost ratio, but also the earning power, is higher for drip irrigated fruit crops compared to that of furrow irrigation. The income from grapes, ber and citrus (Kinnow) increases by about 17 per cent, 28.5 per cent and 29 per cent respectively in the lands where drip irrigation is used. Benefit-cost ratio for grapes, ber and citrus were found to be 1.737, 1.949 and 2.570 respectively for drip irrigation system. Sivanappan *et. al*. (1987) show that the benefit-cost ratio is higher for the established orchards. These ratios for guava, sapota, coconut, sourlime and pomegranate are 1.71, 1.59, 1.44, 2.72 and 1.58 respectively, compared to 1.06, 1.17, 0.97, 1.55 and 1.21, respectively, for new orchards. Dhawan (2002), using NICID data, calculates the benefit-cost ratio for tomato, chilli, cucumber and watermelon as 2.64, 2.03, 1.71 and 3.74, respectively. Also the benefit-cost ratio for the widely spaced crops computes to be higher than other crops.

A study by Tiwari *et. al*. (2003) on the experimental plot in IIT Kharagpur for cabbage (a vegetable crop), however, calculates the benefit-cost ratio of the furrow system to be higher than the drip system - 6.99 for the drip system compared to 8.17 for furrow irrigation. A study by Narayanamoorthy and Deshpande (1997) shows very high ratios for banana, grapes (Nasik), grapes (Coimbatore) and coconut at 4.36, 7.82, 5.32 and 5.85, respectively. Dhawan (2002) questions the results of this study, disagreeing with the methodology for computing these returns.

Field Experience

As mentioned, earlier this study is based on a survey carried out in 12 villages of two *taluks* of Kolar and Sidlaghatta, both in the Kolar district. IDEI has a strong presence in the district for propagating the drip method of irrigation. The survey was based on a personal interview with farmers that use drip irrigation, as well as those that do not. At least four farmers using the drip system were interviewed from each village. There were often more than four farms using the drip system, but not all were available at the time of the survey. Also, the farm sizes of the surveyed farmers were very different, ranging from a low of 1 acre to a high of 45 acres.

Regardless of the size of the farms, most of them were very happy with the system. According to them, there is no maintenance cost involved if the system is handled carefully. Such maintenance involves the routine cleaning of the filter, removing the salt deposits on the in line drip (micro tube design does not have this problem) as the system is very sensitive to clogging and, removing the lateral pipes to clean the land at least twice a year.

14 per cent of the farmers had problems related to rats and squirrels trying to get to the water in the pipes, damaging the laterals. However, this problem was resolved when on the advice of the IDEI supervisor the farmers started keeping pots of water near the mouth of the laterals. 8 per cent of the farmers mentioned a problem of disproportionate water dripping at the end of the lateral. However, all these farmers had installed the first model of the IDEI designed system and have been using them for the last 5 years. Indeed, while 18 per cent of the farmers complained about the design of the old system, they also agreed that the new design is much better in many ways when compared to the old one.

The reasons why many farmers do not use the drip irrigation system are often unrelated to the system itself. For example, a farmer in Nayakara village referred to something very interesting. The government gives a subsidy for the installation of the drip system, but only to those who have bore-wells on their land. This farmer did not have one and hence was not entitled to the subsidy. Farmers can get around this by buying the system in the name of someone who owns a bore-well but that brings up the issue of how long the water can be shared between two farmers since the groundwater is receding on everyone's land. One was unable to put in a drip system due to insufficient funds. Most farmers do not have any complaint about the amount of the subsidy, and often, they do not want 100 per cent subsidy from the government. The only complaint, from 90 per cent of the farmers, is the time taken to get the subsidy, anything from six months to a year.

Methodology

Villages with the maximum area under drip irrigation were selected. The data collected during the survey were the initial cost of the drip system, the labour costs, electricity consumption, yield of leaf, yield of cocoon, area irrigated, cropping pattern *etc.*, for the year 2002-03. The information was collected for both the drip and the furrow systems of irrigation and a cross-section analysis was done for the year 2002-03.

To evaluate the profitability of drip irrigation system and the criterion for investment, we calculate the net present value as well as conduct a cost-benefit analysis. We then do a sensitivity analysis to map the effects of changes in the wage rate, interest rate, cocoon yield and the price of cocoon.

We have assumed that the life of the drip system is 12 years for mulberry production. The current price of the drip kit is Rs. 14825. All calculations are normalized to a land size of 1 acre and for 3 feet by 3 feet spacing of the crop. Throughout, the following have been assumed:

- The installation cost of the drip system includes the costs of the screen filter, PVC pipe, micro tube, labour and transportation cost.
- The yield per crop in case of drip irrigation system is calculated as: the sample average of 348 DFLs (Disease Free Laying) per acre multiplied by the cocoon produce sample

average of 244.6 kgs during the peak season and 200.5 Kgs during the non-peak season. The yield of the cocoon is less in summer compared to rainy season.[7]

- In the case of furrow irrigation, the DFL sample average is 257.3 DFLs per acre, the cocoon yield sample average is 132.6 Kg per 257.3 DFLs during the peak season and 110.5 Kg per 257.3 DFLs otherwise.
- The rate of interest is assumed to be the market rate of 14 per cent per annum.
- The annual repair and maintenance cost is taken as 2.5 per cent of the installation cost. In the case of the drip system, the cost of maintaining a bore-well is therefore added (2.5 per cent of Rs. 30,000) based on Thompson *et al.* 1980, Pitts and Clark, 1991 for calculating the maintenance cost of drip system.
- The electricity cost is the same for both the systems; it is a fixed payment depending on the horsepower (hp) of the motor. For both the systems, farmers use a 7 hp motor.
- The cost of cocoon rearing is also included in the annual operational cost.
- The price of cocoon is taken from Indiastat database. Indiastat reports the price every month, but we have taken the prices corresponding to the five times the crops are brought to the market by the surveyed farmers. These are Rs. 175, Rs. 206, Rs. 173, Rs. 143 and Rs. 169 for June, September, December, February and April, respectively.
- The installation cost of the bore-well is not included in the calculations of the NPV or the cost-benefit ratio. The absence of rivers and canals in Kolar district forces farmers to access groundwater resources. Hence even if they choose the furrow irrigation, they will have to bear the cost of a bore well.

Net Present Value (NPV): The net present value of any investment made is the present value of an equivalent financial

7. Details of Cocoon yield is given in Table 1 & Table 2.

instrument net of its cost. We assume that the operational costs and returns are the same each of the 12-year expected economic life of the drip system, except for the first year where the initial investment cost is included.

$$NPV = \frac{R1}{(1+r)^1} + \frac{R2}{(1+r)^2} + \ldots\ldots + \frac{Rn-1}{(1+r)^{n-1}} + \frac{Rn}{(1+r)^n} - IC$$

NPV = Net Present Value

R1, R2...Rn are the net returns in period 1, 2......n

n is the life of the system

r is the rate of interest

IC is the initial investment for installing the drip system

R is calculated from the difference between the revenue (P) and operating cost (excluding the initial cost) OC; thus R = (Revenue – Operating Cost)

NB = Net Benefit

$$NB = \frac{R1}{(1+r)^1} \ldots\ldots\ldots, \frac{Rn}{(1+r)^n}$$

Benefit-Cost (BC): It is the ratio between the net returns (R) and the sum of costs incurred (OC).

$$BC = \frac{R}{OC}$$

It is used to analysis the economic viability of the project undertaken. If the BC ratio is more than 1, the project is worth undertaking.

Results and Analysis

Drip irrigation system is the ideal alternative for the Kolar district, since water is scanty in the region. Further, since the soil does not have enough moisture holding capacity, drip becomes the perfect solution. The drip system requires an initial fixed installation cost, depending on the type of crop and its spacing. Water retention capacity of the leaf increases due to uniformity in the water supply. With the adoption of drip irrigation technology in Karnataka, farmers were able to irrigate 30 per cent extra land, with 23 per cent water saving.

Viability of the Drip System

The drip irrigation system is beneficial even without any support from the government. With the increasing demand for water in Indian agriculture, an option like drip irrigation is worth considering. Drip is not that important in areas where canal or river water is the source for irrigating the land. Indeed, the conventional way of furrowing is more profitable than drip system if there are no costs of drilling a bore-well or paying for electricity consumption. In the district surveyed, however, there is a shortage of river or rain water and drip irrigation appears as the better alternative.

Drip system of irrigation has produced good results, with not only the evident increase in the yield, but also, less crop damage due to pests. The quality of leaf has also improved after adopting this technology. Due to the alarming water depletion in the Kolar district, the state government of Karnataka has announced an increased amount of subsidy, from 50 per cent to 100 per cent,[8] for the installation of drip irrigation. The increase in subsidy will make the drip system more affordable to the poor farmers in the district.

Drip irrigation also saves time for the farmer, increasing the leisure time available to the farmers. Almost all the Kolar district farmers pointed this out. Many of them have started cattle breeding for extra income; some have started small businesses, while others spend more quality time with their family.

Benefit-Cost Analysis

A benefit-cost[9] analysis is one of the simplest ways to determine the profitability of any project. Any project having a BC ratio more than unity is worth investing. In mulberry, this ratio for drip irrigation is 2.57, which is higher than 1.49 for furrow irrigation (Table 6). This implies that for every rupee spent on the drip system, it gives revenue of Rs. 2.567 while in the furrow system this return is only Rs. 1.486.

8. *The Hindu*, 12 June 2003 – "100 per cent subsidy for drip irrigation in Kolar".

9. The Returns from the mulberry Crop for Drip and Furrow are given in Table 4 & 5. Total cost of mulberry cultivation for one acre of land is given in Table 7.

A part of this difference is due to the fact that under the drip system, the effective cultivable area increases. However, even without this extra area, and hence extra income, the drip system is more profitable (Table 6). There are not many other studies done on mulberry, but a paper by Muralidhara *et. al* (1994) also confirms that the benefit-cost ratio is high for mulberry.

The cost of mulberry cultivation is reduced by 7 per cent once the drip is installed. From this, the farmers are able to save Rs. 5105 per acre annually.

Net Present Value: Net present value assesses the future returns of the project inclusive of deprecation. The NPV of the drip system for mulberry works out to Rs. 7.21 lakh for a 12-year life of the investment. The average annual returns, or the net returns/acre, come out to be Rs. 1.29 lakh. The NPV for the furrow irrigation system, assuming the same life span computes to 1.98 lakh, with the annual net returns of Rs. 35 thousand.

The detailed calculations of NPV are given in the Table 8-9.

Payback Period

The installation cost of the drip system for mulberry at 3 feet by 3 feet spacing is Rs. 14.2 thousand. The annual returns in accordance with the net benefits are Rs. 1.29 lakh. The pay back period for the 3 feet by 3 feet mulberry crop is 2.6 months with a 14 per cent rate of interest and without any government subsidy. This shows that the payback period is very low. Within three crops, the farmers are able to get back the money invested.

Considering the pay back period, the drip system for mulberry seems to be highly advantageous. The State sericulture department could start finance schemes to encourage the small farmers to use the drip system. The private finance companies, also, should come forward to help the farmers in installing the drip system. The local financing sources are too expensive, being available only at rates as high as 36 per cent per annum.

Sensitivity Analysis

Sensitivity analysis was done to find whether the drip system continues to be profitable in adverse conditions like high interest rates, fall in cocoon prices, and hike in labour wage or loss of crop due to climatic disorder or pests. This has to be studied as a comparison with the furrow irrigation system under similar circumstances. The results favour the drip irrigation system (Table 10).

Hike in Interest Rate: NPVs for the drip system were calculated at 24 per cent and 36 per cent interest rates. These worked out to Rs. 4.87 lakh and Rs. 3.41 lakh, respectively. Even with these high interest rates, the payback period is still less than a year, profitable and hence, worth installing. In fact, there are instances of farmers having paid the 36 per cent rate of interest to the local financers for loans to install the drip system. Two farmers, one each from Charuvana Halli Nayakra Halli villages, took loans at interest rates of 3 per cent and 5 per cent per month, respectively. Dealers often charge the 24 per cent rate on credit given to the farmers for buying the drip equipment.

Fall in the Cocoon Price: Cocoon price fluctuations were taken to monitor the effect of competitive pressures due to the advent of Chinese silk in the Indian market. Chinese silk is available at a very cheap price compared to Indian silk. The annual average price of cocoon has declined from Rs. 178.16 per kg in the year 2000-01 to Rs. 167.4 per Kg in 2001-02. The standard deviation (SD) for the monthly cocoon price is 15.96 per cent in the last two years. In the last one year there is a decline of 6 per cent in the price of cocoon. During April to June 2002, the average price of the cocoon has shown a decline of 22 per cent with respect to the average price at the same time last year.

With a 30 per cent fall in cocoon price, the NPV changed to Rs. 3.87 lakh with a payback period of 3.5 months; a 50 per cent fall in price led to a 50 per cent decline in the NPV, which remained positive at Rs. 1.65 lakh with a 12 month payback period. By contrast, for the furrow irrigation system a 30 per cent fall in cocoon price resulted in a NPV of only Rs. 16,462. More importantly, a decline of 50 per cent in the cocoon price resulted in a negative net annual return of Rs. 18,546. The results show that the drip irrigation system is profitable enough to withstand the competitive pressures brought about by the entry of Chinese silk.

Crop Failure: Farmers grow five crops in a year, but due to pests or climatic conditions one crop gets damaged almost every year. Crop failure makes a strong impact on the annual returns of the farmers, which in turn disturbs the investment plan. The sensitivity analysis for crop failure was done on the three maximum yielding mulberry crop — the first crop yield in the month of June, the second yield coming in the month of September, and the fourth yield of February.

The NPV for drip irrigation system was calculated at failure of 1st, 2nd and 4th high yielding crops due to climate or other changes in the same year. If the 1st crop gets damaged the NPV for the system comes down to Rs. 4.79 lakh with the pay back period of 2.8 months. In case, the 2nd crop also gets damaged due to natural calamity or any other reason, the NPV shows a decline of Rs. 1.94 lakh. In the worst condition, were the third good yielding crop, also gets spoiled in the same year, the NPV computes to Rs. –4,036 having the maximum payback period of 2 years and 3 months. In such case, mulberry-cultivating farmers have to be cautious while investing so much money as the money gets blocked for more than 2 years and the earning starts in the 3rd year with a very low start of Rs. 1,148 per annum.

The NPV for furrow irrigation system with 1st crop failure in the year computes to Rs. 67,274 compared to Rs. 4,79,157 for drip irrigation, with the annual net return of Rs. 11,885 only. The NPV for furrow irrigation with two crop failures in the years comes to negative, indicating that the farmers using the furrow system cannot manage with more than one crop failure in a year.

Increase in Labour Wage: Drip irrigation is not a labour intensive technology. However, sericulture requires a lot of labour for the pruning of mulberry leafs and the rearing of cocoon. The NPV for drip reduces to Rs. 7.1 lakh with a 20 per cent hike in wages. In the case of furrow, a 20 per cent increase in wages results in the NPV falling to Rs. 1.6 lakh with annual net returns of only Rs. 29,130.

Clearly, the increase in wage rates makes drip much more attractive than the furrow option. As for operational costs, these rise much faster in furrow irrigation, compared to the drip system.

Comparison of the Economic Viability of both the Systems: The economic comparison of mulberry under furrow and drip irrigation system gives a better idea to the farmers in adopting the later. The CB ratio of drip system is more than furrow irrigation. The cost of drip was fully recovered in the first four crops of the year. NPV of drip system under all circumstances (keeping in mind the sensitivity analysis) was higher than farrow. With the use of drip system there was an increase in total area under cultivation, resulting in higher income with same water usage. The cost of cultivation was also less under drip. Further, net returns of the crop were also higher in drip compared to furrow. Hence, keeping all the domino effects in perspective, it is definite that any day drip system form of irrigation is far better yielding superior results for farmers than the furrow form of irrigation.

Key Findings

- Water table has gone down to 600 ft to 800 ft in many areas of Kolar.
- Mulberry is the main crop cultivated in the district, due to the water shortage there is 10 per cent increase in ragi cultivation.
- Government has failed to provide the alternative sources of water like canals in the district.
- The decision of de-silting the tanks has taken a long time.
- There are no check dams in the district for storing rainwater.
- The silk industry is not doing as well as before.

References

Assouline S., Cohen S., Meerbach D., Harodi T. and Roser M. (2002). "Microdrip Irrigation of Field Crops: Effect on Yield, Water Uptake, and Drainage in Sweet Corn", *Soil Science Society of America Journal*, 2002, Vol 66, 228-235.

Bher Christopher and Guru Naik: *"Applying Micro-Irrigation in the Himalaya: A case study"* on IDE's Experience.

Dhawan B.D. (2000). "Drip Irrigation Evaluating Returns", *Economic and Political Weekly.*

————. (2002). *Technological Change in Indian Irrigated Agriculture.*

Dhuyvetter Kevin C., Lamm Freddie R. and Rogers Danny H. (1994). *"Subsurface Drip Irrigation for Field Corn: An Economic Analysis"*, Irrigation Management Series, November 1994.

Katz Elisabeth, LBL (2001). "Low Cost Micro-Irrigation II", *BeraterInnen News*, February 2001.

INCID (1994). *"Drip Irrigation in India"*, Indian National Committee on Irrigation and Drainage, New Delhi.

Malik D.P. and M.S. Luhach (2002). *"Economic Dimensions of Drip Irrigation in Context of Fruit Crops"*, Paper presented in International Workshop on Economics of Water and Agriculture, December 2002.

Morris Justin R. (1999). *"Evaluating Drip Irrigation in Eastern Vineyards"*, University of Arkanasas, WE 24(4), 16-21.

Muralidhara H.R., D.S. Gundurao, Arun M. Sarpeshkar and R.Ramaiah (1994). "Is Drip Irrigation Viable for Mulberry Cultivation – An Economic Analysis", *Mysore Journal of Agriculture Science*, Vol-28, 256-260.

Nagaraj N., W. Marshall Frasier and R.K. Sampath (2000). *"A Comparative Study of Groundwater Institutions in the Western United States of Peninsular India for Sustainable and Equitable Resource Use"*, Presented at Constituting the Commons: Crafting Sustainable Commons in the New Millenium, the Eighth Conference of the International Association for the Study of Common Property, Bloomington, Indiana, USA, May 31-June 4.

Narayanamoorthy A. (1997). "Economic Viability of Drip Irrigation: An Empirical Analysis from Maharashtra", *Indian Journal of Agriculture Economics*, 52(4), 728-739.

Narayanamoorthy A. and R. S. Deshpande (1997). *"Economics of Drip Irrigation: A Comparative Study of Maharashtra and Tamil Nadu"* mimeo, Gokhale Institute of Politics and Economics, No 47, Pune.

O'Brien Daniel, Rogers Danny, Lamm Freddie (1996). *"An Economic Comparison of Alternative Irrigation Systems on Small and Irregularly Shaped Fields"*, In Proceedings of the Central Plains Irrigation Short course and Exposition, Burlington, CO, Feb 6-7, 1996. 74-88.

Paducah, KY (1996). *"Guidelines for Drip Irrigation and Fertigation of Pines and Hardwoods"*, Paper presented at the First Conference of the Short Rotation Woody Crops Operations.

Pant Niranjan (1999). "Impact of Irrigation Management Transfer in Maharashtra", *Economic And Political Weekly*, March 27-April 2, 1999.

Plusquellec Herve (1998). *"Modernization of Irrigation Systems: The Role of The World Bank And New Opportunities"*, IT IS V Workshop, Aurangabad, India, October 27-29, 1998.

Pundarikanthan N.V. and Santhi C (1995). *"Irrigation Scheduling In A Developing Country"*, Proceedings of the ICID/FAO Workshop on Irrigation Scheduling, Rome, Italy, 12-13 September 1995. http://www.fao.org/docrep/W4367E/w4367e17.htm

Howes Stephn and Rinku Murgai (2003). "Karnataka: Incidence of Agricultural Power Subsidies- An Estimate", *Economic and Political Weekly*, Vol.38, No.16, 1533-1535.

Chakravarty Subhra and Lalita B.Singh (1994). "*Water Economy Through Drip Irrigation*", 20th WEDC Conference.

Pant Niranjan (1999). "Impact of Irrigation Management Transfer in Maharashtra", *Economic and Political Weekly*, March 27- April 2, 1999.

Shrestha Rajendra B. and C. Gopalakrishnan (1993). "Adoption And Diffusion Of Drip Irrigation Technology", *Economic Development and Cultural Change*, 1993, Vol. 41, issue 2, 407-18.

Saad Cury J.C. and *et al* (2000). *"Economic Viability and Selection of Irrigation System Using Simulation and Stochastic Dominance"*, ASAE Annual International Meeting, July 2000.

Sivanappan R.K. (1994). "Prospects of Micro Irrigation in India", *Irrigation and Drainage System*, 8(1), 49-58.

Sivanappan R.K., O. Padamakumari and V. Kumar (1987). *Drip Irrigation*, Keerthi Publishing House, Coimbatore.

Tiwari K.N., Ajai Singh and P.K. Mal (2003). "Effect of Drip Irrigation on Yield of Cabbage under Mulch and Non-Mulch Conditions", *Agricultural Water Management*, Vol 58, 19-28.

Wildung David K. and Wright Jerry (2000). "Micro irrigation of Blueberries in Minnesota", *Irrigation Journal*, May/June 2000.

100 p.c. Subsidy for Drip Irrigation in Kolar – The Hindu, 12/06/03.

Drip Irrigation Improves Fertilisers Efficiency – The Business Line, 06/08/99.

"Market Assessment – Drip and Micro Irrigation system", STAT-USA on the Internet, US Department of Commerce, http://strategis.ic.gc.ca/SSG/dd72705e.html

APPENDIX

Table 1

Details of Cocoon Yield Per Acre – Drip Irrigation

Crop	*DFLs per Acre*	*Cocoon Yield Kg*
1st Crop (June)	348.03	244.6
2nd Crop (September)	348.03	244.6
3rd Crop (December)	348.03	200.5
4th Crop (February)	348.03	244.6
5th Crop (April)	348.03	200.5
Total	**1740.15**	**1134.5**

Table 2

Details of Cocoon Yield Per Acre – Furrow Irrigation

Crop	*DFLs per Acre*	*Cocoon Yield Kg*
1st Crop (June)	257.3	132.6
2nd Crop (September)	257.3	132.6
3rd Crop (December)	257.3	110.5
4th Crop (February)	257.3	132.6
5th Crop (April)	257.3	110.5
Total	**1286.5**	**618.8**

Table 3

Detailed Installation Cost of the Drip Irrigation System for 3' by 3' Spacing

Item	*Units*	*Cost/unit*	*Total Cost (Rs.)*
Screen Filter	1		1500
63 mm PVC Pipe	9	170	1530
40 mm PVC Pipe	12	110	1320
12 mm LLDPE	2300	3	6900
1.2 mm Micro Tube	1500	0.6	900
12 mm Gromate and take off	80	2	160
12 mm Connecter	25	1	25
40 mm Ball Wall	4	100	400
PVC and GI Fitting		800	800
Labour		500	500
Transport		200	200
Total			**14235**

Note: Total no of rows are 74. Laterals are 37.

Table 4

Returns from the Mulberry Crop Per Acre - Furrow Irrigation

Crop	*DFLs*	*Cocoon Yield (Kg)*	*Price*	*Total*
1st Crop	257.3	132.6	175	23205.0
2nd Crop	257.3	132.6	206	27315.6
3rd Crop	257.3	110.5	173	19116.5
4th Crop	257.3	132.6	143	18961.8
5th Crop	257.3	110.5	169	18674.5
Total	**1286.5**	**618.8**		**107273.4**

Table 5

Returns from the Mulberry Crop Per Acre - Drip Irrigation

Crop	*DFLs*	*Cocoon Yield (Kg)*	*Price*	*Total*
1st Crop	348.03	244.6	175	42805.0
2nd Crop	348.03	244.6	206	50387.6
3rd Crop	348.03	200.5	173	34686.5
4th Crop	348.03	244.6	143	34977.8
5th Crop	348.03	200.5	169	33884.5
Total	**1740.15**	**1134.5**		**196741.4**
Additional Produce Earning				**86566.2**
Total				**283307.6**

Table 6

Benefit Cost Ratio for Drip and Furrow System

System	*Benefit*	*Cost*	*Ratio*
Drip	283307.6	110341.1	2.57
Furrow	107273.4	72183.0	1.49
Drip (Without extra cultivable land)	196741.4	81313.0	2.42

Table 7

Cost of Cultivation Mulberry per Acre

	Quantity	*No. of Unit*	*Rs/Unit*	*Drip*	*Furrow*
Cultivation		3	300	900	900
Farm Yard Manure (FYM)		10	800	8000	8000
Chemical Fertiliser					
1st Crop	150 Kg N: P: K	3	430	1290	1290
2nd Crop	50 Kg Urea	1	250	250	250
3rd Crop	150 Kg N: P: K	3	430	1290	1290
4th Crop	50 Kg Urea	1	250	250	250
5th Crop	150 Kg N: P: K	3	430	1290	1290
FYM & Fertiliser Application Labour			1000	1000	1000
Pesticides & Foliar Spray Application charge			75	75	75
Weeding Labour charge		3(Drip), 5(Farrow)	500	1500	2500
Leaf Harvesting Charge		5	1500	7500	7500
Irrigation Labour Charge				0	4800
Transporting		5	2000	10000	10000
Sericulture Cost					
Eggs		5	1500	7500	7500
Raring Labour Cost		5	2800	14000	14000
Bamboo Mount-age Rent		5	500	2500	2500
Bed Disinfectants (A Powder, B Powder, Lime)				3000	3000
Electricity 7hp motor				4500	4500
1% Tax on sale				1128	788
Maintenance Cost				1105	750
Total				**67078**	**72183**
Extra Area Cultivated	0.44				
Extra Cultivation Cost				29028.12	
Sub Total				**96106.12**	**72183**
Drip Irrigation Kit Cost				14235	
Total				**110341.1**	

Table 8

Net Present Value for Drip Irrigation System for Mulberry

N	IC	Operational Cost+ Maintenance Cost + Rearing Cost	Total Cost	Returns	Net Returns	Discount Coefficient (r = 14%)	Net Present Value	NPV
1.	14235	67078	–81313	196741	115428	0.88	101253	721445.9
2.		67078	67078	196741	129663	0.77	99772	
3.		67078	67078	196741	129663	0.67	87519	
4.		67078	67078	196741	129663	0.59	76771	
5.		67078	67078	196741	129663	0.52	67343	
6.		67078	67078	196741	129663	0.46	59073	
7.		67078	67078	196741	129663	0.40	51818	
8.		67078	67078	196741	129663	0.35	45455	
9.		67078	67078	196741	129663	0.31	39873	
10.		67078	67078	196741	129663	0.27	34976	
11.		67078	67078	196741	129663	0.24	30681	
12.		67078	67078	196741	129663	0.21	26913	
Total							**721446**	

Table 9

Net Present Value for Furrow Irrigation System for Mulberry

N	IC	Operational Cost + Maintenance Cost + Rearing Cost	Total Cost	Returns	Net Returns	Discount Coefficient (r = 14%)	Net Present Value	NPV
1.	—	72183	72183	107273.4	35090.4	0.88	30781.1	198621.1
2.		72183	72183	107273.4	35090.4	0.77	27000.9	
3.		72183	72183	107273.4	35090.4	0.67	23685.0	
4.		72183	72183	107273.4	35090.4	0.59	20776.3	
5.		72183	72183	107273.4	35090.4	0.52	18224.9	
6.		72183	72183	107273.4	35090.4	0.46	15986.7	
7.		72183	72183	107273.4	35090.4	0.40	14023.4	
8.		72183	72183	107273.4	35090.4	0.35	12301.3	
9.		72183	72183	107273.4	35090.4	0.31	10790.6	
10.		72183	72183	107273.4	35090.4	0.27	9465.4	
11.		72183	72183	107273.4	35090.4	0.24	8303.0	
12.		72183	72183	107273.4	35090.4	0.21	7283.3	
Total							**198621.9**	

Table 10

Sensitivity Analysis Results of Changes in NPV

Interest Rate	*Net Present Value*	
	Drip Irrigation	*Furrow Irrigation*
Due to Change in Interest Rate		
24 Per cent	487901.0	
36 Per cent	340713.2	
Due to Change in Cocoon Price		
30 Per cent Fall	387361.7	16462.3
40 Per cent Fall	276000.4	–44257.6
50 Per cent Fall	164639.0	–104977.5
Due to Crop Failure		
1st Crop Failure	479157.1	67274.8
1st and 2nd Crop Failure	193948.5	–87339.4
1st, 2nd and 4th Crop Failure	–4036.0	–194668.8
Due to Change in Labour Wages		
20 Per cent Hike	717235.4	164886.6
40 Per cent Hike	713024.8	131151.2
50 Per cent Hike	710919.6	114283.6

Details about Area Under Drip Irrigation in Kolar District

Taluk	*Land (Acres)*
Kolar	1800
Chintamani	500
Srinivaspur	700
Mallore	200
Mulbagilu	250
Sidlaghatta	1600
Chickbalapur	60
Bangarpet	20
Gouribidanur	60
Gudibande	Nil

Current Status of Sericulture in Karnataka State & Kolar District

Particulars	*Units*	*Karnataka*	*Kolar*
Geographical Area	Hectare	19049836	779467
Number of Taluks		175	11
Total Population	Crores	5.27	0.25
Rainfall	mms	1004	744
Area under Mulberry			
Irrigated	Hectare	74056	33280
Rain fed	Hectare	14847	—
Total	**Hectare**	**88903**	**33280**
Number of Sericultural Taluks		175	11
Number of Sericultural Villages		14867	2893
Number of sericultural farmers		254155	71063
Production of DFLs	Lakh Nos	1287.136	574.38
Production of Reeling cocoon			
Bivoltine	Tons	2749	220
Cross breed	Tons	53102	18025
Total	**Tons**	**55851**	**18245**
Production of Raw silk	Tons	6760	2203
Value of the Raw silk	Rs. Crore		321.29
Number of Government Silk Farms		98	8
Number of Grainages			
State		88	15
NSSP		7	1
Private		891	229
Total		**986**	**245**
Number of cocoon markets		65	10
Number of TSC's (General)		246	32
Number of Govt. Silk Filature		5	—
Number of silk exchanges		11	3
Number of reelers		13514	5946
Number of Charka units		10776	3819
Number of cottage basin units		319	4
Number of filature basin units		4380	1999
Number of Multi-end units		104	35

Status of Ground Water Exploitation in Kolar

Name of Block	*No of dug wells feasible*	*No of Borewells feasible*	*Stage of Devpt (%) at present*	*Stage of Devpt (%) after 5 years*	*Category*
Bagepalli	728	1501	57	67	Grey
Bangarpet	868	1815	51	61	White
Chickbalapur			155	165	Dark
Chintamani			78	88	Dark
Gouribidanur	512	1075	67	77	Grey
Gudibande	215	454	48	58	White
Kolar			139	149	Dark
Malur			215	225	Dark
Mulbagilu	295	607	68	78	Grey
Sidlaghatta			80	90	Dark
Srinivaspur	557	1173	62	72	Grey
Total	**3175**	**6625**	**93**	**103**	

Source: NABARD.

10

Bt Cotton in India: A Case Study

SHABANA ZAHOOR[1]

Introduction

The debate on the usefulness of genetic engineering in agriculture is far from over. This technology's usefulness is measured by different sectors in different ways. While the biotechnology industry weighs it in the terms of protection from insect pests, production increment and nutrition improvement, the civil society weighs it on the basis of its impact on farmers' economy, human health, and environment.

One has to do a case by case study in order to appreciate the facts of GM technology. One has to see the difference between what the biotech industries claim and how much is the actual gain? This technology's acceptance in pharmaceuticals is understandable as its effect can be seen immediately. The problem of this technology's acceptance arises in agriculture as issues of human health, environment and economy come into the picture.

The Soil Association's US investigations have found that GM crops have increased the cost of farming and have reduced farmers' profits. Likewise the records from other sources also show lower yields of GM crops from non-GM crops. The major problem for farmers comes in the form of higher costs of technology and reduced profits by lower yields. GM seed costs higher than the non-GM crop seed.

Another burden of GM crops on farmers is to pay "biotech fee" to the biotechnology industry. It further lowers the profitability of GM crops. Farmers using GM seeds in their field cannot re-sow them, which goes against the farmers' right. This is thanks to the

1. The views expressed here are the author's, and should not be taken to represent those of the organization she works with or of any of its associates.

'Terminator Technology"[2] that stops the GM plants to produce fertile seeds. Thus, farmers are physically bound not to re-sow saved seeds. They have to buy new seeds from the biotech firm. These factors reduce the profit from GM crops and simultaneously make the farmers under control of few multinational corporations worldwide.

GM technology can ruin organic farmers too. Internationally, the organic movement has rejected GM because of its potential for genetic contamination and its continued reliance on chemicals.[3] In North America, many organic farmers have been unable to sell their produce because of contamination. Contamination has already forced many organic farmers to give up trying to grow certain crops altogether. A survey by the Organic Farming Research Foundation found that one in 12 US organic farmers had already suffered direct costs or damage because of GM contamination.[4]

The biotech industry employed various justifications, for example alleviating hunger and improving food and feed crop, to get acceptance in society. It did succeed in this area in several countries quite spectacularly. Among the developing countries, India has taken the plunge by welcoming this new technology selectively. In India both public and private sectors are taking interest in GM research of various crops. To take a close look, one has to go through the list of GM crops under research.

In this paper, we take a look at the story of Bt Cotton in India as it was the first GM crop commercially approved for cultivation.

---

2. In 1998, the USDA and Delta and Pine Land, a seed company now owned by Monsanto, came up with a solution for both the concerns about seed copyrights and the potential of superweeds, by creating a sterile seed. While potentially solving one problem, sterile seeds create another. Food security activists dubbed them "Terminator seeds". This approach is in direct conflict with saving and sharing seeds for the next planting season and with naturally breeding hybrids that are suited for the particular bioregion in which they farm. With sterile seeds, farmers are dependent for their livelihood on large agribusiness for the seeds and the corresponding chemicals. This especially impacts the small farmer. Since 1998, this technology has moved rapidly forward. Astra Zeneca has developed a seed that cannot germinate or reproduce without chemicals. Due to their chemical dependence, opponents have dubbed them "junkie plants". (http://www.sfsu.edu/~holistic/document/Down/Food_Health/engineered.htm)

3. "Indian agro experts are of the view that transgenic technology should not be applied to crops selected for organic farming, if the country is to take any advantage of the lucrative $ 36.89 billion global market for organic food". Ashok B. Sharma, *Financial Express,* March 28.

4. *The Ecologist,* July/August 2003, pp 36-37.

Bt Cotton: The Genesis

A new chapter was added to Indian agriculture when the GEAC (Genetic Engineering Approval Committee) of the Government of India permitted the commercial release of Bt Cotton hybrids. The decision evoked a mixed response from both the farming community and the civil society. On the one hand, it was hoped that Bt Cotton would help reduce the pesticide use, increase the yield, and make the cultivation of cotton more economical and environmental friendly. On the other, there also were serious apprehensions that this would lead to increased pest and antibiotic resistance, increased genetic pollution, destruction of biodiversity, and perpetual dependence on transnational agrochemical and seed companies.

The Genetic Engineering Approval Committee (GEAC), the apex body for genetically modified organisms (GMOs) in India, conditionally approved the commercial cultivation of Bt Cotton varieties belonging to Mahyco-Monsanto on 31st March 2002 for a period of three years. The genetic modification rendered in this case is by making the cotton plant resistant to bollworm—one of its common pests. Mahyco-Monsanto had claimed that cultivation of Bt. Cotton would significantly reduce use of chemical pesticides and farmers would gain economically on account of higher yield.[5]

Six States have been granted permission to commercially cultivate Bt. Cotton. This included Gujarat, Maharashtra and Madhya Pradesh in the central zone and Tamil Nadu, Andhra Pradesh and Karnataka in the southern zone. After the first harvest of Bt Cotton, its evaluation went through a roller-coaster ride. Expert agriculture committees set up in Madhya Pradesh, Andhra Pradesh, and Karnataka concluded that GM cotton had failed to live up to the expectation.[6] The government, evaluating the first Bt Cotton harvest, first claimed that the harvest was quite promising. Later, it admitted poor performance and then finally ordered a state-wise review to assess the

5. The Bt gene produces a toxin called 'cry lac' that kills the bollworms – the biggest enemy of cotton. But a study released by entomologists at IARI has cast doubts on the long-term benefits of Bt Cotton. It found that the protection afforded by Bt gene is at best for six years. The study by K. Chandrasekar and G.T. Gujar has found that the bollworm develops "31 fold resistance" to the toxin 'crylac' within six generations/ years. The bollworms also developed cross-resistance to two more toxins called ' crylaa' and 'crylab'. *The Times of India* (2004) "Doubts over Bt Cotton benefits," 11th February.

6. "Snowbolloing by Desai," *Outlook*, 23rd June, 2003.

reasons behind the poor show.[7] Mahyco-Monsanto tried to present a positive picture, saying that Bt Cotton had performed well and yields had increased by 30 percent. This claim was buttressed by a paper published in *Science* by Qaim and Zilberman (2003). They claimed that Bt Cotton showed 87 percent yield increase compared to the non-Bt Cotton. However, the fact was that the paper was based on selected field trial data of Mahyco-Monsanto and was methodologically weak.[8] The planting of illegal Bt Cotton compounded the situation. To make matters worse, because of the absence of a clear-cut government policy, some farmer leaders even asked for a free playground, saying that there should be no regulation of GM crops and farmers should have a free access to such crops!

Responding to the confounding situation *vis-a-vis* the performance of Bt Cotton, different organizations conducted studies in the Bt Cotton growing states and came up with more or less similar results or findings. In the following sections, we analyze the performance of Bt Cotton in the light of the findings of a number of studies.

The Gene Campaign Study

Gene Campaign, a Delhi-based NGO, conducted a field study of Bt Cotton in two states - Maharashtra and Andhra Pradesh. In this study, 100 farming families were randomly chosen for the study. Of the 100 families surveyed, 25 were from Maharashtra and 75 from Andhra Pradesh. These farmers were growing simultaneously Bt and non-Bt varieties of cotton.

The Bt Cotton varieties taken were *Bt*. 162 and *Bt*. 184 and the non-Bt Cotton varieties were the local hybrids Brahma, Banny and Ankur. The findings of the study can be seen in the following tables.

Table 1 shows that:

- The number of bolls per plant was higher in the non-Bt Cotton variety.
- Fibre length was also longer in the non-Bt varieties, which had better grade cotton.

7. "States asked to report Bt Cotton Performance," *The Economic Times*, 17 April, 2003.
8. Suman Sahai, "The Bt Cotton Story: The Ethics of Science and its reportage," *Current Science*, 2003.

Table 1

Bolls and Fibre of Bt. and Non-Bt. Cotton

Item	*Bt. cotton*	*Non-Bt. cotton*
No. of bolls/plant	50 (25-75)	95 (70-120)
Boll size	3.5-5 gm	6-8 gm
Fibre length	30.5 mm	34.5 mm
Cotton quality	B & C	A & B

One of the most significant findings of this study (Table 2) was the indication that this Bt Cotton variety does not offer protection against pink bollworm (*Pectinophora gossypiella*). Pink bollworm attack was found to be severe after 60 to 70 days.[9] (There could be two reasons for this: first, the period of pest attack and the expression of Bt toxin does not coincide; and second, pink bollworm is not susceptible to the Bt toxin).

Table 2

Pest Attack on Bt. and Non-Bt. Cotton

Pest	*Bt. cotton*	*Non-Bt. cotton*
Leaf sucker	Moderate	Moderate
Stem borer	Low	Low
Bollworm	Moderate	Moderate
Pink bollworm	Heavy	Heavy

Table 3

Yield Comparison of Bt and Non-Bt Cotton in quintal/acre

Field Type	*Bt Cotton*	*Non-Bt Cotton*
Low Yielding	2.75 (2 - 3.5)	3.25 (2.5 - 4.0)
Medium Yielding	4.75 (4 - 5.5)	5.50 (5 - 6)
High Yielding	7.50 (6 - 9)	9.00 (7 - 11)

9. Training offered by Monsanto consisted of distributing pamphlets that required the farmers to count the ballworm in his fields and if they exceeded a certain number, then to spray pesticides. Spreading information through such pamphlets has been grossly inadequate for illiterate farmers. This resulted in misinformation and rumours.

Table 3 shows that:

- In all the three types of landholdings (low, medium, and high yielding), yield of non-Bt Cotton was better than its counterpart.
- Cotton traders confirmed the fact that demand for Bt Cotton was low and prices ranged from Rs. 2000 to 2100/qt. whereas non-Bt Cotton was selling at Rs. 2200 to 2350/qt.

Table 4

Comparative Investment in Bt and Non-Bt Cotton in Rs./acre

Input	*Bt Cotton*	*Non-Bt Cotton*
Seed	1,600	400
Fertiliser	2,800 (1500-4000)	2,800 (1500-4000)
Pesticide	1,316 (500-2200)	1,533 (600-2500)
Total	**5,716**	**4,733**

Table 4 shows that:

- Non-Bt came up with lower investment (net investment) than Bt Cotton.
- The seed of Bt Cotton is almost four times more expensive than the local hybrids.
- Yield/acre of Bt Cotton was lower than non-Bt Cotton and the cotton was of poorer quality, thus, fetching a lower price per quintal. Added to this was the higher investment in Bt Cotton fields.

Table 5 shows that:

- Net profit in all three types of fields in Bt Cotton is lower per acre as compared to its counter part- non-Bt Cotton.
- 60 per cent of Bt Cotton growers incurred losses by Rs. 79 per acre.
- The performance of Bt Cotton in the areas studied in Maharashtra and Andhra Pradesh is so poor that majority of the farmers surveyed said they did not want to grow Bt Cotton again.

Table 5

Comparative Income from Bt. and Non-Bt. Cotton

Farm Type	*Bt Cotton*			*Non-Bt Cotton*		
	Farmers (%)	*Income/ acre (Rs.)*	*Net Profit/ acre (Rs.)*	*Farmers (%)*	*Income/ (Rs.)*	*Net Profit/ acre (Rs.)*
Low Yielding	60	5637	-79	35	7394	2661
Medium Yielding	35	9737	4021	58	12512	7779
High Yielding	5	15375	9659	7	20475	15742

The Andhra Pradesh Government Study

Performance of Bt. Cotton in Andhra Pradesh During Kharif, 2002

The GEAC had permitted Mahyco-Monsanto for commercial release of three Bt. Cotton seeds, namely, MECH 12 Bt., MECH 162 Bt. and MECH 184 Bt. Mahyco-Monsanto marketed only first two seeds in Andhra Pradesh (A.P.). Out of 650317 hectares under cotton crop, 3315 hectares were grown with Bt. Cotton during the season 2002-2003.[10]

Department of Agriculture, Govt. of A.P., had issued instructions to all the District Joint Directors of Agriculture of cotton growing districts for conduct of farmer wise survey on the performance. Simultaneously, Acharya N.G. Ranga Agricultural University (ANGRAU) was also requested to submit their report on performance of Bt. cotton.

Survey Conducted by the Department

A.P. Govt. officials (District Joint Directors of Agriculture) conducted the survey in 14 districts of the state. Total number of farmers surveyed was 3709. Evaluation parameters were incidence of bollworm, incidence of sucking pests, yield compared to indigenous hybrids, quality of produce, market value and intention of farmers using Bt. Cotton seeds next year. All the parameters showed a wide range of results:

- Incidence of bollworm ranges from low to high. Low incidence was 33.02 per cent, moderate was 33.59 per cent and high incidence was 32.83 per cent.

10. In India, in just two years the area under the officially approved Bt Cotton has trebled from 72000 hectares to 2.16 million hectares while an illegal variety of Bt Cotton covers nearly 90 per cent of the cotton area in Gujarat.

- Incidence of sucking pests ranges from low to high. Low incidence was 25.90 per cent, moderate was 32.11 per cent and high was 41.79 per cent.
- Yields compared to indigenous hybrids also showed a range from low to high[11]. Yield in low performance was 70.96 per cent, 24.04 per cent was medium yield and 4.98 per cent was high yield.
- Produce quality showed two extremes, good and poor. Only 0.97 per cent produce was of good quality, remaining 98.78 per cent was of poor quality.
- Average and poor were the market values[12] of Bt. cotton. 9.59 per cent was of average market value, while 90.13 per cent was of poor market value. Due to short staple length of lint, less price of Rs. 150 to 200 per quintal cotton was offered.
- Last parameter was to evaluate the intention of farmers taking Bt. next year. Out of 3709 farmers, 65 (1.75 per cent) farmers showed their interest to grow Bt. in next season, 435 (11.72 per cent) were not in favour of it while 3177 (85.65 per cent) did not give their opinion.
- Bt. plants have shorter duration and become mature 30-45 days earlier to non-Bt.
- The study shows average no. of bolls per plant in Bt. 30-32/ plant as compared to 28-30 bolls/plant. But the boll size is relatively small (3-4 gm).

Survey conducted by ANGRAU

ANGRAU did their survey following the system of agro-climatic zones. The entire area was divided into Krishna-Godavari (KG) zone, Northern Telengana (NT) zone, Southern Telengana (ST) zone and Scarce Rainfall zone. We now discuss the major highlights of the survey in various zones.

---

11. Low yield being below 5 quintals/acre, Medium yield being 5-10 quintals/acre, and High yield being 10 quintals and above.
12. For market value, Poor (market value) corresponded to Rs. 1800-2000 per quintal and Good (market value) corresponded to Rs. 2000 and above per quintal.

KG Zone

- Net returns were higher compared to Telengana districts *i.e.*, Rs. 16750 per hectare in Bt. cotton. Though pickings were not completed in non-Bt. cotton.

NT Zone

- Cost of cultivation in Bt. cotton was slightly more than non-Bt. variety.
- Net returns are too low in Bt. cotton (Rs. 4800 per hectare) compared to non-Bt. cotton (Rs. 14880 per hectare).
- 90 per cent farmers who raised Bt Cotton in the year of 2002-2003 did not show inclination to grow it in the following season. Reasons attributed to it are small sized bolls, poor vigour, lack of rejuvenation, short staple length, low yield potential, and low market value.

ST Zone

- Cost of cultivation was slightly more compared to non-Bt. cotton.
- Net returns in case of Bt. was less (Rs. 2,400 per hectare) as compared to non-Bt. cotton (Rs. 18,880 per hectare).
- Less no. of bolls per plant and small sized bolls in Bt. cotton.
- More than 60 per cent farmers felt that attack of American bollworm was less severe.
- More than 75 per cent farmers who raised Bt. cotton were reluctant to raise Bt. cotton in the following season.
- In Medak district the performance of Bt. was better than non-Bt.

Scarce Rainfall Zone

- Farmers found Bt. cotton possessed resistance to bollworm.
- MECH 162 did not show sufficient yield potential on par with hybrid varieties.
- Net returns in Bt. cotton was Rs. 16,800 and in non-Bt. cotton Rs. 22,300 per hectare.

The Research Foundation for Science, Technology and Ecology[13] Study

Research Foundation for Science, Technology and Ecology (RFSTE) conducted a performance study of Bt Cotton in 2002-2003 in Maharashtra, Madhya Pradesh, Andhra Pradesh and Karnataka. The study showed that as claimed, Monsanto's Bt Cotton did not protect the plants from the American Bollworm and they fell prey to fungal diseases like root rot disease or fusarium. Simultaneously, there was also an increase of 250-300 per cent in attacks by non-target pests like jassids, aphids, white fly, and thrips. The yield from Bt Cotton varieties was also very poor. The staple length of Bt Cotton was very short. It fetched a low price in the market.

In Maharashtra and Andhra Pradesh, average yields of Bt Cotton are 1.2 quintals per acre, while it was sold with a promise that it would give 15 quintals of yield per acre. In Madhya Pradesh almost half of the 42 farmers surveyed in some districts—Badwani, Khargaon, Dhar and Khandwa reported that their crop had failed. In the other districts, only one farmer expected a yield of 12.5 quintals. In Karnataka too some farmers in districts—Bellary, Haveri/Dharwad and Sirippupa expected a total failure. The remaining farmers expected the average yield by 3.82 quintals per hectare. Since Bt Cotton was a complete disaster in the southern states of India, the GEAC denied the permission to commercialize Bt Cotton in the northern states.

In RFSTE's view, genetic engineering or the genetic engineering processes through which the Bt Cotton has been developed could be the cause of early maturity of the Bt Cotton plants. The toxin gene, and not environmental conditions, could be causing the early maturity of the Bt crop, since non-Bt varieties and other hybrid cotton plants were healthy and lush green in October while Bt Cotton plants had started reddening. This causes the reduction in yield as plants cannot give yield after November-December. The non-Bt plant gives yield until March.

The failure or drastically reduced yield of Bt Cotton has devastated Bt Cotton farmers. The incomes of Bt Cotton farmers suffered in two

---

13. http://www.greens.org/s-r/33/shiva.pdf

ways: by low yields and by staple size. Mahyco-Monsanto claimed staple size ranging between 26 mm and 29 mm. In actuality, it was hardly 15-20 mm, and thus, fetched the rate of a short staple cotton (around 1500 Rupees per quintal). The normal rate offered for the best quality cotton is Rs. 2000 to 2200 per quintal.

Economic concerns apart, various laboratory experiments and field researches have also demonstrated the adverse environmental impact associated with the cultivation of Bt Cotton.

APCID and DDS Study

In the Warangal district of Andhra Pradesh, about 1500 acres were cultivated with Bt Cotton in Kharif 2002-03. Andhra Pradesh Coalition in Defence of Diversity (APCID), a coalition of over 140 civil society groups in the state and the Deccan Development Society (DDS), decided to initiate a systematic study of the Bt crop[14] in this area in order to understand the facts in the field clearly, and make it available for a transparent public debate. The study was led by two agricultural scientists, Dr Abdul Qayum, formerly Joint Director of Agriculture, Andhra Pradesh, and Kiran Sakkari, who had worked with ICRISAT for three years.

The study included various parameters, from pest resistance to yield performance, and from economics of Bt and non-Bt Cotton to biosafety concerns of Bt Cotton. The following are the key findings of the study:

(a) **Pest attack:** During the first 30 to 35 days after germination, sucking pests like aphids and jassids were absent in both the Bt and non-Bt. But when the crop was about 80 to 90 days old, moderate to heavy infestation of sucking pests were more prominent on Bt than on non Bt crop. Even the dreaded pest *Helicoverpa armigera* was reported at the lowest level till early to late October but from November 2003 onwards infestation increased. Later, from December onwards, pink bollworm infestation was more predominant both in Bt and in non-Bt crops.

14. "Did Bt Cotton save farmers in Warangal? Release of a season long impact study of Bt Cotton."

(b) **Economic fall-out:** The cost of cultivation of Bt Cotton was more than non-Bt Cotton by Rs. 1092.

- Seeds of Bt Cotton were nearly Rs. 1100 more expensive than Non Bt.
- For plant protection, farmers had to spend less, Rs. 70 per acre, in Bt Cotton as compared to Non Bt.
- The average yield in Bt Cotton was 4.5 quintals per acre, while in non-Bt Cotton it was nearly 7 quintals per acre.
- The market price for Bt Cotton was less than non-Bt Cotton by Rs. 100 a quintal.
- All these factors together resulted in Bt farmers netting a return that was nearly Rs. 6663 less than that of Non-Bt farmers. While Bt farmers had a net loss of Rs. 1295 per acre, non-Bt farmers earned a profit of Rs. 5368 per acre.
- While 71 per cent of Bt farmers reported losses, only 18 per cent of non-Bt farmers reported losses.
- In terms of profits, while 29 per cent of Bt farmers reported profits, 82 per cent of non-Bt farmers had gained profit.

(c) **Biosafety concerns:** The study showed that in Warangal district of Andhra Pradesh, "refugia"[15] followed by farmers were not monitored by any regulatory authority. Mahyco-Monsanto had also completely abdicated their responsibility for this. This irresponsibility led to serious biosafety concerns. There is a possibility of genetic pollution since the Bt Cotton pollens can transfer themselves to cotton in adjacent fields.

Simultaneously, the regulatory authority also failed to monitor or control the mixing of Bt with non Bt Cotton at the market yard. To compensate the loss because of Bt Cotton, farmers mixed their Bt Cotton seed with non-Bt

15. Farmers have to divert 20 per cent of their land as an insect refuge, as recommended by the GEAC. If there is no refuge, the insects will quickly develop resistance and the Bt Cotton will fail. Wasting about 20 per cent of the land on managing resistance makes the Bt Cotton even more uneconomical, especially for the small farmers.

seed. This has raised severe anxieties about the entrance of GM crops into the food chain since cottonseed is used as feed for cattle [which can enter the human food chain through milk]. Further, cotton oil is used in cooking.

Overall, the study highlighted the deep disappointment of farmers over the performance of Bt Cotton, and that too in the very first year of its commercial cultivation. Many farmers who grew this crop were angry about its poor performance. They have expressed their anguish over the hype that Bt is a miracle seed that can resist the pest, and thereby improve the yield. The hopes of a large number of farmers have been belied.

(d) Other findings:

- Bt plant height was shorter, had lesser branches, thereby reducing its yield.
- Bt had smaller boll size.
- Bt showed higher characteristics of premature drying and boll shedding.
- Bt was less tolerant to abiotic stress.
- Bt had less number of cotton pickings compared to Non-Bt.
- Bt had twice as many seeds as non-Bt, thus reducing the quantity of lint.

Conclusion

The above studies have made it clear that Bt Cotton did not well in India in very first year of its cultivation. The second year field reports are yet to be published, and hence it remains to be seen if second year response is also unfavorable to the farmers. However, the Bt Cotton juggernaut is moving unhindered in India. As early as April 2004, the GEAC has approved yet another Bt transgenic cotton, RCH 2 for commercial cultivation in the central and southern parts of the country. RCH 2 is developed by Rassi Seeds, a sub-licensee of the US multinational, Monsanto. RCH 2 becomes the fourth Bt cotton seed variety to be released for commercial cultivation after Bt Mech 12, Bt Mech 162 and Bt Mech 184 varieties developed by Monsanto in collaboration with its Indian partner, Machyco was approved in March 2002. The GEAC in its recent meeting also gave permission to Rassi Seeds to conduct largescale field trials for its transgenic cotton varieties developed for cultivation in the northern part of the country, namely Punjab, Haryana and western Uttar Pradesh.[16]

The studies cited in this paper flag many serious issues. Bt Cotton does not offer protection against pink bollworm, which is emerging a major pest in the cotton belt of Andhra Pradesh and Gujarat. The toxin in Bt Cotton is proving to be ineffective against pink bollworm. The Bt technology has no effective provision to fight sucking pests such as aphids and whitefly, which can damage the cotton crop. The economics of Bt Cotton is also not impressive enough. One, the Bt seeds are about four times more expensive than the good local cotton hybrids available to farmers. Two, average yield per acre was found to be lower in case of Bt Cotton in all categories of landholding. Three, the cotton produced by Bt Cotton was found to be of poor quality in comparison to Non-Bt Cotton. Four, Bt Cotton must be grown with a refuge for resistance management. GEAC's recommendation of 20 per cent of the cultivated area to be used for refuge makes the Bt Cotton even more unviable, especially for the small farmers. In the US, farmers have large landholdings and have no problem in setting aside 20 per cent of their holdings as a refuge.[17] Indian farmers are at a disadvantage on this score. Bt Cotton has made the Indian farmers, who have generally smallholdings and a low risk taking capacity[18], vulnerable to economic losses.

---

16. "Rassi Seeds Receives Nod For Cultivation of Bt Cotton," *The Financial Express*, April 4, 2004.
17. According to a report in Nature Biotechnology, up to 30 per cent of American farmers do not follow the refuge requirement.
18. The risk taking capacity of US farmers is very high because of enormous subsidies which amounts to US $ 3.4 billion on cotton alone.

WTO and GMOs

Genetically Modified Organisms (GMOs) are created by transferring genetic material from one organism to another. This process is called genetic engineering, or biotechnology. Although the transfer of genetic material has long occurred through selective breeding and other techniques, new technologies permit more controlled transfers, and transfers of genes from completely unrelated species. Although citizens and governments in different countries all want to ensure that these GMOs do not pose a threat to human health or the environment, they do not agree on the best way to protect against these potential threats.

Trade problems arise when countries have different regulations regarding the testing and approval procedures necessary to place GMOs and their products on the market, or when they disagree about labelling and identification requirements. Some countries ban imports and sales of GMOs and their products altogether. In other countries, a large part of the production of some crops, such as maize or soybeans, is from genetically modified seeds, and is mixed with non-modified varieties during storage, transport and processing. These countries argue it would be unnecessary and very costly to keep GMOs separate, and consider that labelling requirements or import bans are unnecessary trade barriers.

So far, no trade dispute over GMOs has been examined by a WTO dispute settlement panel. Several WTO agreements could apply to the topic, including SPS, but also the TBT Agreement, the Agreement on Trade-Related Aspects of Intellectual Property Rights (TRIPs) and the GATT. An international agreement on *living* modified organisms, the Biosafety Protocol, was negotiated in the year 2000 under the Convention on Biodiversity of the United Nations.

The Bt Cotton Story in India: A Timeline

March 31, 2002	The Genetic Engineering Approval Committee (GEAC) conditionally approved the commercial cultivation of Bt Cotton varieties belonging to Mahyco-Monsanto for a period of three years.
April 19, 2002	The final evaluation report of the Central Institute for Cotton Research (CICR) on Bt cotton field trials showed that these varieties, developed by Monsanto and marketed by Mahyco in India, were still susceptible to jassids, aphids and sucking pests and several crop diseases.
May, 2002	The Department of Biotechnology (DBT) gave the go-ahead signal to the Tamil Nadu-based private seed producing firm, Rasi Seeds Company Ltd (RSCL), for conducting 'multi-location contained replicated research trials in open fields using transgenic Bt Cotton containing the Cry 1A(c) gene' during kharif season 2002.
April 15, 2003	The Gene Campaign study report ("Analysis of First Harvest of Bt Cotton: 2002-2203) revealed that neither State Level nor District Level Committees had been set up

	in either Maharashtra or Andhra Pradesh where Bt Cotton was being commercially grown: A breach of law and a direct violation of the prescribed rules for manufacture, use, import, export and storage of hazardous microorganisms and genetically engineered organisms and cells, under the Environmental Protection Act, 1986.
April 25, 2003	Since Bt Cotton was a complete disaster in the southern states of India, the GEAC denied the permission to commercialize Bt Cotton in the northern states.
June 13, 2003	The Genetic engineering approval committee (GEAC) struck down the plea made by Rasi Seeds for commercial cultivation of its genetically modified (GM) RCH 2 Bt cotton seeds in the South, saying the product needs further field trials and evaluations.
October 27, 2003	Indian agricultural commissioner Dr. C.D. Mayee claimed that Bt cotton cultivation was likely to increase to 1.25 lakh hectares in 2003 as against 40,000 hectares last year.
November 2003	Following the adverse reports on the performance of Bt cotton, Government of India set up a sub-committee under the co-chairman of the Genetic Engineering Approval Committee, GEAC, Sushil Kumar, to review the transgenic crop policy.
November 2003	The GEAC deferred its decision on Mahyco's application for seed production of its seven transgenic cotton hybrids. These hybrids are Bt MRC-6301, Bt MRC-6160, Bt MRC-6304, Bt MRC-6703, Bt MRC-6322, Bt MRC-6918, and Bt.MRC-6928.
January 13, 2004	The Union agriculture ministry asked the Gujarat government to take action against the manufacturers and vendors of spurious Bt cotton seeds.
January 18, 2004	The Agriculture Ministry said that the area under Bt Cotton was negligible. "In 2002-03, the first year of its approval for commercial cultivation, Bt cotton covered an area of only 38,038 hectare area representing 0.51 per cent of the area under cotton in the period. In 2003-04 with good monsoon rains the area under Bt cotton increased to 92,000 hectare. This area coverage under Bt cotton is almost neligible as compared to over 9 million hectare under cotton crop in the country. This points to the low acceptability of Bt cotton by farmers", said an internal report of the agriculture ministry. The agriculture ministry's findings ran down the hype created by US based International Service for the Aquisition of Agri-biotech Association (ISAAA). The ISAAA study has claimed that the Bt cotton area in India has increased to 100,000 hectare in 2003-04, while the government estimate put it at 92,000 hectare.
February 10, 2004	Study released by entomologists at IARI cast doubts on the long-term benefits of Bt Cotton. It found that the protection afforded by Bt gene is at best for six years.
April, 2004	GEAC approves yet another Bt transgenic cotton, RCH 2 for commercial cultivation in the central and southern parts of the country.

Bibliography

APCID and DDS (2003). "Did Bt Cotton Save Farmers in Warangal? Release of a Season Long Impact Study of Bt Cotton," Andhra Pradesh Coalition in Defence of Diversity and Deccan Development Society, Andhra Pradesh.

Economic Times (2003). "States asked to Report Bt Cotton Performance," 17 April.

Financial Express (2003). "Panel Rejects Rasi Seeds' Bt Cotton Bid," June 14, 2003.

Government of Andhra Pradesh (2003). " Performance report of Bt Cotton in Andhra Pradesh during kharif, 2002," Department of Agriculture, Hyderabad.

Liu, Yong-Biao, Bruce E. Tabashnik *et al.* (1999). "Development Time and Resistance to Bt crops," *Nature*, 400: 519.

Morin, Shai, *et al.* (2004). "Three Cadherin Alleles Associated with Resistance to *Bacillus Thuringiensis* in Pink Bollworm," *PNAS*, 100: 5004-5009.

Outlook (2003) "Snowbolloing by Desai," *Outlook*, 23 June.

Qaim, M. and D. Zilberman (2003) "Yield Effects of Genetically Modified Crops in Developing Countries," *Science*, 299, 900-902.

Rowell, Andy (2003). "Debate, What debate?" *The Ecologist*, July/August, 36-37.

Sahai, Suman (2003). *Genetically Modified Crops in India: Some Issues*, Gene Campaign, New Delhi.

————. (2003) *Social and Ethical Concerns about Agricultural Biotechnology*, Gene Campaign, New Delhi.

————. (2003). "The Bt Cotton Story: The Ethics of Science and its Reportage," *Current Science*, 84 (8), 974-975.

Sahai, Suman and Shakeelur Rahman (2003). "Performance of Bt Cotton in India: Data from the First Commercial Crop," Gene Campaign, New Delhi.

Sharma, Ashok (2002). "Bt Cotton Belies Promises: Research," *The Financial Express*, April 20.

————. (2004). "Area Under Bt Cotton Negligible, Says Agriculture Ministry," *The Financial Express*, January 19.

————. (2004). "No Transgenic Tech For Organic Crops, Say Experts," *The Financial Express*, March 28.

————. (2004). "Rassi Seeds Receives Nod For Cultivation of Bt Cotton," *The Financial Express*, April 4.

Sharma, Manju, *et al.* (2003). "Agricultural Biotechnology Research in India: Status and Policies." *Current Science*, 84 (3): 299-301.

Shiva, Vandana and Afsar H. Jafri (2004). "Failure of GMOs in India," *Synthesis/Regeneration* 33 (Winter).

Suresh, N. (2004). "GEAC Needs a Make Over," *Biospectrum*, Vol. 2, Issue 1, January.

Times of India (2004). "Doubts over Bt Cotton benefits," 11, February.

11

Information Technology and Rural Development in India[1]

NIRVIKAR SINGH

Introduction

It may seem paradoxical that modern information technology (IT), associated in our minds with developed country markets and capital-intensive methods of production, has any relevance for a country where many millions still lack basic needs. Nevertheless, there are many efforts underway in India and other developing countries to demonstrate the concrete benefits of IT for rural populations, and to do so in a manner that makes economic sense.[2]

This paper outlines the conceptual and empirical case for the use of IT in India's rural development. Section 2, provides a broad discussion of the potential role of IT in broad-based economic development. Section 3 examines the conceptual issues from the perspective of demand for, and supply of IT-based services to rural populations in a developing country. Section 4 discusses the lessons of some of the efforts underway in India, including the work of Aksh, Drishtee, ITC, n-Logue and TARAhaat. Section 5 is a brief conclusion.

---

1. This research has been supported by grants from the Rajiv Gandhi Institute of Contemporary Studies, International Development Enterprises (India), and the Division of Social Sciences and the Academic Senate of the University of California, Santa Cruz. I am indebted to S. Sivakumar of ITC, P.G. Ponnapa of n-Logue, Ranjit Khosla of TARAhaat, and Satyan Mishra of Drishtee, for providing me with detailed information on their respective organizations, and for their extensive cooperation. I have received valuable suggestions and guidance on this research from Bibek Debroy and especially from P.D. Kaushik, who has been a valued collaborator on related work. I alone am responsible for remaining errors and omissions. Finally, I am grateful to all those individuals who generously gave their time at various sites I visited around India.

2. See Singh (2002) for a broader discussion of the potential role of IT in India's development.

IT, Economics and Development[3]

In abstract, there are two types of potential economic gains from the use of IT. First, there are both static and dynamic efficiency gains. Static gains are one-time, and come from more efficient use of scarce resources, allowing higher consumption in the present. It is useful to distinguish two kinds of static efficiency gains. One kind pertains to increases in operating efficiency, while the other comes from reduced transaction costs. In both cases, the channel for gains is through more effective and lower cost information storage, processing and communication. Dynamic gains come from higher growth, potentially raising the entire future stream of consumption.

The second type of potential benefit comes from reductions in economic inequality, to the extent that such reductions are an agreed-upon social goal, and therefore a social benefit. The two types of gains may conflict, if growth requires increased inequality, or they may be mutually reinforcing, where broad sharing of the benefits of growth enhances the rate of growth. We can discuss the role of IT in achieving greater economic gains along both dimensions, without having to commit to a particular position on the relationship between inequality and growth. However, a focus on using IT for rural development is, at least on the surface, supportive of reduced inequality along with increased efficiency and growth.

Of course, benefits that are measurable as increased market-based economic activity, and hence show up in national accounts statistics, are not the only component of development. Development can also include improvements in the capabilities of the population, such as education, health and nutrition, independently of any direct or indirect economic impact. The ability to participate in democratic decision-making also falls into this category. Broad-based improvements in capabilities can also have positive impacts on long-run economic well being, but this is not a necessary condition for desiring such improvements. The role of IT in effecting improvements along non-economic dimensions is also considered in this paper.

Turning to specific impacts, note that IT involves the electronic processing, storage and communication of information, where anything

3. There is a growing literature on this topic: see Kaushik and Singh (2004) for references.

that can be represented in digital form is included in the term 'information'. Thus news, entertainment, personal communications, educational material, blank and filled-out forms, announcements, schedules, and so on are all information. Software programs that process data (searching, tabulating, and calculating, for example) are also information in this sense, representing a particular kind of intermediate good. We can use standard economic characterizations to classify the different kinds of information. For example, entertainment, personal communications, and sometimes news, are final goods. Educational material, job announcements, or some kinds of news (weather news for farmers, for example) are intermediate goods, typically used for improving income-earning opportunities.

Information goods typically have the characteristic that one person's use does not reduce their availability for another person. Thus, a message or weather news can be viewed by many people, simultaneously or sequentially. Depending on the content of the news or message, different people may place different valuations on the information. Only friends and relatives may be interested in a personal message, all farmers in a district may be interested in local weather news, and so on. The ability to share information among users can impact the feasibility of providing it on a commercial basis. IT dramatically increases shareability of information, and this affects the economics of private provision of information goods and services.

The government may provide information goods because they are shareable and non-excludable (pure public goods). The classic example of a pure public good is national defense, but such goods may also be local in nature, such as public parks or law and order. Of course many local shareable goods can be provided exclusively, in which case private provision is a feasible alternative, in a club-like arrangement. Here, government provision may be justified more on equity grounds than on the basis of failure of private provision. In some cases, government financing through taxes or statutory user charges can be combined with outsourcing of delivery to private providers to achieve both equity and efficiency goals.

Often, private provision is feasible, but neglects the spillover benefits that it creates, in which case, government subsidization may be socially beneficial. For example, primary education has private economic benefits that people are willing to pay for, but it can also have substantial non-economic benefits to the individual and to others in the society (improved understanding, ability to make sound judgments, political decision-making capacity, and so on). Additional roles of government that are important to bring out are in redistribution to achieve equity objectives, and in regulation of private activities through licensing and certification. In both cases, the government also uses economic resources, and IT has a potential role in increasing the efficiency of government.

For both government and private provision, one of IT's main direct benefits is in increasing efficiency by economizing on resource use in the operations of firms as well as in market transactions. Information that would otherwise be conveyed through face-to-face contact, post, courier, print delivery, telegraph or telephone may instead be communicated in digital electronic form via the Internet. Efficiency gains from Internet use are not automatic: the telephone, in particular, is an efficient means of communication for many types of information. IT also requires new investment, so the benefits of trips, time and paper saved must be weighed against the costs of installing and maintaining the new infrastructure. Efficiency benefits of IT are not restricted to the communication itself. IT can improve the efficiency of the telephone network, and it can make it possible to track and analyze communications. Word processing, maintaining accounts, inventory management, and other such activities that may not require long-distance communications are also made more efficient by IT.

Experience with Internet use in developed countries suggests that information exchange related to the completion of market transactions is especially valuable. The ability of IT-based communications (combined with storage and processing) to bring together buyers and sellers more effectively represents major potential gains. These gains can come about through lower search costs, better matching of buyers and sellers, and even the creation of new markets. The successes of auction and employment websites in the US illustrate these gains. In the rural Indian context, farmers selling their crops and buying inputs, parents seeking matrimonial alliances for their children, and job seekers are all potential users of Internet-based matching services.

Efficiency gains of IT can also come about through the enabling of new goods and services. In many cases, the new good is related to something available earlier, but is presented in a form that reduces costs and expands the size of the market. For example, recorded music is a mass-consumption item, whereas only a small minority of the population could afford or have access to live performances by the highest quality musicians. Educational material is another example where recording and duplication can replace more expensive, skilled-labour-intensive alternatives for delivery. The possibilities for interactivity with IT-based educational materials illustrate the advantages of IT over older technologies based only on recording and duplication. Interactivity also implies personalization, in that an individual can select the precise content that he or she wishes to see. This feature also distinguishes IT-based content from what was available through previous technologies. Finally, the sheer volume of information that is accessible through IT is much greater than before: this also allows new kinds of services to be provided at a cost that is affordable to larger segments of the population.

We have outlined the potential static efficiency benefits of IT, but the direct dynamic benefits in terms of higher growth are harder to identify. Of course, if IT economizes on current resources, more is available for investment, which can increase growth. If IT increases the efficiency of education delivery to the broader population, this investment in people (human capital acquisition) is also likely to lead to higher growth. IT may also have positive impacts through impacts on the innovation process. For example, IT can make innovation easier by allowing simulation and low-cost testing of new designs or searching through possible chemical compounds for beneficial drugs. Finally, IT may speed the diffusion of innovations through better communications, which may stimulate further innovation – though this last channel is speculative.

An important barrier to realizing the economic benefits of IT is the often-substantial up-front cost of investment in new infrastructure – both hardware and software. In developed countries such as the US, large potential customer bases and efficient capital markets help overcome this barrier. Hardware and software designed for developed country markets can easily be adapted to serve higher income consumers in developing countries, but this leaves out the majority of the population in developing countries. Thus, one potential consequence of IT is an exacerbation of inequality, as only higher income groups enjoy its benefits – this is the so-called 'digital divide'.

On the other hand, because government-provided goods and services, including redistributive transfer payments, are often aimed at lower income groups, to the extent that IT can increase the efficiency and effectiveness of government, the benefits of IT will be more widely spread, partly reducing 'digital divide' concerns. However, achieving these benefits requires more than just internal use of IT: beneficiaries of government services (particularly the economically disadvantaged) must be able to access IT resources also. While governments may invest in such front-end interfaces with citizens (and have done so in developed countries), the cost of doing so for governments in developing countries may be prohibitive. Such governments typically already have difficulties in raising sufficient resources through taxes and user charges.

While successful examples of implementation of 'e-governance' initiatives exist[4], there is a conceptual alternative. This comes from recognizing the fact that citizens typically incur private costs (often substantial) in availing of government-provided services. If the use of IT can reduce such costs, even low-income individuals may be willing to pay at least some fraction of the cost savings, and there is scope for private provision of intermediate services that reduce the cost of access to government. Of course, this idea is not specific to IT: private intermediaries already help in filling out forms, getting access, and so on.[5] One difference that IT can make is in reducing costs even further, often by an order of magnitude. In broad terms (as is also the case with electronic marketplaces and job-matching boards), IT changes the scope and nature of intermediation.

Private providers may therefore have a role in delivering IT-based information services that are complementary to government services, as well as in providing conventional private goods and services. However, the private individual benefits that determine the prices charged by private providers may not reflect the overall social benefits of provision. As discussed earlier, these may include benefits such as greater awareness and participation in the political process. In such cases, there may be a role for government subsidization of private

4. In India, these include Bhoomi in Karnataka, e-seva in Andhra Pradesh, Lokmitra in Rajasthan, and the CHOICE Project in Chattisgarh. See also Bhatnagar and Schware (2000) for further examples.

5. In some cases, government officials themselves illegally take on these intermediary roles, demanding 'speed money' or other payments.

provision. This assumes that government provision is likely to be less efficient than private provision, which seems to be true in some cases in developing as well as developed countries. In either case, richer information flows increase the transparency with which the government operates, thereby promoting better monitoring, and potentially – depending on whether electoral and legal institutions are effective – greater accountability. The ultimate payoff is more efficient delivery of government services.

Looking at the case of India, in cities and larger towns, cyber-kiosks have already begun to proliferate. Urban population densities, income levels, cultural attitudes and telecom infrastructure all seem to be sufficient for the commercial success of these enterprises. The falling cost of hardware and the availability of a variety of English language software have also supported this trend. Finally, the government's belated opening up of Internet service provision to competitive entrants has been a crucial supporting development. In non-Internet IT-related services, IT education has clearly taken off in cities as well, inspired by India's success in software exports.

In rural areas and smaller towns, however, the various demographic and socioeconomic factors such as income levels, cultural attitudes, and geographic and social fragmentation may not be present in configurations that would easily enable the diffusion of commercial access to various IT-enabled services. Furthermore, the market power of traditional rural intermediaries may act as a barrier to partial innovations in how matching of buyers and sellers is conducted. Finally, vernacular language requirements and different demand patterns imply the need for software that is tailored for fragmented rural markets. In the next section, we examine the technical and organizational issues in implementing widespread rural IT use in India.

Rural IT: Issues and Conceptual Framework

We examine the potential for rural IT use, both from supply and demand perspectives. On the supply side, we examine the technical and organizational issues that arise for delivering IT-based services to rural populations in India. On the demand side, we examine the potential benefits that IT can bring to these populations, if the implementation is successful. We begin with the demand side, as a way of motivating the supply side issues.

Figure 1

Rural Household Economic Decisions

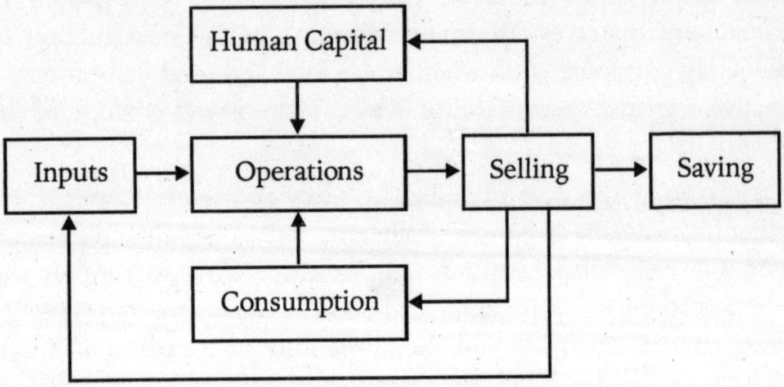

Potential sources of demand for IT-based services can be framed in terms of a simple flow diagram representing the decisions of rural households. We will treat a typical household as engaged in farming, though this will not be true for all of them. Figure 1 presents a simplified representation of the various economic decisions.

Beginning from the left of Figure 1, input decisions include material inputs such as seeds, fertilizer and pesticides; and capital inputs such as tractors and land (whether through purchases or rentals); as well as the credit required for such purposes. The focus of analysis will be market transactions for inputs. In all cases, there is a potential for benefiting through improved information about prices, quality and availability. Labour is also an important input, but the labour market has special characteristics that reduce the importance of such information in rural contexts.

Operations include decisions with respect to quantity and timing of inputs. A crucial aspect of agricultural operations is risk management, as both the weather and pest incidence are extremely variable. *Ex ante* decisions in the face of uncertainty, as well as *ex post* responses to realizations of uncertainty are both important. Predictive and technical information are both important for agricultural operations.

Continuing to the right of Figure 1, marketing of outputs primarily requires price information. Increasingly, producing for sale also requires knowledge of quality requirements in different markets. Selling of produce provides income for consumption, investment and inputs (the reverse arrows in the figure), as well as generating information that affects input and production decisions.

Non-production decisions of households can be roughly divided into pure consumption activities, as well as human capital investment in education and health. The boundary is fuzzy, since even basic food consumption has nutritional impacts and therefore a human capital component. These activities generate impacts on operations, since they affect the quality of decision-making, as well as household labour inputs: we indicate this with the vertical arrows. While poorer households may be severely limited in their consumption, a significant proportion of rural households in India have incomes sufficient to support some discretionary consumption. In some cases, consumption may be only superficially discretionary – social norms may dictate spending on activities relating to marriage and other life cycle events.

Finally, the rightmost box captures household saving, again something that is not feasible for all rural households, but is an activity of growing importance. Saving may be for consumption smoothing, investment, or precautionary reasons.

Even this simplified and summary picture of rural households' economic activity illustrates that they engage in a broad range of transactions and decisions with economic impacts. What is noteworthy besides this complexity is that many decisions are made with very limited information, and that market interactions are often subject to high transaction costs, due to imperfections in information, as well as high transportation costs, inefficient intermediation and time delays. High transaction costs will always prevent marginal transactions from being undertaken; in extreme cases, the market may fail to function at all. Given this scenario, the role of IT can be understood in terms of reducing transaction costs, as well as improving the efficiency of decision making within households (both as producers and as consumers).

Reductions in communication and transaction costs are particularly beneficial where they can allow new markets to develop, in the sense that existing goods and services, otherwise restricted to urban areas, or to a very limited segment of rural populations, now can be offered to broad cross-sections of the rural population. Examples include financial services, particular types of education, health services, long distance communications, and expertise on a range of production-related decisions. Whether this can be done in a sustainable manner depends on the supply conditions for IT-based rural services.

It must be further understood that the activities outlined, in Figure 1 and the accompanying discussion, take place within a particular institutional environment. This includes private actors as well as governments. For example, farmers may obtain credit and inputs, as well contract their output, to private 'commission agents,' even in the presence of government procurement and government-run local markets. Governments play a major role in subsidizing inputs, providing infrastructure, and enforcing property rights. To the extent that these activities are also subject to inefficiencies, it may be the case that, in order to be successful, IT-based interventions geared towards rural households will have to simultaneously alter the institutional environment, or else achieve sufficient scale and scope in order to impel changes in it. We will take this up later in the paper.

Turning to the supply side, we can illustrate the various stages of decision-making and delivery of IT-based services in terms of a typical value chain, as shown in Figure 2. At each stage of the chain, the IT components include a mix of hardware, software and services. In addition, the creation of an organizational structure and value network is a critical first step, while managing human resources and customers is vital for successful final implementation.

Figure 2

Value Chain for IT-Based Services

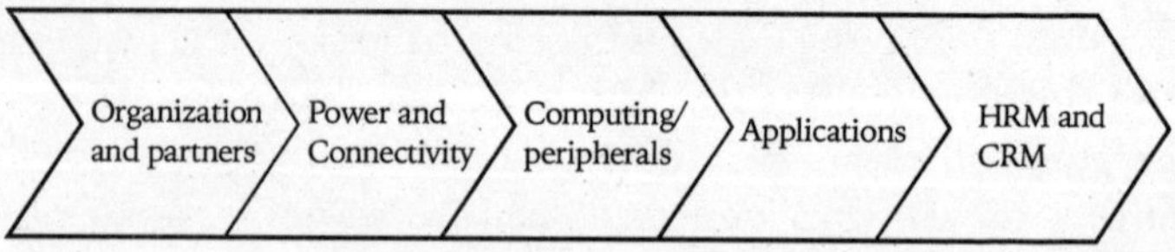

We next discuss each of the components of the value chain in Figure 2. The organizational structure typically requires commercial goals of profitability to be built in. This is easily done through a standard corporate structure. It is clear that, for scalability, some minimum size of the organization is required. In addition, there are fixed costs of innovation that can be spread more effectively across a larger organization. Social goals can be incorporated in two ways. For organizations that are dedicated specifically to rural IT-based services delivery, controlling ownership of the corporation by a non-profit entity provides the social focus. For existing corporations with broader businesses, social goals may enhance reputation, meet corporate social responsibility guidelines, or otherwise be consistent with the mission and values of the organization. In other words, including social goals may make good bottom-line business sense.

For both types of organizations, building the right capabilities requires some effort. Creating what amounts to a brand new infrastructure for rural IT service delivery requires a broad mix of skills, and finding talented and trained people who can be effective in a role that mixes entrepreneurial tasks with corporate line responsibilities, all in an unfamiliar rural environment, can be a challenge. One solution to the potentially insurmountable problem of collecting the necessary talent and skills is to enter into partnerships with other organizations that may provide specific pieces of the overall package that is needed: application software, content, maintenance services, technology, marketing, and so on. These partnerships can pose their own problems, particularly in goal alignment and consequent performance monitoring requirements. Of course all these organizational issues are well recognized in management writing and experience: what is important is to recognize their criticality in a setting that has more typically been the arena of pure 'social service' entities such as governments and NGOs. It is also critical to recognize that the organizational innovation required in this case is an order of magnitude greater than the task of selling consumer goods in rural areas, something that is now quite well accepted in India. The greater complexity and variety of the services being delivered through IT is the root cause of this difference.

The second stage of the supply chain in Figure 2 concerns access to electric power and Internet connectivity. In both cases, a major constraint is the failure of the public sector to deliver adequate power and telecommunications to rural India. Privatization has helped in the case of telecommunications, as has technological change. In fact, innovation in digital communications technologies is the foundation of all rural IT-based service delivery. While conventional telephone connectivity has often proved inadequate for Internet access in rural areas, because the quality of existing voice lines is too poor to sustain data transmission, several innovations provide alternatives that are likely to be cost effective. These include wireless in local loop (WLL), fiber optic cables, and high-powered versions of Wi-Fi (802.11 wireless standards). The Internet boom in the United States clearly played a role in pushing down costs and speeding innovation in fiber optics and wireless transmission. In some cases, VSAT satellite connectivity has been used for Internet access, but it is not very cost effective. The major challenges for connectivity are likely to be regulatory, having to do with interconnection to the main network, and with maintenance, rather than with the fundamental technological choices and implementation.

Electric power is more of a problem, and this is true throughout India. Battery backups are a very partial solution to the lack of reliable power supplies, and solar technologies may be more promising in the near future: they are already in use in existing rural IT efforts. The difficulty is that having to rely on these alternatives and backups unnecessarily raises costs of operation. Of course this is true for all of India's economy. It is well recognized that the power sector is the major bottleneck, with capacity well short of demand, and the quality of transmission and distribution remaining poor.

The third stage of the supply chain is the most straightforward, because of the standardization of components of desktop computing and peripherals, rapid technological improvements, falling costs of production, and, most recently, price reductions resulting from changes in tariffs on imported hardware. It is now possible to fully equip a single-computer rural Internet kiosk for less than Rs. 50,000, including CD drive, printer, scanner, power backup, and web cam. Potentially, the highest cost component is the operating system, since Windows enjoys a virtual monopoly on the desktop. However, Microsoft seems to have concessional pricing for socially oriented developing country initiatives, and this helps to reduce costs. The operating system is still typically in English, but as long as simple drills can take kiosk operators to local language applications and content, this is not a substantial usage barrier. One can conclude that this stage of the supply chain is easiest to implement, with a highly standardized, almost cookie-cutter approach – although ongoing maintenance can be a challenge. The major business decision is whether to have more than one computer per kiosk, but experience suggests that one is sufficient for almost all situations, at least in the beginning.

The next stage of the supply chain, namely applications, presents more challenges. The range of possible applications is vast. Many IT-based services require non-IT logistics or processes as complements. Availability of local language software becomes more of a constraint. There is much more variation across localities, not just regions. Delivery of services or development of content often stretch the resources and expertise of the primary provider, and require varied partnerships or other contractual relationships. Deciding the sequencing, scope and sophistication of various applications can be a major challenge, since many of the services are being offered for the first time, or are being delivered in novel ways that challenge existing institutional frameworks and relationships. Pricing for low income markets, where market penetration is limited in any case, and where some services may be perceived as public goods that are traditionally unpriced, presents another major challenge. In the case of financial services or government records or services, substantial government cooperation may be required, raising political and bureaucratic hurdles. In some ways, of course, the essence of the success of the rural IT-based-service business model depends on the selection, quality and pricing of the services being offered. What is interesting is that a substantial amount of learning has occurred in this arena, in just a few years.

The final stage of the value chain in Figure 2 refers to human resource management (HRM) and customer relationship management (CRM). In this context, these more general terms take on specific focuses. Training of rural kiosk operators, whether they are formal franchisees or independent farmer operators, becomes a key aspect of the delivery model. Training the field personnel at various levels (village and district hub) is also critical. Gathering customer information on usage patterns (nature and timing of use), revenue streams, responsiveness to pricing, social acceptance, and so on is also vital, as these are brand new markets in terms of the nature of service delivery. Furthermore, being able to respond to this information with appropriate and timely changes in strategy is also necessary for successful implementation.

One might expect that a 'labour surplus' developing economy such as India's would not have a problem with the more labour-intensive tasks at either end of the value chain as it has been mapped in Figure 2. However, it seems that these value chain activities are the most difficult to carry out successfully, because those with the requisite skills are more likely to be taken up by more traditional corporate organizations, in urban environments. This does not minimize the challenges associated with technical implementations and adaptations for rural areas, whether in software, hardware and maintenance. However, solutions in these cases are often one-time and replicable, whereas building organizational expertise involves much more of a situation-specific or local approach.

We have so far provided a general and abstract discussion of the various aspects of supply and demand of rural IT-based services. In the next section, this discussion is made more concrete and specific, through an assessment of several initiatives in India.

Implementation: Cases, Impacts and Lessons

The discussion of several rural-IT initiatives is based on field visits conducted over a two-year period, from December 2001 to December 2003, as well as discussions with various members of each organization.[6] The goal is not to provide an exhaustive description or analysis of any single organizational effort, but to use the conceptual framework of the previous section to bring out common features as well as differences. Nevertheless, it is useful to describe each initiative separately, rather than organize the discussion according to value chain components or demand-side factors, as this provides a better sense of each overall effort.

Drishtee

Drishtee.com had its origins in Gyandoot, a government project in Dhar district of Madhya Pradesh, in central India. Gyandoot provided an intranet for 33 village information kiosks, offering a range of mainly e-governance-related services. The most prominent of these is land record certificates, which are needed by landowners for

---

6. It is important to reemphasize that the following is a subjective assessment, and does not reflect the views of any of the individuals or the organizations they represent.

transactions such as sale or leasing of land. While Gyandoot was a specific local initiative, involving heavy support from the District Collector, Drishtee has attempted to take that model and rapidly replicate it across the country. Currently, Drishtee has over 100 rural Internet kiosks in several states, run by franchisees according to a revenue sharing arrangement. In Drishtee's case, a kiosk has, at least initially, just one computer. The set-up cost is in the range of Rs. 50,000.

Drishtee is a commercial organization, with specific social objectives of targeting benefits to the rural poor built into its vision and strategy. Drishtee has developed some software on its own, but also relies on various partners for software development, as well as, in some cases, other partners for management of district hubs, from which kiosks in a district are managed. Thus Drishtee's model involves not only franchising individual kiosks, but also potentially franchising district hubs. Partnering with local district hub 'channel partners' allows Drishtee to expand faster without creating a bulky organization, spreads risks, and also insulates Drishtee from some of the commercial pressures that might conflict with social objectives. At the same time, it reduces Drishtee's ability to monitor and implement the achievement of social objectives. This tension between commercial success and meeting social objectives is a general challenge for all the rural IT initiatives examined here. Despite some challenges, Drishtee appears to have built a capable but lean organization, with learning having been systematized in a manner that makes it transferable across locations, permitting more effective scaling up.

Electric power and telecom connectivity have posed challenges for Drishtee, since it is a pure startup, without resources for heavy investments in infrastructure. It uses standard battery backup for power interruptions, and has relied mainly on dial-up Internet access, though it is experimenting with Wi-Fi for district-level intranets. In some cases, it has set up kiosks even without phone connectivity, relying on physical delivery of information. Software has also been developed that economizes on bandwidth for information exchange, making the constraint of dial-up access less severe.

As we have noted, the software and hardware for basic kiosk operations are quite standardized, and their cost has been falling. Drishtee was able to get concessional terms for using the Windows operating system. Various local language software applications have been developed, for e-governance, market price information, buying and selling, and so on.

With the origins in Gyandoot playing a role, simple e-governance, such as making government forms available and allowing a variety of complaints to be relayed to the district level government, has typically been the lead service in setting up operations in a new district. In this context, informal partnerships with district level government officials (both state and local) have been very significant. For example, in Sirsa and Jaipur districts, Drishtee has been able to act as a significant intermediary for information exchange between the district government and constituents. It obviously remains limited in its ability to improve the internal functioning of government. Nevertheless, Drishtee's approach can be viewed as achieving the right kind of 'embedded autonomy' at the local level, to use Peter Evans' term, meaning a societal structure with coherent institutions that are autonomous, but nevertheless connected through institutionalized channels for continual negotiation of goals and policies (Evans, 1995, p. 12).

Expanding the range of services has meant tying up with content partners, particularly organizations such as Agriwatch, which provides a substantial quantity and range of agricultural information to farmers. Agriwatch is essentially developing into a large-scale Internet portal for farmers, and Drishtee's role can be seen as providing last-mile access to this rich information, through its kiosks. It is difficult to quantify the benefits of this service, but its popularity with farmers suggests that it is valuable. Related examples from the cases of ITC and n-Logue will provide a more definite assessment of these benefits.

Drishtee's pricing scheme for e-governance services follows a set model. The full cost of a transaction such as obtaining, filling out and submitting a government form is estimated, including imputing the value of time spent in travel. The kiosk owner's fee for this is then set at about 10 percent of the estimated transaction cost, also taking into account possible willingness-to-pay considerations in choosing "pricing points" such as Rs. 5, 10 or 20. Assuming that these fees can cover the full cost of the kiosk owner and Drishtee (which depends largely on generating sufficient volume) the saving in transaction costs is substantial. The savings in such cases are generated by reductions in travel and time costs. There may also be benefits in terms of improving the effectiveness of transactions (e.g., if a complaint through this channel is more likely to be addressed), but these are harder to quantify.

In the case of other services, such as matching buyers and sellers, or providing horoscopes or matrimonial advertising, additional services require partners who can provide software, maintenance, content or other components of the complete service. Education has played a limited role in Drishtee's offerings, though kiosk owners have often used the presence of a computer and peripherals to offer computer training, as well as other offline services such as printing and games. The benefits in these examples are reductions in transaction costs for existing transactions, improved quality of successful matches, and potentially most significant, completion of activities (e.g., training, entertainment, communications) that would otherwise not take place because of high transaction costs.

Finally, Drishtee has appeared to learn rapidly with respect to the selection and training of kiosk owners, and eliciting the preferences of rural Internet kiosk users. This partly reflects the organization's own structure and character. As a lean start-up, it seems to have attracted people who are relatively in tune with rural market environments. The process has not been painless, and there are still challenges in managing operations that are spread across several states, but Drishtee's ability to manage its own human resources and the end users of its services has grown over time.

In sum, Drishtee has emerged as a typical start-up. Without very substantial financial resources, it has still managed to expand, and it has built an organization with strong competencies in what may be broadly termed 'rural IT based service delivery.' This judgment holds despite Drishtee's lack of any clear strength in technology, applications, partnerships or ability to scale. In all these dimensions, it is 'good enough,' but it appears to have built a strong, low-cost organization from scratch, one that may be well suited to delivering at least some components of the overall service. This competence is discussed further in the context of Aksh, a former Drishtee partner.

Aksh

Aksh is essentially a fiber optic cable company, with its core competence in laying and maintaining cable. Its revenue model is driven by the content and data that can be delivered over this cable. Therefore it has an interest in increasing such content delivery. While urban areas in India have seen substantial penetration of cable TV, through a model (now in transition) of largely unregulated local operators, the rural market remains largely unserved. The bottleneck has been the lack of last mile infrastructure, since there is a significant percentage of rural households (especially in richer districts) that can afford cable TV. Aksh, along with other companies such as Reliance, has received licenses for laying a new fiber optic network in rural areas.

In the case in point, Aksh rapidly laid a large fiber optic network in rural Jaipur district (excluding the city itself). It initially partnered with Drishtee for the development and maintenance of kiosks that would act as distribution points for cable TV access, as well as Internet kiosks. The Drishtee franchise model, interface and services were adopted, but with the brand name of "Gramdoot." Aksh therefore appeared in the value chain as the provider of connectivity, with Drishtee handling all the other value chain stages illustrated in Figure 2. However, this asymmetry between Drishtee and Aksh was fairly quickly reversed, and now Aksh stands as the main service provider, with Drishtee reduced to the role of providing software and related services.

There are several reasons for this shift in the business relationship. Most obviously, Aksh's far greater size, resources and hardware capabilities give it an advantage in setting up and maintaining the hardware aspects of the kiosks. The rapid expansion of kiosks in Jaipur, with over 100 being set up within six months, stretched Drishtee's human resources beyond their limits. It was also not feasible to hire and train large numbers of people for servicing the kiosks. Second, the needs of the cable TV business, and some degree of competition that emerged with another cable TV provider in the same district created additional problems of maintenance (e.g., Aksh's cables were cut by the competitor) and conflicts in terms of priorities for bringing Internet-based services online – essentially, Internet services were the tail of the cable TV dog. Finally, Aksh's incentive was to control and brand the effort to score points for corporate social responsibility.

In any case, the model of rural IT-kiosks managed by a large company with incentives to provide access to large numbers of rural households appears to be scalable and sustainable. Cable TV over fiber optic networks provides a strong revenue base, and a range of Internet-based services and content can be provided through partnerships. As companies such as Drishtee also scale up, they may be more effective in providing the necessary scale for ongoing management of the kiosks, including training services and customer relationship management. For now, providing software is easier for start-ups in such cases.

The history of Aksh's initiative means that the range of services provided in their kiosks, the revenue model, and pricing structures currently follow the Drishtee model. Hence the earlier discussion of benefits transfers over to this case. The importance of cable TV revenues, however, suggests that these kiosks may emphasize a range of entertainment services more than utility services such as agriculture-related information or e-governance. It is conceivable, however, that kiosk operators will be able to span the entire range of services. The bandwidth available will certainly support a full range of offerings, and the issues will be managerial attention and the perceptions of rural users. One important implication of greater bandwidth is that video interactions are possible, and Drishtee and Aksh have been able to test several communication services based on this. The power of video over text is in increasing the richness of information exchange, as well as greatly increasing the attractiveness and acceptance of all the services offered by the kiosks.

n-Logue

While Aksh and Drishtee are mostly active in north India, n-Logue has its origin and chief presence in the south. It is a for-profit corporation, with majority ownership residing with a nonprofit organization. The main impetus for n-Logue came from the IIT Chennai research group headed by Professor Ashok Jhunjhunwala. This group has been responsible for a stream of hardware and software innovations that enable rural IT-based service delivery, through connectivity and applications.

The core innovation at the heart of n-Logue's operations is a WLL technology, Cordect, which provides joint wireless Internet and voice connectivity. The kiosk-level hardware is relatively inexpensive, and adds only marginally to the overall cost of a kiosk. However, the construction of WLL towers and maintenance of the WLL hub is relatively costly, and this fixed cost requires a substantial density of kiosks within a particular radius of the tower. The n-Logue model is designed to achieve this density, with kiosks generating returns from fairly small user populations (somewhat smaller than in the case of Drishtee and Aksh). Another constraint on this connectivity model is the requirement of clear lines of sight, and therefore relatively flat topography. Nevertheless, large parts of India are still suitable for this implementation. Furthermore, n-Logue has progressed well beyond being simply a connectivity provider, to delivering a range of services – these can be adapted to different connectivity technologies. N-Logue is the second largest organization in this field, supporting over 500 rural-IT kiosks.

The WLL technology does provide several strengths. It overcomes lack of dial-up connectivity, and provides an extra revenue stream for kiosk operators, through voice calls. Furthermore, it has greater bandwidth than traditional fixed line dial-up, which allows a wide range of applications to be delivered. In particular, the IIT Chennai group has been able to develop video applications that are sufficiently compressed to work within the constraints of the WLL.

In general, the close links with the IIT Chennai group have given n-Logue access to a range of software innovations for delivery and implementation of various applications in the fields of education, health and agriculture. For example, web cams have been used for remote diagnostics for diseases of people, animals and plants. A considerable amount of local language software has been created quite rapidly and effectively. The university connection is important, and stands out as a model for other providers to emulate.

N-Logue has also been able to leverage its university connections to build strong partnerships across the board. The Tamil Nadu government has been strongly supportive of n-Logue's operations in Madurai district, where numerous innovations have been piloted and showcased. MIT's Media Lab has also been involved in the initial stages, and ICICI Bank is piloting various financial services products in kiosks in Madurai. In Nellikuppam district, n-Logue has partnered with EID-Parry to improve sugar farmers' access to information, and reduce their transactions costs in dealing with Parry's large sugar factory in the district, through improved tracking and settlements of payments. In this case, the factory chimney has also served as a base for the tower, and the control hub is housed in the factory, substantially reducing fixed costs. Parry plans to use those kiosks that are under its own brand (several dozen in total) to offer processed foods to farmers.

N-Logue also appears to have developed a very capable organization, and has expanded beyond Tamil Nadu into other southern states, as well as the west and north of India. One advantage that emerged in discussions was the relative ease of establishing organizational capabilities, training kiosk operators, and serving rural communities in the south relative to the north of India. This reflects higher proportions of the population with basic education, greater population densities, and, in general, a more structured and stable civil society. A factor that seemed to emerge in all cases was the greater average success of women kiosk operators, possibly reflecting the fact that there is greater untapped potential for rural women, given their otherwise more restricted employment opportunities.

Overall, n-Logue has several strengths compared to Drishtee, in terms of access technology, software applications and partnerships. Nevertheless, the two organizations are quite similar in terms of the range of services offered, and their ability to deliver close to an 'end-to-end' solution. Their social goals are more salient than those of Aksh, and each has achieved a substantial geographic reach and partnership capability. There are some differences in emphasis in terms of applications, services, and revenue models (Drishtee relies more on overall revenue sharing, whereas n-Logue charges mainly for connectivity). In each case, however, there has been a demonstration that rural IT-based services are commercially feasible, and as a corollary, provide quantifiable economic benefits. Since estimates of the overall market size suggest that it can support at least 50,000 kiosks (roughly one per 10,000 people), and these two organizations, plus Aksh, have less than 1,000 kiosks, there appears to be substantial room for further growth.

ITC

ITC stands out as a large Indian corporation serving global markets. Its kiosks are called e-choupals, and they have several differentiating features. The key distinguishing factor is that the e-choupals are totally designed to support ITC's agricultural products supply chain. This gives them a focus that is not present even in EID-Parry's kiosks in Nellikuppam. In addition, the e-choupals are totally owned and set up by ITC, with the operators not having any investment or risk of their own. Furthermore, e-choupal operators are, because of the focus, always substantial farmers, and therefore always male. All these features make the e-choupals different from the previous three initiatives.

The e-choupal initiative has involved a clear focus and strong direction from the head of ITC's International Business Division. ITC has been able to turn its substantial organizational and managerial capabilities toward this initiative. Management trainees are heavily immersed in the e-choupal model as part of their inculcation into ITC's workings. There are four kinds of e-choupals, tailored very specifically for four different products: shrimp, coffee, wheat and soybeans. The first two of these involve large commercial farmers, and the focus is on creating Internet access to global market information to guide production and supply decisions. There are a few dozen of these e-choupals. In the case of wheat and soybeans, there are many small farmers, and over 2,000 e-choupals have been set up, in several states of India.

The description here is based on soy-choupals. Wheat-choupals are somewhat similar, with the final market and products being somewhat different. Soybeans are pressed to extract oil, which is sold domestically, while the remainder is exported as animal feed. Thus they are a cash crop, without the regulated market conditions or subsistence consumption associated with a food grain such as wheat. Soy-choupals are used as registry points for procurement of soybeans. Actual procurement is done at factories and warehouse hubs, but the initial logging in is done through the e-choupal, which provides price information and therefore price certainty. In fact, the e-choupal price acts as a floor price for procurement – the factory or warehouse price can be higher. E-choupals also provide access to local market (*mandi*) prices and global market price information on soybeans and derivative products, to allow farmers to compare prices. They give access to operational information, developed by ITC experts, pertaining to cropping, seeds, fertilizer, and so on.

E-choupals are set up by ITC, with solar power backup and VSAT connectivity. The equipment cost for the e-choupal is borne by ITC, with the selected farmer providing the location. In addition to the adoption advantages that come from using a farmer with high social status as the operator, the house should be spacious and sturdy enough to house all the required equipment, including the VSAT and solar panel on the roof. E-choupal farmers take an oath to serve the village, and they are trained by ITC. While there is an important element of social pressure and pride of work, the operators also receive commissions on soybean shipments booked through the e-choupals. This provides substantial revenue to the e-choupal operator.

The narrow (at least initial) focus of the e-choupals and the substantial commitment of financial and human resources by ITC has made rapid expansion possible, as well as quick acceptance by farmers. The narrow range of applications has limited software requirements, and operators bear no risk in the ITC model. The longer-term goal is, however, to use e-choupals and warehouse hubs as sales points for soybean oil, tractor rentals, and eventually a range of ITC-produced consumer goods.

The initial benefits of the ITC effort include a substantial reduction in transaction costs, from 8 per cent of a transaction, down to 2 per cent, approximately. It is estimated that these gains are shared roughly equally between ITC and individual farmers. Some of this gain may be at the expense of traditional intermediaries, who operate in *mandis*, but much of it comes from genuine efficiency gains, including clearer quality guidelines and measurement, greater timeliness and reduced waits, quicker payments, and reduced uncertainties. To some extent, traditional intermediaries are co-opted in the new process, by being hired to perform tasks such as handling payments at ITC's receiving points.

Clearly the use of information technology is just a part of ITC's overhaul of its supply chain, but speedy delivery of complex information pertaining to market conditions makes IT essential. It might be asked what acts as a check on ITC's market power in this process. Clearly, the traditional *mandi* system, with its accompanying government regulation and oversight, acts as continuing competition. More significantly, ITC's concern with its reputation acts as a disciplining device. Finally, the long term goal of selling back to farmers as customers also gives ITC an incentive to cultivate relationships with individual farmers. In fact, farmers view ITC as treating with greater respect and dignity than is the case in traditional *mandi* interactions.

It is quite conceivable that the ITC model will not broaden significantly beyond the two-way flow of agricultural produce from farmers to ITC, and processed foods, consumer goods and inputs from ITC to farmers, without extending to e-governance, entertainment, health or education-related services. Instead, other firms may provide these services in similar locations to ITC e-choupals.

TARAhaat

TARAhaat has evolved in a somewhat unusual manner. It achieved well-publicized success with Internet kiosks in Bundelkhand in Uttar Pradesh. These kiosks were very much along the lines of those implemented by Drishtee and n-Logue, with a mix of e-governance services, market price information, and so on. TARAhaat's long-range plans include a comprehensive portal for rural information services and an extended vision of its 'TARAkendras' as community centers. However, in its expansion into Punjab, at the invitation of the administrator of Bathinda district, its model evolved quite differently.

While the Bundelkhand model had used VSAT connectivity, this was not economical for a commercially sustainable expansion. While Punjab is a high-income state with relatively good infrastructure, the level of telephone connectivity turned out to be too poor for practical Internet use. Other issues arose with the substantially greater investment required by TARAkendra operators, since the model assumed that each kiosk with have three or four computers. Perhaps the greatest problem was in building an organization for implementation. While TARAhaat is a subsidiary of Development Alternatives, an established NGO, it is set up as a corporation, with social goals meant to be enforced through ownership by the nonprofit parent. The expansion of TARAhaat required building an organization from scratch, and this turned out to be a slow process. There were also problems with establishing effective partnerships with local and state government, and TARAhaat has mostly gone it alone.

TARAhaat does have an educational content partner, called TARAgyan. In association with various partners, TARAgyan is developing local language content and software for use in TARAkendras. Basic IT education is an important part of TARAgyan's actual and potential offerings, but it is not the exclusive focus. In fact, there has been a substantial diversification into developing materials for English language instruction, rural marketing, personality development, and so on. This development was initially very slow, though it may be picking up steam.

The constraints faced by TARAhaat pushed its Punjab effort in the direction of locating in *mandi* towns rather than villages, and focusing on offering offline education rather than a full array of IT- and Internet-based services. Thus, the few dozen TARAkendras in Punjab have emerged as quite distinct from the Internet kiosks of the other organizations discussed in this paper. It is conceivable that TARAhaat will end up occupying a very distinct niche in small town India, quite different from a direct impact on the rural, agricultural part of the country.

Interestingly, Punjab may have been the wrong place to try to create efficiency improvements in agriculture, since there are relatively strong market and related institutions for existing crops such as wheat, rice, cotton and sugar cane. Efficiency gains in Punjab agriculture are more likely to come about through the intervention of the government to create a new infrastructure to support alternative, higher value-added crops, or through concerted efforts by large agribusiness firms such as ITC.

Conclusions

This paper has briefly surveyed several initiatives to provide IT-based services in rural India. I have provided a broad overview of the economic impacts of IT, and gone on to examine demand side and supply side issues of successful implementation. In particular, I have suggested that there is a broad range of services that can be provided to a cross-section of rural households, even at relatively low levels of income. This creates challenges for implementation by posing choices for organizations, but also opportunities for creating niches. I have also provided a framework in terms of the supply side value chain, and used this to discuss the implementation of rural IT-based initiatives by several organizations.

All the organizations discussed in the paper face common issues of implementation, but differ in terms of how they have been handled. There are differences in scale, connectivity technologies, services offered, revenue models, organizational structures, and so on. Clearly, focused efforts with substantial financial and organizational backing have a good chance of success. However, even startups that have put together the required competencies and resources through partnerships and slow organization building appear to have room in this market.

There appears to be enough evidence now that it is commercially feasible to use IT to deliver services to rural populations either at costs that are lower than previous delivery methods, or in ways that make it possible to achieve delivery where none was earlier cost effective or feasible. Initially, the static savings from reductions in transaction costs may be of the order of a few percent of value added. However, the benefits from enabling new transactions should be an order of magnitude greater. In the long run, bringing rich information to the population of rural India, whether in the form of education, market prices, market opportunities, and more, can only have positive impacts on the material well being of rural masses.

References

Bhatnagar, Subhash and Robert Schware (2000). *Information and Communication Technology in Development: Cases from India*, New Delhi: Sage Publications.

Evans, Peter (1995). *Embedded Autonomy: States and Industrial Transformation*, Princeton: Princeton University Press.

Kaushik P.D., and Nirvikar Singh (2004). Information Technology and Broad-Based Development: Preliminary Lessons from North India, forthcoming, *World Development*.

Singh, Nirvikar (2002). Information Technology as an Engine of Broad-Based Growth in India, in *The Information Economy in India*, ed. Parthasarathi Banerjee and Frank-Jürgen Richter, London: Palgrave/Macmillan, 24-57.

12

ICT and Poverty

BIBEK DEBROY

Introduction

Information and communication technology (ICT) is a bit like *Janus* in India. On the one hand, there are studies that estimate India's exports of information technology (IT) products and services will shoot up to 50 billion US dollars in 2008, accounting for 30 per cent of exports and 7.5 per cent of GDP.[1] This is the face of *Janus* that encompasses the link between NASDAQ and Indian stock market prices, talks of call centres and medical transcription services moving to India, wishes to tap the comparative advantage of 30 million Indians who possess a working knowledge of English and harps on the fact that 40 per cent of H1-B visas granted by the United States go to Indians. Certainly for the urban educated youth, to H1-B or not to H1-B is often the question, despite the recent IT slowdown in the United States and elsewhere. And despite the anti-sourcing backlash in the United States and elsewhere.

However, 30 million is only 3 per cent of India's population and there is another face of *Janus* as well. That is the development dimension. Despite fifty years and more of planned development, India ranks 127th out of 175 countries in the human development index (HDI).[2] The adult literacy rate used to be only 52 per cent and has now inched up to 65 per cent.[3] The combined (primary, secondary

1. These are essentially NASSCOM-McKinsey type reports, NASSCOM standing for the National Association of Software and Service Companies. Such figures have also been quoted in UNDP's *Human Development Report (HDR)* for 2001.
2. That India has recently moved from the low human development category to the medium human development category is not terribly important, except as a minor signal.
3. These are Census figures, not those from HDR. The Census of 1991 had 52 per cent, the Census of 2001 shows 65 per cent.

and tertiary) gross enrolment ratio is only 56 per cent. 26 per cent of the population is under the indigenous poverty line, 34.7 per cent is under the international poverty line of 1 US dollar per day.[4] 47 per cent of children under the age of five are under-weight. Only 28 per cent of the population has access to improved sanitation, 16 per cent or more do not have access to safe drinking water. The infant mortality rate is stuck at 70 per thousand and refuses to decline further.

Pockets of Deprivation and Developed Country Status

India is a large and heterogeneous country and such figures look worse if one brings in the regional and gender dimension. The poor and backward States of India have conventionally been referred to as the BIMARU (Bihar, Madhya Pradesh, Rajasthan and Uttar Pradesh), with a pun on the word *bimar*, which in most Indian languages, means sick or ill. With a further division of States, Bihar now has Jharkhand, Madhya Pradesh now has Chhatisgarh and Uttar Pradesh now has Uttaranchal.

Post-1991 reforms, disparities in growth across States have increased and will increase even further. In States like Gujarat and Maharashtra, real State domestic product has grown at rates of 8 per cent and more. So despite a relatively higher rate of population growth, such States have registered per capita income growth rates of 6 per cent and more and this has beneficial effects on poverty and unemployment. But among the BIMARU States, real State domestic product has only grown at around 3 per cent in Bihar and Uttar Pradesh (and in Orissa among the non-BIMARU ones) and a relatively high rate of population growth has thus contributed to per capita income growth rates of 1 to 1.5 per cent. There have been limited beneficial effects on poverty and unemployment. There are variations in literacy levels as well. According to the 2001 Census, Bihar has an

4. The 26 per cent needs explanation, since it is not a HDR or WDR (*World Development Report*) figure. Poverty figures can only be estimated once expenditure data are available. These are collected by the National Sample Survey (NSS) Organization. Unfortunately, NSS collects data with large samples at infrequent intervals, 1993-94 and 1999-2000 being the two latest years. In between, there are the somewhat more unreliable thin samples. HDR and WDR figures still reflect thin sample data. The 26 per cent figure is from the 1999-2000 NSS large sample.

overall literacy rate of 47.5 per cent, the only State that has a figure lower than 50 per cent. To a large extent, the literacy problem is a female literacy problem and overall literacy will not improve until female literacy improves. Among major States, female literacy is still remarkably low in Chhatisgarh, Andhra Pradesh, Orissa, Madhya Pradesh, Rajasthan, Uttar Pradesh, Jammu & Kashmir, Jharkhand and Bihar. In Jharkhand and Bihar, this figure is lower than 40 per cent. District-wise figures from the Census are not yet available. But when they are, there will be districts where the female literacy rate is lower than 10 per cent.

Increasing inter-State disparities across India has received some attention and the question of convergence versus divergence across States is often debated. Did the reform decade of the 1990s accentuate inter-State disparities? And what can be done to ensure that trickle down benefits of growth percolate to all regions and some backward areas are not bypassed? India is not *sui generis* in raising such questions. The divergence between North-West China and the Southern Coastal Provinces has probably received much more attention.

Divergence or convergence is of course a function of the variable used to measure it. The two most commonly used indicators are growth in per capita State domestic product (SDP) or the poverty ratio (head count ratio). On the former, the growth records of Gujarat or Maharashtra in the 1990s are hardly comparable to the growth records of Orissa or undivided Bihar and Uttar Pradesh (UP). If growth in per capita SDP is the yardstick, then inter-State disparities existed in the 1980s as well. But the conclusion that these disparities increased in the 1990s also seems fairly robust. Similarly, on poverty ratios, Goa, Punjab or Haryana are hardly comparable to Orissa or undivided Bihar. Arguably, the post-1991 reforms shifted the focus of policy change from the Centre to the States. In a federal country, most factor markets are either on the State or Concurrent Lists. Hence, the agenda of second-generation reforms includes items that require changes at State level. Agriculture, social infrastructure and most areas of physical infrastructure are cases in point. If reform inclinations vary across States, it logically follows that so must growth rates. And this is compounded by the phenomenon that many faster growing States tend to have lower rates of population growth. Sick public sector units (PSUs) also tended to be concentrated in certain geographical regions and these are not the regions that have exhibited high (private sector driven) employment growth in the 1990s. To compound matters further, most new entrants to the labour force are concentrated in States that aren't growing fast.

In discussing inter-State disparities, the East versus the West or the North versus the South dichotomy is often emphasized. This East versus the West dichotomy, with a vertical line drawn through Kanpur, has some validity, subject to the caveat that undivided UP is an extremely heterogeneous State, with the Eastern parts somewhat different from the Western, NOIDA being an obvious example. The North versus the South dichotomy, with a horizontal line drawn through the Vindhyas, also has some validity, with growth rates in Tamil Nadu, Karnataka and Andhra Pradesh picking up in the 1990s. But like all generalizations, these hide as much as they reveal. The identification of poverty and backwardness with the BIMARU (Bihar, Madhya Pradesh, Rajasthan and Uttar Pradesh) States, with a pun on the word "bimar", is a bit more robust. However, Rajasthan clearly no longer belongs to the classic BIMARU fold and MP also seems to be climbing out. Conversely, Orissa exhibits many BIMARU characteristics. And how do Uttaranchal, Jharkhand and Chhattisgarh fit into the BIMARU identification?

More importantly, why is one interested in identifying pockets of deprivation? While not negating the possibility of differential relative growth rates across the country or attempting to neutralize it, the answer must be that one is interested in policy interventions that ensure uniform access to market opportunities across the country, quite apart from the socio-economic tensions that marginalization leads to. Liberalization does not mean an abdication of the State's responsibility. Instead, it should be interpreted as a refocusing of State intervention, with an emphasis on social (education, health) and physical (power, water) infrastructure, or even governance. The tension over better performing States effectively cross-subsidizing States that have relatively inferior track records needs to be viewed in this light. However, development or deprivation does not necessarily follow State boundaries, which are at best, administratively determined. Unfortunately, policy intervention in India is too centralized. This doesn't only mean overwhelming emphasis on the

Centre in Centre-State relations, as all States invariably argue, it also means negligible emphasis on decentralization and devolution within States, a point that States rarely make. Hence, while policy intervention is indeed needed to tackle problems of poverty and deprivation, identification of backward regions needs to go beyond State boundaries. And indeed, it is not very difficult to identify India's worst districts, mostly, but not exclusively, concentrated in India's BIMAROU (with Orissa included) States.[5]

Eight Millennium Development Goals were set out, for attainment by the year 2015. These are the following. (1) Halve, between 1990 and 2015, the proportion of people whose income is less than $1 a day. As a further objective, halve, between 1990 and 2015, the proportion of people who suffer from hunger, measured as prevalence of underweight children or the proportion of population below minimum levels of dietary energy consumption. (2) Ensure that, by 2015, children everywhere, boys and girls alike, are able to complete a full course of primary schooling. (3) Eliminate gender disparity in primary and secondary education preferably by 2005 and in all levels of education no later than 2015. (4) Reduce by two-thirds, between 1990 and 2015, the under-five mortality rate and obvious indicators for the under-five mortality rate, the infant mortality rate and the proportion of one-year-old children immunized against measles. (5) Reduce by three-quarters, between 1990 and 2015, the maternal mortality ratio. (6) Halt by 2015 and begin to reverse the spread of HIV/AIDS. As an additional goal, halt by 2015 and begin to reverse the incidence of malaria and other major diseases. (7) Integrate the principles of sustainable development into country policies and programs and reverse the loss of environmental resources. In addition, halve, by 2015, the proportion of people without sustainable access to safe drinking water. (8) Develop an open, rule-based, predictable, non-discriminatory trading and financial system.

The first five goals are more specific, with quantifiable targets, than the last three. And on the first five, India is on course for all but

---

5. Bibek Debroy and Laveesh Bhandari edited, *District-Level Deprivation in the New Millennium*, Rajiv Gandhi Institute for Contemporary Studies and Konark Publishers, 2003 and "Multidimensional Poverty in India: District Level Estimates" in Aasha Kapur Mehta, Sourabh Ghosh, Deepa Chatterjee and Nikhila Menon edited, *Chronic Poverty in India*, Chronic Poverty Research Centre, Indian Institute of Public Administration, 2003, are two such recent attempts.

the health ones. However, that is at the all-India level. In government quarters, the refrain that India will become a developed economy by 2020 is often heard. The expression "developed" economy is never defined. Shouting from the rooftops that India will become a developed economy by 2020 gets us nowhere, without a precise roadmap for that transition.

At the very least, India's per capita income has to graduate from the present level of 500 US dollars a year. (India's purchasing power parity per capita income may be higher at 2840 US dollars, but that is neither here nor there.) A lunar mission won't make India developed. The World Bank doesn't use expressions like developed. Today, India is a low-income country. Whatever definition of developed one uses, to become "developed" by 2020, India must graduate to lower-middle-income status. Anything beyond that is unachievable, like aiming for the moon. Lower-middle-income status requires a per capita income of 1500 US dollars in today's dollars. A per capita income growth of 6 per cent will get us almost there by 2020. Since the annual average rate of population growth will be around 1.3 per cent, India requires an income growth of at least 7.3 per cent. The Tenth Plan (2002-07) talks of increasing annual real GDP growth to 8 per cent. The Indian economy's track record during the Eighth Plan (1992-97) suggests that 8 per cent is indeed feasible. While the Eighth Plan had an annual average growth rate of 6.8 per cent, in the three years from 1994-95 to 1996-97, growth crossed 7 per cent and in 1996-97, it even crossed 8 per cent. However, since then, growth has slackened.

More importantly, growth cannot afford to bypass the poor. The all-India poverty ratio may have dropped to 26 per cent. However, poverty ratios are still fairly high in Assam, Bihar, Madhya Pradesh, Uttar Pradesh, Orissa and some North-Eastern States. At a simple level, poverty ratios have dropped in easier States and easier districts, thanks to the poverty reducing aspects of growth. Regional disparities have increased and the rate of poverty reduction has slowed down after the mid-1990s. Poverty continues to be high in hardcore States and districts.

In addition, poverty has dropped because of growth, not because of the government's anti-poverty programmes. There is an alphabet soup of more than 200 centrally sponsored schemes (CSSs), mostly directed against poverty. Planning Commission documents have established that these are of doubtful utility, with the Indira Awaas Yojana (IAY) performing better than the others. With leakage, high administrative costs and success judged through expenditure rather than actual improvements in outcomes, these anti-poverty programmes do little for the poor, although they exist in the name of the poor.

India will not become developed as long as poverty and deprivation remain endemic. Consider the following. Globally, India accounts for:

- 36 per cent of the world's poor living on less than $1 a day;
- 20 per cent of the world's out-of-school children
- 20 per cent of the world's gender gap in elementary education (6-14 years);
- 25 per cent of the world's maternal deaths;
- 23 per cent of the world's under-5 child deaths;
- 30 per cent of the world's deaths from poor access to water and sanitation.
- 260 million people live in poverty.
- 296 million people are still illiterate. 189 million of them are women.
- 1.8 million infants die each year, and most of these deaths are avoidable.
- 47 per cent of children under 3 years of age are malnourished – nearly twice the levels reported by Sub-Saharan Africa.
- There are striking regional disparities. Kerala has an infant mortality rate of 11, compared to Orissa's 90. The rural infant mortality rate is 72, compared to the urban figure of 42. The proportion of fully immunised children varies from 11 per cent in Bihar to 89 per cent in Kerala. Less than 15 per cent of women are illiterate in Kerala and Mizoram. On the other hand, 66 per cent of women are illiterate in Bihar. The proportion of under-weight children varies from 21 per cent in Sikkim to 50 per cent or more in Maharashtra, Rajasthan, Uttar Pradesh, Bihar, Orissa and Madhya Pradesh.

The point is a simple one. Does ICT help the cause of the poor and the deprived, especially in these backward States and backward districts? Can ICT help in achieving the UN Millenium Declaration's goals on development and poverty eradication? Will it help to halve the proportion of people living in extreme poverty or those suffering from hunger or those without access to safe water? Will it ensure that all children are enrolled in primary school? Will it empower women and eliminate gender disparities in education? Will it help to reduce maternal, infant and under-five mortality rates? Will it help to provide universal access to reproductive health services? Will it help to prevent HIV/AIDS or serve the cause of environment protection?

The argument should not be advanced too strongly. ICT is only a tool, it cannot be expected to solve all the development problems of the world, problems that have plagued us for generations. But these developmental objectives are certainly the yardsticks against which ICT needs to be evaluated. The point about a North-South digital divide, which is increasing, is often made and is a valid point. However, there is a North-South divide of a different kind and that is a North-South divide within India. Out of India's 1.4 million Internet connections, more than 1.3 million are in Delhi, Karnataka, Maharashtra and Tamil Nadu. Per thousand people, Maharashtra may have 43 telephone lines. But Orissa has only 9. It is not surprising that although HDR 2001 classified India as a dynamic adopter of IT, India's technology achievement index (TAI) ranked it only 63rd out of 72 countries.[6] After all, Bangalore is the only hub.

The Italian economist and sociologist Vilfredo Pareto (1848-1923) is now mostly remembered for a test he set out in welfare economics, the so-called Pareto efficiency or Pareto optimality test. But Pareto also did some work on income distributions (the Pareto law), exhibiting a consistency in income and wealth distributions across history and across societies. Stated somewhat simplistically, Pareto found that regardless of the variable whose distribution one was examining, 80 per cent of the population obtained 20 per cent of the asset, while 20 per cent of the population obtained 80 per cent. This 80:20 distribution is the issue. We know what ICT offers the 20 per cent. What does it offer the 80 per cent? Before answering this

6. Other than dynamic adopter, the other categories are leaders, potential leaders and marginalized.

question, we need to talk about the reform agenda of liberalizing or liberating the social sector.

The Social Sector

Liberating the Social Sector from What?

Textbooks on the Indian economy describe India as a developing economy and then go on to enumerate the characteristics of a developing economy. Invariably, there is the statement that two-thirds of India's citizens live in rural areas, suggesting that is bad. Why should there be this normative value judgement about living in the rural areas? After all, 23 per cent of the US population lives in rural areas and there are no such negative connotations there. The negative connotation of rural has nothing to do with the Census definition of rural, defined in terms of number of inhabitants or pattern of work. Instead, rural in India connotes a complete lack of social and physical infrastructure. On top of this, there are class and caste (SC/ST) biases, not to forget gender biases. Stated differently, given a choice, would one like to be born as a SC woman in a remote district of undivided Bihar or Rajasthan? That is the state of the social sector from which one needs liberation.

The post-1991 period is an era of liberalization. It is also an era of abdication by the State. However, the citizen, especially the poor citizen, has legitimate expectations on the part of the State. Primary education, rural health care, clean drinking water, sanitation and rural roads - these are all examples of sectors where classic arguments about market failure and State intervention continue to be true. Barring rural roads, which belong to the realm of physical infrastructure, the others are what one may broadly describe as the social sector. Ergo, the social sector is one where State intervention continues to be necessary. To this list of citizen expectations, one should also add the rule of law, something that is often ignored. Given judicial delays, the poor citizen is crowded out of the court system. Rather perversely, the poor citizen is crowded into the jail system. Out of the jail population of 280,000, more than 200,000 are under-trial prisoners who have been in jail for longer than the maximum sentences prescribed for such petty crimes.

And while talking about getting the State into social sectors, one should not forget the issue of getting the State out of unsocial sectors.

By that, one means the government machinery of clearances, licences, permissions and procedures. This plagues the citizen from birth to death[7] - birth certificates, death certificates, land records, caste certificates, the list is endless. There can be no objection to the idea of clearances *per se*. However, any machinery requires oil and grease and the government machinery is no different. The objection is to non-transparency and discretion in decision making, thus contributing to bribery and corruption. And there is the obvious point that rent-seeking is not distributionally neutral, because it tends to hurt the small relatively more than it hurts the large. There are economies of scale in bribe-giving. We not only need to get the State out of the commanding heights, we need to get it out of the demanding heights as well. And while on the provision of social sector services, one should also mention that secession of the successful does take place. For example, richer sections can afford to privatize many of these services.

Having said this and acknowledged the importance of State intervention in social sectors, some points need to be made to ensure that the preceding 50-odd years of State failure don't continue to recur. First, there is an issue of resources. Governments in India are bankrupt and this is a serious problem at the State government level, where most social sector spending should take place. The worry is not about the fiscal deficit *per se*, but about the fact that the fiscal deficit is driven entirely by the revenue deficit. Planning Commission's *National Human Development Report* has some figures on composition of public spending across States in 1998-99. The only States which spent more than 20 per cent of total expenditure on capital expenditure were Arunachal Pradesh, Manipur, Mizoram and Delhi.[8] As a per centage of State Domestic Product (SDP), the only States that spent more than 6 per cent on education were Arunachal Pradesh, Himachal Pradesh, Jammu & Kashmir, Manipur, Sikkim and Tripura. The only States that spent more than 3 per cent of SDP on health were Arunachal Pradesh and Sikkim. Hence, there is a revenue issue as well as an expenditure one. Does non-recovery of costs of public services or non-taxation of high-income agricultural households further the

7. Thankfully, Eliot's third bare fact seems to be excluded.

8. The distinction between revenue and capital expenditure and between plan and non-plan expenditure can be artificial. But that is not a terribly important point.

cause of the social sector or the cause of the poor? Do high salaries and pensions for government employees improve health and education outcomes? In most States, salary-related expenditure is between two-thirds and three-fourths of revenue receipts.

This thus leads to the second point. Without addressing efficiency of public expenditure, arguments that public expenditure on education should be increased to 6 per cent of national income or public expenditure on health should be increased to 3 per cent of national income are neither here nor there. Increments to school-teachers who don't teach increase expenditure on education. But they don't improve education outcomes. Chalks, textbooks, blackboards and mid-day meals might, but there is no money for these.[9] There are several issues connected to efficiency improvements. There is the government budget making process itself, which judges success in terms of expenditure and not in terms of improvements in outcome.[10] There is leakage, aided by non-transparency and complete lack of accountability. In a scenario of depression and unemployment, Keynes talked about digging ditches (that had no use) and then filling them up. We have improved on Keynes. There are any number of roads that haven't been built and any number of wells that haven't been dug. They only exist on paper. Decentralization facilitates accountability and there are success stories in education, perhaps less so for health.[11] Accountability also improves if Right to Information Acts are enacted, without caveats that hide the information under the garb of official secrets or public interest.

Third, public funding of social sectors need not necessarily be equated with public provisioning, because subsidies are not antithetical to the idea of injecting competition. Incidentally, competition through private sector entry is often restricted by regulatory systems. The license-permit *raj* may have disappeared for manufacturing, but it remains for social sectors. Studies have also

9. Mid-day meals seem to improve retention rates, in the sense of reducing drop-outs. The impact on enrollments is less certain.

10. Action Taken Reports (ATR) have now become part of the Union Budget. But ATRs will tell us how much has been spent on the *Pradhan Mantri Gram Sadak Yojana*, not how many roads have been built as a result. Should there be any Central social sector programmes at all?

11. Decentralized committees are also subject to predatory capture and some of the euphoria about *panchayats* needs to be qualified. But because there are fewer layers, there should be less leakage.

established[12] that the argument that the poor are unwilling to pay higher prices is fallacious. Higher prices are acceptable, provided quality improves. And in education, we also know that private budget schools don't necessarily charge higher fees and deprive the poor. With cross-subsidization, scholarships are possible and because administrative expenses are much lower, user charges don't shoot up. Depending on geographical and demographic factors, private sector entry in social sectors is possible and so are public-private partnerships. Subsidies are best delivered in the hands of recipients, so that there is no leakage. Subsidies in the name of the poor are not the same thing as subsidies for the poor.[13] For example, there can be vouchers for targeted poor that the recipient can take to whichever provider he or she wants. That delinks public funding from public provisioning, as does the idea of retaining ownership in public hands, but handing over management to private parties. If this can work for roads, why can't it work for primary schools and health care centres? There are bound to be backward areas where geographic and demographic considerations preclude private sector entry. Even there, in instances of classic market failure, subsidies should be linked to tangible improvements in outcomes. Monopolies are never efficient. This proposition is also true of public sector monopolies. Hopefully, 55 years down the line, this lesson has finally been grasped. There are still no clear explanations as to why the literacy rate has improved from 52 per cent in 1991 to 65 per cent in 2001,[14] the fastest increase since Independence. From what one hears anecdotally, one would like to think that this improvement is because the lesson has been learnt. There has been greater decentralization, accountability and transparency, coupled with increased private sector entry. Interpreted thus, liberalization has led to greater liberation.

In general, there is dissatisfaction, disenchantment and cynicism on the part of citizens with the three organs of State prescribed in the

12. See, for example, the surveys done by Public Affairs Centre, Bangalore or Administrative Staff College of India, Hyderabad. Or for that matter, the toilets built by Naandi in Andhra Pradesh.

13. If present explicit subsidies are converted into direct cash transfers for households below the poverty line, each poor household would get around Rs 8000 per year. With implicit subsidies, the figure is higher and obviously, very little actually reaches the poor.

14. The argument that the Census definition of literacy is inadequate, doesn't get very far. Despite this inadequacy, there is no denying that the literacy rate has increased significantly.

Constitution - the legislature, the executive and the judiciary. In the context of social sectors, this primarily means the executive. However, cynicism doesn't get us very far, unless countervailing pressure is exerted by civil society. This seems to be happening for urban education and urban municipal services, but has not snowballed sufficiently elsewhere. The 20 million people who work for the government[15] are unlikely to be agents of change, left to themselves. The pressure has to come from without.

The ICT Tool

The efficacy of ICT as a tool for removing poverty is crucially dependent on the efficiency with which the State performs its core governance functions in physical and social infrastructure.

Conceptually, there ought to be no problem. Whichever form of deprivation one has in mind, in the last instance, it can always be distilled out in the form of asymmetry of access to information. Had there been equal access to information, many of the problems of poverty and deprivation would have disappeared. ICT is essentially an information tool and for the first time in India's developmental history since independence in 1947, we have an extremely powerful tool that can remove this asymmetry in access to information. Obvious instances of this are in sectors like health, education, public governance, empowerment, right to information and disintermediation of the agricultural distribution chain. The last is especially important for a country like India, where two-thirds of the population is employed in the rural sector. And poverty in India is fundamentally a rural problem, urban poverty being largely a spillover of rural poverty. Rather paradoxically, India is also a country with one of the longest agricultural distribution chains in the world. For typical agricultural produce, the farmer will not obtain more than around ten cents a kilo for his product. Yet that same product will be sold to the retail consumer for one and a half dollars a kilo. While disintermediation was in any case desirable, ICT helps the process.

At an anecdotal level, there are success stories and it is worth mentioning a few. Dhar is a backward district in Madhya Pradesh State. A government funded Gyandoot project was started for Dhar

15. Centre, State, local bodies and PSUs.

district, with cyber-kiosks or information centres (*soochanalays*) set up in rural villages under the control of local village bodies (*panchayats*) and networked to district headquarters.[16] Villagers obtain access to information about prices for crops through these information centres and caste and land certificates can be produced. Grievances can be e-mailed to administration. The kiosks are also used to impart education to school children and offer them career-related advice. In Pondicherry, the Chennai-based M.S. Swaminathan Foundation provides information through local centres on weather forecasts, tides, wind directions and heights of waves to coastal villages that obtain a livelihood from fishing. In Warana district in Maharashtra, information centres record transactions with sugar and milk cooperatives and provide information on harvesting times, expected yields and the results of crop sampling. In Thiruvarur in Tamil Nadu, e-governance has made the government delivery system more accountable. Old age pensions and records, land records, community, birth and death certificates have been computerized. These are available faster, as are government loans and the government is more responsive to complaints. As is inevitable, rent-seeking through middlemen has been weeded out. Such experiments have also taken place in Ratlam district in Madhya Pradesh, Hamirpur district in Himachal Pradesh, the Sonepat and Sirsa districts of Haryana and in Kerala. There are also direct employment benefits that these information centres lead to.

The Confederation of Indian Industry and the Boston Consulting Group (BCG) recently brought out a document depicting what India might be like in 2010.[17] This depicts four possible images as metaphors for India in 2010. The document has nothing to do with ICT, but the images are useful. The first image is that of buffaloes wallowing. "The buffaloes continue to wallow in the swamp. It is time to move on. Who can goad them? The herdsboy yells to them that they will go hungry if they do not make a move. One or two attempt to get out of the water. But they are surrounded by others. So they give up." The second image is that of wolves prowling. "The land has become a wild jungle. Bands of wolves roam. Small animals, and even

---

16. This project won the Stockholm Challenge Award.

17. *Scenarios For India 2010, Putting It Together Again*. This slim document is undated. It can be downloaded at www.ciionline.org or www.bcg.com.

big animals, live in fear of these marauding bands. Who can control them? Only the well muscled and armed tiger is safe." The third image is that of birds scrambling. "Grain is strewn in the courtyard for the birds. They have been waiting for the food. They scramble for it. The pigeons flap their wings and push the smaller sparrows aside. The sparrows hop around the pigeons hoping they will get to eat also. The pigeons peck away at the grain with no concern for the sparrows. A peacock arrives and the pigeons also retreat. The food is over. The peacock and even the pigeons fly off contentedly. The sparrows have gone hungry. May be tomorrow they may have a chance." Finally, there is the metaphor of fireflies arising. "At first, a few bright lights emerged from the darkness. Then many more. Soon the countryside is alight with dancing fireflies. It is wondrous to see how such tiny beings can transform the night. Where did they come from?"

One would like to think that what is happening in India in ICT represents the metaphor of the fireflies rising. But this would do violence to the truth. It is tempting to be optimistic, because there is hype about the successes. They tend to get talked about much more and attract media attention. However, there are failures as well. And just as the successes have lessons in terms of their possible replication elsewhere, so do the failures – hopefully, in their non-replication. Nyala village in Rajasthan is an example of such a failure, a village that generated a lot of hype when President Bill Clinton visited it. This was supposed to be a model village, with e-learning and e-business. USAID donated five Dell computers, but they lie unused. Some of them are yet to be unpacked. It is because there are examples like Nyala that the metaphor of fireflies rising is inappropriate. But equally, the metaphors of buffaloes wallowing or wolves prowling are also inappropriate. What one has is the birds scrambling and the challenge is to convert this metaphor into one of fireflies.

The issues that shape the contours of this challenge are easily listed.

First, there is an electricity issue. One reason why computers in Nyala lie unused is that the village only gets three hours of electricity a day. That too, erratic. ICT forms part of the broader issue of infrastructure and at a sweeping level of generalization, infrastructure reforms in India have got stuck, barring the somewhat high-profile area of telecom. The arguments for reform are well known. The present system of subsidies through inappropriate user charges (in power say) make investments (both public and private) unviable and contrary to populist perception, don't benefit the poor at all. On an average, transmission and distribution (T&D) losses are around 25 per cent. But these are State Electricity Board (SEB) figures and are unreliable. Once power distribution reforms generate more accurate figures, as in Orissa, one discovers that T&D losses are in excess of 45 per cent and this is nothing but a euphemism for theft of power, stolen not by the poor, but by the rich. The implicit cross-subsidy is regressive. Unfortunately, despite this recognition, or perhaps because of this, reforms have got stuck. There are also transient problems of lack of reform in other infrastructure areas like telecom, where government monopolies and lack of competition still continue in some areas. However, these are transient problems, because there are clear time-frames for these monopolies to end in the not too distant future.

Second, there is a hardware cum software issue. The ICT infrastructure has to be installed in villages. Where is this hardware going to come from? Who will provide it? Usually, a lot is made of the hardware costs, but such costs are probably less significant than is commonly made out to be. For instance, a switch to Linux rather than Windows brings down hardware costs and old machines, which are often donated gratis, can be used. This is over and above the consideration that Linux makes the development of local language applications easier. Using Linux, the Indian Institute of Science, Bangalore, has developed a handheld Internet appliance that sells at less than one-third the price of an entry-level Pentium III PC. This is known as the Simputer. Connectivity and bandwidth problems are also solvable. For instance, Wireless Local Loop Technology can be used. Once the hardware is installed, software has to be available in vernacular languages and there must be local language based applications, so that users identify the benefits associated with using ICT.

Third, there is the question of who is going to do all this, the delivery issue. Understandably, there is a great deal of skepticism in India about centralized government-administered delivery. Primary education is a good example. As was mentioned earlier, in the 1991 Census, India had a literacy rate of 52.2 per cent. In 1951, India had a literacy rate of 18.3 per cent. So over a period of 40 years, the literacy rate improved by 34 per cent, or 0.85 per cent per year. In 2001, the Census shows an overall literacy rate of 65 per cent. This is an improvement of 1.3 per cent a year and has never happened before.[18] How has this improvement come about? Historically, primary education has been assumed to be the responsibility of the government. It is not the case that schools are not available. If one has in mind primary schools, there are very few habitations that do not have schools within a range of 1 kilometre. It is not the case that children can't go to school because they have to work. At least at the primary school level, there is very little evidence of work pulling children out of school. It is not the case that parents are stupid and there is no demand for education. If returns on primary education are upwards of 20 per cent, as they are, no parent will want children to be out of school. The issue is thus related to quality, quality imparted by government schools and government schoolteachers. In fact, there is evidence to show that parents are willing to pay, if quality of education is good enough.

The following story concerns a Mumbai slum. There is a government school in the slum and children don't attend school. This is not because they have to work. The government school functions in the mornings and at 11.00 A.M. the municipal water supply arrives. It is important to queue up for water, since there will be no further water supply in the course of the day. This is the sum total of work children have to do. The government school has been asked several times to switch to classes in the afternoon. Apparently, government rules prevent this switch. Along comes a NGO (non-government organization) with a proposition. Let us use the government school's infrastructure in the afternoon. We will run a school then. Thankfully, the authorities agree and this school is running famously. Free textbooks obtained by enrolling in the government school are used to study in the NGO-run school in the afternoon. There is also the true story of another NGO that runs schools for children on railway platforms. These children polish shoes when there is a train on the platform and school is dissolved for that period. Once the train leaves,

18. There are indeed people who argue that definitions of literacy don't capture much, they have no functional tests. True, but the definition hasn't changed much. And even if the definition is unsatisfactory, as long as it does not become more unsatisfactory, an improvement is an improvement.

the school functions again. The point thus is lack of flexibility and adaptability in government run schools, even if children do actually work. The government schoolteacher doesn't teach, he is not accountable to users, he draws salaries from district headquarters. If salaries or increments of such teachers are increased, that shows up as an increase in government expenditure on primary education. India spends around 3.5 per cent of national income on education. This public expenditure can certainly be increased and obvious comparisons with expenditure on defence can be made. But the more important point is that expenditure on education is inefficient. 97 to 98 per cent of expenditure on primary education goes towards wages and salaries. There is no money for chalk, blackboards or textbooks. The government has concentrated on increasing inputs into the education process through wages and salaries. There has been no attention to outcomes. What is true of education is also true of anti-poverty programmes run by the government. The PDS (public distribution system), which runs a system of ration shops, ostensibly for the poor, is another example. There are substantial leakages and not more than 20 per cent of what is spent in the name of the poor actually reaches target beneficiaries. There are two primary reasons for the sharp increase in literacy between 1991 and 2001 – greater NGO involvement and decentralization of government, with greater accountability to users. The Education Guarantee Scheme (EGS) in Madhya Pradesh is an example of the latter.

To get back to the point, it is understandable that the government needs to finance and subsidize the ICT process. However, there is no reason to presume that if the government finances a process, it necessarily has to run cyber-kiosks on its own. It is possible to delink the two functions. But on the financing itself, two questions arise. The combined fiscal deficit of the Centre and the States is more than 10 per cent of GDP, the worst since reforms started in 1991. The Centre and the States are both bankrupt. If one considers the Centre, three items of revenue expenditure add up to more than tax and non-tax revenue. These three items are interest payments, subsidies and defence expenditure. As was mentioned earlier, the subsidies don't benefit the poor, they leak away, even if they are introduced in the name of the poor. The present subsidies amount to Rs. 300 billion a year. If these were directly given as cash transfers to households below the poverty line, each poor household would receive around Rs. 8000 a year. Obviously, this is not happening. The situation is no different at the level of the States. The trade-off is fairly simple. For the costs of running one government car, ten primary schools can be run in villages. Thus, the issue of subsidizing ICT is linked to the broader issue of reforming government expenditure, which is part and parcel of the reform process. Within education, there is also the question of what the government decides to subsidize – primary or higher education. Unlike East Asia, India has subsidized higher education at the expense of primary education and economic wisdom now argues that this should not be done. However, had it not been for the earlier distorted policy of subsidizing higher education, the present software and H1-B boom would not have happened.[19]

Hypothetically, it is possible to argue that the ICT boom can be engineered without government subsidies. Commercial streams of revenue can be used to cross-subsidize non-commercial activities like primary education or healthcare. Detailed data are not available. But at the anecdotal level, none of the present private experiments suggest that is plausible in the short-run, since commercial revenue streams don't materialize immediately. Even if current or revenue costs don't need subsidies and projects need to be deliberately designed so that they eventually become self-financing, subsidization of capital costs is necessary. This is certainly true of rural areas, perhaps less so in urban areas. However, the present anecdotal evidence also suggests that any attempt to push ICT in a top-down approach is doomed to failure. There has to be a sense of ownership created at the local level, through involvement of local NGOs, employment of local people to man the information centres and contributions from local bodies through land or housing. For example, a few of the successful information centres are run in village temples. To the extent that e-governance is an integral component, citizens' right to information is also an issue and a few Indian States (Goa being the first) have enacted Right to Information Acts.

Finally, a comment on the education system is also in order. The knowledge-based economy of the 21st century, with its emphasis on

19. There is the minor question of India suffering from a skilled manpower shortage now, not only because of the software exodus, but also because teachers have increasingly begun to emigrate. Obviously, a tax on emigration or an H1-B type export quota is out of the question. But this is yet another argument as to why higher education should not be subsidized, because those subsidies eventually benefit developed countries.

intellectual property rights, requires innovation and invention, the ability to think and question. The ability to take risks. Unfortunately, the entire Indian educational system, from kindergarten right up to universities is designed to encourage conformity and stifle innovation and creativity. It discourages failure, and hence, also discourages success. This educational system was primarily designed to serve colonial rule and needs transformation. It has always needed such a transformation, but ICT imparts a greater urgency to the need.

In sum, from an Indian perspective, the ICT phenomenon can be interpreted as a paraphrasing of www as where, who and why. Where will it happen? In urban areas alone, or will the benefits trickle down? In the parts of India that lie to the west of a vertical line drawn through Kanpur in Uttar Pradesh, or will it percolate to States that have been bypassed by the reform process? Who will do it, private initiatives or the government, or a combination of the two? How does one delink government finance and government delivery? How can the government be decentralized and made suitably accountable? And finally, the why of the education system.

13

Incidence of Child Labour

Theory, and Evidence from India[1]

SHUBHASHIS GANGOPADHYAY
WILIMA WADHWA

Introduction

Basu and Van (1998) develop a model where child labour is associated with low adult wages. In their paper, if adult wages can be increased, child labour can be prevented. The strong point of their paper is that they do not use selfish parents as an explanation for the incidence of child labour. For a given level of parental altruism, they have two possible equilibria — a low adult wage equilibrium where children work and, a high adult wage equilibrium where children do not work. There is an exogenously given minimum level of consumption that the household must have. If the household earnings fall below this level, children go out to work to augment earnings. A major policy conclusion of their paper is that, an effective ban on child labour rules out the equilibrium where children work.

In this paper, we extend their analysis in a number of different directions. There are three reasons for doing this. First, we want to develop a model that is empirically testable. If parents are equally altruistic towards their children in every society, then one has to find an explanation of why different societies have different incidences of child labour. Indeed, even within the same economy, different sectors report different amounts of child labour. For instance, in rural India, 7 per cent of the children work, compared to around 3 per cent in urban India (Gangopadhyay and Wadhwa, 1999).

1. This paper is based on a study done by the authors for the International Labour Organization, and while the second author was visiting the Indian Statistical Institute, Delhi Centre. Balwant Bisht, Achintya Ray and S. Gayathri provided excellent research support. However, the authors bear complete responsibility for any remaining error.

Second, and this is related to the differential incidence of child labour in different sectors, we want to endogenize the threshold level of consumption below which children are sent out to work. In other words, even though households are equally altruistic in all sectors, the environment in which they operate may be crucially important in determining what they perceive to be a minimum standard of living. This is prompted by the observation that the poverty line, used to measure the poverty status of a household, is a very subjective concept. It does have an objective component, like the minimum amount of nutrition as worked out by the biologists. However, when it comes to other basic amenities, like housing, clothing, health care, *etc.*, different societies have different perceptions on the minimum amounts needed.

Third, we want to be able to come up with policy prescriptions in the event that a ban, though feasible otherwise, is not fully enforceable. Given that much of the child labour occurs in developing economies, where institutional and legal structures are weak, enforcement issues are important when discussing the legal banning of child labour. Given that sending children to work is a household decision, if one knows how these decisions get formed, one can devise policies that make it beneficial for households not to send their children to work. Such a mechanism is always more fruitful in societies characterized by weak enforcement of laws.

Our approach in this paper is to develop a simple theoretical model that explains the extent of child labour in a particular sector. The decision to send children to work is made in the household and depends on household preferences. All decision makers have identical preferences but face different economic environments. The decision to send children to work can be broken up, conceptually, into two parts: whether to have working children in the household and, if so, how much work should they do. The answer to the first question allows us to describe a threshold such that all households on one side of it have no working children, while those on the other side have children working at varying, but positive, degrees of intensity. If this threshold is an observable variable, targeting households that require inducements to reduce child labour becomes that much simpler.

The productivity of the adult, relative to the child, plays an important role in our model. We distinguish between two types of productivity changes — one that increases the productivity of both adults and children, and another, that increases adult productivity relative to the child. While the first can be brought about by improvements in economic infrastructure, or factors complementary to labour, the latter is dependent on the social infrastructure that improves the health, training and awareness of the adults. Since both can be affected through government policy, it is important to know which is more desirable in its effect on the incidence of child labour.

We then go on to test the empirical implications of the model with Indian data. Every five years, the Indian National Sample Survey Organization (NSS) conducts a 'large' sample survey of about 0.12 million households throughout the country. The survey asks detailed questions on the consumption pattern of households and the employment status of every member of the sampled households. All relevant demographic factors of each of these members, like age, sex, level of education, relation to the head of the household, etc., are also recorded. The data set we use for our analysis is for the year 1993-94 which is the latest available.[2]

Our major findings are that the threshold consumption level, in real terms, below which children go out to work, is higher in urban areas than in rural areas. This apparent anomaly, when all parents are equally altruistic towards their children, can be explained with the help of our theoretical model. We also find that increased adult productivity, proxied by the education level, reduces the incidence of child labour. Furthermore, we demonstrate the importance of the mother's education in reducing child labour, regardless of whether she works or not.

Incidence of Child Labour

We use the latest available 'large sample' household consumption and employment data of the National Sample Survey Organization.[3]

---

2. The most recent large survey was conducted in 1999-2000. However, the data are yet to be released to researchers.

3. An alternative data source are surveys conducted by ORG (Operations Research Group). Indeed, as Weiner (1991) and Groetart and Kanbur (1995) show different estimates of child labour are obtained depending on the data source. We concentrate on the NSS data set since it gives a much larger sample and has detailed information on other family characteristics as well.

The survey period is from July 1, 1993 to June 30, 1994 (also known as the 50th round). Consumption and employment surveys are carried out each year, but the large samples, of more than a hundred thousand households, are done every five years. The survey uses two sets of questionnaires, one for household consumption and household demographic characteristics (Schedule 1) and the other (Schedule 10) for employment and demographic characteristics of individuals in the households surveyed in Schedule 1. In these data, a household is defined to be a set of individuals who obtain food from the same kitchen. Consequently, a live-in maid, for instance, will be counted as a member of the household where she works. On the other hand, a villager working as a migrant labourer in the city will not be counted as a member of the village household.

The assumption in our theoretical model (developed in the next section) is that parents do not want to send their children to work, or the household suffers a utility loss if their children work. Some evidence of this is brought out by the following statistics: adult unemployment is mostly among the non-poor; poor households have very few non-working adults, both unemployment and the proportion of out of labour force adults is higher in non-poor households; the participation of women in the work force is much higher in households where the children work (Gangopadhyay and Wadhwa, 1999). All of this is consistent with the hypothesis that children are sent out to work as a last resort. Alternatively, parents are altruistic towards their children.

Altonji, Hayashi and Kotlikoff (1997) reject the hypothesis of altruism using PSID data for the US. However, their study considers parent's behavior towards adult children, those aged more than 18 years. In this paper we look at children in the age group 5-14. Typically parents tend to be more protective or altruistic towards younger children, for whom they also take most of the decisions. This may be due to a sense of responsibility or societal pressures. While children above 18 are treated as independent decision-makers by most societies, almost every society expects parents to act as guardians of minors.

Since we assume that parents are altruistic, our analysis has to be confined to children who are related to the head of the household. Many affluent households have domestic help, and often, they are within the age group 5-14. A parent is unlikely to be worried about such a child's welfare in the same way as he, or she, would care about her own children.[4] Also, our theoretical model focuses on children who work to augment family incomes. In the empirical analysis, therefore, we consider only those children who are earning wages and leave out the children helping in household chores. In short, we consider those members who are in the age group 5-14, are related to the head of the household and work as wage labour.[5]

An important part of our analysis is the level of economic distress that forces parents to send their children to work. The usual method of measuring the economic distress of a household is to check whether the household is above or below the poverty line. In India, all poverty calculations are consumption based. A household is considered to be poor if the value of consumption of its members falls below the poverty line. We use the consumption data for poverty calculations, as in Dubey and Gangopadhyay (1998).

The first obvious question is who are the working children. More than 6 per cent of all Indian children work outside the household (Table 1). However, while the proportion of working children (7.25 per cent) is higher for those households who are below the poverty line (BPL), more than 5 per cent of children in non-poor (above poverty line, APL) households also work. Thus, child labour as a phenomenon occurs in both APL and BPL households.

One could, of course, argue that the APL households where the children work are non-poor because the children are working. The NSS data set does not have information on household income, or the wages received by the working children. We are, thus, unable to test directly whether the working children in the non-poor households are helping the APL families to stay above the poverty line. Another argument that can be made is that the poverty line is not a true measure of economic distress, as viewed by the households. In other words, the poverty line underestimates the value of the minimum consumption needs and, hence households above the poverty line also have to send their children out to work.

4. In the data set, the relation of each member in the household, to the head of the household, is recorded.

5. Observe that this will include children working in household enterprises.

Table 1

Distribution of Child Labourers

(Per cent)

	All India	Rural	Urban
Work	6.32	7.33	3.03
No Work	93.68	92.67	96.97
APL			
Work	5.51	6.80	1.91
No Work	94.49	93.28	98.09
BPL			
Work	7.25	7.90	4.72
No Work	92.75	92.10	95.28

Notes: The sample includes all children in the age group 5-14 years who are related to the head of the household.

Children are classified as workers if they work outside the house or in a household enterprise.

APL: Above the poverty line; BPL: Below the poverty line.

Neither of the two alternative explanations in the previous paragraph can, however, explain the difference in the nature of incidence in the rural and urban sectors. The proportion of children working in the rural sector is more than double that in the urban sector. On the other hand, while 7.9 per cent of all rural children belonging to poor households work, the corresponding figure for the urban sector is only 4.7 per cent. This difference is more marked in the APL households — while 6.8 per cent of children in rural APL households work, only 1.9 per cent do so in the corresponding urban households. This difference is significant because, the poverty calculations in India take into account the difference in prices as well as the difference in the consumption baskets between the rural and urban sectors, as well as the differences across geographical space (Dubey and Gangopadhyay, 1998). Caiumi and Perali (1997) report a similar finding for female labour. In particular their simulations show that urban households allocate more time to leisure and household activities as compared to rural households. They find this consistent with employment evidence since in general all female labour can be employed on the farm. This characteristic, which differentiates labour opportunities among rural and urban households, could also account for the higher incidence of child labour in rural areas.

Nevertheless, if child labour is a household decision, one will have to consider it as an outcome of household characteristics. In other words, there could be other factors that influence the incidence of child labour, apart from economic distress and presence of labour opportunities. Alternatively, one could look at a household's perception of distress as being the outcome of various factors both inside and outside the household. That is, different households may perceive economic distress as such at different income/consumption levels. One obvious factor affecting the perception of economic distress is the level of awareness among the parents regarding the need to train children so that they can be more productive as adults. Behrman *et. al.* (1977 and 1994) and Miller *et. al.* (1997), among others, establish the influence of family background on the schooling-income relationship. Family background influences include resources available within the household, role models provided by parents and their peers and the direct and indirect encouragement given by parents. In fact, many would also argue that the mother plays a large role in the development of the child — the more educated the mother, greater is the child's mental and physical development, at all levels of income classes. While the mother's education is a factor internal to the household, one external factor that acts as an incentive to send the child out to work is the wage a child can receive. *Ceteris paribus*, if the child wage is high, the parent may be induced to send the child out to work.

Since there could be more than one factor affecting the household's decision regarding child labour, and different households experience varying amounts of these factors, it is possible that an exogenously defined poverty line may not be the correct threshold to consider as a determinant of child labour. The moment we appreciate this, we realize that it is not surprising that there is so much difference in the rural-urban incidence of child labour in India. For example, Indian urbanites are generally more educated than their rural counterparts, and women are better educated in the cities than in the villages (Dubey, Gangopadhyay and Wadhwa, 1999). On the other hand, the productivity of child labour is likely to be higher in the cities, which might act in an opposing direction to the other two factors.

In the next section, we develop a simple model of household behavior to determine incidence of child labour. We then derive some empirically testable propositions from it.

The Model

Supply of Child Labour

Each household has 1 unit of labour time, of which θ is adult labour and $1-\theta$ is child labour. Adult labour is γ times more productive than child labour, i.e., one unit of adult labour-time is equivalent to $(1/\gamma)$ units of child labour time, where $\gamma > 1$. Each household has non-labour income z, $z \geq 0$, and $z \in [0,1]$.[6] Henceforth, households are arranged so that they can be indexed by their non-labour income. The distribution of *z* is denoted G(*z*).

A1: G(.) is uniform for $z \in [0,1]$

Household welfare, *V*, depends on the total household consumption (income) and the extent of child labour utilized to obtain that consumption. Assuming that all income is consumed, as in Basu and Van (1998),

$$V_Z = V(a, c; z) = \ln(aw_a cw_c + Z) + \beta(1-\theta-c) \qquad ...(1)$$

where *a* is the amount of adult labour-time, *c* is the amount of child labour-time, w_a is the adult wage, and w_c is the child wage. We also have $\beta > 0$, implying that household welfare decreases with child labour. β can be used as a measure of the degree of awareness of the household decision maker, about the importance of keeping children away from work. In general, societies seem to have different attitudes to child labour. In some societies, it is routine to send children to work if they do not want to go to school, or cannot cope with the school curriculum. This cuts across income, or wealth, classes. Even a wealthy shopkeeper will make the son help in the shop if he is not doing well at school. On the other hand, in the southern Indian state of Kerala, even the poorest families will keep their children at school, regardless of how they are performing there. The long history of royal and state patronage of education in Kerala, has resulted in parents wanting to keep their children in school.

All households are price takers, and treat w_a and w_c as given. As in Basu and Van, we do not have any labour leisure choice for adult labour time, so that for any positive w_a, adults will work full time, i.e.,

6. Suppose that there is a finite maximum amount of non-labour income in the economy. Normalizing by this maximum value, we can always define *z* to be in [0, 1].

$a = \theta$. We are assuming, therefore, that when it comes to child labour, households utilize it only after adult labour is exhausted. The determination of the amount of child labour in a household is obtained through the maximization of (1) by a choice of c. The amount of child labour c_z^*, in household type z, is given by,

$$c_z^* = \max\left\{\min\left[(1-\theta), \left(\frac{1}{\beta} - \frac{\theta w_a}{w_c} - \frac{z}{w_c}\right)\right], 0\right\} \quad \text{...(2)}$$

Equation (2) follows directly from the necessary condition for an interior maximum of (1) and that, the maximum and minimum amounts of child labour are (1-θ) and zero, respectively. In Basu and Van (1998), the decision regarding child labour was a zero-one choice. Here, in addition, we are solving for the actual amount of child labour.

Define

$$z_h \equiv \min\left\{\max\left[\frac{w_c}{\beta} - \theta w_a, 0\right], 1\right\} \quad \text{...(3)}$$

$$z_l \equiv \min\left\{\max\left[\frac{w_c}{\beta} - \theta w_a - (1-\theta) w_c, 0\right], 1\right\} \quad \text{...(4)}$$

Since adult (child) labour is homogeneous and receives the same wage, and since all households determine the amount of c in the same way, we can describe the incidence of child labour by the household's non-labour income, which, in our model, is the only thing that distinguishes one household from another. Thus, z_h is the threshold non-labour income, above which all households have zero child labour. z_h is obtained by setting c_z^* to zero, and observing that c_z^* continues to be zero for all households with $z \geq z_h$. Similarly, $c_z^* = 1-\theta$ for all $z \leq z_l$. Our first Proposition is a formal statement of these points.

Proposition 1: $c_z^* = 0$ for all $z \geq z_h$, $c_z^* = 1-\theta$ for all $z \leq z_l$, and

$$c_z^* = \frac{1}{\beta} - \frac{\theta w_a}{w_c} - \frac{z}{w_c}$$

for $z_l < z < z_h$.

The value of z_h is the threshold non-labour household income above which children do not work and below which, children work at least some part of their time. This may suggest that as soon as one knows the non-labour income distribution, one will be able to identify the households with working children. However, observe that this threshold is a function of not only observables like the wage rates, but also of unobservables like β. On the other hand, if we can empirically identify the threshold, then we can infer the marginal loss to household utility when children go out to work.

Proposition 1 allows us to derive the aggregate supply of child labour, $C^s(w_a, w_c)$, given w_a and w_c as,

$$C^s(w_a, w_c) = \int_0^{z_l}(1-\theta)dG(z) + \int_{z_l}^{z_h}\left[\frac{1}{\beta} - \frac{\theta w_a}{w_c} - \frac{z}{w_c}\right]dG(z)$$

Using A.1, this reduces to

$$C^s(.) = \begin{cases} (1-\theta)w_c\left[\frac{1}{\beta} - \theta\frac{w_a}{w_c} - \frac{1-\theta}{2}\right] & \text{if } 0 < z_l < z_h < 1 \\ 1-\theta & \text{if } z_l = 1 \\ 0 & \text{if } z_h = 0 \end{cases} \quad ...(5)$$

Demand for Child Labour

There are many small and identical producers who are perfectly competitive in both the labour and product markets. The aggregate production relation, *Q*, is given by

$$Q = Kf(\gamma A + C) \quad ...(6)$$

where *A* is the aggregate adult labour time, *C* is the total child labour time, *K* is the amount of capital, $\gamma \geq 1$ and is the extent to which adult labour time is more productive than an equivalent amount of child labour time. There are two things worth noting while interpreting this aggregate function. First, γ can be thought of as all productivity factors embodied in adult labour, like skill, human capital, etc., while *K* represents all disembodied, complementary (to labour) factors, like physical capital. If we assume that child labour is unskilled or, only adult labour possesses human capital, then $\gamma > 1$. Also, while physical capital improves the productivity of both adults and children, human capital embodied in adults improves only their productivity.

A.2: $f'(.) > 0, f''(.) < 0$, and $\left[1+\frac{f''(.)\gamma A}{f'(.)}\right] > 0.$

Define $Q_{jk} \equiv (\partial^2 Q / \partial j \partial k), j, k = A, C, \gamma, K$. It immediately follows from A.2 that the marginal productivity of both adult and child labour are positive but diminishing. Also, $Q_{A\gamma} > 0$ and $Q_{C\gamma} < 0$. In other words, while γ increases the marginal productivity of adult labour, it has the opposite effect on child labour. To see why this is happening, define effective labour time $L = \gamma A + C$. Given $f''(.) < 0$, it implies that the marginal productivity of L is declining in L. L can increase if any one of γ, A, or C increases. So, all three will have a negative effect on $f'(.)$. What A.2 ensures is that the direct effect of γ on adult labour productivity at the margin is positive and outweighs the negative effect of the diminishing marginal productivity. There is no such direct effect of γ on child labour and the indirect effect is negative.

Let the product price be unity. Profit maximization with both adult and child labour being used implies the following necessary conditions:

$$Q_A \equiv \frac{\partial Q}{\partial A} = K\gamma f'(.) = w_a \qquad ...(7)$$

$$Q_C \equiv \frac{\partial Q}{\partial C} = Kf'(.) = w_c \qquad ...(8)$$

From equations (7) and (8) we know that

$$w_a = \gamma w_c = \gamma K f'(.). \qquad ...(9)$$

For the rest of the paper we assume an equilibrium with positive amounts of child labour, *i.e.*, equations (7), (8) and (9) hold.

Model Results

In this section we investigate how z_h, w_c, w_a, and the amount of child labour is affected, in equilibrium, by changes in the various parameters we have used in our model. In particular, we want to check the effect on child labour of K and γ. An equilibrium is denoted by the vector $(A^*, C^*, w_a^*, w_c^*, z_h^*, z_l^*)$, where the superscript * denotes an equilibrium value. It is also easy to see that if $C^* > 0, A^* = \theta$, i.e., children work only after all adults have been hired.

Proposition 2: Suppose we have an initial equilibrium with $0 < C^* < 1 - \theta$ and $A^* = \theta$, which imply that $w_a^* = \gamma w_c^*$ and $0 \leq z_l^* < z_h^* < 1$. Then,

$$\frac{\partial w_a^*}{\partial K} > 0, \frac{\partial w_c^*}{\partial K} > 0, \frac{\partial z_h^*}{\partial K} > 0, \frac{\partial C^*}{\partial K} > 0 \text{ and } \frac{\partial w_a^*}{\partial \gamma} > 0, \frac{\partial w_c^*}{\partial \gamma} \gtrless 0, \frac{\partial z_h^*}{\partial \gamma} \gtrless 0, \frac{\partial C^*}{\partial \gamma} < 0$$

Proof: See Appendix.

Both *K* and γ have a positive effect on adult wages. However, the effect of the increase in adult productivity on child wages is ambiguous. As adult productivity goes up, adult wages go up, implying less pressure to send children to work. This reduces the supply of child labour. On the other hand, employers have less need for child workers as effective adult labour is higher and the marginal productivity of total labour is diminishing. Thus, there are two opposite effects on child wage — lower supply tending to increase wage, and lower demand tending to reduce it. The aggregate effect, therefore, is ambiguous.

An important result is that, γ and *K* have opposite effects on the incidence of child labour. As mentioned before, one can interpret γ as adult skill and *K* as disembodied physical capital. Our Proposition states that improved adult skill reduces child labour while increased physical capital, being complementary to labour, increases child labour. Urban areas have more physical infrastructure than rural areas, suggesting that the incidence of urban child labour should be higher than that of rural child labour. On the other hand, labour in cities tends to be better educated as compared to their rural counterparts (Dubey, Gangopadhyay, Wadhwa, 2001) and this should have a dampening effect on urban child labour. The next proposition shows that it is possible to find combinations of simultaneous increases in γ and *K* which lead to an increase in z_h^* and a *fall* in C^*. That is, while the total incidence of child labour goes down, *comparatively richer* households, whose children did not work before, now send their children to work. This happens essentially because the absolute productivity of child labour (w_c^*) increases, i.e., the increase in *K* dominates the impact on a child's marginal productivity due to an increased γ.

Proposition 3: Let K_0 and γ_0 be the initial values of K and γ, respectively. Suppose we have an initial equilibrium with $0 < C^* < 1 - \theta$, $A^* = \theta$, which implies that $w_a^* = \gamma w_c^*$ and $0 \leq z_l^* < z_h^* < 1$. Now suppose that both K and γ change from their initial values, such that $dK = \eta$ and $d\gamma = \varepsilon$ with

$$\frac{\eta}{\varepsilon} = (-)\frac{K\theta[f''(.)M - f'(.)]}{f'(.)M}$$

where

$$M = \frac{1}{\beta} - \theta\gamma - \frac{1-\theta}{2}$$

and all the functions are evaluated at the initial values. Then $dC^* = 0$ and $dz_h^* > 0$, where dC^* and dz_h^* measure the combined effects of the changes in K and γ.

Proof: See Appendix.

This Proposition has some important implications. We have already argued that the nature of the incidence of child labour is different for rural and urban areas. In most developing countries, urban areas are better served by economic infrastructure compared to rural areas, urbanites are better educated than their rural counterparts and there is greater awareness in the cities regarding child labour. These factors create different effects on child labour and may explain the reasons why there may exist vast differences in the rural and urban incidence of child labour. While it is difficult to measure the actual amounts of *K* and γ, Proposition 3 suggests that increases in both γ and *K* can lead to a lower incidence of child labour. On the other hand, the same changes can also lead to relatively richer households, who were initially not sending their children to work, to now do so.

Recall that z_h was the threshold above which no household sent their children to work. This Proposition tells us that observing this threshold is not sufficient to infer about the quantity of child labour in the aggregate. It is perfectly possible for a higher threshold level to be associated with a lower aggregate amount of child labour. This implies that it is not enough to count whether children are working but more important to know whether their working time reduces their ability to do other things, like attending school, for instance.

Empirical Results

At the very outset, we need to make a point regarding the correspondence between the theoretical model and the empirical analysis that we now set out to do. In the previous two sections, the total amount of child labour in each household was equal to 1–θ. We did not say anything regarding the number of children in the household. Thus, when the incidence of child labour in a household is positive but less than 1–θ, one interpretation is that not all children of that household are working. It is possible that in one situation a greater number of households have working children compared to another situation, but the total amount of child labour is lower in the first case. This is because in the second case, a larger number of children per household are working, albeit in a smaller number of households. It is instructive to keep this interpretation in mind when evaluating the empirical results. Indeed, the data set we are using does not allow us to completely determine the hours worked by a child. Moreover, in many households, there are both working and non-working children.

Recall that our model rests on two basic assumptions. First, the child is not a decision maker in the household — the head of the household takes all the decisions. Given the data we are using, the household head is mostly a parent of the children in the household. Our second building block is that all parents (heads of households) are altruistic towards their children (β > 0 in the model). Thus, whether or not the child works can be modeled as a function of the child's household characteristics. From the theory, the incidence of child labour can be linked to three parameters of interest, *K*, γ and β. *K* is capital, or more generally, a proxy for all factors that are complementary to labour. *K* can also be interpreted as infrastructure, or technological parameters that increase the output, *ceteris paribus*, from a given amount of labour. This interpretation is helpful in understanding the differences in the incidence of child labour in the rural and urban sectors. In most developing countries, urban areas are better served by economic infrastructure compared to rural areas. According to our model, this actually *increases* child labour (Proposition 2). However, the data suggests otherwise, as the incidence of urban child labour is lower than in rural India.

The apparent anomaly can be explained through the difference in (marginal) productivity of adult labour in the two sectors, γ. Dubey, Gangopadhyay and Wadhwa (2001) demonstrate that adult labour in urban India seems to be more productive than similar labour in rural areas. Sviekauskas (1975) gives a possible explanation for such a phenomenon to be generally true in developing countries. We account for these factors by considering the rural and urban sectors separately in the empirical analysis.

In addition to physical capital and infrastructure, labour productivity can also be affected by human capital. Assuming that child labour is unskilled to begin with and children can acquire only limited skills on the job, human capital has to be associated with adult labour. However, it is difficult to directly measure the levels of human capital. One thing is obvious, though; as adults become more skilled, the gap between adult labour productivity and child labour productivity will increase. Theoretically, this is captured by higher values of γ.

We use education to be a determinant of productivity. In particular, we look at the degree of educational qualification of the head of the household (CGEDUHD). Higher is the education of the head, the greater is his or her income earning capability and, therefore, lower is the need to send the child to the workplace. About 10 per cent of all households surveyed had women as heads of households. Many of the women heads, educated or not, were not employed or involved in any income earning activities. Consequently, we do not consider women headed households in our analysis.

In addition to the education of the head, we also consider the education of the spouse (CGEDUSP). Existing literature suggests that an educated mother brings up educated children. While a father spends most of his time working outside the house, a mother, by virtue of spending greater amounts of time at home, has a bigger impact on the child's development. Consequently, the mother's education has a larger impact on the children. In our sample, less than 0.5 per cent of the children belong to households where the head has no spouse. Moreover, a similar small proportion of households have female heads with a live-in male spouse. Both these types were dropped from the sample. Consequently, when we are using the spouse's education as an explanatory variable, we are, indeed, correcting for the education of the female spouse.

The educational levels of the parents can be thought of as a proxy for the parameter β in our model. In general, better-educated parents will have a preference for sending their children to school rather than to the work place. Human capital of parents apart from improving the parents' productivity, γ, and, thus, reducing child labour directly, also improves the general awareness of the parents about the advantages of educating children.

Table 2 presents some interesting statistics regarding the relationship between the mother's (spouse of the head, more technically) education and the work status of the child. As the education of the spouse increases, the proportion of working children decreases. For instance, 7.85 per cent of all children with illiterate mothers were working. This figure falls to 1.21 per cent for mothers who have a high school degree. The education of the head also results in lower proportion of working children.

Table 2

Percentage of Working Children by Parents' Education

	All India	*Rural*	*Urban*
CGEDUSP			
Illiterate	7.85	8.45	4.34
Up to Primary	3.05	3.32	2.48
Up to High School	1.21	1.73	0.78
Graduate and above	1.33	0.54	1.42
CGEDUHD			
Illiterate	9.53	10.03	5.84
Up to Primary	5.38	5.81	3.74
Up to High School	2.26	2.90	1.25
Graduate and above	1.09	1.61	0.83

Notes: CGEDUSP : Education of the spouse
CGEDUHD : Education of the head of the household

Our basic hypothesis is that parents are altruistic. We have also suggested that educated mothers will be more inclined to send their children to school. If both of these are correct, then one expects that mothers will themselves work to add to household income, if necessary, rather than send their children to work. And, even if the household is poor, an educated spouse will be less willing to send her children to work. Observe that our hypotheses do not imply that the incidence of working children will be lower in households with working mothers. All that it says is that, the spouse will be more inclined to work, before the child is sent out to work. It is, therefore, consistent with the observation of a lower incidence of working children belonging to households where the spouse decides not to work. Table 3 combines the education of the spouse and her work status, with the incidence of working children in the household. Across the board, the proportion of working children is higher for working mothers, compared to those outside the labour force, in each education category. And, of course, the proportion of working children goes down with the mother's education. For instance, 11.8 per cent of all children with illiterate working mothers were also working. This figure falls to less than 2 per cent for graduate working mothers. These figures tie up with our underlying hypothesis that parents are altruistic. If able-bodied, but non-working, adults are available in the household, it is unlikely that altruistic parents will send their children to work.

Table 3

Percentage of Working Children by Mother's Work Status

	All India	*Rural*	*Urban*
Working Mothers			
Illiterate	11.78	12.23	7.31
Up to Primary	5.91	5.63	7.11
Up to High School	2.06	2.56	1.16
Graduate and above	1.77	1.32	1.83
Non Working Mothers			
Illiterate	5.50	5.98	3.50
Up to Primary	2.20	2.45	1.76
Up to High School	1.06	1.51	0.75
Graduate and above	1.16	0.18	1.26

In our theoretical model, as in Basu and Van (1998), children work in order to augment household resources. Our data also point in this direction — as many as 70 per cent of the urban working children do so in order to supplement household income. Therefore, an important determinant of the probability of a child working would be the economic status of the household the child belongs to. In terms of our model, there is no child labour in households with non-labour income in excess of z_h. However, we do not have income data for the households in our dataset. Therefore, we have to work with the household's average per capita total expenditure (PCTE). A household is classified as being poor if the per capita consumption of the household is below the poverty line. Thus, a natural cutoff to consider as a proxy for z_h is the poverty line. However, economic distress is determined within the household. Therefore, while economic distress may be perceived in one household at the poverty line, another household may perceive it well before consumption falls below the official poverty line. In what follows, we investigate whether or not there is such a threshold, and in particular, how it is related to the poverty line. To do this, we employ a variety of dummy variables. We divide the PCTE below the official poverty line into four quarters. Thus, DQ1PLINE is equal to one for a household whose PCTE is less than one-fourth the poverty line. Similarly, DQ2PLINE is a dummy variable for households whose PCTE is half the poverty line, while DQ5PLINE corresponds to PCTE which is 25 per cent more than the poverty line.

Finally, we control for two other household characteristics in our model estimation: the household size (HHS) and the ratio of dependent adults to total adults in the household (DEPAD). Since, our premise is that parents are altruistic we expect both these variables to have a negative effect on the probability of child labour. The larger is the household size, the greater is the number of individuals capable of augmenting household income and, thus, reducing the need for sending children to work. Similarly, if there were dependent adults in the household, the decision-maker in the household would put these individuals to work before sending the children out to work.

To sum up, we model the probability of a child (defined as an individual in the age group of 5 to 14 years) working as a function of

- Economic status of the household (DQxPLINE, x=1,2,3,..)
- Education of the head of the household (CGEDUHD)
- Education of the spouse (CGEDUSP)
- Number of dependent adults in the household (DEPAD)
- Household size (HHS)

The dependent variable (DCWKG) is binary, and is equal to one if the child is working.

Rural Sector

The estimation results for the rural sector are presented in Table 4. We report marginal effects of each of the independent variables (evaluated at the mean). The reported z statistic and associated probability are for the underlying coefficient, however. The first thing to note is that the critical level of consumption, below which the child goes to work, is DQ2PLINE. DQ2PLINE differentiates between households whose PCTE is below a level that is half the poverty line. Higher consumption thresholds like the poverty line and DQ3PLINE turned out to be insignificant determinants of the probability of a child working. What this means is that the average PCTE of the household has to fall below half the poverty line before the poverty status has a significant effect on the probability of children in that household working. This reinforces our basic presumption that parents are altruistic. If they can avoid sending a child to work they will. On the other hand, it also suggests that poverty status alone may not be able to explain why children work. As we have already observed, children from rural APL households also work.

Table 4

Probit Results for the Rural Sector

	Dependent Variable: DCWKG			
Explanatory Variable	*dF/dx*	*Standard Error*	*z*	*P > |z|*
DQ2PLINE	0.010	0.005	2.18	0.03
HHS	0.002	3.0E-04	–6.31	0.00
CGEDUHD	–0.009	6.7E-04	–13.61	0.00
CGEDUSP	–0.011	0.001	–10.42	0.00
DEPAD	–0.077	0.003	–22.87	0.00
Sample				73002

Notes: DCWKG: Binary variable that takes a value of one if the child is working and zero otherwise.

DQ2PLINE: Binary variable that takes a value of one if the household's consumption expenditure is less than half the poverty line and zero otherwise.

HHS: Household size.

CGEDUHD: Education of the head of the household.

CGEDUSP: Education of the spouse.

DEPAD: Number of dependent adults in the household.

The education of both the head of the household and his spouse have a negative and significant effect on the probability of the child working. This is an interesting result since the education of the mother is a significant determinant of child labour even while controlling for the education of the father. This reinforces our hypothesis that the mother plays a significant role in deciding whether her children go to the workplace or to school. An educated mother realizes the value of education and encourages her children to go to school. Further, if the household is in dire straits and additional income is needed, an educated spouse is likely to enter the labour market before she allows her children to do so. This is because the probability of her finding a job is higher than that of her relatively less trained children. Thus, apart from the altruistic motive of parents, it could also be the case that more educated parents prefer to send their children to school because the parents are in a better position monetarily to support the household.

As expected the coefficients of HHS and DEPAD are negative and statistically significant. More individuals or dependent adults in the household lower the probability of children in that household working. This once again confirms our hypothesis that parents are altruistic.

Urban Sector

Table 5 presents the estimation results for the urban sector. The results obtained are different from those for the rural sector in three important aspects.

First, the economic status of households in the urban sector affects the probability of child labour even before the household falls below the poverty line. We find that the binary variable DQ5PLINE, which classifies households as being below (per capita) expenditure levels 1.25 times the official poverty line, is significantly and positively related to the probability of a child working. Coefficients of higher consumption thresholds were insignificantly different from zero.

If economic distress affects the incidence of child labour in the household, then what determines economic distress is different in the urban sector from that in the rural sector. Taking the poverty line as the standard of comparison, the perception of economic distress appears at higher levels of per capita household consumption in the urban areas. One argument could be that the urban poverty line is underestimated and the rural overestimated. Or, one could argue that, the urban sector has more job opportunities than the rural sector. Hence, *ceteris paribus*, economically distressed households can rise above poverty levels by sending children to work, something that is more difficult in the rural sector.

Table 5

Probit Results for the Urban Sector

	Dependent Variable: DCWKG			
Explanatory Variable	*dF/dx*	*Standard Error*	*z*	*P > |z|*
DQ5PLINE	0.003	0.002	2.06	0.04
HHS	–6.3E-05	3.1E-04	–0.21	0.84
CGEDUHD	–0.005	5.0E-04	–10.27	0.00
CGEDUSP	–0.003	5.8E-04	–4.46	0.00
DEPAD	–0.038	0.003	–12.84	0.00
Sample				39892

Notes: DCWKG: Binary variable that takes a value of one if the child is working and zero otherwise.

DQ5PLINE: Binary variable that takes a value of one if the household's consumption expenditure is less than 1.25 times the poverty line and zero otherwise.

HHS: Household size.

CGEDUHD: Education of the head of the household.

CGEDUSP: Education of the spouse.

DEPAD: Number of dependent adults in the household.

Second, if we compare the magnitude of the marginal effects of the head of the household's education and that of the spouse, we find that the coefficient of the spouse's education is about half of the head's coefficient. In the rural sector the two coefficients were approximately equal (Table 4). In other words, in the urban sector, the head's education has a much larger effect on preventing child labour than the education of his spouse. One immediate explanation is that *ceteris paribus,* an educated urban male has a higher productivity than the similarly educated rural male (Gangopadhyay and Wadhwa, 2001). Higher productivity implies higher income and a lower likelihood of sending children to work. The spouse's education, therefore, has a lower additional effect.

Another explanation could be that the urban male prefers an educated spouse. Therefore, correcting for the male head's education is sufficient information about the spouse's education. Consequently, once we correct for the head's education, the spouse's education has a small additional effect. In the rural sector, an educated man may be married to either an educated woman or an illiterate one. In other words, in the rural sector, the level of education of the male head may not be related to that of his spouse. On the other hand, should the spouse also be educated, the children are more likely to be sent to school.

Table 6 gives the spouse's education level by the education of the head. For instance, more than 32 per cent of graduate urban heads have spouses with a graduate degree as well. In rural India, on the other hand, the corresponding figure is less than 6 per cent. If we look at the same category of heads, but now consider those among them who have spouses with at least a middle school degree, the difference between the rural and urban sectors continues to be large. In the rural sector it is around 54 per cent (48.3 + 5.6) and in the urban sector it is 82 per cent.

Table 6

Distribution of the Head's Education by Spouse's Education, %

	CGEDUHD			
CGEDUSP	*Illiterate*	*≤ Primary*	*≤ High School*	*≥ Graduate*
Rural				
Illiterate	96.32	71.53	46.41	21.93
Up to Primary	3.25	25.96	29.58	24.18
Up to High School	0.41	2.51	23.69	48.31
Graduate and above	0.02	0.00	0.31	5.58
Urban				
Illiterate	90.05	55.96	26.84	6.12
Up to Primary	7.63	35.34	29.12	11.90
Up to High School	2.31	8.63	41.26	49.71
Graduate and above	0.02	0.07	2.78	32.28

Notes: CGEDUSP: Education of the spouse.
CGEDUHD: Education of the head of the household.

Third, in the urban sector, the household size is not a significant determinant of the probability of child labour. The rationale for including this variable was that a larger household size would tend to reduce the probability of a child seeking work since there would be more members to contribute to the household kitty. Urban households tend to be smaller than rural households. Consequently, DEPAD is a sufficient statistic for explaining the incidence of child labour, in the urban sector.

Conclusion

This paper extends the paper by Basu and Van (1998) to allow for different households having different incidence of child labour even when they face similar labour market conditions. It also enables us to explain why different sectors within the same economy have differing amounts of child labour in the aggregate. These theoretical extensions allow us to empirically test certain important hypotheses about child labour. We do so using Indian household data.

Our major finding is that the hypothesis that poor children work is too simplistic. We show that while poor rural families above a certain threshold consumption do not send their children to work, in urban families this threshold is much higher and, indeed, well above the poverty line. Our theoretical model gives an explanation for this phenomenon. Greater availability and use of factors complementary to labour increase the demand and use of child labour. On the other hand, improvement in adult productivity alone reduces the aggregate use of child labour. We argue that urban areas, compared to rural, have more of both types of factors. The empirical results support our theoretical conclusions.

Another finding is that mother's education has a significant positive impact on reducing child labour. This coupled with the fact that increased adult productivity, with no improvement in child productivity, reduces child labour, highlights the importance of education and skill generation among parents to control the use of children in the workforce.

References

Altonji, Joseph G., Hayashi, Fumio and Kotlikoff, Laurence J. (1997). "Parental Altruism and Inter Vivos Transfers: Theory and Evidence." *Journal of Political Economy*, December 1997, 105(6), 1121-66.

Basu, Kaushik and Van, Pham Hoang. (1998). "The Economics of Child Labor." *American Economic Review*, June 1998, 88(3), 412-27.

Behrman, J., Taubman, P. and Wales, T. (1977). "Controlling for and measuring the effects of genetics and family environment in equations for schooling and labor market success," in P. Taubman , ed., *Kinometrics: the Determinants of Socioeconomic Success within and between Families*. Amsterdam: North Holland, 35-96.

Behrman, J., Rosenzweig, R. and Taubman, P. (1994). "Endowments and the Allocation of Schooloing in the Family and in the Marriage Market: The Twins Experiment. *Journal of Political Economy*, December 1994, 102(6), 1131-74.

Caiumi, Antonella and Perali, Federico. (1997). "Female Labor Force Participation: A Comparison between Urban and Rural Families." *American Journal of Agricultural Economics*, May 1997, 79(2), pp. 595-601.

Dubey, Amaresh and Gangopadhyay, Shubhashis. (1998). *Counting the Poor: Where are the Poor in India?* Delhi: Sarvekshana Analytical Series, volume 1, CSO.

Dubey, Amaresh, Gangopadhyay, Shubhashis and Wadhwa, Wilima. (1999). "Female-Headed Households in India: Incidence, Poverty and Socioeconomic Characteristics." Mimeo, Indian Statistical Institute.

————. (2001). "Occupational Structure and Incidence of Poverty in Indian Towns of Different Sizes." *Review of Development Economics*, February 2001, 5(1), 49-59.

Gangopadhyay, Shubhashis and Wadhwa, Wilima. (1999). "Employment and Poverty," A Report for the International Labor Organization.

Grootaert, Christiaan and Kanbur, Ravi. (1995). "Child Labour: An Economic Perspective." *International Labour Review*, March-April 1995, 134(2), 187-203.

Miller, Paul, Mulvey, Charles and Martin, Nick. (1997). "Evidence on Gender Differences from a Sample of Australian Twins." *Economica*, February 1997, 64(253), 119-36.

Sviekauskas, Leo. (1975). "The Productivity of Cities." *Quarterly Journal of Economics*, August 1975, 89(3), 393-413.

Weiner, Myron. (1991). *The Child and the State in India: Child Labor and Education Policy in Comparative Perspective*. Princeton, NJ: Princeton University Press.

Appendix

First, maximize $V_z = V(a,c;z) = \ln(aw_a + cw_c + z) + \beta(1-\theta-c)$ subject to (a) $c \geq 0$ and (b) $c \leq (1-\theta)$.

If λ_a, λ_b are the Lagrange multipliers for the constraints (a) and (b), respectively, we get

$$\frac{1}{aw_a + cw_c + z} w_c - \beta + \lambda_a - \lambda_b = 0, \text{ where } \lambda_a, \lambda_b \geq 0.$$

If we have an interior solution, then both $\lambda_a, \lambda_b = 0$ and we have $c_z^* = \frac{1}{\beta} - \frac{aw_a}{w_c} - \frac{z}{w_c}$. If $\lambda_a > 0$, then $\lambda_b = 0$ and we have $c_z^* = 0$; if the opposite, we have $c_z^* = (1-\theta)$. This gives us equation (2) of the text.

Proof of Proposition 2:

Consider the following four first order conditions for a unique interior equilibrium. Since we are using the superscript '*' to denote equilibrium values, the variable values in these equations should be starred. However, we suppress them for ease in notation.

$$C = \left[\frac{1}{\beta} - \theta\frac{w_a}{w_c} - \frac{1-\theta}{2}\right](1-\theta)w_c \qquad \text{...(a1)}$$

$$z_h = \frac{w_c}{\beta} - \theta w_a \qquad \text{...(a2)}$$

$$w_a = \gamma K f'(\gamma\theta + C) \qquad \text{...(a3)}$$

$$w_c = K f'(\gamma\theta + C) \qquad \text{...(a4)}$$

(a1) is the same as equation (5) in the text, excepting that we are using C to represent both the supply and demand for child labour as they are equal in equilibrium and, the fact that the solution is interior, i.e., $0 < z_l < z_h < 1$. (a2) is equation (3) in the text given the range of values of z. (a3) and (a4) follow from equations (7) and (8) and the fact that for positive amounts of child labour, adult labour must be fully exhausted. This implies that the aggregate amount of adult labour is θ.

Totally differentiating the equations (a1)-(a4) around the equilibrium, we get

$$\begin{bmatrix} 1 & \theta(1-\theta) & (1-\theta)[\frac{1-\theta}{2}-\frac{1}{\beta}] & 0 \\ 0 & \theta & -\frac{1}{\beta} & 1 \\ -\gamma K f''(.) & 1 & 0 & 0 \\ -Kf''(.) & 0 & 1 & 0 \end{bmatrix} \begin{bmatrix} dC \\ dw_a \\ dw_c \\ dz_h \end{bmatrix}$$

$$= \begin{bmatrix} 0 & 0 \\ 0 & 0 \\ \gamma f'(.) & K[f'(.)+\gamma\theta f''(.)] \\ f'(.) & K\theta f''(.) \end{bmatrix} \begin{bmatrix} dK \\ d\gamma \end{bmatrix} \qquad \ldots(a5)$$

Let the first matrix on the left hand side of (a5) be denoted D. Then,

$$|D| = 1 - Kf''(.)(1-\theta)\left[\frac{1}{\beta} - \gamma\theta - \frac{1-\theta}{2}\right] > 0,$$

given A.2 and the fact that the solution is interior. The interior solution implies c>0. Hence, using (a1) and observing that (a3) and (a4) imply that $\gamma = (w_a / w_c)$, we get $|D|>0$.

We can now solve for the changes in equilibrium values with respect to K and γ.

$$\begin{bmatrix} \frac{dC}{dK} \\ \frac{dw_a}{dK} \\ \frac{dw_c}{dK} \\ \frac{dz_h}{dK} \end{bmatrix} = \frac{1}{|D|} \begin{bmatrix} f'(.)(1-\theta)\left[\frac{1}{\beta} - \gamma\theta - \frac{1-\theta}{2}\right] \\ \gamma f'(.) \\ f'(.) \\ f'(.)\left[\frac{1}{\beta} - \gamma\theta\right] \end{bmatrix}$$

$$\begin{bmatrix} \dfrac{dC}{d\gamma} \\ \dfrac{dw_a}{d\gamma} \\ \dfrac{dw_c}{d\gamma} \\ \dfrac{dz_h}{d\gamma} \end{bmatrix} = \frac{1}{|D|} \begin{bmatrix} -Kf'(.)\theta(1-\theta)+Kf''(.)\theta(1-\theta)\left[\dfrac{1}{\beta}-\gamma\theta-\dfrac{1-\theta}{2}\right] \\ -K^2f'(.)f''(.)(1-\theta)\left[\dfrac{1}{\beta}-\dfrac{1-\theta}{2}\right]+K[f'(.)+\gamma\theta f''(.)] \\ Kf''(.)\theta[1-(1-\theta)Kf'(.)] \\ -K\theta\left[f'(.)\left(1+\dfrac{\gamma\theta f''(.)}{f'(.)}\right)-f''(.)\left(\dfrac{1}{\beta}-Kf'(.)\dfrac{(1-\theta)^2}{2}\right)\right] \end{bmatrix}$$

The signs of the changes in equilibrium values, given in the Proposition follow from:

(a) an interior solution, implying that $C>0,\ 0<z_l<z_h<1$;

(b) since C>0, the amount of adult labour is θ and,

(c) A.2 holds

Proof of Proposition 3:

Write

$$C^* = \left(\frac{1}{\beta}-\gamma\theta-\frac{1-\theta}{2}\right)(1-\theta)w_c^*$$

Knowing that the equilibrium values depend on K and γ, we can write

$$C^* = \phi(K,\gamma) \Rightarrow dC^* = \phi_K dK + \phi_\gamma d\gamma$$

where, $\phi_j \equiv \dfrac{\delta\phi}{\delta j}$, $j=K,\gamma$. From Proposition 2,

$$\phi_K = \frac{f'(.)(1-\theta)M}{1-Kf''(.)(1-\theta)M} \text{ and } \phi_\gamma = \frac{-K\theta(1-\theta)[f'(.)-f''(.)M]}{1-Kf''(.)(1-\theta)M}.$$

For $dC^*=0$, we must have

$$\phi_K dK + \phi_\gamma d\gamma = 0 \Rightarrow \phi_K\eta + \phi_\gamma\varepsilon = 0 \Rightarrow \frac{\eta}{\varepsilon} = \frac{-\phi_\gamma}{\phi_K}$$

Plugging in the values of ϕ_K and ϕ_γ, we get the relationship between η and ε. Observe that both η and ε have the same sign.

Thus, if K goes up, and γ goes up by a corresponding amount, the total amount of child labour stays the same.

To show that z_h goes up, we write

$$z_h^* = \varphi(K,\gamma) \Rightarrow dz_h^* = \varphi_K \eta + \varphi_\gamma \varepsilon$$

Plugging in the values of $\frac{dz_h}{dK}$ for φ_K and $\frac{dz_h}{d\gamma}$ for ϕ_γ from Proposition 2, we get

$$dz_h = \frac{Kf'(.)\theta \frac{1-\theta}{2}[1 - Kf''(.)(1-\theta)M]}{M|D|}\varepsilon > 0\,.$$

14

Organic Farming – Sustainable Step Towards Food Safety, Production and Consumption

SUGATA GHOSH

Introduction

Food is the single most important component for the determination of human well-being as it is the supplier energy for life support to the human body. At the same time, food is a highly sensitive political issue. It is also a public health issue, a key determinant of whether humans achieve health or ill-health. Food is however also a commodity that can be traded, driving and being driven by national and international trade policies. In this last sense it is different from other commodities and manufactured products in that it has an 'organic' or natural base that distinguishes it economically, environmentally, and culturally from other products. Its biological role in human health also sets it apart from other commodities.

The world has definitely come a long way so far as feeding the population is concerned. Food production of the world has increased at a slightly higher rate than the rate of population growth since 1950. The cultivators across the globe produced three times as much grain output in the 90s as they did in the 50s. The per capita food production index of the world increased by almost 24 per cent between 1989-91 and 1997. The daily per capita calorie supply has gone up from 2336 calories in 1970 to 2751 calories in 1996. However, the distribution of food production and land productivity has been very uneven across different regions. Persistence of hunger in the world in recent times is not due to the limits of capacity of the ecosystems to produce food, but due to the distribution process.

The current food system has led to a situation where enough food is being produced to feed the world despite population growth. Yet in 1994-96, 19 per cent of developing countries' population was under-nourished. According to the FAO, around 800 people suffer from chronic food security in the world [FAO 1999]. Although the relative proportion of the under-nourished shrank significantly over the past 30 years, the absolute number of hungry people decreased only slightly – in some parts of the world in recent times even increasing. The rapid rate of population growth only aggravates the problem. The medium variant projections of the UN state that the global population will increase from 6 billion today to 7.5 billion by 2020, and a majority of the increase will occur in the low and middle-income countries with a concomitant rise in food requirements. Moreover, the developing world with a growth rate of over 4 per cent in per capita income will add to the demand for food, both in terms of quantity and quality. It is estimated that the global food demand will increase by almost 75 per cent by the next generation. In a study of soil and climate for 117 countries across Africa, Asia, and Latin America, it was estimated that only 19 countries with an approximate population of 109 million would not be able to feed their expected population during the early 21st century from their own land. This is despite the fact that they could use every hectare of their useful land and get the highest technically possible yield. According to the study, the total food output of the 117 countries could be multiplied by 16 times, provided there is no soil erosion, all cultivable land is used for agriculture, conditions of elastic supply of agricultural inputs, perfect weather and idealized management prevail.

However, the key features of the modern-day food economy include:

- Rapid economic concentration in all the food sectors, both through organic growth and mergers and acquisition within and cross border;
- Fragmentation of markets and a seemingly endless pursuit of new niche markets;
- Comparatively rapid and commercially driven changes in diet and taste;
- Ceaseless pursuit of quality control via supply chain management;
- Intensification both on and off the land, designed to get land and capital to yield more;

- Transformation of foods and food processes across sectors, not just the nature of farming and storage but also of cooking;
- Growth of size and influence of the distributors and retailers within the food system, representing a transition from the producer to retail power;
- Ideological tension over the state's role, both over responsibilities of law enforcement and for education of the public on food matters;
- Difficulty in managing the consumer body politic, with a growth of consumerism threatening predictability of dominant forces within the food system;
- Promotion of brands as a response to the consumer desire for certainty;
- Ever more sophisticated use of the 'consciousness' industries such as advertising, marketing, and product placement and sponsorship to increase the brand value;
- New inequalities within and between countries creating modern forms of food poverty even in rich countries;
- Centralization of decision-making nationally, regionally, and internationally, with tensions amongst all levels.

While most of the food eaten today is still nationally or regionally produced, already, there is a tendency for food exports to rise. This tendency is being accelerated by high degrees of concentration in national home markets, a process that encourages regionalization rather than globalization. This also encourages the emergence of 'core and cluster' economic patterns that are financial pressure to expand. They have three major choices:

(a) Further internationalization

(b) Vertical integration

(c) Entry into new sectors

The food sector is experiencing all the three strategies; experiencing gigantic mergers and acquisitions. Consequently, it is not surprising that world politics and governance are increasingly being challenged by one major issue – the ability to provide safe and adequate food to its population - the issue of food security.

To ensure a certain level of food security, there is a need to understand the food needs, and the importance of maintaining the integrity of natural ecosystems while answering those needs. This ensures that food can be made available in a safe and sustained manner. Any policy or strategy for food production and consumption must address these issues. Given the present situation where the natural resources are being exploited to the brink, the highly degraded state of the environment and the fast changing quality of life, the discussion on food and nutrition should atleast try to address the following issues:

(a) What are the needs that we want the 'food' to answer?

(b) What are the modifications we need to make in the pattern of production and consumption to answer those needs?

(c) How do we make those changes?

Any discussion on the nature, production, distribution and consumption of food must, at the outset, examine the definition and connotation of food. The pattern of production, distribution, and consumption of food has to ensure that the need according to this definition is fulfilled. The definition of food should go beyond the description of food quality. It must include the specifications about the production and consumption, and also mention the ethical, political, ecological, social, and economic implications. Only then can its production and consumption be influenced to move in a sustainable direction. Therefore, a comprehensive definition of food, has to satisfy three important requirements:

Food should be natural consisting of organic food elements in their natural, unaltered state; it should be whole, complete and unfragmented, neither refined nor enriched; and it should be poison free, organically grown, free from poisonous chemical residues and additives. [Capra 1982]

These requirements of food, apparently, are extremely simple but are at the same time extremely difficult to obtain in recent times. If the food production and consumption are to be made sustainable, then it must satisfy our evolutionary, ethical and ecological needs - the 3Es. The next step is to examine the use of resources efficiently to answer these needs. The other critical issue when it comes to food production and consumption is sustainability of human health and safety on which the sustainability of the society rests. Food production and consumption must not only ensure genetic integrity, and health and safety of the present generation but also for the generations to come. This needs to be sought not only from making nutritious, whole and chemical-free food available, but also from making sure that in the process the integrity of natural systems is not conquered.

Given this, the need really is to search for sustainable food production practices, be it agriculture, fishing *etc.* that, is a model of social and economic organisation based on an equitable and participatory vision of development. This model would recognize the environment and natural resources as foundations of any economic activity. The process is sustainable only when it is ecologically sound, economically viable, socially just, culturally appropriate, and based on a holistic approach.

The focus of this paper is to examine one of the most talked about, yet not commercially practiced way of sustainable agriculture – organic farming. To understand the strength and weaknesses, possibilities and future of this type of farming, it is essential to understand where we are at present and what is wrong with our existing practices in order to correct them.

Current Methods

While this section is by no means an exhaustive descriptor of the existing practices of food production and consumption, we will try to examine the impact of current practices and put the various issues in perspective as the main focus of this paper.

Production

Food is, and always has been, central to trade and exchange. Crops, food, tastes and cultural predilections for foods have traveled far from their botanical origins, often becoming global commodities, usually as a result of colonial trading relations. What is new about this current phase of globalization is the pace and scale of change and the systematic manner in which control can be executed. The scale on which institutions – government or the corporate – are able to think in recent times is unprecedented. They are able to organize the planting and distribution of crops more holistically and speedily than before.

Up until the Green Revolution, agriculture was marked by traditional practices of small firms, labour-intensive practices such as manuring, limited tillage, riding, terracing, composting organic matter, and recycling plant products into productive process, that enhance soil conservation and fertility. But with the advent of the western model of large scale, mechanized, and high-yielding corporate agriculture and its promotion as being the only effective solution to feed the world population, the Green Revolution emerged as the only strategy. The governments of the developing nations immediately adopted this strategy as the best possible answer to the problems of feeding the increasing population as well as addressing food security. The concept of crop diversity took a nosedive and the Green Revolution concentrated only on wheat, corn and rice. Consequently, there was more than a double increase in the average yield of these three crops. But the result wasn't the same in areas with low rainfall and in the most fragile ecological zones, where people subsisted on crops such as sorghum and millet. The greatest beneficiaries of this trend were the petro-chemical industry supplying the fertilizer and pesticides; the food industry built on wheat and corn and the chemical industry providing the additives, preservatives, *etc*. While it was definitely good for certain constituents of the economy, the Green Revolution failed to deliver its benefits in the truest sense.

Once the basic excitement subsided, issues regarding environmental degradation, deteriorating human health, and economic losses were being raised, and search for something to replace industrial agriculture began. At this juncture, advances in the studies of biotechnology came into the picture and it helped build the Green Revolution. Biotechnology featured an industrial farming system; the breeding of new crop varieties that could effectively use massive inputs of chemical fertilizers, and the use of toxic pesticides.

Biotechnology offers a tool for enhancing productivity by removing constraints that create a higher genetic production potential and protect crops against biotic and abiotic stresses that destabilize production. Through recombinant-DNA technology [where the encoding DNA sequences are from one source and the controlled elements of expression from another], one can not only transfer genes across species barriers but also tailor genes and their controlling elements to achieve expression at the specifically selected time and in the desired organ. As a result, it is now routine to manipulate metabolic pathways for bringing about dramatic changes in phenotypes.

Since it involves use of biological organisms, biotechnology is considered to be more ecologically responsible route that could be useful in increasing food production. Genetically engineered micro-organisms and toxins derived from genetically engineered micro-organisms were introduced as safer alternatives for pest control than the use of chemicals.

But indiscriminate release of these biological controls into the environment disrupted the integrity of the natural ecosystems by interfering with the indigenous pray-predator relationships. They accelerated the emergence of resistant pest strains.[1]

To have a better understanding of the situation, let us have a look how biotechnology through genetic engineering affects adversely the food security and the environment:

1. Genetic engineering destroys biodiversity, which is a major source of food and erodes the genetic basis of food production. There are four ways in which genetic engineering destroys the biodiversity in agriculture.
   (a) It pushes out crop diversity and narrows the genetic base of agriculture to only a few crops.
   (b) It accelerates the expansion of the monocultures of these crops.
   (c) It leads to the destruction of on-farm biodiversity through use of broad-spectrum herbicides like Round-up associated with Round-up ready Resistant crops.
   (d) It threatens the survival of species especially through the ecological impact of Bt. Crops.

---

1. Genetic material from the bacterial strain Bacillus thuringiensis (Bt) used as a biological control agent, was introduced into corn and cotton to produce transgenic Bt cotton and Bt corn. This led to Bt resistant populations of boll weevils and corn borers. Pollen from herbicide resistant canola has pollinated weeds in the mustard family (Cruciferae) creating new herbicide resistant weeds. [Gopalan 2001].

The global trends of the growth of genetically engineered crops is as follows:

40 per cent Soybean	40 per cent Conola
25 per cent Corn	40 per cent Tomato
40 per cent Tobacco	40 per cent Potato
40 per cent Cotton	

A glance at the above figures shows that this can hardly provide food security to rice-eating Asians or sorghum-eating Africans. The trend clearly indicates a clear narrowing of the genetic basis of our food supply. The currently commercialized staple food crops are only two. On the other hand, it also pushes the expansion of non-food crops such as cotton and tobacco, leading to larger areas going out of food production and hence aggravating food insecurity. The Green Revolution had narrowed down the basis of food security by displacing diverse nutritious food grains and spreading monocultures of rice, wheat and maize. However, it had focussed on staple foods and their yields – the genetic engineering revolution is undoing the narrow gains of the Green Revolution, both by neglecting the diversity of staples and by not addressing the issue of yields.

The genetically engineered-based cropping systems are based on expanding monocultures of the same variety evolved for a single function response. During the last part of the 90s, 1.9 million acres were planted with only two variants of Bt. cotton and 1.3 million acres were planted with the same Round-up Ready soybean. As the biotechnology industry is globalizing, these monoculture tendencies are increasing, thereby further displacing agricultural biodiversity and creating ecological vulnerability.

2. Genetic engineering maintains and deepens the monoculture paradigm of the Green Revolution and industrial agriculture, which focuses on a single function of single species, and fails to take yields of diverse species and diverse functions into account.

The argument of increased food availability through industrial breeding, including genetic engineering, is illusionary on four counts.

(a) Industrial breeding both in genetic engineering and the Green Revolution focuses on partial aspects of single crops rather than total system yields of multiple crops and integrated systems.

(b) Industrial breeding focuses on yields of one or two global commodities, not on the diverse range of crops that people eat in different regions. It also lays more emphasis on quantity per acre than nutrition per acre. In effect the nutrition per acre has come down globally through various ways of industrial breeding. It is also responsible for the displacement of diverse high nutritional value crops with HYVs of lower nutritional value crops. The table below demonstrates the nutritional value of crops; wheat and rice contain the least nutritional value, but make up most of the world's agriculture displacing the more nutritionally valuable crops.

Nutrition Content of Different Food Crops
(All values per 100 gm of edible portion)

Crop	*Protein (gms)*	*Minerals (100gms)*	*Calcium (mg)*	*Iron (100 gms)*
Bajra	11.6	2.3	42	5.0
Ragi	7.3	2.7	344	6.4
Jowar	10.4	1.6	25	5.8
Bengal Gram	17.1	3.6	202	10.2
Green Gram	24.0	3.5	124	7.3
Rajma	22.9	3.2	260	5.8
Wheat	11.8	0.6	23	2.5
Rice	6.8	0.6	10	3.1

Source: National Institute of Nutrition, Hyderabad, India.

(c) Industrial breeding including genetic engineering uses natural resources intensively and wastefully. If productivity is defined on the basis of resource use, industrial agriculture has very low productivity. It also undermines food security by using up resources that could have been used to produce more food, if they had not been wasted in a non-sustainable system of production.[2]

(d) Ecological alternatives can increase food supply through biodiversity intensification instead of chemical intensification and genetic engineering.

3. Genetic engineering is not aimed at crop improvement for food security. The most dominant genetic engineering application is herbicide resistant seeds, which on a global scale means increased use of chemicals, not necessarily more food. The dominant tools of genetic engineering will increase non-sustainability of agriculture and make agriculture more vulnerable to crop failure due to pests, diseases and weeds, thus increasing food insecurity.

   The two most prevalent applications of genetic engineering in agriculture are herbicide resistance and pest resistance. In particular, the most widespread transgenic crops are

---

2. To assess the real productivity of a farm system from the perspective of the farmer and the perspective of the soil we need to measure the Biodiversity Based Productivity not just the price or yield of single commodity or single output. We also need to calculate

   (a) The value of diverse outputs from diverse species and their diverse functions

   (b) The value of internal inputs provided by diverse farm outputs (such as straw for organic manure)

   (c) The costs of purchased inputs such as fertilizers, pesticides, and herbicides

   (d) The ecological costs of external chemical inputs

   In a polyculture diversity based internal input based farming system the returns the farmers get are:

   $\Sigma O_i + I_j$ where O_i are the diverse outputs of the farming system and I_j are the internal outputs provided by on-farm diversity.

   In an industrial monoculture, the returns to the farmer are

   $O_1 - \Sigma O_i - 1 - \Sigma E_j - \int I_x (E_j)$ where

   O_1 is the single commodity output.

   $O_j - 1$ are the outputs lost in the shift from diversity based systems to monocultures.

   E_j are the external inputs.

   $I_x (E_j)$ are the ecological impacts of external inputs.

   The higher productivity of diversity-based systems indicates that there is an alternative to genetic engineering and industrial agriculture – an alternative that is more ecological and more equitable.

Monsanto's Round-up Ready crops, which are resistant to Monsanto's herbicide Round-up and Monsanto's Bt-crops, which are genetically engineered to produce Bt toxins. In the context of the small diverse farms of the developing nations, both these applications are neither sustainable nor they can offer food security to the rural producers.

Weeds and pests in agriculture are symptoms of non-sustainable agricultural practices. The Green Revolution or chemical agriculture has led to an increase in weeds, pests, and disease occurrence. Herbicides and pesticides are toxic chemicals aimed at controlling weed and pest problems in crops. However, these reductionist 'solutions' have also proved non-sustainable. Herbicide residues in soils have led to decline in yields, and pesticide use has led to an increase in pest occurrence both through killing of predators and through emergence of pesticide resistance in pests. Genetic engineering is now deepening the reductionist paradigm of controlling pests through the creation of herbicide resistant and pest resistant crops. These applications account for more than 80 per cent of the biotechnology research in agriculture. Moreover, evidences are already available that rather than controlling weeds, pests and diseases, genetic engineering is on its way to create super weeds, super pests and super viruses.[3]

It is these concerns about the ecological costs of genetic engineering that provided the impetus for the Biosafety Protocol under the Convention on Biological Diversity.

---

3. (Bt.) is a naturally occurring organism Bacillus thuringiensis that produces a toxin. Researchers are now adding genes for Bt.toxins to a wide array of crops to enable the plants to produce their own insecticide. Research has shown the following discrepancies in this method;

   a. The Bt. plant does not merely use 'sunshine, air, and soil nutrients' as claimed by the developers.

   b. The so-called 'biodegradable protein' is actually a toxin that the gene continuously produces in the plant.

   c. Insect pests like the cotton bollworm, which destroys cotton, can actually evolve resistance because of continuous release of the toxin and hence become 'super pests'.

The Bt.crop does not affect just one specific insect pest. The beneficial insects like bees and ladybirds can be seriously affected.

4. The substitution of tropical crops through biotechnology also causes major dislocations and displacement in the developing nations, thus contributing to hunger among rural producers.

   One of the areas of application of the new biotechnology is the substitution of biological products and agricultural commodities supplied by the developing nations. This has a serious impact on the national economy and employment. Plant tissue culture offers increased possibilities of substituting agricultural specialties with industrially produced inputs. Many high value plant-derived products used for pharmaceuticals, dyes, flowerings, and fragrances are vulnerable to displacement due to the current applications. The impact of successful production of substitutes is being felt by countries, which have, in an earlier international division of labour, been made dependent upon exports of the natural products concerned. This is so because they have hitherto enjoyed resource endowment comparative package due to the specific conditions needed for the growth of the plants concerned.

   The case of vanilla is a good example of the potential of biotechnology to displace or eliminate traditional botanical exports, and to transfer agricultural production from the South to the laboratories and factories of the North. 98 per cent of the vanilla supplies come from four island nations: Madagascar, Reuman, the Comoros, and Indonesia. Madagascar accounts for 75 per cent of the supply, with 70,000 small farmers involved in the production. The substitution of vanilla production will seriously affect the livelihoods of the producers as well as the country's export earnings.

5. Food security includes food safety. The exclusion of concerns for food safety through the resistance to labelling of genetically engineered foods by the biotechnology industry and the denial to consumers of the right to know and the right to choose have also increased the food insecurity.

   In recent times, genetic engineering is primarily promoted by the private sector, especially by the global corporations. Since concerns of biosafety interfere with the market of expansion of genetic engineering in agriculture, there are primarily five ways through which the industry tries to suppress the safety debate and biosafety policy and manufacturing the exclusion of biosafety.

(a) The first method is by invoking 'sound science', which is equated, with industry friendly science and treating industry independent science as 'junk science'. Industry has always followed the science and never vice-versa – this simple truth has to be remembered.

(b) The second method is by the political construction of 'substantial equivalence' of Genetically Engineered Organisms [GEOs] and natural products.

(c) The third method is by treating contained, artificially constructed experiments as 'field trials' that prove safety. Safety under laboratory conditions for research by scientists using crippled organisms is very different from safety under market conditions for production undertaken using robust organisms. Further, existing field tests for safety and risk assessment are not designed to collect environmental data, and test conditions hardly proximate production conditions that including commercial scale, varying environments and time scale.

(d) The fourth method is by treating the labelling of genetically engineered foods which guarantees consumers the 'right to know' and the 'right to choose' as the interface in free trade.

(e) The fifth method of exclusion is by not allowing the space for alternatives such as organic farming, which provide safe food.

6. The monopoly control on seeds through intellectual property rights and the growing concentration of ownership control over the entire agricultural system increase food insecurity for the economically weaker farmers. This is because these farmers cannot afford to buy agrichemicals and patented seeds, and pay royalties each year and is hence pushed off the land.

There are two ways in which farmers' rights and freedoms related to agricultural systems and seeds are being eroded. First, seed legislation forces farmers to use only 'registered' varieties. Second, farmers are forced to give up their inalienable rights to save, exchange, and improve seeds through the 'intellectual property rights'.

Another issue of concern is - broad species patents. In March 1994, the European Patent Office granted an extraordinarily broad patent to Agracetus Corporation, a subsidiary of W.R. Grace, which was later on acquired by Monsanto. The patent covers all transgenic soybean varieties and seeds, regardless of the genes used and all methods of transformation. To top it all, while Monsanto had originally challenged the patent, it has withdrawn the same after buying Agracetus.

Agracetus's soybean patent claims:

"A soybean seed which will yield upon cultivation a soybean plant comprising in its foreign gene effective to cause the expression of a foreign gene product in the cells of the soybean plant." [Claim 17, patent no. EP 301749]

The situation could be best explained by the comment made by Dr Geoffrey Hawtin, Director General of the International Plant Genetic Resources Institute in Rome, Italy at such patenting:

"The granting of patents covering all genetically engineered varieties of a species, irrespective of the genes concerned or how they were transferred, puts in the hands of a single inventor the possibility to control what we grow on our farms and in our gardens. At a stroke of a pen the research of countless farmers and scientists has potentially has been negated in a single, legal act of economic highjack."

The latest in the attempt at total control is the 'terminator technology' developed jointly by the US Department of Agriculture and Mississippi based Delta and Pine Land Seed Company (now owned by Monsanto). The technology switches a plant's reproductive processes off so that the harvested seed will be sterile if farmers attempt to replant it.

The farmers are forced to buy seed every year and, hence, create a permanent market for the biotechnology industry.

What we can see from the discussion is that the totalitarian structures that are being put in place to launch genetic engineering as the dominant technology for food production do not feed the hungry nor save the planet!

Distribution

Another area of concern in this total process is the distribution process of food, which has reached abysmal proportions in the present society. Currently the majority of the people do not have any link whatsoever with the place of production. Consequently, there was a need for a system that would deliver the food to the consumer from the place of production without any wastage or spoilage. The gap gave birth to the food processing industry.

Food processing makes all kinds of food available throughout the year in total contradiction to the evolutionary and cultural characteristics of food. Let us have a look at some of the prominent features of this industry, which could also be termed as the features of the present global distribution process.

(a) Very frequently, due to the increasing distance between the point of production and consumption, food has to be transported from the point of production to the central point of storage. In this entire distribution chain there is whole gamut of wholesalers and retailers who play an active role in the pricing process of the food items.

(b) At the storage point, there is a need to apply chemicals to food such as grains, pulses, spices *etc.*, to prevent pest/ rodent attacks. For fresh/perishable foods like vegetables, meat etc. they may either have to be preserved with chemicals or refrigerated or processed in various forms.

(c) The requirement for storage and shelf-life has given birth to another significant issue and that is of irradiation. The use of radiation in food processing has been looked upon as a viable way of non-chemical preservation that destroys microorganisms and other pests. The technique is not only unnatural but also changes the colour and taste, degrades the nutritive value of the food product, and results in formation of potentially dangerous radiolytic compounds. The process depends upon radioactive isotopes, one of which, Cesium 137, is an unavoidable decay product of nuclear fission.

(d) Food processing industry is also providing tremendous support to a gamut of other industries such as refrigeration, chemical and petrochemical industries manufacturing preservatives, pesticides, additives, *etc*., packaging material, transportation, and advertising.

Some of the major issues facing the present distribution practices, therefore, include:

(a) Socio-economic impact due to the non-equitable food distribution: The wholesalers and retailers are in total control of the system including the pricing mechanism. A whole range of middlemen, who apply their margin/ markups on the production cost, are the only ones to benefit from the process. The consumer pays an extra amount of 25-50 per cent, as markups while the producer (farmers) are hardly able to recover their cost of production.

(b) Ecological and health impact of the processed foods: Apart from the straightforward environmental impacts of the processing part itself, the ancillary industries such as packaging, additives, refrigeration *etc*. create a tremendous impact on the environment. For example, styrofoam, tetrapacks, plastic, and various forms of packaging require land for final disposal as solid waste, particularly styrofoam, which is neither biodegradable, nor can it be recycled. Medical research has already stared to show the negative effects of the consumption of processed food. Pesticides and metal residues in food, chemicals in the form of preservatives, and adulterants from the distribution system cause extensive damage to human health.

(c) Ethical issues of depriving farmers of their costs, and compromising consumer health and safety: Issues of ethics in advertising foods, particularly, those aimed at children are being discussed extensively today. Companies claim qualities through advertisements with no scientific basis and products may arrive in countries even before the health warning is issued! Human health is, thus, undermined and compromised.

Consumption

With the process of globalization in the forefront in recent times, there is hardly any link left between the consumer and the producer. Consequently, what we have lost is the connection with nature and the sense of appreciation of the act of farming, which sustains human beings.

The following features could be termed as the prominent ones, features that mark the present-day global consumption process.

(a) Food, in present times, does not really answer the evolutionary, cultural or ethical needs of the community. Rather, it is typically defined and evaluated in terms of its quality (appearance, nutritional composition, and texture) and has been reduced to a set of numbers in terms of calories and the recommended daily allowance of various constituents. Consequently food is described as 'low calorie', 'fat free', '100 per cent natural,' *etc*. The holistic character of food in terms of its ability to provide sustenance, physical and mental well-being has, thus, been reduced to a set of faddist terms.

(b) Increased globalization has taken the speed and dimension of integration of consumer markets to an abysmal height. It is characterized by constant flow of new products, fierce competition to sell to the consumers worldwide and aggressive advertising. The consumer has a plethora of foods to choose from, and with the increasing affluence, the demand for meat, poultry, and seafood is rising. This trend has deep implications on food security, since large tracts of farmlands are increasingly being used as feed for the table animals. On the other side, a tremendous pressure is created on the land to produce seasonal vegetables, fruits and grains so that they can be processed and made available throughout the year.

(c) In the present-day food economy, it is not the consumer who has too much a choice but the store shelf that determines what the consumer should feed on! It simply follows the basic principle of consumerism – Buying what you do not want, with money you do not have, to impress people you do not know!

The consumer, while making a choice about food, has to make a safe selection from the supermarket shelf that contains processed food, genetically modified foods, dairy and meat products containing growth hormones, irradiated food, *etc*. To make this choice, the predominant source of information is commercial advertising, which in many cases is incomplete and inadequate. As a result, at times this information has proved to be quite deceptive. Protecting consumer rights on food safety and product information, thereby, has become extremely complex.

(d) The gap between the consumption level in developed nations of the North and the developing ones in the South is becoming larger every day. Per capita consumption rates in Germany are 15 times those in India [von Weizsacker *et al* 1997]. Calculations of 'ecological footprints'[4] show that if all six billion humans on the planet consumed at the rate of the Netherlands or the Germans, there would be a need for three planets to satisfy the requirements of human beings!

---

4. Everybody (from a single individual to a whole city or country) has an impact on the Earth, because they consume the products and services of nature. Their ecological impact corresponds to the amount of nature they occupy to keep them going. In this report, we quantify, nation by nation, the biologically productive areas necessary to continuously provide their resource supplies and absorb their wastes, using prevailing technology. In other words, we calculate the "ecological footprints" of these countries.

   Ecological footprint calculations are based on two simple facts: first, we can keep track of most of the resources we consume and many of the wastes we generate; second, most of these resource and waste flows can be converted to a biologically productive area necessary to provide these functions. Thus, ecological footprints show us how much nature nations use. However, in reality this footprint is not a continuous piece of land. Due to international trade, the land and water areas used by most global citizens are scattered all over the planet. It would take a great deal of research to determine where their exact locations are. To simplify, the occupied space is calculated by adding up the areas with world average productivity that are necessary to provide us with all the ecological services we consume.

A very significant proportion of global environment degradation could be directly attributed to the overconsumption in the northern countries.

(e) The consumers in recent times also face a new phenomenon called 'green marketing'[5] along with the corporate environmentalism, which conspicuously aims at changing the pattern of consumption but never by its overall reduction.

Given this trend in consumption patterns and consumerism, the long-term viability of our current food production and consumption needs to be relooked.

A Sustainable Alternative

Alternative practices of food production and consumption are being practiced in many parts of the world including India. Irrespective of the area of practice, the common feature is that mostly it is done at the small community level or as an individual initiative. The practices include organic and ecological farming, biodynamic farming, permaculture, *etc.* Consumer groups are forming initiatives in the form of networks and some of the main forces driving these initiatives are:

(a) Concern for health and safety

(b) Consumer need for quality goods and value for money

(c) Recognition of ecological degradation and respect for the integrity of natural ecosystems

(d) Religious and cultural beliefs

(e) In some cases, faddism and pleasure of exclusivity.

The most widespread initiative that has emerged as a result of these driving forces is Organic Agriculture. The term 'organic farming' was first used by Northbourne in his 1940 book *Look to the Land.* Organic farming is one of the several approaches towards sustainable agriculture. Indeed, many of the techniques used in organic farming, such as inter-cropping, mulching, and integration of crops and

---

5. Green or Environmental Marketing consists of all activities designed to generate and facilitate any exchanges intended to satisfy human needs or wants, such that the satisfaction of these needs and wants occurs, with minimal detrimental impact on the natural environment. [Polonsky 1994b, 2]

livestock, are practiced under various agricultural systems. What makes organic agriculture unique is that, under various laws and certification programmes, almost all synthetic inputs are prohibited[6] and "soil building" crop rotations are mandatory. If properly managed, organic farming reduces or eliminates water pollution and helps conserve water and soil on the farm. However, it must be noted that until the Green Revolution in the mid-1900s, the distinction between organic and non-organic food production systems did not exist. The farming practices that are being labelled as 'alternative' in the recent times were the norms.

I will discuss the concept of organic farming, global opportunities, and constraints of organic agriculture. I will also discuss a few consumer initiatives in the world to examine how the consumer as a 'market force' can proactively influence the production and consumption pattern. A note is also included on the situation of organic agriculture in India. The paper covers a multifarious approach involving policy changes, regulatory efforts, and other economic instruments to steer food production and consumption in a more sustainable pattern.

Definition of Organic Agriculture

An organic label indicates to the consumer that a product was produced using certain production methods. In other words, organic

---

6. No synthetic products can be used in organic farming although, where direct intervention is required, non-synthetic substances like sulphur, and biological pest controls may be used. Mineral fertilizers should be regarded as a supplement to, and not a replacement for nutrient cycling within the farm. Here is a list of permitted, restricted, and prohibited supplementary nutrients.

Permitted	*Restricted*	*Prohibited*
Rock phosphate	Leather meal	Fresh blood
Feldspar	Borax	Urea
Magnesium limestone	Epson salts	Slaked lime
Rock potash	Sulphate of potash, magnesium	Quick lime
Fish meal		
Wood ash		
Calcined aluminum phosphate		
Calcium sulphate (gypsum)		
Ground chalk with limestone		
Meat, bone, hoof, and horn meals		

is a process claim rather than a product claim. An apple produced by practices approved for organic production may very well be identical to an apple produced under other agricultural management regimes.

Several countries and a multitude of private certification organizations have defined organic agriculture. In the past, differences in these definitions were significant but the demand for consistency by multinational traders has led to a great uniformity. The International Federation of Organic Agriculture Movements (IFOAM), a non-governmental organization internationally networking and promoting organic agriculture, has established guidelines that have been widely adopted for organic production and processing.

Most recently, the Codex Committee on Food Labelling has debated "Draft Guidelines for the Production, Processing, Labelling and Marketing of Organically Produced Foods". Adoption of a single definition for organic agriculture by the Codex Alimentarius Commission is expected at its next meeting in June 1999. According to the proposed Codex definition, "organic agriculture is a holistic production management system which promotes and enhances agro-ecosystem health, including biodiversity, biological cycles, and soil biological activity. It emphasizes the use of management practices in preference to the use of off-farm inputs, taking into account that regional conditions require locally adapted systems. This is accomplished by using, where possible, agronomic, biological, and mechanical methods, as opposed to using synthetic materials, to fulfil any specific function within the system."

Organic agriculture is one of the several approaches to sustainable agriculture and many of the techniques used (*e.g.* inter-cropping, rotation of crops, double-digging, mulching, integration of crops and livestock *etc.*) are practiced under various agricultural systems. What makes organic agriculture unique, as regulated under various laws and certification programs, is that: (1) almost all synthetic inputs are prohibited, and (2) 'soil building' crop rotations are mandated.

The basic rules of organic production are that natural inputs are approved and synthetic inputs are prohibited. But there are exceptions in both cases. Certain natural inputs determined by the various certification programs to be harmful to human health or the environment, are prohibited (*e.g.* arsenic). Also certain synthetic inputs determined to be essential and consistent with organic farming philosophy are allowed (*e.g.* insect pheromones). Lists of specific approved synthetic inputs and prohibited natural inputs are maintained by all certification programs and such a list is under negotiation in Codex. Many certification programs require additional environmental protection measures in addition to these two requirements. While many farmers in the developing world do not use synthetic inputs, this alone is not sufficient to classify their operations as organic.

Opportunities and Constraints

Markets

The demand for organic products has created new export opportunities for the developing world. While some consumers express a preference for locally grown organic foods, the demand for a variety of foods year-round makes it impossible for any country to source organic food entirely within its own borders. As a result, many developing countries have begun to export organic products successfully (*e.g.* tropical fruit to the European baby food industry, Zimbabwean herbs to South Africa, and six African nations export cotton to the European Community). Typically, organic exports are sold at impressive premiums, often at prices 20 per cent higher than identical products produced on non-organic farms. However, the ultimate profitability of organic farm varies, and a few studies have assessed the long-term potential for such market premiums. Nevertheless, under the right circumstances the market returns from organic agriculture can potentially contribute to local food security by increasing family incomes.

Entering this lucrative market is not easy, however. Farmers are denied access to developed country organic markets for two to three years after beginning organic management. This is so because such countries do not certify land and livestock as organic before that time (2-3 years), arguing that it is necessary for the purging of chemical residues. Under the Draft Codex guidelines, however, products produced on land under organic management for at least one year but less than the two-three year standard can be sold as "transitional organic", although a few markets have yet to be developed for such products.

In most cases, farmers and post-harvest businesses seeking to sell their products in developed countries need to hire an organic certification organization to annually inspect and confirm that these farms and businesses adhere to the organic standards established by the various trading partners. The cost for this service can be expensive, although it varies in relation to farm size, volume of production, and the efficiency of the certification organization (for example, IFOAM certification costs a maximum of 5 per cent of sales value, but where local certification organizations exist, it reduces to 2 per cent of sales value). Few developing countries have certification organizations within their borders, and even when sufficient resources are available to pay for certification, farmers often lack the information to find credible inspectors.

While most developing-country traders have focused on export markets in the developed world, domestic market opportunities for organic food or eco-food may also be exploited. In China, for example, there is a growing market for "green food" which, according to government grading standards, is produced without certain pesticides and fertilizers using biological methods. Chinese farmers also export organic food such as tea to the Netherlands, soybeans to Japan *etc.*

Whether the intent is to sell organic products domestically or abroad, reliable market information is difficult to obtain. There is virtually no systematic production or market survey data being collected with which to assess the rate and pattern of organic market growth. In particular, no projections for the markets in the developing world have been made, nor have markets systematically been identified for developing country exports. Estimates of the public's willingness to pay premiums, the impact of regional attitudes and tastes, and the incidence of market fraud have not been undertaken.

Pricing

An argument against organic agriculture is that organic food is more expensive, therefore, low-income families and people in the third world would not be able to afford it. While it is true that organic food has a price premium, this price difference is the result of higher demand for organic products, and does not necessarily reflect a higher cost of production. According to the Wallace Institute report, organic production of grains and soybeans in the mid-west was more profitable than the conventional production in at least half the cases studied, even without factoring the higher prices that organic soybeans bring in the market (sometimes more than twice as much as conventional soybeans). There are still situations though in which organic systems appear to depend on price premiums to remain profitable such as the case of high-value tomato crops in California. The higher cost of production that was found in the SFAS (discussed later) project is attributed mainly to the increased labour requirements for weed control in organic systems.

However, these studies overestimate the relative costs of organic production. Federal commodity programs and subsidies are geared towards large-scale chemically-intensive agriculture, and artificially inflate figures for industrial agriculture. Furthermore, this type of economic comparison ignores external costs that the conventional agriculture creates. The World Resources Institute, an environmental policy think tank, reports that when measured with the traditional cost analysis methods, the average farm shows an $80 per acre profit. After accounting for all the external costs of soil loss, water contamination and environmental degradation caused by farming practices however, the average farm shows a $29 per acre loss instead!

A number of European nations have started to factor in these expenses into their agricultural support programs. In several European countries, such as Denmark and Sweden, farmers get government support during their conversion to organic farming and continue to receive support for the environmental services they provide to their communities such as wildlife corridors and the elimination of toxic runoffs that contaminate underground water sources. These programs helped foster an almost 100-fold increase in organically farmed land in Europe, from 29,000 acres in 1986 to 2.4 million acres in 1996. Similar programs in the US could help the conversion of more farms to organic methods. It is to be noted that these price supports do not have to be subsidies, rather a compensation to organic farmers for each of the ecological and social services that they provide.

Farm Productivity

Farmers will probably experience some loss in yields when converting their operations to organic production. There is a period of time between the discarding of synthetic inputs and sufficient biological activity being restored to the land (for example growth in beneficial insect populations, nitrogen fixation from legumes *etc.*) during which pest suppression and fertility problems are typical. The degree of yield loss varies, however, and depends on factors such as the inherent biological attributes of the farm, farmer expertise, and the extent to which synthetic inputs were used under the previous management system. Wherever soil fertility is low and biological processes have been seriously disrupted, it may take years to restore the ecosystem to the point where organic production is possible. In such cases other sustainable approaches, which allow judicious use of synthetic chemicals, may be more suitable start-up solutions. One strategy to survive the difficult transition period involves converting farms to organic production in partial installments so that the entire operation is not at risk.

Most studies find that organic agriculture requires significantly greater labour input than the conventional farms. This is especially true in areas of low ecological potential. However, when labour is not a constraint, organic agriculture can benefit the underemployed labour in the rural communities. Furthermore, the diversification of crops typically found on organic farms, with their various planting and harvesting schedules, may distribute labour demand more evenly, which could help stabilize employment. Land tenure is also critical to the adoption of organic agriculture. It is highly unlikely that tenant farmers would invest the necessary labour and sustain the difficult conversion period without some guarantee of access to the land in later years when the benefits of organic production are attainable.

Soil-building rotations need to be designed both from the economic and the technical points of view; uses must be identified for all the crop and livestock products produced. As in all agricultural systems, diversity in production increases income-generating opportunities and can, as in the case of fruits, supply essential health protecting minerals and vitamins to the family diet. It also spreads the risks of failure over a wide range of crops. It is possible that, even on farms where the organic crop yields are lower than those produced under systems using high levels of inputs, the overall economic yields of the farm will be competitive, since organic systems benefit from market premiums and sometimes, lowered input costs.

The insights generated by organic farmers in their search for site-specific production strategies can be of great benefit to non-organic farmers interested in expanding their management options. However, organic farmers still face huge uncertainties. A lack of information is an obstacle to organic conversion (for example, surveys find that 63 per cent of sub-Saharan African farmers and 73 per cent of North American (US and Canada) organic farmers cite a lack of knowledge as the greatest barrier to adoption). Extension personnel rarely receive adequate training in organic methods, and studies have shown that they sometimes discourage farmers from converting to these methods. Furthermore, institutional support in developing countries is scarce. Professional institutions with a capacity to assist farmers throughout the production, post-production, and marketing processes are non-existent in many developing countries. While there are helpful research results that could immediately be extended to farmers, much more are needed. In 1990, the FAO sponsored a conference where organic research needs were identified (such as economics of stockless farms, animal husbandry, nitrogen cycling, *etc.*); however, these challenges have largely gone unmet.

Comparisons of Organic and Conventional Chemical Farming Systems: Case Studies

A survey of recent studies comparing the productivity of organic practices to conventional agriculture provides an excellent example of the wide range of benefits we can expect from the conversion to sustainable agricultural methods. The results clearly show that organic farming accomplishes many of the FAO's sustainability aims, as well as shows promise in increasing the food production ability.

Sustainable Agriculture Farming Systems Project (SFAS) at UC, Davis

An ongoing long-term comparison study, SFAS is an interdisciplinary project that compares conventional farming systems with alternative production systems that promote sustainable agriculture.

The study examines four farming systems that differ in crop rotation design and material input use: a two-year and a four-year rotation conventional system, an organic and a low-input system.

Results from the first eight years of the project show that the organic and low-input systems had yields comparable to the conventional systems in all crops that were tested - tomato, safflower, corn and bean, and in some instances yielding higher than the conventional systems. Tomato yields in the organic system were lower in the first three years, but reached the levels of the conventional tomato yields in the subsequent years and had a higher yield during the last year of the experiment (80 t/ha in the organic system compared to 68 t/ha in the conventional system in 1996). Corn production in the organic system had a higher variability than the conventional systems, with lower yields in some years and higher in others.

Both organic and low-input systems resulted in increases in the organic carbon content of the soil and larger pools of stored nutrients, both of which are critical for long-term fertility maintenance (Clark, 1998). The most important limiting factor in the organic system appeared to be nitrogen availability. The organic system relied mainly on cover crops and composted poultry manure for fertilization. One possible explanation for a lower availability in the organic system is the high carbon inputs associated with nitrogen to build soil organic matter, thus reducing nitrogen availability for the organic crops. During the latter 2 years of the experiment, soil organic matter levels appeared to be stabilized resulting in more nitrogen availability. This was in agreement with the higher yields of organic crops that were observed during those last two years. The organic systems were found to be more profitable for both corn and tomato among the 4-year rotations mainly due to the higher price premiums.

Farming Systems Trial at the Rodale Institute — Soybean Study

Initiated in 1981, the Farming Systems Trial compares intensive soybean and maize production under a conventional and two organic management farming systems.

The first organic cropping system simulates a traditional integrated farming system. Leguminous cover crops are fed to the cattle and the resulting manure is applied to the fields as the main source of nitrogen. In the second organic system, the leguminous cover crops are incorporated in the soil as the source for nitrogen before corn or soybean planting.

Corn yields were comparable in all the three cropping systems (less than 1% difference) (Drinkwater, 1998). However, a comparison of soil characteristics during a 15-year period found that soil fertility was enhanced in the organic systems, while it decreased considerably in the conventional one. Nitrogen content and organic matter levels in the soil increased markedly in the manure under the fertilized organic system and declined in the conventional system. Moreover, the conventional system had the highest environmental impact, where 60% more nitrate was leached into the groundwater over a five-year period than in the organic systems (Drinkwater, 1998).

Soybean production systems were also highly productive, achieving 40 bushels/acre. In 1999 however, during one of the worst droughts on record, yields of organic soybeans were 30 bushels/acre, compared to only 16 bushels/acre from conventionally grown soybeans (Rodale Institute, 1999). "Our trials show that improving the quality of the soil through organic practices can mean the difference between a harvest or hardship in times of drought" writes Jeff Moyer, farm manager at the Rodale Institute in Kutztown, Pennsylvania (Rodale Institute, 1999). He continues, "Over time, organic practices encourage the soil to hold on to moisture more efficiently than conventionally managed soil." The higher content of organic matter also makes organic soil less compact so that root systems can penetrate more deeply to find moisture. These results highlight the importance of organic farming methods and their potential to avert future crop failures both in the US and in the rest of the world.

Broadbalk Experiment at the Rothamsted Experimental Station, UK

One of the longest running agricultural trials on record (more than 150 years) is the Broadbalk experiment at the Rothamsted Experimental Station in the United Kingdom. The trials compare a manure-based fertilizer farming system (but not certified organic) to a synthetic chemical fertilizer farming system. Wheat yields are shown to be on average slightly higher in the organically fertilized plots (3.45 tones/hectare) than the plots receiving chemical fertilizers (3.40 tones/hectare). More importantly though, soil fertility, measured as soil organic matter and nitrogen levels, increased by 120 per cent over 150 years in the organic plots, compared with only a 20 per cent increase in the chemically fertilized plots.

Organic Grain and Soybean Production in the Midwestern United States

A comprehensive review of a large number of comparison studies of grain and soybean production conducted by six Midwestern universities since 1978 found that in all of these studies organic production was equivalent to, and in many cases better than, the conventional one (Welsh, 1999). Organic systems had higher yields than conventional systems, which featured continuous crop production (no rotations) and equal or lower yields in conventional systems that included crop rotations. In the drier climates such as the Great Plains, organic systems had higher yields, as they tend to be better during droughts than the conventional systems. In one such study in South Dakota for the period 1986-1992, the average yields of soybeans were 29.6 bushels/acre and 28.6 bushels/acre in the organic and conventional systems respectively. In the same study, the average spring wheat yields were 41.5 bushels/acre and 39.5 bushels/acre in the organic and conventional systems respectively.

While comparing the profitability of farming systems, the study found that organic cropping systems were always more profitable than the most common conventional cropping systems if the higher premiums that organic crops enjoy were factored in. However even when the higher premiums were not factored in, the organic systems were still more productive and profitable in three of the six studies. This was attributed to lower production costs and the ability of the organic systems to outperform the conventional systems in drier areas, or during drier periods.

The author of the report remarked: "What is most surprising is how well the organic systems performed despite the minimal amount of research that traditional agricultural research institutions have devoted to them."

Comparison of Conventional and Organic Farms in California, US

Lastly, a study that compared ecological characteristics and productivity of 20 commercial farms in the Central Valley of California gives us a better understanding of how a conversion to organic system would fare in a commercial farm setting.

The farms compared had a fresh market tomato production. Tomato yields were shown to be quite similar in organic and conventional farms (Drinkwater, 1995). Insect pest damage was also comparable in both cases of organic and conventional farms. However, significant differences were found in soil health indicators such as nitrogen mineralization potential and microbial abundance and diversity, which were higher in the organic farms. Nitrogen mineralization potential was three times greater in the organic fields compared to conventional fields. The organic fields also had 28% more organic carbon. The increased soil health in the organic farms resulted in considerably lower disease incidence. Severity of the most prevalent disease in the study, tomato corky root disease[7], was found to be significantly lower in the organic farms.

Environmental Impacts and Sustainability

The explicit goal of organic agriculture is to contribute to the enhancement of sustainability. Nevertheless, negative impacts may occur and organic agriculture is not an exclusive method for sustainable farming. The soil and water protection and conservation techniques of sustainable agriculture used to combat erosion, compaction, salinization, and other forms of degradation are evident in organic farming. The use of crop rotations, organic manure and mulches improves soil structure and encourages the development of a vigorous population of soil micro-organisms. Mixed and relay cropping provide a more continuous soil cover and, thus, a shorter period when the soil is fully exposed to the erosive power of the rain, wind and sun. Terracing, to conserve moisture, and soil are used in appropriate situations and particular attention is paid in the irrigated areas to on-farm water management. Properly managed organic farming reduces or eliminates water pollution and helps conserve water and soil on the farm (although improper use of manure can seriously pollute water). A few developed countries compel or

7. Soil-borne diseases and pests are generally less severe in alternative than in conventional systems. The mechanisms of root disease control in alternative systems vary with location and environment. For example, corky root (Pyrenochaeta lycopersici) and Phytophthora root rot (P. parasitica) of tomato were less prevalent in organic than conventional farms in central California. These differences were associated with differences in soil biological properties for corky root and soil physical properties for Phytophthora root rot. Corky root usually does not kill plants, but may reduce yields. Corky root suppression was correlated with higher diversity and abundance of actinomycetes after incorporation of cover crops (CCs) in organically managed soils, but effects of longer rotations at organic farms could also contribute to the observed differences.

subsidize farmers to use organic techniques as a solution to the water pollution problems (*e.g.* Germany, France).

Organic farmers rely on natural pest controls (biological control, plants with pest control properties *etc.*) rather than synthetic pesticides which, when misused, are known to kill beneficial organisms (natural parasites of pests, bees, earthworms), cause pest resistance, and often pollute water and land. Reduction in the use of toxic synthetic pesticides, which the World Health Organization (WHO) estimates to poison three million people each year, should lead to improved health of farm families.

Organic farmers aim to make the maximum use of the recyclable fertility in the on-farm crop residues (straws, stovers, and other non-edible parts) either directly as compost and mulch or through livestock as farmyard manure. Eliminating the use of synthetic nitrogenous fertilizer greatly lowers the risks of nitrogen contamination of water. Crop rotation is a widely used method of fertility maintenance and pest and disease control, which is used in large- and small-scale farming in both the developed and developing countries, especially under intensification. Fodder legumes are well-known fertility-building crops and are grown on vast areas in sub-tropical Asia and semi-arid regions for the dual purpose of feeding livestock and adding nitrogen to the farm fertility cycle. Grain legumes may also produce a reasonable crop without the nitrogenous fertilizer. Leguminous crops in rotations add various amounts of nitrogen to the overall farm system through biological fixation; other nitrogen-fixing plants such as Azolla may also be used.

Biological nitrogen fixation is a powerful technique but it often requires some addition of minerals to the soil, especially phosphorus. Most certification programs restrict the use of mineral fertilizers, which may be necessary to supplement the organic manure produced on the farm. Natural and organic fertilizers from outside the farm are used (*e.g.* rock phosphate, potash, guano, seaweed, slaughterhouse by-products, ground limestone, seaweed, wood-ash). While most certification programs prohibit the use of sewage sludge and night-soil they are still used in some places. However, sludge may contain many contaminants, including heavy metals, which can have a deleterious and cumulative effect on the soil, while night-soil contains human pathogens and must be carefully composted before use.

Crop rotations encourage a diversity of food crops, fodder and under-utilized plants; this, in addition to improving overall farm production and fertility may assist the on-farm conservation of plant genetic resources. Integrating livestock into the system adds income through organic meat, eggs and dairy products, as well as draught animal power. Tree crops and on-farm forestry integrated into the system provide shade and windbreaks while providing food, income, fuel and wood. Integrated agri-aquaculture may also be found within diverse organic agricultural systems. Economic objectives are not the only motivation for organic farmers; their intent is often to optimize land, animal, and plant interactions, preserve natural nutrient and energy flows, and enhance biodiversity, all of which contribute to the overall objective of sustainable agriculture to preserve natural resources and ecosystems for future generations.

The Capacity to Feed the World

Organic management practices promote soil health, and water conservation and can reverse environmental degradation. The emphasis on small-scale family farms has the potential to revitalize rural areas and their economies. Counter to the widely held belief that industrial agriculture is more efficient and productive, small farms produce far more per acre than large farms. Industrial agriculture relies heavily on monocultures, the planting of a single crop throughout the farm, because they simplify management and allow the use of heavy machinery. Larger farms in the Third World also tend to grow export luxury crops instead of providing staple foods to their growing population. Small farmers, especially in the Third World, have integrated farming systems where they plant a variety of crops maximizing the use of their land.

They are also more likely to have livestock on their farm, which provides a variety of animal products to the local economy and manure for improving soil fertility. In such farms, though the yield per acre of a single crop might be lower than a large farm, the total production per acre of all the crops and various animal products is much higher than the large conventional farms.

Even in the United States, the smallest farms, (27 acres or less) have more than ten times greater dollar output per acre than larger farms *(US Agricultural Census, 1992)*. Conversion to small organic farms therefore, would lead to sizeable increase in food production worldwide. Only organic methods can help small family farms survive, increase farm productivity, repair decades of environmental damage and knit communities into smaller, more sustainable distribution networks — all leading to improved food security around the world.

The magazine '*Nature*' reported the results of one of the biggest agricultural experiments ever conducted.[8] A team of Chinese scientists had tested the key principle of modern rice-growing—planting a single, high-tech variety across hundreds of hectares—against a much older technique: planting several breeds in one field. They found, to the astonishment of the farmers who had been drilled for years in the benefits of "monoculture", that reverting to the old method resulted in spectacular increases in yield. Rice blast—a devastating fungus, which normally requires repeated applications of poison to control—decreased by 94 per cent. The farmers planting a mixture of strains were able to stop applying their poisons altogether, while producing 18 per cent more rice per acre than they were growing before.

Two years ago, another paper published in *Nature* showed that yields of organic maize are identical to yields of maize grown with fertilizers and pesticides, while soil quality in the organic fields dramatically improves.[9] In trials in Hertfordshire, wheat grown with manure has produced consistently higher yields for the past 150 years than wheat grown with artificial nutrients.

Professor Jules Pretty of Essex University has shown how farmers in India, Kenya, Brazil, Guatemala and Honduras have doubled or tripled their yields by switching to organic or semi-organic techniques.[10] A study in the United States reveals that small farmers growing a wide range of plants can produce ten times as much money per acre as big farmers growing single crops.[11] Cuba, forced into

---

8. Youyong Zhu, Hairu Chen, Jinghua Fan, Yunyue Wang, Yan Li, Jianbing Chen, Jinxiang Fan, Shisheng Yang, Lingping Hu, Hei Leung, Tom W. Mew, Paul S.Teng, Zonghua Wang and Christopher C. Mundt, "Genetic diversity and disease control in rice", *Nature*, 406, 718-722 (2000).
9. David Tilman, "The Greening of the Green Revolution," *Nature*, 396 pp 211-212, 19th Nov 1998.
10. Jules Pretty, Feeding the world? *Splice*, the magazine of the Genetics Forum. August/September 1998, Volume 4 Issue 6.
11. Peter M. Rosset, The Multiple Functions and Benefits of Small Farm Agriculture In the Context of Global Trade Negotiations. Policy Brief prepared for "Cultivating Our Futures," the FAO/Netherlands Conference on the Multifunctional Character of Agriculture and Land, 12-17 September 1999, Maastricht, The Netherlands. Co-published by: Transnational Institute, Paulus Potterstraat 20, 1071 DA, Amsterdam.

organic farming by the economic blockade, has now adopted it as policy, having discovered that it improves both the productivity and the quality of the crops its farmers grow.[12]

Organic Farming in India

Sustainable agricultural practices like organic or ecological farming are not new to India. Although the Green Revolution has impacted the large rice and wheat-producing belts in the country, there are pockets in the country, particularly tribal areas, and marginalized farms where agriculture has always been chemical free, sustainable, 'organic' farming [for details, see, Alvares 1996]. The formal organic farming movement began in the mid-1980s with a conference organized by the Association for the Propagation of Indigenous Genetic Resources (APIGR). In recent times, a large number of groups and individuals in India are part of the movement with ARISE based in Auroville, Pondicherry, being the principal network for promoting organic farming within the country. A number of farmers' movements such as the Shetkari Sanghatan of Maharashtra, the Karnataka Rajya Raitha Sangha, and the Bharatiya Kisan Sabha have all taken up the cause of ecological/organic farming.

Production

Presently, in India, the percentage of total produce from organic farming is about 1.5 per cent. India's 'organic production' touched 14,000 tones in 2002. That for a country that produces over 200 million tones of foodgrains! Of this exports stood at meager 11,000 tones in 2002. This include seven broad categories of coffee, tea, spices, rice, wheat, pulses, oilseeds, fruits and vegetables, cashewnut, cotton, and herbal extracts. The domestic sales were even bleaker. A miserable 1000 tonnes—barely 0.0006 per cent of its total food consumption.

In nearly all the States in the country, organic farming is being practiced, but the focus is on coffee, tea, pepper, cardamom, cotton,

12. Renee Kjartan, Castro Topples Pesticide in Cuba. Washington Free Press, August 7, 2000. Also note that food production in Punjab and Haryana, the Indian States long celebrated as the great success stories of modern, intensive cultivation has all but collapsed. The new crops the farmers there have been encouraged to grow demand far more water and nutrients than the old ones, with the result that, in many places, both the ground water and the soil have been exhausted. [Sharma, 2000].

and fruits, all aimed at the export market. Once again, food crops, particularly subsistence crops such as millets and other cereals, are not the focus and neither is the local human population. Thus, food security, community integrity, and integrity of the ecosystem which is the purpose of this alternative form of food production, ceases to be at the heart of the system.

In India, there are three main types of farmers engaged in organic agricultural production.

(a) Farmers who mostly follow the indigenous knowledge and technology developed over the past hundreds of years. They normally grow for their own consumption and have little surplus.

(b) Farmers with medium to small-size holdings. These can be divided into two groups: those working to revive the Vedic practices coupled with the Ayurvedic tradition of the health system with scientific exposition; and others who follow modern agricultural organic systems, such as Steiner's biodynamic agriculture or Fukuoka's 'Nature farming', for example. They usually have marketable surplus as well some amount for export.

(c) Private companies that have responded to market demands in the North by organizing large-scale conversions to organic systems. By going organic they add more economic value to the crops, which are already cultivated in a manner similar to the organic systems. They are actively engaged in promoting organic agriculture for export.

Distribution

The heart of the production-consumption cycle is the food having to reach the consumer. In recent times, this distance between the producer and consumer is so large that people have no personal connection with food. Increasingly, alternatives are emerging through farmers' markets, community supported agriculture, and the direct marketing strategies of small farmers. As a result, consumers are beginning to connect with the people growing their food, and with food itself as a product of the farmer's cooperation with nature.

The distribution models range from exclusive stores/outlets selling organic food[13] to formation of cooperative buyers' groups set up to exclusively source organic foods.[14] While the focus of the former is to maintain the exclusivity of such products, the latter aim to make organically/sustainably grown food available to a larger consumer population. In such cases, prices have to be reasonable and customers must be sure that any premium that is being paid is for products that are truly organically grown.

Consumer cooperatives that directly source food from producers thereby minimising the length of the distribution chain and making the process more sustainable have set up by consumer groups. This has taken place both for organic and non-organic foods and other consumer goods.

Small groups of people in urban areas are also attempting to do collective buying particularly of vegetables and fruits from farms located on the outskirts of cities to obtain healthier produce. One such group was the Green Cross in Mumbai, where the intention was to first source fresh vegetables and fruits from the farmers located in Vasai on the outskirts of the city for a small group of people. Having developed a relationship with the producer and establishing a captive urban market, the intention was then to slowly convert the conventional farming practices here to ecological and sustainable farming practices.

Apart from consumers' cooperatives, producers' cooperatives are being formed for the equitable distribution of organically grown food. In Aurangabad, Maharashtra, the Institute for Integrated Rural Development has set up a producers'/farmers' cooperative, which has proved to be successful in ensuring fair prices to the farmers while

---

13. In Mumbai, one of the earliest outlets for organic food was the 'Health Shop' set up by Kavita Mukhi in 1990. Several other outlets grew shortly, who primarily sourced their product from the 'Health Shop'. However, all of them cater primarily to consumers who can afford to pay premium prices for these products.

14. During 1995, a national chain of ethical and environmental supermarkets cooperative called 'Out of this World' was set up in the UK. Starting with an initial membership of 18000, their products, mostly food and beverages, are to meet the following criteria: healthy eating through consumption of whole food and organically grown produce; fair trade; animal welfare; environmental sustainability and community development. The shops are made with materials chosen for their functionality and minimal environmental impact. Each of their shops stock produce from local farmers and suppliers as well as community-based farms thus ensuring sustainability of the local producers. Currently the chain has three outlets.

ensuring delivery of organically grown produce to the consumer. The cooperative chooses the crops to be grown, establishes the price of produce and through a consumer cooperative run entirely by women, called Organic Link, it distributes its produce to the member households.

Another alternative distribution model that has emerged is that of a large independent wholesaler and retailer of natural and organic foods. Distribution of natural, whole organic foods which started as a small one-room outlet in 1970, SUMA, is currently the largest independent wholesaler and distributor of organic and natural foods in the UK promoting vegetarian food.[15]

Consumption

Consumers play a critical role in creating a sustainable food system. Through their purchases, they send strong messages to the producers, retailers, and others in the system about what they think is important. Food cost and nutritional quality has always influenced consumer choices. Consumers have to be brought in contact with the producers using sustainable practices to market their goods so that it is available to a wider public and the process becomes viable.

What really are the alternatives available given the plethora of food products that sell 'ease of cooking', 'convenience', 'nutrition and quality', 'wholesome food'? The consumer has to select safe and healthy food from a shelf of genetically engineered foods, organic foods, health foods, whole foods, *etc*. What used to be a western overconsumption pattern is fast becoming prevalent in developing

15. SUMA is the UK's largest independent wholesaler and distributor of quality vegetarian, fairly traded, organic, whole and natural foods. One man started SUMA in the early 1970s who sold rice and lentils from his front room in Leeds. Such was the demand that SUMA grew rapidly into a seven-employee business. These people became the founder members and SUMA was registered in 1977 as a common ownership workers cooperative. Today SUMA is a multi-million pound company that operates out of a 60,000 sq ft warehouse in Elland, West Yorkshire. From here their product lines are distributed to independent retail shops, supermarkets, institutions (hospitals, schools, prisons), community groups. SUMA has pioneered major new products and categories in the UK, recycled paper toilet tissues, dairy-free margarines, organics, fair-trade and introduced leading environment friendly brands such as Ecover to the UK. SUMA has been growing and changing while maintaining the founding principles: equality of wages for all jobs; multi-skilling and job variety; personal development within the company; ethical business; 100 per cent employee-owned and managed; democratic decision-making processes; equal opportunities; environment friendly products; and common ownership. [www.suma.co.uk]

countries with increasing numbers of shopping malls and supermarkets. The only way out is to make an informed rational choice. In the absence of any coherent or respected 'labelling' scheme, shoppers are, as ever, entirely at the mercy of the producers' and advertisers' cleverly worded and often spurious or misleading claims. Nobody expects the average shopper to be able to perform a full life cycle analysis and environmental impact assessment of their prospective purchase on the shop-shelf or supermarket aisle.

Take the case of the Health Awareness Centre in Mumbai, which is into its tenth year of existence. The Centre has provided an alternative healthier lifestyle even to those with chronic illnesses through promotion of natural, holistic food consumption practices and an alternative way of life – a 'sustainable health model', the responsibility of which rests entirely with women in this centre.

Religion and culture have played an important role in the choice of foods. In Mumbai, for example, a group of Jains (about 10 dedicated families) driven by their religious beliefs, source organically grown food from Karnataka and distribute it among themselves. The group called ASAL typically sources cereals, pulses, sugar, etc, in amounts adequate for their needs. The grains, condiments, oil, *etc.*, are transported to a central warehouse from where they are distributed to the member consumers. No chemicals are used at any stage of production or distribution. Increasingly they have been receiving enquiries for their produce from religious organizations for mass feeding in functions.

Alternative consumption patterns thus can be seen as largely isolated events occurring in pockets.

The Problems

In preparation for this paper, some of the discussed initiatives were examined closely through discussions with the practitioners and participants of these initiatives. The various arguments that emerged from such initiatives not being the norm can be categorized as follows: premium pricing; authenticity of produce; strong multinational and market forces; lack of right policy and governance support; and conditioning of overconsumption in lifestyles.

Pricing

One of the most important constraints faced by the producers and consumers of organic foods is the high price. Farmers charge a premium of at least 10-15 per cent over the local '*mandi*' price.

In India, production of ecologically grown produce is actually profitable to producers. Inputs required are lower compared to conventional farming and they can actually afford to sell it at a price lower than the market price for conventionally grown produce. Labour costs are much lower here, thereby reducing cost of inputs *vis-à-vis* European countries, therefore the costs of organic farming should be on par if not lower than conventional farming. These findings have been drawn from a global study in Asia and other countries by IFOAM.

Discussions with both producers and distributors of organic produce showed that the main causes of high pricing are: high demand and low supply; no systematic price structure; absence of a structured marketing system; often used as a value addition by producers that serves as an incentive; and serves to attract consumers biased towards premium products.

Due to the absence of a marketing system, there is no public awareness of organic *vs.* chemically grown produce. In the wholesale markets, very often organic and non-organically grown produce are mixed due to this lack of awareness. In India, roughly 30 per cent of the organic produce is exported and 70 per cent is marketed along with the normal produce. So not all farmers get the premium price on the organically grown produce.

Individual organic food outlets and health shops in metro cities like Mumbai have problems of overheads, which are high due to real estate costs. All these costs contribute to the high cost of the products. Since the demand and supply are not in place and the market is unreliable, some of the outlets find that the spoilage factor is high although the shelf life of organically grown produce is higher than for other non-organic produce. This is another reason for the high price.

Another issue that is contributing to the premium pricing is the cost of certification. We need to remember that till date the process of certification for any organic product is absolutely central – the price and acceptability to the customer depends upon this to a great extent. To certify the soil/system as organic, there is a cost. This cost is internalized into the production cost, which, also contributes to the rising price. For example, the current expenses to obtain an organic certification in India works out to be around Rs. 20,000 (includes travel and transportation, report preparation and certification for a single product.)

Experienced practitioners of organic farming are of the belief that if the process is producer-driven rather than consumer-driven then costs of organic farming are reasonable. If the middlemen are reduced and the distance between the producer and consumer shortened the system is bound to be more efficient and cost-effective. The most optimal model would probably be a producer cooperative selling to a marketing cooperative.

Authenticity

As I have mentioned before, certification of an organic productivity is quite central. There is no labelling system in place in India, and hence consumers are not able to differentiate and discriminate between the various types and categories of foods. Additionally riding on the organic food wave is a number of 'greenwash' outlets and vendors who charge a premium for produce that might not be organic. Even at the well known outlets such as the Health Shop (now Nature Options) in Mumbai, produce is not obtained from farms certified as organic instead it is by word of mouth and through personal visits and inspection that it is ascertained whether the produce is organically grown or not.

Due to the absence of a system, organic produce is mixed with non-organic and the authenticity of the produce is not known. Though several public and private sector certifying authorities have been constituted of late, there are still a couple of problems that creates problems. First, not all of them are duly accredited by the IFOAM – thereby reducing the acceptability of their certificates; second, the cost involved to obtain a certificate also deters most of the producers.

Lack of Policy Support

One of the greatest problems with organic agriculture has been the oppressive institutional policies that have constantly undermined the system. There is no policy level or governance support to establish a marketing and distribution system for organic produce in the country.

In January 1994, *Business Standard* reported that the Government of India (GoI) was allocating Rs 26 crore for promoting organic farming in the country. This was earmarked in the Eighth Plan and the programme was to involve *Krishi Vigyan Kendras*, farm universities and NGOs. Discussion with organizations engaged in organic farming revealed that the Ministry of Agriculture, GoI does not provide any support for organic farming. But the ray of hope is that with the Uruguay Round of GATT agreements, agricultural subsidies are slowly being lifted from 2002. So, farms must slowly move towards organic farming to prevent sudden exposure to high costs when subsidies from fertilizers and pesticides are lifted.

Surprisingly, the Ministry of Commerce, GoI, on the other hand, was promoting organic farming in a big way particularly for organic cotton. The Ministry has developed a suit of policies to encourage organic farming but it is entirely aimed at crops for the export market.

All bank loans are for pure crop farmers, in other words—monoculturists. The farmer who nourishes his/her soil with organic compost or recycled wastes is not even eligible for insurance, let alone subsidies.

The State Support

Suddenly, for some reason there have been a whole lot of activities aimed towards the organic sector from the government quarters. The Government has created a national organic logo through APEDA [Agricultural and Processed Food Products Export Development Authority].

In order to promote organic farming in the country in view of its great export potential and also because of its eco-friendly nature, the National Steering Committee, under the Chairmanship of Secretary Commerce, approved the National Programme for Organic Production. Under the National Programme for Organic Production (NPOP), documents such as National Standards, Accreditation Criteria for accrediting, inspection and certification agencies, Accreditation Procedure, Inspection and Certification Procedures have all been prepared and approved by the National Steering Committee. These documents were prepared on the basis of the guidelines evolved by the representative international organization, International Federation for Organic Agricultural Movement (IFOAM), EU Regulations, and Codex standards.

The National Steering Committee has designated the following statutory boards/authorities as Accreditation Agencies:

(a) Agricultural and Processed Food Products Export Development Authority (APEDA)

(b) Coffee Board

(c) Spices Board

(d) Tea Board

(e) Coconut Development Board and

(f) Directorate of Cashew and Cocoa Development.

The Planning Commission has set up a Working Group on Organic and Biodynamic Agriculture. The Department of Commerce has established National Organic Standards. APEDA has already submitted an application on 30 June, 2001 through the Advisor (Agriculture & Marine), Mission of India to the EU, Brussels for inclusion of India in the list of third countries under Article 11 of the EU regulations No 2092/91 so that India's National Programme for Organic Production gets recognition under the EU regulations. APEDA's membership with the International Federation of Organic Agricultural Movement (IFOAM), Germany, has been revived to keep in touch with the developments taking placed the world over in the organic sector. APEDA is also proposing to take up membership of International Accreditation Forum, Inc., US, to gain equivalence for our NPOP with the similar programs of US, Japan, Canada, and Australia.

Some amount of activity is also being noticed in the forms of customer awareness programs, exporters' meets, framing the operational instructions, state and NGO-level cooperation, *etc.*

Policy Considerations

Public-Private Partnerships

The environmental and economic benefits of organic agriculture have captured the attention of several countries; however, only a small number have enacted policies to assist the organic sector. Most assistance has been developed by the private sector, especially the NGOs. This private-sector infrastructure is not only recognized by countries, but is also encouraged to a large extent.

Farmers and consumers in almost all countries rely on a system of private self-organized producer organizations and independent certifiers, which have, over the years, provided an economically efficient mechanism of certification. The degree to which private organizations are significant is indicated by the fact that IFOAM has some 650 individual and institutional members in over 100 countries, 75 per cent of which are in developing countries. However, the network of private certifiers needs to expand; as mentioned earlier, many developing countries still lack certification organizations.

Organic programs, as well as the Draft Codex guidelines, maintain evolving "input lists" of acceptable inputs for organic production, processing aids, and ingredients. Countries, in consultation with the civil society organizations, can propose their own input lists to Codex, and negotiations will probably take place over what ultimately is acceptable in the international marketplace. Many developing countries have not drawn up material lists and generally lack the resources and training to effectively participate in the international standard-setting processes.

Engaging in international trade requires quantities of goods well beyond the production capacity of individual small organic farmers. NGOs have supported farmers in their efforts to establish appropriate organizations for collecting, processing and marketing organic products. Countries could support NGOs in building organizations that play a key role in disseminating the best practices and ensuring that farmers use adequate production and post-production techniques.

Technical Support

Northern developed countries have invested by far the most in organic agriculture research, but even so, the contribution is minimal compared to overall research in agriculture (less than 0.01 per cent of the US Department of Agriculture research budget is directed to organic agriculture). The lack of extensive formal organic research combined with the highly site-specific nature of organic agriculture, suggests that it would be most advantageous for farmers themselves to participate in the locally based, applied field research. Experience with the FAO-initiated Integrated Pest Management (IPM) Farmer Field Schools and community forestry projects has shown that farmers, whether owners or tenants, large or small, can practice good scientific methods if they are given orientation and technical support. Countries could also undertake market research. The USA, for example, analyzed the market for organic goods in more than 20 countries, with a focus on opportunities for US exports.

Draft Codex guidelines, as well as most national and private organic standards, disallow genetically engineered organisms (GEOs), including transgenic crops, in organic production. By providing consumers with a non-GEO produced alternative organic agriculture has secured an important market, at the same time relieving much of the pressure to impose out-right bans on GEO-produced food. While current biotechnology applications have been rejected for organic production, it is possible that future scientific developments and further discussions may produce technologies acceptable to consumers (such as the value of tissue culture in producing disease-free planting materials).

Direct Assistance

Interest in environmental protection and the preservation of small family farms has led developed European countries to subsidize organic production to varying degrees. The subsidies can provide significant encouragement (such as UK provides up to £450 per hectares during the conversion period for designated land areas, while the European Community subsidies have helped 15 per cent of Irish organic farmers develop dairy operations). Interested communities would have to be advised on organizational aspects, on procuring and commercializing the necessary inputs, and marketing any surplus produce (*e.g.* seed and planting material of adapted varieties, suitable livestock genitors *etc.*).

Consumer confidence in the integrity of organic claims is essential if goods are to be sold at a premium. Because organic products cannot be distinguished from conventional products, consumers depend entirely on certifiers to truthfully distinguish organic from non-organic goods. Countries could better enforce organic standards by punishing those who engage in fraudulent activities as well as undertaking systematic tracking, and measuring of fraud and its impact on the market.

Required Policy Measures

Any recommendations or strategies to steer food production and consumption in a sustainable direction must follow a multi-pronged approach since the same is governed and directly influenced by multiple forces. The challenge is to use a range of well-targeted policy measures and approaches, which can ensure that the growing concerns regarding food safety, food security, environmental protection, and the viability of the rural areas are met in ways that maximize benefits, are most cost-effective, and avoid distortion of production and trade.

The FAO during its 1996 World Food Summit recommended "...political and administrative framework within which food production can increase without leading to widespread environmental damage should have the following main elements:

- Initiation of dynamic, participatory land-use planning processes that identify and mitigate the risks of natural-resource degradation and other environmental impacts.
- Social and economic policies that improve the capacity of food producers in the poorer areas to manage efficiently their soil fertility, soil moisture, pest populations and biological diversity through holistic management systems. In many cases, success will depend on first addressing major social or economic constraints such as the equitable distribution of productive resources, access to capital, or unemployment.
- Greater investment in human capital and rural infrastructure including the improved use of information and communication technology and training and empowering agricultural advisers to work with farmers to apply environmentally sound production methods.
- Ongoing assessment, monitoring and evaluation of environmental impacts due to food production practices"

(*Food Production and Environmental Impact*, World Food Summit, FAO, 1996, http//www. fao.org/wfs/final/e/ volume2/t11a-e.htm).

Keeping these basic principles in mind one can frame a set of policy measures that would definitely help:

General Measures

- Identify and recognize the already existing organic and traditional agriculture production systems based on polyculture and diversity. In the process of promoting sustainable agriculture, the government must take cognisance of and respect the multi-functionality of agriculture. The first step in the entire process is for producers and consumers to understand the true definition of food, and then promote practice-oriented agronomic and economic research, by which we can improve the understanding of organic farming systems and of the environmental, economic and social impact of farming.
- Define a clear policy for sustainable agricultural development. Incorporate organic agriculture as a central part of overall policy. Fractured and part policies, particularly from the government, do not provide any benefit to the sector.
- Support to farmers converting to organic agriculture, or for the introduction of certain technologies such as water and energy conservation. They should also be adequately informed about the importance of conservation of these resources. Resources such as energy and water are extensively subsidized by national governments in a number of developing countries. As a result of which no amount of promotion of alternate non-conventional sources of energy or water conservation measures can bear fruition. There is no incentive to conserve these resources.
- Recognize the important interdependence of healthy societies, the economy, and the environment. The absence of recognition of this interrelationship between economic and environmental policies, particularly in developing economies, has resulted in extensive wastage of resources – financial resources, human power, and time. On one hand, extensive resources are committed to environmental management programs and plans developed in an attempt to conserve natural resources, on the other hand, economic policies are formulated in direct contradiction to this wherein utilization of natural resources are heavily subsidized. In effect this amounts to subsidizing pollution because many subsidies actually reduce the cost of overexploiting or polluting the environment.

Economic Measures

- Reform national economic indicators for the agricultural sector to reflect depletion and degradation of natural resources. Implement the "Polluter Pays' principle: Internalize "external" costs for environmental and health risks in the price of products.[16]
- Eliminate subsidies that encourage natural resource degradation or depletion. Let us take the case of free electricity for farmers in some states of India. This is probably one of the most distortionary subsidies in recent times. Apart from creating extensive energy demand and hence stress on natural resources such as water, coal or natural gas, the costs incurred will have to be cross-subsidised by other consumers or through resources allocated by the state. The same is the case with the production of chemical fertilizers such as urea.
- A local certification programme that is well supported by a national organic movement can strengthen the identity of a country's organic sector and give fresh impetus for various joint activities. Reducing the cost of certification can be another motivation for developing countries to set up a local certification agency. The development of domestic organic markets can be facilitated if local certification is available. Another way of doing is to promote – Community Certification, which involves the communities taking charge of the certification process themselves.[17]

Food and Markets

- Eliminate agricultural support programs that create

---

16. The Polluter Pays Principle was first widely discussed in the United Nations Conference on Environment and Development held in Rio de Janeiro of Brazil in June 1992. All the attending representatives of the countries and nations endorsed the principle.
17. The community certification involves the communities taking charge of the certification processes themselves and working on a non-profit but no subsidy basis. Such certification process look at the farmers' commitment to the stewardship of soil, growing food in an environmentally sensitive way rather than a set of technical standards like whether a certain kind of bone meal was added to the soil or not. [Satheesh, 2003]. World Organic Congress'03 hosted by IFOAM at Victoria, Canada had a remarkable theme: "Cultivating Communities". The motto "Cultivating Communities" highlighted the role of organic agriculture in sustaining healthy, vibrant communities whether they are communities of microorganisms in the soil, communities of beneficial insects in the orchard or rural and urban communities anywhere in the world. A major item of discussion was Community Certification.

commodity surpluses and lower global commodity prices in the name of export production and global markets.

- Abolish distorting incentives, such as government programs, that finance only industry-dominated partnerships for pesticide or synthetic fertilizer promotion programs or special incentives for exports.
- Prioritize safe food crops and investment in the food sector. Offer incentives to the private sector to make hassle free and secured investments.
- A central element of the organic farming method is the efficient use of on-farm and local resources: farmyard manure, indirect crop protection, local seed, *etc*. Organic agriculture pursues a course for promoting the powers of self-regulation and resistance, which soil, plants and animals possess naturally. Develop local and regional food processing and local food markets. Promote sustainable consumption patterns and local food. Promote local and regional food processing. Reduce the distance between the point of production and consumption to ensure greater food security. Time and again it has been proved through local action that all efficient resource management/utilization is best done this way, be it water or land.[18] This can also help in responding to shift in dietary patterns as greater access to fresh produce improves.[19]

18. '*Pani Panchayat*' at Ralegan Siddhi in Maharashtra, micro-watershed management in various parts of the country, joint forest management by the local community in Madhya Pradesh and many more are all evidence of the efficiency and sustainability of decentralized resource management.
19. Consumer cooperatives such as the *Mumbai Grahak Panchayat* and the Nippon Ecology Network [NEN] in Japan are proof of how efficient distribution systems can be effective by reducing the distance between producer and consumer through elimination of middlemen to a large extent. Marketing and distribution then becomes cost-effective. In Mumbai, over 17,000 households now belong to the *Mumbai Grahak Panchayat*, which has developed an interesting model of distribution of groceries to its members based on the principle of collective buying, and no-loss-no-profit. It is a collective purchasing system that procures directly from the producer/vendor, eliminates/minimizes the 'middlemen' and provides good quality foods and other products at a competitive price. This movement has been operational since 1975. [Gopalan, 2001] Similarly, Nippon Ecology Network (NEN) in Japan also focuses on ensuring safe and fairly priced foods and other goods. The NEN operates a weekly organic food home delivery service for over 25,000 households. Recently, the Green Purchasing Network bringing together over 1,000 companies, public authorities and citizen groups to promote the choice of sustainable goods and services across Japan have supplemented this. The NEN is a women's initiative and has become a large movement in Japan.

Research, Extension, Farming Education and Information Exchange

- Give first priority to research in organic agriculture, livestock and food crops.
- Link research, extension and farmers closely.
- Reform extension service and agriculture education and re-train staff both in knowledge and methodology of organic or ecological farming.
- Support farm-based research, farmer-to-farmer exchanges and other participatory methods.
- Include a clear commitment to government-NGO partnerships and to the democratic process. Also provide a clear commitment to and inclusion of women, small farmers, indigenous people and other possibly disadvantaged groups.
- Support producers' associations, women and community organizations to play a leading role in development.

Access to Resources

- Provide the basic security to the farmer who is actually the closest to the entire agricultural production system. Secure farmers' land tenure and his rights to develop and save seeds. The terminator technology should not eradicate the role of the farmer from the entire system. Efforts should also include genuine land reforms, tariff protection for staple foods so that farmers receive fair prices, and the reversal of biases in policies for credit, technology, research, education, subsidies, taxes, and infrastructure, which unfairly prefer large farms at the expense of smaller ones.
- Make credits accessible for organic projects and production. The system of not providing credits to biodiverse farmers should be changed.

Conclusion

Today, the inability to achieve environmentally sound and sustainable food production is primarily the result of human inaction and indifference rather than natural or social factors. Compounding the shorter-term problems of damage to soil, water, forests and fisheries are longer-term prospects of climate change, loss of biological diversity and the pressure of an increasing human population.

Genetic modification has increased production in some crops. But the evidence we have suggests that the technology has so far addressed too few challenges, in few crops of relevance to production systems in many developing countries. Even in developed countries, a lack of perceived benefits for consumers, and uncertainty about their safety, have limited their adoption. The scale of investment involved, and the attraction of advanced science, may distort research priorities and investment. Genetic modification is not a good in itself, but a tool integrated into a wider research agenda, where public and private science can balance each other. Most of the short-term successes may be derived from marker-assisted breeding and diagnostics rather than from transgenic crops *per se*.

Relying on technology or policy tools alone is not sustainable. It must be combined with participation, equity, dialogue, enabling mechanisms, and gender empowerment. Steering research in the right direction and developing adequate and international agreements. On safety and access is a difficult and responsible task. While we are most aware than ever of the need to manage international public goods responsibly, the political tools to do so are weak, and, in a globalized economy, the voices of small and poor producers and consumers go often unheard. Ultimately the political action, if it is to be effective, must result in governance prepared, and mandated, to govern in the interests of citizens as full human beings in the real living world, not simply as economic units of production and consumption.

Last but not the least, economists and policy makers have moral responsibilities to speak for the weaker segments of the society, because they at times best understand the likely results of not doing so.

References

Alvares, Claude (ed) (1996). *The Organic Farming Sourcebook*, The Other India Press in association with Third World Network, Malaysia.

ACC/SCN (2000). *Fourth Report on the World Nutrition Situation: Nutrition Throughout the Life Cycle*, United Nations Administrative Committee on Cordination (ACC) Subcommittee on Nutrition (SCN), Geneva.

AIBA (2000), Biotechnology Parks, AIBA, Delhi.

Amoore, L. (2000). "International Political Economy and the Contested Firm", *New Political Economy*, 5(2), 183-204.

Bail, C., R. Falkner and H. Marquard (2002). "The Cartagena Protocol on Biosafety: Reconciling Trade with Environment and Development?" *Earthscan*, London.

Barton, J. (2000). "Intellectual Property Rights: Reforming the Patent System", *Science*, 287, March 17, 'Policy Forum', 1933-34.

Bendell, J. (2000). "Civil Regulation: A New Form of Democratic Governance for the Global Economy?" in J. Bendell (ed), *Terms for Endearment: Business, NGOs and Sustainable Development*, Sheffield, UK, Greenleaf.

Biermann, Frank (2001). "Big Science, Small Impacts – in the South? The Influence of Global Environmental Assessments on Expert Communities in India", *Global Environmental Change. Human and Policy Dimensions*, Vol 11, Number 4: 457–88.

BIO (2002). "Open letter to President George W. Bush on BIO's Legislative Priorities for 2002", Biotechnology Industry Organisation, http://www.bio.org/issues/bush2002.asp.

Bozeman, Barry (2001). "Public Value Mapping of Science Outcomes", draft concept paper, October, Centre for Science, Policy and Outcomes (CSPO), Washington, DC.

————. (2002). "Public-Value Failure: When Efficient Markets May Not Do" in *Public Administration Review*, March/April. Vol 62, No 2: 134-51.

Bud, R. (1995). "In the Engine of Industry: Regulators of Biotechnology, 1970-86" in M. Bauer (ed), *Resistance to New Technology*, CUP, Cambridge.

Byerlee, D. and K. Fischer (2001). "Accessing Modern Science: Policy and Institutional Options for Agricultural Biotechnology in Developing Countries", *IP Strategy Today* 1 (Available from http://www.bio developments.org/ip/index.htm).

Brown, L.R. (1996). *Tough Choices*, Worldwatch Environmental Alert Series, W W Norton, New York.

Capra, F. (1982). *The Turning Point: Science Society and the Rising Culture*, Flamingo, London.

Carr, S. and L. Levidow (2000). "Exploring the Links between Science, Risk, Uncertainty, and Ethics in Regulatory Controversies about Genetically Modified Foods", *Journal of Agricultural and Environmental Ethics*, 12, 29-39.

Chaturvedi, Sachin (2002) "Agricultural Biotechnology and New Trends in IPR Regime: Challenges before Developing Countries", *Economic and Political Weekly*, March 30.

DBT (1990). Recombinant DNA Safety Guidelines, Ministry of Science and Technology, Government of India, New Delhi.

————. (1994). Revised Guidelines for Safety in Biotechnology, Ministry of Science and Technology, Government of India, New Delhi.

————. (1998). Revised Guidelines for Research in Transgenic Plants and Guidelines for Toxicity and Allergenicity Evaluation of Transgenic Seeds, Plants and Plant Parts, Ministry of Science and Technology, Government of India, New Delhi.

————. (1999a). Addendum to the "Revised Guidelines-August 1998", Issued September 24, Ministry of Science and Technology, Government of India, New Delhi.

————. (1999b). "Counter Affidavit on Behalf of The Union of India-Respondent No 1 to the Writ Petition", Supreme Court of India, Extraordinary Original Jurisdiction, Civil Writ Petition No 71/1999.

Dhillon, B.S. and G.J. Randhawa (2000). "Evaluation of Transgenic Crop Varieties for Biosafety and Agronomic Performance – Some Considerations", paper presented at the Biosafety Training Seminar, National Bureau of Plant Genetic Resources, August 14-27.

E P Act (1986). The Environment (Protection) Act, 1986, Union Ministry of Environment and Forests, Government of India. November 19, vide Notification No G S R 1198(E), *Gazette of India No 525*, dated 12-11-86.

Expert Panel (2000). "Recommendations on the Establishment of Research and Development Facilities for Evaluation of Indian and Imported Transgenic Plant Material in India", A panel of experts report, coordinated by the University of Delhi, New Delhi.

Ghosh, P.K. and T.V. Ramanaiah (2000). "Indian Rules, Regulations and Procedures for Handling Transgenic Plants", *Journal of Scientific and Industrial Research*, (Vol 59, February, pp 114-20).

GoI (2000). "Large-Scale Field Trials for Transgenic Cotton Allowed", Press Release, Government of India, July 20 (Press Information Bureau: New Delhi).

Gopalan, Radha (2001). "Sustainable Food Production and Consumption: Agenda for Action", *Economic and Political Weekly*, April 14.

Gupta, Aarti (1999). "Framing 'Biosafety' in a Transnational Context: the Biosafety Protocol Negotiations under the Convention on Biological Diversity", (ENRP Discussion Paper E-99-10, Kennedy School of Government, Harvard University, Cambridge, MA).

————. (2000a). "Governing Trade in Genetically Modified Organisms: The Cartagena Protocol on Biosafety" in Environment, Vol 42, No 4: 23-33.

————. (2000b). "Governing Biosafety in India: The Relevance of the Cartagena Protocol", discussion paper 2000–24, Kennedy School of Government, Harvard University, Cambridge, MA. Available at: http://www.environment.harvard.edu/gea

————. (2001). "Advance Informed Agreement: A Shared Basis to Govern Trade in Genetically Modified Organisms?" Indiana Journal of Global Legal Studies, Vol 9, No 1: 265-81, Available online at http://ijgls.indiana.edu

————. (2002). "When Global is Local: Negotiating Safe Use of Biotechnology in a Multilateral Context", in Globalising and Localising: Knowledge Cultures of Environment and Development, edited by Sheila Jasanoff and Marybeth Long-Martello, forthcoming.

Hannis, M. (1998). "The Myth of Green Consumerism: Consumption, Community and Free Markets", Lancaster University MAVE Programme, http://www.lancs.ac.uk/users/philosophy/mave/mh_2.htm.

Hare, J. (1998). "Crisis in Agriculture Cultivating Disaster: US Farm Policy Fiasco", *Multinational Monitor*, July-August, Vol 10, Nos 7 and 8.

HT (1998a). "Terminator Stares India in the Face: Deadly Seed May Sneak into the Country, Warn Social Scientists", *The Hindustan Times*, August 21.

————. (1998b). "Govt to Keep Door Shut on Terminator Seeds", *The Hindustan Times*, December 2.

————. (1998c). "AP Bans Monsanto's Bollgard Field Tests: Farmers Term Experiments as Attempt to Introduce Terminator Gene", December 9.

Kapur, Arvind (1999). "Opportunities in Agricultural Biotechnology" in TERI: 80-92.

————. (undated). "Globalisation and the Seed Distribution System: The Impact of Globalisation and of Domestic Market Reforms on the Seed Distribution System in Developing Countries", unpublished manuscript, ProAgro PGS, New Delhi.

Kloppenburg, J.R. (1988). *First the Seed: The Political Economy of Plant Biotechnology*, 1492-2000, Cambridge University Press, Cambridge.

Mashelkar, R.A. (1999). "Economics of Knowledge" 16th Dr. C.D. Deshmukh Memorial Lecture, India International Centre, New Delhi.

Meadows, D.H. *et al* (1972). *The Limits to Growth*, Pan Books, London.

Mruthyunjaya and Ranjitha, P. (1998). "The Indian Agricultural Research System: Structure, Current Policy Issues and Future Orientation", *World Development*, 26: 6, 1089-1101.

Mubashir, Ellora (1999). "Introducing Transgenic Crops in India: A Joint-Venture Approach", in Joel I. Cohn (ed), *Managing Agricultural Biotechnology: Addressing Research Programme Needs and Policy Implications*, (New York: CABI Publishing, in association with International Service for National Agricultural Research, The Hague).

Nair, Rashmi (2000). "Safety Assessment of Transgenic Crops with Special Emphasis on Toxicity and Allergenicity", paper presented at the Biosafety Training Seminar, National Bureau of Plant Genetic Resources, New Delhi, August 14-27.

National Bureau of Plant Genetic Resources (2000). "Orientation Course: Biosafety Considerations for Evaluation of Transgenic Crops – Emerging Themes and Recommendations", held from July 17-26, Schedule and paper presentations, New Delhi.

Newell, P. (2002). "Biotechnology and the Politics of Regulation", working paper 146 (Biotechnology Policy Series No 2), Institute of Development Studies, Brighton, UK.

Oxfam (1999). "Genetically Modified Crops World Trade and Food Security", November (http://www.oxfam.org.uk).

Persley, G.J. (ed) (1999). *Biotechnology for Developing-Country Agriculture: Problems and Opportunities*, IFPRI 2020 Vision Focus 2 (10 Briefs), IFPRI, Washington DC.

Pimbert, M.P. and T. Wakeford (2002). "Prajateerpu: A Citizens, Jury/Scenario Workshop on Food and Farming Futures for Andhra Pradesh, India", IIED, London and IDS, Sussex.

Pimbert, M.P., T. Wakeford and P.V. Satheesh (2001). "Citizens' Juries on GMOs and Farming Futures in India", Low External Input and Sustainable Agriculture (LEISA) 17(4), 27-30.

RFSTE (1999a). Writ Petition (Civil) No 71 of 1999, in the matter of Research Foundation for Science, Technology and Ecology (Petitioner) versus Union of India and Others (Respondents). Supreme Court of India, Extraordinary Original Jurisdiction, Filed on January 16.

————. (1999b). Common Rejoinder Affidavit to the Counter Affidavits filed by the Union of India through Ministry of Science and Technology (Respondent No 1), Maharashtra Hybrid Seeds Company (Respondent No 2) and Monsanto Biotech (India) (Respondent No 3). Writ Petition (Civil) No 71/1999. Supreme Court of India, New Delhi.

————. (2000). "US Government Dumping Genetically Engineered Corn-Soya Mix on Victims of Orissa Super Cyclone", RFSTE Press Release, dated June 2, New Delhi.

Rules (1989). "Rules for the Manufacture, Use, Import, Export and Storage of Hazardous Microorganisms, Genetically Modified Organisms or Cells", issued by the Union Ministry of Environment and Forests, Government of India, vide Notification No GSR 1037 (E) dated December 5, 1989, Union Ministry of Environment and Forests, New Delhi.

Tata Energy Research Institute (1999). "Genetically Modified Plants: Benefits and Risks", proceedings of a workshop held on June 24, (New Delhi: TERI publications).

————. (2000). "Stakeholders' Dialogue on Agricultural Biotechnology: Biosafety and Economic Implications", proceedings of a workshop held on November 25, 1999 at the Tamil Nadu Agricultural University, (New Delhi: TERI publications).

The Hindu (1998). "Panel to Check Field Trials of Terminator Gene Technology", November 25.

————. (1999a). "Panel to Ensure Biosafety Recommended", January 8.

————. (1999b). "Terminator Technology Vital for Farmers' Interests", January 13.

————. (1999c). "Officials Welcome Seed Trials by Monsanto", January 14.

————. (1999d). "Monsanto Justifies Trials in India", February 23.

————. (1999e). "Debates over Monsanto's Field Trials", February 24.

Van Dusen, Eric (2000). "Challenges for Biosafety Regulation in Developing Countries", Viewpoint, June 12, Science, Technology and Innovation Programme, Harvard University.

Available at http://www.cid.harvard.edu/cidbiotech/comments/ UNDP (1998) *Human Development Report 1998*, Oxford University Press, New York.

Visvanathan, S. and C. Parmar (2001). "A Biotechnology Story: Notes from India", Centre for the Study of Developing Societies, Delhi,http://www.ids.ac.uk/ids/env/BiotechnologyStory.pdf.

von Weizscker, E., A.B. Lovins and L.H. Lovins (1997). "Factor Four: Doubling Wealth, Halving Resource Use", *Earthscan*, London.

Wright, Susan (1994). *Molecular Politics: Developing American and British Regulatory Policy for Genetic Engineering, 1972-1982*, University of Chicago Press, Chicago.

15

Coping with New Environmental Issues Concerning Agriculture Exports

MOHAMMED SAQIB

SECTION 1

TARIFF AND NON-TARIFF ISSUES IN WORLD TRADE

Despite the significant achievements of the trading system in reducing tariff barriers to trade, as early as 1970, General Agreement on Tariff and Trade (GATT) Contracting Parties expressed their dissatisfaction with the emergence of new non-tariff barriers (NTBs). In the 1970s, a GATT Working Group was established to evaluate the impact of NTBs on international trade, and reached the conclusion that technical barriers were the main form of NTBs that faced exporters. The term 'technical barriers' refers to product standards. Other forms of NTBs may include quotas, import licensing arrangements, *etc.*[1]

While a number of GATT provisions already addressed technical barriers, their scope was deemed to be insufficient to tackle the growing concerns. During the Tokyo Round, a Standards Code was drafted to govern the preparation, adoption and application of technical regulations, and standards and conformity assessment

1. Since the signing of the General Agreement on Tariffs and Trade (GATT) in 1947, tariffs have been bound for a large number of industrial and agricultural goods, and have declined significantly. Tariff binding means that a tariff level for a particular product becomes a commitment by a WTO Member and cannot be increased without compensation negotiations with its main trading partners. The Uruguay Round alone (1986-93) increased the percentage of bound product lines from 78 to 99 per cent for developed countries, from 21 to 73 per cent for developing countries, and from 73 to 98 per cent for economies in transition. It also resulted in substantial tariff reductions, occasionally to zero. Through a parallel process of 'tariffication', the trading system has initiated the conversion of all non-tariff import restrictions to tariffs for transparency, paving the way for their binding and gradual decline.

procedures. Negotiated during the Uruguay Round, the new Agreement on Technical Barriers to Trade (TBT) has built upon, as well as strengthened, the Standards Code. Whereas the Standards Code was a plurilateral agreement (with only limited membership), the Agreement on Technical Barriers to Trade applies to all World Trade Organization (WTO) Members. It came into force in 1995, with the entry of the WTO.

The Agreement on Technical Barriers to Trade (TBT) allows members to apply standards (both mandatory and voluntary) for the protection of human health or safety, animal or plant life, of health, or the environment. This Agreement also requires sound science and fulfillment of the least trade restrictiveness test. Even voluntary standards (such as eco-labels) have to follow a code of good practice based on the above principles. Rules are laid down for the conformity assessment here also. The Agreement does not consider standards set by any particular international setting organization as acceptable. In practice, however, ISO standards are considered compatible unless certain trade rules and certain jurisprudentially developed practices are not followed in setting them. For example, standards based on non-product related process and production methods and those differentiating between like products may not be acceptable.

The TBT Agreement is premised on an acknowledgement of the right of the WTO members to develop technical requirements, and to ensure that they are complied with. However, the Agreement has, as its objective to ensure that unnecessary obstacles to international trade are not created. This is achieved through a delineation of a number of legitimate objectives for which mandatory technical requirements may be developed. This is also achieved by a number of principles that govern the preparation, adoption, and application of mandatory and voluntary requirements and conformity assessment procedures, such as non-discrimination, avoidance of unnecessary obstacles to international trade, harmonization, equivalence of technical regulations and of the results of conformity assessment procedures, mutual recognition of conformity assessment procedures, and transparency. The scope of the Agreement extends to the central and local governmental standardizing bodies as well as to the non-governmental ones.

The Agreement on the application of sanitary and phytosanitary measures (SPS) is an elaboration of the GATT rules as they relate to the measures necessary to protect human, animal or plant life or health. Under this Agreement, member countries are required to base their SPS measures on scientific principles and refrain from maintaining measures without sufficient scientific evidence. Exceptionally, measures could be taken without sound science provided they are provisionally adopted, additional sound science is sought and the measure reviewed within reasonable time based on risks that non-fulfillment may entail. This provision was tested in three WTO cases in recent times. Broadly speaking, the 'precautionary principle' was not allowed to be expanded beyond what is already available in this provision. Also, it was considered essential to consider the risks that non-fulfillment would entail in adjudging the compatibility of the measure with the WTO rules. The Agreement encourages harmonization of the SPS measures and considers the standards set by three international standard setting bodies as acceptable standards. These are the Codex Alimentarius Commission, the International Office of Epizootics, and the International Plant Protection Convention. Equivalence is encouraged and conformity assessment guidelines are laid down. Special and more favourable treatment provisions exist for developing countries, but they apply only in name.

Under the TBT Agreement, special and differential treatment for developing countries is authorized. Such treatment includes: ensuring that the technical regulations, standards, and conformity assessment procedures of the developed countries do not create unnecessary obstacles to the developing country exports (including their expansion and diversification), not expecting developing countries to use international standards (since these, for instance, may be inappropriate for their level of technological development); ensuring that developing countries participate representatively in international standardizing bodies and international systems for conformity assessment; preparing international standards for the products that are of export interest to them; and, allowing them (particularly the least-developed among them) to obtain certain time-limited exceptions from obligations.

In addition, the Agreement calls upon the developed countries to provide the developing countries with technical assistance. Such assistance may be directed towards helping developing countries prepare their own technical regulations, meet the technical requirements of their export markets, establish national standardizing bodies and participate in international ones, establish bodies for conformity assessment with technical regulations and standards, access the conformity assessment systems of other countries, and become members of international bodies. Priority is to be given to the needs of the least-developed countries.

Non-tariff measures are often characterized by the use of non-product-related process and production methods (NPR-PPM), which have process implications and are based on value judgements that differ across countries. Such standards enforced in the developed country markets are not necessarily the best option in the developing countries. Standards vary from country to country due to factors such as differences in pollution assimilative capacities, degrees of industrialization, population densities, social objectives and priorities attached to the environment.[2] Principles 7 and 11 of the Rio Declaration also endorse this. Environmental measures also depend, to a significant extent, on the use of the "precautionary principle" and on risk-assessment techniques, which may be highly specific to the country making the decision, and may lend themselves to protectionist trade policies.

The developing countries are more vulnerable to the adverse effects of environmental measures on market access and competitiveness. This is because of lack of infrastructural and monitoring facilities, limited technology choices, inadequate access to and relatively more expensive environmental friendly raw materials, or even information. In addition, small and medium enterprises (SMEs) are the predominant exporters and there is an increasing emergence of environmental standards in the sectors of export interest to them.[3] They are at a disadvantage even with respect to the positive trading opportunities generated by environmental measures, because

2. UNCTAD, Policies and Mechanism for Achieving Sustainable Development, TD/B/1304, para 61, Geneva, 1991.
3. UNCTAD, TD/B/WG.6/10 paras 42-69.

exploitation of such opportunities requires skill and technology, which they sorely lack. UNCTAD has concluded that developing countries' exports may become vulnerable to external environmental requirements on account of their scale and sectoral composition.[4]

Trade measures are not the first best option for meeting global environmental objectives. Sustainable development is a much larger issue, encompassing efficient allocation of global resources, domestic environmental priorities in light of the states' contribution to the national and global environmental degradation, poverty alleviation, capacity of developing countries, and so on. An individual country might achieve sustainable development by safeguarding and enhancing existing market access. Scarce revenues preserved in this way might then be requisitioned through domestic policies for environmental protection purposes. Environmental policies, standards, and regulations can have varying impacts on the competitiveness of the developing and the developed countries. The effects on SMEs are particularly significant, often in sectors that are of particular export interest to the developing countries.[5]

Studies show that, in certain sectors, existing market access is being eroded on account of environmental measures, or environmental measures in the making have the potential to restrict developing countries' access to foreign markets. In the former case, an UNCTAD study[6] points out that about one-third of the value of the total exports and about half of the value of the manufactured exports of the developing countries originate in sectors that are potentially affected by environmental requirements; 60 per cent of the manufactured exports of the Asian developing countries are so affected.[7] Of particular importance is the impact of environmental measures on SMEs in such countries.[8] UNCTAD has reported that the SMEs share half of the total exports in a number of Asian developing countries. In India, the share of SMEs in the exports of textiles and leather is about 80 per cent. Further, the potential to expand the share of SMEs

4. UNCTAD, TD/B/WG.6/10, para 70.
5. UNCTAD, TD./B/WG.6/L.7, paras 21-23.
6. UNCTAD, TD/B/WG.6/10.
7. *Op. cit.* para 47. Also see para 48 and 53.
8. *Op.cit.* para 53-61.

in exports is very large in these countries. For example, while SMEs in Bangladesh account for 80 per cent of the total exports in a number of sectors, they export only 4 per cent of their output. Wherever additional investments are required for only exports, because the domestic market does not require such standards, there is an absence of economies of scale[9] and market access is hindered.

Measures such as eco-labeling, packaging, eco-taxes, *etc.*, affect market access. Eco-labels freeze technology choices, discourage product development and affect SMEs more than the large enterprises, because of difficulties in technological adaptation as well as in information requirements for effective monitoring. The fact that most eco-labels are voluntary does not change the fact that they are *de facto* non-tariff barriers affecting exports from the developing countries. Similarly, packaging regulations may be based on considerations that go beyond the borders of the importing market.

In addition to the issue of safeguarding existing market access, jurisdictional issues also need to be tackled. Negotiations under the multilateral trading system and panel decisions on these issues have upheld Principle 12 of the Rio Declaration that "unilateral actions to deal with environmental challenges outside the jurisdiction of the importing country should be avoided.[10] This is also affirmed in Chapter 2 of the Agenda 21 of UNCED.[11] Moreover, trade displacement caused by unilateral measures taken pursuant to an MEA is also of concern, particularly to the developing countries, and some safeguards against these trade effects should exist within the framework of the international trade rules. This has become all the more important on account of the emerging WTO jurisprudence whereby long standing principles like those relating to the concepts of like product, extra-territoriality, and extra-jurisdictionality are being gradually diluted.[12]

The use of PPM-based mechanisms needs special safeguards. More transparency or consultations in the process of standard formulation,

9. *Op.cit.* paras 63-64.
10. *Trade Rules and Environmental Controversies during the Uruguay Round and Beyond*, Peter P. Unimonen (1995). Also see Tuna-Dolphins Panel Report I and II, US Gasoline Panel and Appellate Report etc.
11. See United Nations (1993).
12. See, for example, the Shrimp-turtle case.

unless there is an obligation to take such comments into account, would be insufficient in granting market access. All these standards can act as non-tariff barriers to trade because of the following:

(a) The cost of compliance may be high.

(b) The technologies and raw materials required may not be available domestically.

(c) They may be totally inappropriate to the conditions of the exporting country.

The notion that income effects are of overwhelming importance in the context of developing countries is borne out by empirical evidence.[13] The above observations apply equally to removing non-tariff barriers in areas where developing countries have comparative advantages. In fact, removing tariff escalation, coupled with other non-tariff barriers, is also likely to restore production in accordance with the comparative advantage. According to the Brundtland Commission report, producing in accordance with comparative advantage is much more likely to be environmentally beneficial. There are many developing regions having better environmental absorptive capacities than developed regions for sectors like wood products, fisheries, and agriculture. Granting enhanced market access to these regions will not only enhance incomes but also engender balanced environmental protection.

Finally, enhanced market access for developing countries could be provided by phasing-in of environmental-friendly products or packaging from developing countries. An example is the environmental-friendly jute packaging used in India and Bangladesh. Some Organization of Economic Cooperation and Development (OECD) nations have enacted packing regulations requiring less environmental-friendly packaging than jute only because their consumers are not sufficiently familiar with it and it may be difficult to recycle[14] this product. When sustainable funds are being set aside in the OECD markets for recycling technologies, it should be possible to use some of these funds for recycling jute, and giving encouragement to jute packaging for environmental protection. Similar

13. WT/CTE/W/25, dated 22nd March 1996.

14. UNCTAD, TD/B/WG.6/Misc.7, para 45.

environmental-friendly products could be identified elsewhere for granting improved market access. Apart from niche-market products, it is necessary to look into additional market access across the board. The solutions to the environmental concerns may be found in the larger markets as well.

SECTION 2

SETTING OF RULES AND STANDARDS

GATT and the WTO

The GATT has been the beacon of the multilateral trading system since 1948. As a result of the Uruguay Round of multilateral trade negotiations, the WTO came into being in 1994 and came into force on 1st January 1995, subsuming GATT under itself. GATT reflected the environmental concerns of the international community through Article XX. This Article allows member countries to deviate from their obligations under the Agreement, *inter alia,* in the case of three types of trade measures relevant to the environment. These are measures necessary to protect human, animal or plant life or health; measures relating to the conservation of exhaustible natural resources if such measures are made effective in conjunction with the restrictions on domestic production or consumption, and measures necessary to secure compliance with laws or regulations not otherwise inconsistent with the GATT rules. However, such unilateral measures have to pass a composite trade test. This trade test has three components, *viz*., no arbitrary discrimination, no unjustifiable discrimination, and no disguised trade protection. It is often called the "least trade restrictiveness" test. Jurisprudence has shown that the second of these measures has become the most potent tool for taking GATT-compliant unilateral trade measures pursuant to the environmental objectives.

The GATT jurisprudence was historically based on the concept of non-discrimination between 'like products'. Thus, two "tuna-dolphin" cases held that so long as the product exported is tuna, the exports cannot be restricted because "purse seine" nets are used and as a consequence, more dolphins are trapped in the nets. The panels carved out a strict "necessity" test for measures taken for protection of human, animal, or plant life or health. Similarly, the measures taken for conservation of exhaustible natural resources had to be "primarily aimed at" conservation. With the emergence of the WTO, the jurisprudence has evolved beyond these concepts. The "reformulated gasoline" case in 1996 relaxed the latter test; a measure "also relating" to conservation, such as protecting the ambient quality of air over American cities, would pass muster. The "shrimp-turtle" case in 1998 widened the environmental window even further. Now the concept of "like product" seems to have been dropped altogether; a distinction can be made between shrimps harvested using a specific technology or device and those harvested without it. India was a party to this case and won it, but only on the basis of the "least-trade restrictiveness" test, specifically on the ground that the US measure amounted to "arbitrary discrimination."

WTO has environmental protection as one of its preambular objectives. It exhorts member countries to conduct their trade relations while keeping in view the optimal use of global resources in accordance with the objective of sustainable development. This seeks both to protect and preserve the environment and enhance the means for doing so in a manner consistent with their respective needs and concerns at different levels of economic development. Many WTO Agreements have environmental concerns built into them.

The Agreement on Subsidies and Countervailing Measures (ASCM) allows subsidization to promote adaptation with environmental laws without the fear of countervailability. The doctrine of optimal utilization of resources is indirectly built into the Agreement by rendering subsidies to units in economically disadvantaged regions that are also non-countervailable. The Agreement on Textiles and Clothing (ATC) also indirectly incorporates this doctrine by seeking removal of quotas. Similarly, the Agreement on Agriculture seeks removal of export subsidies as well as domestic support measures considered to render agriculture unsustainable. The Agreement on Trade-Related Aspects of Intellectual Property Rights (TRIPs) allows denial to patents on inventions whose commercial exploitation adversely affect animal, plant life or health, or could seriously prejudice the environment.

International Standards Organization (ISO)

ISO is the most important of international standard-setting organizations. It is a world federation of 123 national standards bodies, an international non-governmental organization with a majority of its members coming from the public sector. Its core business is the development, approval, and promulgation of consensus-based international standards. Unlike the WTO, the majority rule determines decisions in this organization.

ISO develops standards through 200 technical committees split into about 650 sub-committees and 2000 working groups. It also develops guides for standard setting. In preparing these, the ISO interfaces with specific users of standards, including those in the private sector. All its standards and guides are voluntary in nature. However, given its credibility as the most internationally accepted organization, ISO standards have considerable trade effects due to their wide use in the international trade. Therefore, those who can afford it, do apply for ISO certification.

ISO certification is a costly process by Indian standards. Certification may cost anything between Rs. 1,00,000 to 5,00,000, apart from the cost of maintaining the certificate. While the ISO 9000 series is the general quality certification standard of ISO, there is also an environmental management standard, *viz.*, ISO 14000 series. India has about 5000 ISO 9000 companies. About 100 companies have taken ISO 14000 certification.

Codex Alimentarius Commission

The Codex Alimentarius Commission, a UN body, compiles agreed-upon standards, guidelines and other recommendations into the Codex Alimentarius (the Codex Food Code or CFC). The CFC attempts to create harmonized standards. Prior to the SPS Agreement, the CFC could be adopted, applied and/or ignored at the discretion of a government. However, the CFC has now been adopted within the SPS Agreement as the benchmark. Thus, countries not imposing standards higher than CFC standards have the right to seek these standards for their imports. Codex Alimentarius has incorporated the Hazard Analysis Critical Control Point (HACCP) plans and principles as an integral part of the CFC. Volume V^{th} of the Food Code sets standards for a number of fish and fish products.

Hazard Analysis Critical Control Point (HACCP)

The HACCP system is being increasingly used as a food safety system all over the developed world. HACCP is not the magic bullet that solves all food safety problems. It is, when properly applied, a set of preliminary steps and principles that gives a systematic method for identifying significant hazards and properly applying preventive measures so that food-borne hazards are prevented, eliminated, or reduced to an acceptable level. With emerging international and national agreement on HACCP principles, their application is intended to create commonality of understanding in the development, implementation, and maintenance of a food-safety system. Many food processors, for example, require their suppliers to have a HACCP system for production of ingredients that they supply. The intention is to implement effective and documented systems that eliminate or reduce the likely occurrence of food-borne hazards. The application of HACCP offers widely understood principles for identifying significant risks and their control.

However, the HACCP does not cover only pathogenic bacteria. In applying HACCP, all food-borne hazards are to be considered. There are a number of hazards that can originate during production. Some examples of biological food-borne hazards that can originate during production include *Salmonella, Campylobacter jejuni, E. coli, Listeria monocytogenes, Yersinia enterocolitica, Cryptosporidium parvum,* and *Trichinella*; among chemical hazards, pesticides and drugs are the most common.

An important definition in HACCP is for Critical Control Point (CCP), defined as "a point, step or procedure at which control can be applied and a food safety hazard can be prevented, eliminated, or reduced to an acceptable level." Therefore, if the identified food safety hazards are to be controlled through the HACCP system, there must be a step or steps in production where control can be applied and there must be an associated preventive measure.

It is essential that scientifically documented steps and preventive measures are identified. If this criterion cannot be met, then the HACCP system cannot be developed. The HACCP system can only be developed through proper application of the preliminary steps and principles of HACCP. An essential prerequisite to HACCP is the adoption of Good Manufacturing Practices (GMPs). The biggest problem in the HACCP Plans is the lack of true CCPs.

Biological hazards are particularly difficult to deal with. For example, we know that proper heating times and temperatures will kill *E. coli*; therefore, this can be a CCP. However, at present there is not enough information about the sources and control of *E. coli* to be able to apply preventive measures.

Thus far, research has not provided for the reduction or elimination of pathogens at the preprocessing stage. There are possible interventions that could be considered as preventive measures on which a CCP could be based. However, these interventions need considerable research before they can be applied on a practical basis in the HACCP system for actual production.

SECTION 3

THE INDIAN FRAMEWORK

The Export and Import Policy (EXIM Policy)

The EXIM Policy of India is drawn up for a period of five years, with some changes being effected in an annual review in April and some other changes as and when necessary. There is a negative list each for exports and imports comprising prohibited, restricted (licensed), and canalized items. India's domestic environmental concerns (health and conservation-related) and multilaterally agreed environmental measures (such as CITES and Montreal Protocol) are implemented through these lists. There are many export-promotion measures built into the EXIM Policy, including the grant of special import licenses for firms having ISO certification. There is a separate chapter on quality, where ISO-compliant firms are rewarded and quality complaints are addressed.

The Export Promotion Councils and certain (Commodity) Boards and (Export Development) Authorities are given special status in the EXIM Policy. They grant membership to the exporters based on which the exporters become eligible to get certain licenses and benefits, like duty-free advance licenses for inputs for export production, and the benefit of deemed exports. Other relevant incentives include duty concession on import of capital goods used for export production, duty free imports for 100 per cent export-oriented units and units in the export processing zones, some fast track mechanisms for import clearances, and additional benefits for export and trading houses showing export performance beyond a certain threshold.

Rules and Regulations on Product Standards

The Ministry of Food and Consumer Affairs is the main Government agency dealing with product standards, although each Ministry/Department also has its own system of framing and notifying product standards. The state governments also have their own systems of adoption of standards, notably in the area of weights and measures. For the products under consideration in this paper, the main Rules and Regulations are contained in the Prevention of Food Adulteration Act, the Export Quality Control, and the Inspection Act and regulations for spice quality. A notable point in product standardization in India is that while the enforcement agencies have systems in place to enforce these rules in domestic units, effective or not, there is little possibility of enforcing them on imported goods. One reason could be that the Indian consumer market was comparatively closed till recently, and very few imported goods came in. With the passage of time, it would be advisable for the concerned agencies to devise systems to enforce these rules on imported goods. In recent times, the imported goods seem to get even better than national treatment as they are seldom subjected to the same enforcement procedures as the domestic units producing like goods. It is understood that an exercise to review the packaging rules has been initiated by the Ministry of Food and Consumer Affairs in order to apply the same rules to imported goods as are applied to the domestic goods.

Export Promotion Institutions

The Government has been laying emphasis on export promotion since the late 1960s. One result of this emphasis has been the proliferation of Export Promotion Councils and Authorities. These agencies have been playing a twofold role for product promotion. The first role has been that of nodal agencies for disbursement of export subsidies, a function that has considerably declined after liberalization and the removal of subsidies like the Cash Compensatory Scheme. The second role has been that of acting as the nodal point for interaction between the industry and the government. Some of these agencies, notably the Marine Product Export Development Authority and the Agriculture Produce Export Development Authority, have been actively involved in the implementation of policies relating to product standards, as we shall see in due course.

Standard Setting Bodies

The Bureau of Indian Standards (BIS) is the chief standard-setting body in India. It sets voluntary standards that, when met, indicate the quality of product. Compliance with the standard is denoted by the use of the "ISI" mark. The BIS is also the guiding organization behind most of the mandatory standards set by the Government agencies. Notably, the BIS is also the inquiry point of India under the WTO Agreement on TBT.

Enforcement Bodies

The Export Inspection Council is the chief enforcement body for exports, and the one relevant to the present paper.

SECTION 4

ENVIRONMENTAL REQUIREMENTS

Environmental measures cover a broad spectrum and include, *inter alia*, charges and taxes for environmental purposes, requirements relating to products including standards and technical regulations, eco-labeling, packaging, and recycling requirements. Such measures have significant effects on the access, particularly of developing countries, into markets prescribing the measures. The positive effects, or opportunities, are not always easy to exploit and require expertise, technology, and resources, which may not always be available to the developing countries. The negative effects include expenditures to adapt to new standards, acquire necessary technology and expertise, and establish the necessary administrative apparatus required in the receiving country. Acquiring or replacing packaging and other materials that are unavailable in the exporting country present another cost. Such negative effects should be mitigated or eliminated altogether for improving developing countries' market access. In fact, ways of providing additional market access to developing countries should be explored.

This section examines the effects of environmental measures on market access for selected Indian products. It studies the impact of stringent regulations in the food processing and agro-product sectors in some developed countries on Indian exports, addressing questions regarding not only the viability of compliance costs, but also their justification on environmental grounds. Some market access barriers related to NPR-PPMs having few transboundary effects are identified, and their impacts on costs, their effects on the local environment studied, as also the necessity or otherwise of meeting such standards. The HACCP standards are specially considered in examining the above issues and sectors.

Marine Products

The Indian Seafood Industry and Exports

The Indian Seafood industry is about 45 years old. It started in 1953 with the first shipment of shrimps to the USA. Until 1960, Indian exports in the fisheries area consisted mainly of dried fish, dried shrimp, shark fins, and similar products. The markets were largely confined to the neighbouring countries like Sri Lanka, Burma, and Singapore. Around the late 1960s, USA, France, Australia, Canada and Japan stated emerging as important markets for frozen and canned items. Processing plants with modern machinery for freezing and canning sprang up mainly for exports. During the 1980s, canned items have slowly disappeared, and frozen items have become predominant.

There are 404 factories registered with the Marine Products Export Development Authority (MPEDA) and over 625 active exporters, of which over 380 are manufacturers/exporters and 245 are merchant exporters. The total installed freezing capacity is around three million metric tonnes per annum. The total current production is around 3,80,000 metric tonnes per annum. Consequently, the industry's capacity utilization is only around 14 per cent. The factories are located all along the coastal states. 95 per cent of the units are in the small-scale sector. The industry employs over five million people directly and indirectly. These include a highly skilled and competitive work force. Women are predominant in certain processes of the labour force such as peeling.

Japan is the principal importer of Indian seafood, followed by the EU and the USA. Japan's share of Indian seafood exports is 45.8 per cent in value terms. It is followed by the EU (19.2 per cent) and the USA (10.6 per cent).

Marine products (fish, shrimp, squid, lobster, crab, etc.) constitute India's largest single agricultural export. Indian exports of marine products stood at US $1123 million in 1996-97 (Directory of Agricultural exports July 1997). The importance of marine exports for India is substantial. India's share of the total world market is 2.52 per cent (MPEDA). It represents an important potential growth area for the Indian economy, and a source of foreign exchange. Though the industry contributes only 3.4 per cent to India's foreign exchange earnings, it contributes over 7 per cent of the Net Foreign Exchange Earnings (*Source: Seafood Manufacturers Association*).

The marine exports are nevertheless at some risk, partly because of the failure to attain or adhere to international standards. India's marine exports attract automatic detention in USA. Automatic detention refers to a situation where the product must be sampled and tested before it gains entry into the country. This means delays, storage costs, and possibly, a substantial refusal rate. According to the estimates, fisheries products detained in the US are valued at US$ 14 million (or 15 per cent), out of total exports of US$108.2 million to the country in 1996-97 (*Source: Chemonics-ACE Project1998*).

In August 1997, the European Commission banned fishery products from India. The ban stated that:

- [European] Community inspection in India has shown there are serious deficiencies with regard to infrastructure and hygiene in fishery establishments and there is not enough guarantee of the efficiency of the controls by the competent authorities.
- There is a potentially high risk for public health with regard to the production and processing of fisheries products in this country.
- The results of checks of the community border inspection ports on fishery products imported from India have indicated that these products may be contaminated by micro-organisms, which may constitute a hazard to human health.
- Import of fishery products from India must, therefore, not be further allowed.

The Indian Government, faced with the EC ban, issued an Order dated 21 August 1995 that specified elaborate process standards, because, *inter alia*, "it is necessary to maintain the highest quality standards as per the health requirements of the importing countries that would encompass the standards like unified directive No. 91/493/EEC dated 22 July 1991 of the European Community ...." As a result of the EC ban on Indian fisheries products, and as a condition for the partial lifting of that ban, certain seafood processing plants and freezer vessels have been re-inspected and approved for exporting to the EC countries. Currently, about 90 out of 404 plants in the country are approved for export of fishery products to the EC.

The European standards are higher than the HACCP standards discussed above. The Seafood Exporters Association of India claims to have spent US$25 million on upgradation of their facilities to meet the regulations. An appropriate training of the personnel involved in various stages of production and processing also need to be addressed. Many of the standards adopted in the Order dated 21 August 1995 are either not relevant for the product quality or are too stringent given Indian fishing conditions. The legitimate objective, if any, of the standards could be met through less cumbersome and costly procedures. Some examples of the Standards applied through this Order, which clearly exceed HACCP standards, are given below:

- Fishes/fillets of uniform size and colour shall be packed together.
- The (shrimp) can exterior shall be free from major dents, rust, and seam distortions.
- 'Potable water' means water used for processing, which means tolerance levels as per EEC Directive No. 80/778-EEC.
- Sufficient supply of potable water ... shall be provided.
- Non-slip floor that is easy to clean ... structures and fixtures must have limber holds that are large enough not to be obstructed ... Walls and ceilings that are easy to clean ....
- Adequate ventilation ... proper vapour extraction ...
- Adequate lighting
- The immediate approaches of the processing areas shall be concreted or tarred or tufted to prevent wind-blown dust.
- The layout of different sections shall be in such a way as to facilitate the smooth and orderly flow of work to prevent possible cross contamination.
- The floor of the food handling and cold room areas shall be waterproof.

- Walls shall be free from projection and all pipes and cables shall be neatly covered. Junctions shall be rounded off.
- All window sills shall be sloping inwards.
- An anteroom should be provided to the cold rooms/storage.
- Potable water or clean sea water shall be used for all purposes.
- Staff must wear clean working clothes with headgear, which completely covers the hair.
- When recruited, any person working on and handling fishery products shall be required to prove, by a medical certificate, that there is no impediment to such employment.

The EC-approved plants are normally bigger plants with a capacity of more than 10 tonnes per day. Before entering the plant, one must exchange one's shoes for rubber boots, and put on a hair cover, facemask, and gown. Each plant has a chilling room with a temperature of -28 degree C. These factories are spotless with excellent facilities. EC-approved plants are as good as, and in some cases better than, any plant in Europe or USA. The floors are of marble and spotlessly clean, the equipment is stainless steel, the temperature is very comfortable, workers are in uniform, there is enough space to work comfortably, and water is provided for periodic cleaning of hands and raw materials. There are in-house peeling facilities. Every effort is made to reice the shrimp, or to put them in the freezer in brine, between steps in processing. The workers are similarly garbed, and while the women deheading the shrimp do not wear gloves (because they are too easily punctured), chlorine baths are always within reach for hand dipping. There are more than adequate changing, rest, and washroom facilities for the workers.

The plants have proper record keeping, and clean and well-equipped microbiological laboratories. A microbiologist staffing one such facility and consulted for this study, said regular checks of the incoming material and finished products are undertaken. According to her, the most common occurrence is the presence of *coliform* bacteria, but *salmonella* is rarely found. The first step is to wash the shrimps in cold brine, hence, contamination is removed. There are some 84 processing units like this in the country, out of a total of 404. Just to be sure, microbiological tests are also done at external laboratories for the confirmation of results.

A second type of unit includes those that have applied for EC approval. These are units exporting to the EU before the ban came into effect, and now exporting to the USA, Japan, and other places. These units also have facilities of a good standard. However, they lack marble floors. Polythene is provided for shoe and head covering. The change rooms and laboratories are not luxurious, but are designed for good hygiene. They are also equipped with laboratories. They have all the features required by the HACCP manual, but may be of a lesser standard than the EC norms. Their main handicap is infrastructure; for example, while they may lack change rooms of the size required by the EU, hygienic standards are not compromised.

The third type is typically run by small companies with an annual turnover of around Rs. two crore. These are small structures. They do not have in-house peeling facilities, and get peeling done from outside. They do have laboratories, but few are functional. They are inferior to EC-approved units. They have plenty of water and cleaning facilities. The hygiene conditions are apparently not bad, but the scope for contamination is quite high. These companies export to countries like China.

The exporters surveyed said that the concept of standards is good, but its adoption in totality for a developing country is rather difficult. For example, while potable water is in short supply in the Cochin area, the EU standards require that even floors and ceilings should be washed by potable water. There is also a social angle, namely that the neighbours of these facilities do not have enough water even for drinking. It is not easy to use 1,00,000 litres of water every day without attracting their resentment. The units, of course, often have their own treatment plants for potable water. They feel that EU norms are too strict, and in some cases, irrelevant for product safety. They have been asked to follow norms that even European plants do not follow. In this sense, double standards apply. For example, 62 tests are required to check water standards. For some of these tests, the equipment does not exist in India.

Adherence to these norms also increases the cost of production. Earlier production was mainly in bulk; the equipment required was plate freezers, refrigeration equipment, and facilities for processing and cold storage. But the EU requirement of infrastructure to meet the standards involves heavy investment in the equipment and buildings apart from operating costs. It is now necessary for each factory to have a potable water system, continuous power supply (standby generators), effluent treatment plants (ETPs), flake ice machines, chill rooms, and laboratories. It is estimated that such upgradation involves an expenditure of rupees one to two crore per unit as a fixed cost. The banks are not willing to give loans. They want to see the performance for the last three years. The last few years were bad because of the EU ban on exports from India. When a loan is granted the cost, at 18 per cent interest plus other running costs, is prohibitive.

As far as ongoing costs are concerned, overhead costs for a medium-sized plant can increase total costs by as much as five times. In one of the sample companies, the processing cost has gone up from Rs. two per kg to Rs. seven per Kg.

A crude breakdown of the increased compliance cost is:

1. The number of records to be maintained per day has gone up to 160. Earlier only 2 people were employed as record keepers; now there are 16. On an average salary of Rs. 2,000 per month, the wage for record keepers alone has reached Rs. 28,000 per month.
2. The number of operators has increased from 8 to 16 because of additional machines like ETPs, chilled rooms, flake ice machines, etc.
3. Earlier, peeling was done on contract by outsiders at Rs. 1 per kg. Since EU enforces in-house peeling, the cost has gone up from Rs. 1 to Rs. 7 per kg.
4. Water consumption has increased five times.
5. Power consumption has increased three times.
6. Overall, the general overheads have increased because of better quality staff, equipment, dress, *etc.*

According to the exporters, and confirmed by MPEDA, the compliance cost for meeting the EC norms is 15-40 per cent of the FOB value. The cost is more for the existing units. According to MPEDA, about two-thirds of the units will ultimately upgrade themselves to the EC norms, while the rest will perish. This may result in some unemployment and social tensions.

Another problem is that coastal fishing has virtually reached its saturation point. Any further growth may not be sustainable. The exporters are pleading for permission to shift to deep-sea fishing. However, the Government studies have found that the fragile marine ecosystem in areas where shrimp is found would be disturbed. So, permission is no longer being given for deep-sea fishing. These trends further affect exporters, in addition to the problems they face in meeting the EC norms. The ire against the EC norms is accentuated, particularly because the exporters find many of the details neither necessary nor implementable. Conducting 62 tests on the water to be used to process fishes is a standard they do not consider justifiable on the ground of hygiene alone. Similarly, they find the specifications for the size of washrooms unnecessary.

Aquaculture

In view of the sustainability issues about shrimp harvested from the sea, there has been a gradual shift to aquaculture in India. This shift was assisted by the MPEDA by providing technical assistance beginning in 1977-78. As a consequence, the export of cultured shrimp in the total exports of shrimp has moved up to 42.9 per cent in quantity terms and 66.4 per cent in value terms by the year 1997-98. The total area under shrimp farming at the end of 1997-98 is estimated to be 1,41,591 hectares. Of this, more than 50,000 hectares are under traditional shrimp farming practices in the states of Kerala, West Bengal, and Karnataka. The rest is scientific farming with the active assistance of MPEDA. The potential area for shrimp farming along the coast in India is estimated to be 1.2 million hectares, of which only about 10 per cent is currently being utilized. There is, therefore, a lot of scope for improving the production.

Environmental issues have emerged in aquaculture also, but these are domestic environmental concerns rather than international sustainability issues. The concerns have arisen in view of the reports of the ecological and environmental effects of aquaculture in the South-East Asian countries. Experts, however, observe that the concerns are misplaced so far as India is concerned. According to them, the apprehension that shrimp farming causes degradation of coastal zones is vague and baseless. In fact, setting up fish farms in the coastal zone has helped in protecting the zone as most of these units have taken care to construct proper bunding with granite on the outer area facing the sea coast. In a way, these farms protect coastal zones against sea erosion during the monsoon. Aquaculture units are set up in fallow areas where land is inundated with saline or brackish water and the units do not encroach upon the traditional fishing or farming zones.

Concerns were also raised about the acute shortage of drinking water in the coastal areas, and the suspicion that aquaculture could have

Contd...

...*Contd*...

contributed to it. But, as per the report submitted by the National Environmental Engineering Research Institute (NEERI) to MPEDA, after a detailed study and analysis, "there is no seepage of drinking water wells because of shrimp farms, as the shrimp farms mostly remain in hard clayey soil and the seepage is almost nil or in its minimum percentage".

The NEERI study also found that salinity did not change outside a distance of 25 metres of the fish farm. Deterioration of ground water quality was not observed around the pond sides. Even so, the MPEDA promotes the setting up of a buffer zone concept as per the requirements of the site conditions.

Unlike Taiwan, the Philippines, etc., India does not use ground water for aquaculture. Aqaculture also checks environmental pollution and degradation, because imported and costly seeds are used, resulting in economic use.

Effluents from shrimp farms are biodegradable. However, intensive culture systems aimed at intensive levels of production could have pollutants in the form of heavy metals (e.g. mercury, cadmium), pesticides, and petroleum products. The Government of Orissa has banned aquaculture around the Chilka lake because of this. The solution to this problem is to discourage intensive culture systems. The MPEDA recommends a farming system that is sustainable in its technical assistance programmes.

In fact, aquaculture provides an environmental "win-win" in coastal Kerala, where rice and shrimp crops can be rotated on the same land. In fact, this has been the traditional practice in that area. Aquaculture cannot be performed during the monsoon, and takes only three to four months. On the other hand, rice can be grown only during the monsoon. It is a fact that aquaculture farmers have purchased land at premium from traditional agriculture farmers, and to that extent there is a shift from agriculture. This should be checked, at least in the interior region, and can be done by the states concerned through the state's Land Utilization Act.

The environmental issues for aquaculture are in fact of a different kind. For example, degradation of aquaculture land due to pesticide residues discharged from agriculture land threatens aquaculture activity. Effluents from industrial belts along the coast may also contribute to the degradation. Because fish cannot survive in polluted water, policy makers should ascertain the areas that need corrective measures by looking at the acquaculture units in the area.

The costs for aquaculture have been ascertained. Capital costs per unit of 180 hectares amounts to Rs 180,000. Other costs include power (Rs. 20 per kg), feed (Rs. 70 per kg), watch and ward (Rs. 10 per kg), interest on loan (Rs. 60 per kg) and misc. (Rs. 20 per kg). On the other hand, the returns are Rs. 280, 000 per 180 hectare farm or Rs. 300 per kg. Clearly it is a profitable business and can provide a lot of employment (650 person days per hectare as compared to 50 person days in traditional farming). In Orissa, the exporters claim that the 8 per cent sales tax by the state government is a burden, which cannot be recovered even from exports, and renders them less competitive in the export markets.

Indian Spices

History and Current Trends

India has been an exporter of spices since the beginning of the civilization. The country now dominates the global market for spices. Of the total world imports of 450,000 tonnes, India's share alone is one-third, with the export value exceeding US$ 340 million. Total world trade in spices amounts to just one fifth of the Indian production. India produces over 60 varieties of spices including pepper, cardamom, ginger, turmeric, chilies, garlic, and several seed spices like coriander, cumin, celery, fennel, and fenugreek.

For many years, Indian exports consisted mainly of bulk-packaged raw spices. Now, with the changing market trends and consumer preferences, the focus has shifted to a variety of valued added and ready-to-cook consumer-packed products. Ground spices, blended spices, curry mixes, and natural food colors are some of the new exports. Spice oils and oleoresins are now an Indian specialty.

The essential constitutions of spices, which provide the aroma, flavour, pungency, and colour, make up a very small part, often less than 10 per cent, of the weight of the whole spice. The balance of the spice mainly functions as the intermatrix and protective sheath for these essential ingredients. The essential ingredients may be obtained by solvent extraction, resulting in an extract called the spice oleoresin. The volatile constituents of the spice known as the essential oil, are part of the oleoresin, but may also be obtained directly from the raw spice by steam distillation. These spice oil and oleoresins have many advantages over raw spices; particularly in being free of contamination and of high anti-bacterial quality.

The Spices Board recognizes the international trend towards cleaner, hygienic, and wholesome spices. It also recognizes that regulatory authorities in many countries have clamped down stricter regulations on imported food. The Spice Board has spearheaded an all-out campaign for excellence in Indian spices, involving all segments of the industry. The Spice Board regularly runs quality surveys on spices at all operational levels – farmers, traders, processors, packers, and exporters. The crops covered are pepper, ginger, turmeric, chilies, fennel, and cumin. The states of Kerala, Tamil Nadu, Andhra Pradesh, Maharashtra, Gujarat, and Rajasthan have been brought under the survey.

One plant visited was a large, 6 floor, modern plant on several acres of company land in their spice enclave, where chilies were being processed. This plant meets all HACCP and Codex Sanitation requirements. It is comparable to spice processing plants anywhere in the world. The company is old and big enough to have long term relationships with its farmers, and the incoming spice is required to be of high quality. The raw spice is stored in a separate building and fumigated to kill any insects before it is allowed entry into the plant.

There are five floors of machinery to wash, agitate, crush, cut, sterilize and powder spices. One machine blows air through the cut up chilies to remove extraneous matter and small stones; even the best products need this treatment. It was learnt that aflatoxin contamination was a recurrent problem with chilies that had to be continually monitored.

Small-scale production with many farmers, brokers and processors is likely to face the most problems. Unlike the case in developed countries where the bulk of agricultural production is large-scale and handled by a few people using large machines, India's agricultural system is based on many small farmers or fishermen using less sophisticated technology.

In the spice industry, for example, there are few pepper plantations. Small producers have arrangements with large-scale processors who purchase their entire crop. The processor has good control over the quality of the raw material he uses and the large-scale producer who controls all his labour can readily produce a uniform product. There is at most only a single broker involved. The processor usually has a contract directly with the importer and this agreement is periodically renewed so that a long term trust and relationship is established. But such large producers account for only about 5 per cent of the pepper crop; the rest come from mostly small farms.

The typical farmer will plant a little pepper, a little cardamom or some chilies, *etc.*, along with his other crops. He will sell these crops to village merchants and they in turn will sell it to town dealers and brokers. A processor or producer-processor (depending on the spice) will eventually purchase the combined lots. The final lot of spices that comes to the processor may be the product of dozens of lots of varying quality from as many different farms.

There is an inherent chance of contamination in such a process. Given a large number of farmers, the combined lot can get contaminated even if all of them have fairly good quality control. For example, if each farmer is 90 per cent efficient in avoiding contamination, combining 7 independent lots from 7 such farmers is more than likely to be contaminated (0.9=0.478) then a single farmer's lot. If the farmers are 80 per cent efficient, it only takes four such lots to increase the chances of contaminating the combined lot to greater than 50 per cent (0.8 = 0.41).

A prominent exporter of spices narrated an interesting episode concerning rat droppings. Black pepper and rat droppings are of the same colour and size; their separation becomes very difficult. The sieves normally used for clearing black pepper of waste debris did not help and complaints continued for a while. A clever employee realized that the shape of rat droppings (oblong) is different from black pepper (round). So a special sieve and a special skill in stirring the pepper did the trick. The rat droppings fell down and the unadulterated pepper remained on the sieve. The message was spread and quality complaints were contained.

Different quality standards for export and domestic products add to the problems. The majority of India's spice crop is sold domestically. There are no spice rules for domestic crops, and no mandatory inspections. The quality control for domestic spices is strictly voluntary, but forward-looking agencies like the Spices Board are attempting to educate consumers in India to the value of quality spices. Similarly, firms marketing branded spices are quite quality conscious. A logo is being introduced that will be seen on the labels of spices produced by processors that have earned Spices Board Certificates. (The presence of two quality standards, one for domestic crops and one for exports, however creates a dilemma for the farmer.)

Currently there is little, if any, price differential between domestic and export spice prices. The farmer is left to wonder why he should bother with sanitation, cleanliness and the controlled use of pesticides when he has to pay for it out of his own money, and can expect little or no return for his efforts. There is really no incentive for the farmer to comply with the sanitation efforts except his own conscience. And in many cases he is not trained or educated to be aware of the benefits of sanitation to his customers. He has been handling spice in the same way for generations.

Lack of awareness of the impact of globalization on trade at the level of the small producer is the next problem. Regulatory and development agencies are aware of the challenges of global trade. Regulators in Delhi, probably most EIA personnel in the country, and most food processors are also well-informed. HACCP is known, if not yet practiced, throughout the country. There are training courses on HACCP by various industry associations, the Agricultural and Processed Food Export Development Authority (APEDA), and the

Food and Agriculture Organization (FAO) trains trainers in courses throughout India.

The problem is that this awareness has not yet been transmitted to the small producers. They need to be informed of the benefits of complying with the stricter food handling and food pre-processing standards. If the small producers can be made to realize how changing their practices will help them in their businesses, they will be receptive. This is the message from experts who have seen similar situations in Indian agriculture in earlier times for different products. The conversion of India's grain agriculture to better and more productive varieties through the farmer's use of better seeds is a case in point. It is not impossible to gain farmer's acceptance for an agricultural practice if it can be seen to improve yields or price acceptance in the market place. But such incentives need to be provided and explained.

In the context of standards, it is evident that education at the grassroots level has to be facilitated. This is because the food regulatory system in India is a very weak link in the food control system. While individual companies and possibly some food product industries can produce export-worthy products, it is very hard to argue that the current regulatory system can be relied upon to assure of equivalence.

The "equivalence" guidelines of many countries require a comparison of the entire regulatory infrastructure between countries. This includes a comparison of the national food safety laws, the standard setting, inspection, laboratory, enforcement and internal monitoring infrastructure. Food safety law must prohibit the introduction of adulterated food into commerce; it must establish what constitutes adulteration and misbranding; it must authorize national regulatory agencies with the power to set standards, conduct inspections and take enforcement action. This requirement assumes that there is only one standard both for exported and domestic food. It does not contemplate the situation in India, where the standard and regulatory agencies are different for imported and domestic food.

The agencies governing the safety of exports should be identify existing and potential health problems associated with food, and establish scientifically-based processing requirements and guidelines. Through the EIA (Export Inspection Agency) and the export promotion bodies (*e.g.* MPEDA and the Spices Board), India does a reasonably good job in this area and should be able to meet this requirement. The inspection infrastructure should be made capable through training and experience to conduct mandatory inspections of commercial entities that prepare, pack and handle food.

Not only is this area seriously undermanned at present, but there is also a question about the credibility of the system. Evidently, certificates of inspection can be purchased without much difficulty. It is not clear what fraction of export consignments is being inspected, but it is certain that many are not inspected effectively.

Laboratories must be capable of analyzing samples to determine the presence and quality of adulterants likely to affect food, including pathogens, toxins, chemicals and parasites. Only three government laboratories and none of the private government approved laboratories were visited, but there is a case for enhancing the capacity of the laboratories. The few laboratories were generally adequate, but did not have the state of the art equipment required, for example, to test for adulterants at the scale of parts per billion. The system of private accredited laboratories may be better than the under funded government laboratories that operate under the Prevention of Food Adulteration Act, 1954 (PFA) to examine domestic food samples.

Enforcement personnel must be capable of reviewing findings from inspections, and making rapid determinations as to whether regulatory action is necessary. Where regulatory action is necessary the enforcement arm should have available to it a range of actions designed to remove infringing products from distribution and prevent a recurrence of the problem. On paper the enforcement authority in India appears adequate, but its implementation is poor. Sanitation rules are not consistently enforced; it also appears that HACCP controls are not being applied in all facilities.

India needs to face this challenge and improve the safety of its exports. But this will not be an easy task. India may have to explore whether a possible decrease in her exports, due to the failure to obtain an equivalence agreement, can be avoided. One possible way is to tighten control over the export of infringing products, by cracking down on exporters who ship such products. These exporters destroy the reputation of other producers and shippers, thus making it tougher to gain entry into the western market. The Indian export-import policy includes a chapter on quality where complaints of this nature can be dealt with; appropriate mechanisms should be developed and implemented, to ensure confidence that quality will be monitored.

Another potential solution is to establish associations of food producers in certain industries that are sanctioned by the government to assure the quality and safety of their products. It could be easier to gain control over product quality and safety in specific industries if the industry is involved. It is the exporters' business that is being harmed; this fact alone should supply sufficient motivation.

Last but not least, an intensive exercise should be undertaken to study indigenous processes and their effectiveness for product quality, safety and standards, and the process standards 'imported' for adoption here should be tested against these standards and modified appropriately to apply domestically. Thereafter, if the exporters face market access problems, 'equivalence' should be negotiated with the trading partner(s) in that market.

Processed Foods

An initial study of the fresh fruit sector was attempted, by looking at a large grape unit. It had an export of Rs.10 crore of which 90 per cent went to the UK. The unit operator said he felt discriminated against, as compared to exporters from some other countries. The duty in Europe for India is 18 per cent, for Chile 3 per cent, and South Africa 0 per cent. In addition to in-house tests conducted by the exporter, importers conduct a survey or test costing US$300, before accepting each consignment. In cases where the importer is unhappy with the results (and this operator suspects an uneven application of the test), the importer may either reject the consignment, or accept it but ask for heavy price discounts. The exporter is compelled to agree, as the goods are perishable.

The exporter pointed out many capacity problems. First, he has difficulty getting market information, and government authorities are of no help in this regard. He could not even find out, for example, the weather in Chile or how much is produced there. He learnt that foreign governments assist his competitors in negotiating good prices with shipping companies for bulk exports. In India, there is no such facility and freight becomes a competitive disadvantage. The only incentive available from the government is the packaging incentive. However, the government has put a ceiling of Rs. 100,000 per company on this incentive. This discourages producers from growing into large companies. In any case, Indian grapes fetch lower prices than their competitors because of their quality and the fear of pesticide residues.

It was decided to focus on processed foods rather than fresh fruit. Peanuts, mango pulp, apple juice and mushrooms were studied.

Peanuts

Peanut exporters feel that foreign markets put non-tariff barriers on their exports of agricultural products in order to sustain their domestic agriculture, which involves higher costs than in India. Exporters also face having to make distress sales when buyers refuse shipments, based on domestic import standards. They feel, therefore, that Indian exporters have to depend on the domestic market or the SAARC region for business sustenance. Their customers have informed them that new, stricter will apply after 31st December, 2000 in foreign markets.

Some of the problems faced by exporters appear to be genuine. For example, they find that different testing procedures and conformity assessment standards are required in different markets. Each test costs Rs. 6000. Nobody has informed them of the justification for most of the tests. In fact, the European Union tests exports from Egypt and India, and not exports from the USA and Argentina.

Another problem is that while there is no import duty on 50 kg bags, there is a duty on 5 kg bags. This is because the foreign markets want to discourage retail consignments. They also face problems regarding genetically modified peanuts. While some years ago, one foreign market encouraged use of GMOs, now another market has asked for an assurance that the peanuts supplied are without GMOs.

A more detailed study was done on the issue of aflatoxin presence in peanuts, as this appeared to be a major threat to peanut exports. The EU Commission in Brussels has specified tolerance limits for aflatoxin contamination in peanuts, and also testing methods. The proposed levels are 10 ppb (5ppb B1) for raw material and 4 ppb (2ppb B1) for consumer ready products. The new proposed sampling plan is similar to the Dutch Code, *i.e.* the analysis is to be done based on a three-test Dutch code methodology from a randomly drawn 30 kg sample. The new procedure is much more rigorous than is currently in force, as should any of the three tests be found to be over the limit, the lot will be rejected.

This step is unwarranted from the scientific angle (as submitted by various agencies/governments). Laboratory test with small animals such as touts and rats that were fed highly contaminated feed (B1) on a daily basis have concluded that aflatoxin can cause cancer of the liver. But there is no clear evidence to prove that aflatoxins are carcinogenic in humans. This should be viewed against the backdrop of the fact that should a shipment of peanuts be found to contain aflatoxin, this does not mean that all peanuts are contaminated since aflatoxin is concentrated on very few nuts. Statistically, one would expect to find one contaminated nut in a sample of say, 5000 to 10,000 uncontaminated nuts. Experts have concluded that 75 per cent of the lots rejected under the proposed procedure would be below the established tolerance, *i.e.* 75 per cent of the rejected lots would be uncontaminated material.

Further, the world over, especially the peanut supply origins like Argentina, China, India, South Africa, U.S.A., Vietnam etc. where peanut consumption is very high, nowhere has there been any findings that aflatoxin in peanuts led to increases in cases of liver cancer.

A JECFA report says that aflatoxin contamination of foodstuffs is very low among EU nations, and only a few members of the population suffer from hepatitis B. Considering the estimated risk at 20 ppb, it will be 0.0041 cancer cases per 100,000 population annually. Considering the risk at 10ppb, it will be 0.0039 cancer cases per 100,000 population annually. This shows that the downward adjustment of the standard from 20 ppb to 10 ppb would bring a reduction of the estimated cancer risk only by approximately 2 cancer cases annually per 1 billion people. It seems improbable that there would be any measurable risk differential between the hypothetical standards (20 and 10 ppb) in populations with a low hepatitis B incidence like in the EU countries. And consider the possibility that denial of export market to farmers of a developing country like India could result in starvation deaths in multiples of the estimated harm to life in Europe.

The JECFA had previously recommended that maximum permissible aflatoxin levels should be fixed as low as possible. But now, on the basis of further data, it has modified its recommendation to reducing the intake as far "as is reasonably possible". Further, it should be noted that the JECFA's risk estimates are based on data that made no allowance for the substantial reduction in aflatoxin contamination achieved by mechanical removal of the nut skins and by the use of optical and electronic methods for sorting the nuts. The risk computations are thus based on aflatoxin levels that are no longer applicable. This new data should be taken into account when finally specifying the future EU tolerance limits. For example, the Codex Alimentarius Commission had proposed a maximum limit of 15 ppb.

Sampling Procedure

The proposed sampling plan is similar to the Dutch Code (3x10 kg). The analysis is to be derived from a 3-test Dutch Code methodology from a randomly drawn 30 kg sample. The new procedure is much more rigorous than is currently in force, as should any of the three tests be found to be over the limit, the lot will be rejected.

In the case of bulk raw nuts, the implementation of a regular monitoring policy presents difficulties because the aflatoxin will seldom be evenly distributed throughout a given batch and only a few nuts may be contaminated. For example, the contamination rate is estimated at 1:10,000 for groundnuts (peanuts).

The question is how large the sample should be in order to ensure that the test yields reliable data on the degree of aflatoxin contamination. Opinions differ on this point.

The FAO has recommended testing a single 20 kg sample for aflatoxin content from a batch of between 15 and 24 t. The FAO is of the opinion that this sampling procedure would yield results that are reliable enough to eliminate the risk for the consumer, and that stricter requirements would bring no significant safety measure.

Meanwhile, the EU Commission wants three samples of 10 kg each tested from a batch of between 15 and 24 t. According to the new regulation, the whole shipment will be rejected if only one of the three samples exceeds the tolerance level. It would be far more logical to calculate an average value from all three samples as an end result. On the basis of the risk estimate computed by JECFA, several experts object that the new procedure would mean an unnecessary waste of good product without actually benefiting consumer safety. It is also certain that this practice would lead to adverse effects on prices. The EU regulation is also criticised because it fails to specify how the sampling and testing of the final products circulating in the trade should be performed. Uniform criteria, binding on all EU member states, are also necessary for these products.

The implementation of the EU Commission's proposals would endanger the export of peanuts to the EU member countries. The planned tolerance limits of 2 ppb aflatoxin B1 and 4 ppb total aflatoxin in finished products are so low that they would almost certainly cause insurmountable difficulties and immense costs for production and export to the EU countries. Producers within the EU itself would also suffer unreasonably from these regulations. While the WHO is proposing a limit of 15 ppb for all aflatoxin, the EU Commission is insisting on an upper limit of 10 ppb for the raw nuts, despite the fact that the aflatoxin content decreases during subsequent processing of peanuts. The latest JECFA study published in June 1997 demonstrates clearly that an increase in the upper limit for all aflatoxin from 10 ppb to 20 ppb would involve a theoretical risk of only two additional cases of liver cancer annually per one billion people.

The European Snack Association's Nut Working Group has already expressed concern about the testing programme and analytical methodologies through CIAA (the European Food and Beverage Association). The American Peanut Council has submitted documents showing significant increase in costs and rejections arising from the use of a multi sample system. In the UK, where approximately one-quarter 25 per cent of the peanuts imported into Europe are consumed, the Ministry of Agriculture has stated that the proposals were more stringent than required by current UK regulations, and could result in unacceptable costs to both industry and enforcement, without any prospect of improved consumer safety. Despite these protests, the revised draft of the sampling plan still recommends a multiple sampling system. It is evident that such a change will have very serious implications for the peanut industry. It is also significant to note that the EU proposal possibly contravenes the GATT/WTO agreement, as it will erect artificial barriers and seriously discriminate against a number of producing countries, particularly third world and developing countries including India. Consider these facts:

- Europe represents 47 per cent of world imports of groundnuts and groundnut products - a value of $1.4 billion.
- Assuming all of Europe moves to a multi-test plan, the increase in cost of testing alone will be $4 million. This does not include re-testing costs in Europe.

- The UK government reported that compliance with the proposed EU directive would average 8 per cent of turnover (£ 3.2 million).
- Exporters will lose the ability to ship goods to an alternate European market. As a consequence, the overall cost of the lot would have to be priced with consideration for recovering the cost of the rejected goods, which must be diverted for crushing, or sold at a significant discount for animal feed.
- Exporters may be forced to absorb the costs for additional cleaning, re-sorting, and blanching of rejected lots of peanuts. The implication for increased costs of doing business in the European market could be more than $200 million, according to JECFA.

Testing Plan Comparison - Cost Implications For Peanuts

Current Single Testing Procedure	Proposed EU Multi-Testing Procedure
Average cost per metric tonne: $800	Average cost per metric tonne: $800
Cost of testing : $50/lot (Lot = 20 tonnes)	Cost of testing : $200/lot (Lot = 20 tonnes)
Rejection: 30%	
(Based on experience of USA	
and Argentine testing under the Dutch Code of Practice)	
Final Cost US $ 802/MT	Final Cost US $ 1157/MT

- Scientific data has documented that reducing aflatoxin levels for raw material (e.g. from 15 ppb total to 10 ppb total) has little or no effect on the levels of aflatoxin found in the finished product.
- There is no justification for restrictive aflatoxin levels on the basis of consumer protection, given the fact that aflatoxin levels in raw materials can be substantially reduced through processing.
- Introduction of rigorous, expensive import requirements puts undue burden on suppliers, distorting trade: it will

limit the volume and number of origin suppliers who can routinely meet the criteria. This could, quite obviously, result in an artificial trade barrier and the possibility of a WTO action.

- Rigorous testing programmes are extremely difficult to monitor and enforce. If not applied uniformly, both suppliers and importers are at a disadvantage. In a crop year when supplies are short, there may be an effort to manipulate results or encourage alternative import schemes through markets where surveillance may not be as stringent.
- Assuming the need to increase pricing to take the anticipated rejections into account, European importers will be forced to consider the following options:

- Blanch peanuts prior to importation (which adds costs to raw materials and raises issues with regard to splits and shelf-life).
- Move production to a non-EU site, where stringent testing of raw materials is not mandatory, leading to job losses in both the manufacturing sector and ancillary business.

  - This stringent system will increase the price of raw material in Europe.
  - Lastly, none of the European countries produces peanuts. To bring about such stringent import restrictions on a commodity for which they have to fully depend on other origins, without giving any heed to the suppliers, other experts, the WTO and JECFA, may prove to be more troublesome than effective.

In conclusion, the proposed legislation will be counter-productive both to the buyer as well as the seller, apart from paving the way for numerous problems and bottlenecks for no good reason. In other words, the risk that non-fulfilment would entail is not commensurate with the costs incurred.

Mango Pulp

There are only nine major exporters of mango pulp in the country. Sourcing is done primarily from Chittoor District of Andhra Pradesh and Krishnagiri District of Tamil Nadu. Exports of mango pulp in quantity and value terms for the last three years for which figures are available is given in the chart below.

Year	*Quantity (MT)*	*Value (Rs. Lakhs)*
1995-96	36023	8461
1996-97	40302	10501
1997-98	45874	12531

The Agricultural and Processed Food Export Development Authority (APEDA) has taken firm export promotion steps for mango pulp. Implementation of HACCP was done by APEDA, with some financial assistance from the Ministry of Food Processing Industries. 12 processing units in Chittor District were taken up in the year 1997-98. Subsequently, 12 units in the Krishnagiri district of Tamil Nadu have been taken. About Rs. 3,500,000 have been spent for this so far.

The following were the stages and steps involved in the implementation:

- Identifying improvements in the mango pulp processing units and assisting them in carrying out the same;
- Development of entire quality assurance documentation, including HACCP plan and essential ISO 9000 requirements;
- Training for personnel of units at three levels;
- Top Management;
- Supervisors/chemists/operational staff;
- Contractual and other labourers/workers; and
- Assisting in getting the units certified through the third-party certification body.

The compliance costs for implementing HACCP would have been prohibitive, had APEDA not come to their rescue with both financial and technical assistance. All the participating units have implemented HACCP in the Chittoor District. Five units were assessed and certified by International Standards Certification (ISC) South Asia Pvt. Ltd. during the 1998 mango season. Six units of Chittoor District and 6 units of Krishnagiri District were assessed during the 1999 mango season. All of the participating units of Chittoor District have been recommended for certification after the certification audit by the National Sanitation Foundation (NSF). In Krishnagiri District, Quality Assurance Service (Australia) carried out a certification audit of 6 units, and all of these were recommended for certification. Small units have not been able to take benefit of APEDA's efforts. There have been problems in applying HACCP at the farm level because of the nature of farms and practices in India.

The quality norms under the Prevention of Food Adulteration Act (PFA) of India do not fully match with Codex. For example, PFA does not cover rules for the various tests for water as required under Codex. According to some small exporters, HACCP has not been followed in the pulp industry! There is a general awareness about HACCP, but they think it has not been passed as a law so far and they do not have to worry about it yet, especially because there is no consumer insistence in India for such standards. They admit that HACCP will certainly increase market accessibility, but they will have problems in adopting them. Some of the problems pointed out were:

(a) Land holdings of orchards are small and contractors procure the raw material, so it will be impossible to keep records at the field level as required for HACCP. The general age of orchards ranges between 3 – 100 years, so it will be difficult to keep control;

(b) The industry is seasonal (3 months per year) so keeping permanent staff. The cost of training new staff every year is also prohibitive;

(c) Meeting the standards will be more viable for large plants or industrial houses that deal in multiple products, work throughout the year and have their own orchards. But most of the units are small in this sector and HACCP will not suit them;

(d) As far as financial aspect of HACCP compliance is concerned, units that are setting up now, will not have any problem. It does not cost much for new units, but the old units will have to revamp their infrastructure. It is a costly affair; according to rough estimates, HACCP compliance will increase costs by 40 per cent;

(e) Financial institutions do not fund HACCP activity;

(f) The main markets are Gulf countries and they are only interested in cheap prices, not HACCP; and

(g) ISO certification is expensive, costing Rs. 1.5 lakhs per audit. The surveillance audit is every six months and costs Rs. 10,000 per person-day.

Another main quality issue for mango pulp is pesticide residue. Other quality issues for Indian mango pulp, which is darker brown in color than other varieties, are the poor quality of packaging materials, namely plastic bags, metal tins and drums. Bags are sometimes punctured, tins rust or impart an unpleasant metallic taste, and the tin or drum is often damaged during shipment. The reason for packaging problems is the low quality of packaging materials available in the domestic market. The imported tin is good in quality but adds to costs. According to exporters, they do not have the technology or the technology is costly and they do not have the economies of scale to meet the costs. They feel that packaging should not be considered a health hazard.

Testing is a major problem for these units. There are a number of institutions but they are spread all over the country and quite expensive. CFTRI charges Rs. 3000 per test and SGS charges 0.27 per cent of f.o.b. value of the consignment. Laboratories in India are not equipped with equipment based on new technology required for the complicated tests necessary to comply with HACCP. Foreign health authorities are moving from parts per million (ppm) to parts per billion (ppb). Indian laboratories are not equipped to do these tests. There are differences in test results in India and Europe, due allegedly to methods of testing, rather than to poor quality. One recent consignment of egg powder was rejected in Germany due to residue. It later passed the test in Spain and was sold there.

In Europe, only "natural food" imports are encouraged i.e. no sugar should be added. Although sugar is a natural product, added sugar attracts an import duty increase of 13 per cent (from 6.5 per cent without sugar to 19.5 per cent with sugar). Sugar is added in Europe because there is a surplus of beet sugar, a subsidized product in Europe. Buyers are interested in buying pulp with sugar, but are dissuaded by the higher duty. All the ex-colonies of France, Portugal and Spain do not pay duty on food items. However, all ex-colonies of UK have to pay duty.

Successful exporters feel that the quality of Indian food has to be monitored for exports, and that APEDA should introduce licensing. Small scale units, they claim, should not be encouraged to export because they are often fly by night operations. FPO (Food Product Order) has issued 4,700 licenses for food processing units, out of which twenty-one are large units, 156 are medium, and the rest are small scale. 90 per cent of these units are making mango pulp while the rest are licensed for other items like gherkins.

Exporters tend to develop and nurture long-term relationships with buyers. If quality or other problems arise, buyers often help by sorting out the problems at their end. Where customs is a problem, buyers are clearly motivated by their interest in consignments.

Quality becomes a major hurdle when buyers have excess stock, or the prices of the goods have fallen in the international market below the agreed or contracted price. In such cases, exporters sometimes have to accept price discounts, especially because of the perishable nature of the goods.

As the ministry responsible for trade promotion, the Ministry of Commerce takes interest in export operations. But the problems faced by exporters are often quality or health related, where the Health Ministry should be involved. Even in business negotiations, foreigners want an assurance from the Health Ministry, which is not easy to obtain. There is a need to create better policy coherence here. Because the Health Ministry is responsible for the development of Codex standards, exporters feel that that Ministry could consult producers to their benefit, while attending Codex meetings and formulating domestic standards. Food laws emphasize economic considerations and not safety. The basic thrust of food laws is thus misplaced so far as export promotion is concerned.

Apple Juice

There is hardly any export of Juice from India. HPMC is the biggest player in Apple Juice. Juice export is not feasible because of government's price support policy (MIS Scheme). Exporters have to procure for the government on a price higher than market price. There have been on and off exports of apple concentrate to Germany, Italy and the US, but this was done through third parties; no direct exports were reported.

India has a lot of potential in fresh and processed food, but it suffers on two accounts:

(a) Productivity is very low. India has one of the lowest productivity of apples in the world, due mainly to lack of advanced technology. India's productivity is 6-8 metric tonnes/hectare compared to world productivity of 30 metric tonnes/hectare. It is. We seem to be reluctant to import technology, especially in agriculture.

(b) State government subsidies act as a disincentive to higher productivity. Subsidies are given on procurement price, fertilizers, water, *etc*. Subsidies would be better focused on transferring technology from lab to field.

There are two systems of standards: (1) the Prevention of Food Adulteration Act (PFA), and (2) Codex and ISO 9000. The level of tolerance under the PFA is higher than Codex or standards in other countries. For example, the allowable level for heavy metals and radiation content in India is 250 ppm, while in it is 100 ppm. Codex tolerances are even lower.

The estimated use of pesticides is 250 tonnes/year for all crops in Himachal Pradesh. But under PFA there is no testing required, the technology used is outdated and does not give reliable results. India's production price of apple concentrate is Rs. 40 per kg, while the international selling price is Rs. 20-22 per kg. China is the main competitor. We do not know the subsidy structure in China but they give flexible conditions to the buyer (e.g. buy now, pay later).

However, in District Kinnaur of Himachal Pradesh, there is no fertilizer or pesticide use and apples are being grown organically by compulsion. One exporter shipped a trial order of 294 boxes of fresh Kinnaur apples to the UK through Anza Corporation of New Zealand in 1997. He never heard from New Zealand after that. Unfortunately, the apple was not marketed as organic, although actually it was. A better marketing infrastructure would have seen the organic Kinnaur apple targeted at the premium export market.

Mushrooms

Background

India produced about 40,000 tonnes of all types of mushrooms in the year 1997, not including the edible wild mushrooms harvested from nature. The marketing of mushrooms harvested from nature is handled by traders/exporters in big cities who collect the mushrooms from the growing areas through local contacts.

There are fourteen large-scale white button mushroom units/export oriented units located at the following places. Approximate installed production capacity is also shown.

i)	Flex India Limited, Dehradun, U.P.	-	2000 TPA
ii)	Ponds India Limited, Ooty, Tamil Nadu	-	4000 TPA
iii)	Agro Dutch, Lalru (Ambala), Haryana	-	3500 TPA
iv)	Trans Chem, Pune, Maharashtra	-	3500 TPA
v)	Saptrishi Agros, Madras, Tamil Nadu	-	3500 TPA
vi)	Premier Explosive, Hyderabad, A.P.	-	3500 TPA
vii)	Sugham Agros, Near Hyderabad, A.P.	-	3000 TPA
viii)	Vishal Agrotech, Indore, M.P.	-	3000 TPA
ix)	Zauri Agrotech, Goa	-	100 TPA
x)	Techtran Agro India, Hyderabad, A.P.	-	2000 TPA
xi)	Bharati Agritech, Gurgaon, Haryana	-	500 TPA
xii)	Mandeep Mushrooms, Gurgaon, Haryana	-	500 TPA
xiii)	Chail Mushrooms, Tanda, Punjab	-	500 TPA
xiv)	Dinesh Agros, Pune, Maharashtra	-	1000 TPA

All the above units are presently in production. Some are selling fresh mushrooms in markets in India, while most of the EOUs are exporting. There are scores of other smaller units growing mushrooms in environment-controlled cropping rooms in various parts of India. Seasonal growers, who produce mostly for local markets, also form a large portion of growers.

The EU and USA are very large producers of mushrooms. They are also the largest importers. The EU production of mushrooms is estimated at about 1 million tonnes and that of USA at about 375,000 tonnes in equivalent-to-fresh form. The imports of mushrooms into USA and EU are estimated at about 84,000 tonnes and 143,000 tonnes respectively in 1996. The major exporting countries to EU have been Bulgaria, Poland, and China. EU has allocated quotas to the mushroom exporting countries to put quantity restrictions on exports to EU at reduced custom duties, ranging from 12% to 23% for mushrooms supplied in various forms. Export into the EU outside the allocated quota attracts heavy duties, to an extent that landed prices increase from an average of US $2.46/kg to US $4.60/kg. With that kind of duty structure outside the quota, it is difficult to export mushrooms to the EU. India does not enjoy a separate quota at present but it has been placed in the residual group with other countries and allocated 4.52% of the total import value, as against 31.25% for China and 59.76% for Poland.

Quotas on mushrooms are an uncorrected vestige of the past, when the agriculture sector was not covered by GATT disciplines. The tariffication process built into the Agreement on Agriculture of the WTO is yet to result in quota free access of mushrooms to EU markets. Multilateral efforts are required to expedite this process. In the meanwhile, India needs to submit a representation to the EU to have an exclusive quota fixed. The quotas allocated to Poland and other countries have been regularly left under-utilised, to the extent of 21,000 to 22,600 tonnes in the last couple of years. India should make representations to be allowed to fill up the under utilised quota through a separate allocation.

A severe restriction in productivity had been experienced initially by most of the growing units all over the country. Some of the bottlenecks identified during interaction with the industry are elaborated below.

a) Technology gap: Mushroom growing in India started with the use of primitive technology for compost making and crop raising in the late sixties and early seventies, resulting in low yields per unit weight of compost. The compost was prepared from cereal straws and animal waste by a long outdoor fermentation process in a single phase, without use of steam pasteurisation. An average mushroom yield (6-8 kg/100 kg) of compost was harvested in 6-8 weeks of cropping, and the crop was raised in makeshift cropping rooms. This was followed by a second phase of activity: a modern mother composting unit was established at Solan with FAO assistance. Compost was prepared using an advanced, two-phase method. A rich substrate was prepared from cereal straws and poultry manure. The compost produced in this way doubled the productivity of mushroom per unit weight of compost, which is considered a big leap for the growing mushroom industry in India.

   With increased exposure of scientists and workers to modern growing methods, and more and more people taking to the profession, the mushroom industry started taking shape.

   Then came the establishment in 1983 of the National Research Centre for Mushrooms, by the Indian Council of Agricultural Research at Solan, H.P. This gave a fillip and encouragement to the industry. Concerted efforts began for popularising the improved methods of cultivation, screening of improved strains for use by Indian seasonal growers, and addition of more mushrooms to the list of cultivated mushrooms in India. The information on improved technology was still not available to the common grower or entrepreneur in India.

After composting was accomplished by the grower, information on raising a healthy crop of mushrooms was another bottleneck. The grower would collect spawn from some source and not know about the growing parameters, nor was the modern cropping room available to him.

In the late eighties and early nineties, modern cultivation units were established with the help from various companies from Europe, whose interest was in selling the machinery. This led to the construction of modern mushroom units, but the question remained who would manage them. At that point, the Indian industry took a beating: unit after unit failed to produce mushrooms to the level of profitability. Some time was taken to tune the production parameters, until economic yields were obtainable by most of the units in India. By the time this was achieved, the international market came crashing down and has not improved.

b) Role of Govt. institutions: The research and development (R&D) support available in the country caters more to the needs of small or marginal mushroom growers, both for information and training. The average yield per unit weight of compost has been increased to 16-20 kg/100 kg of compost in 6 weeks of cropping. But for becoming globally competitive, yield increase combined with reduced cultivation costs is the goal.

c) Exploitation by foreign machinery sellers and consultants: Foreign machinery sellers supplied machines used in labour starved countries in Europe, on an as-is-where-is basis. In addition to selling the machinery, they also offered the technical know-how for cultivation of white button mushrooms in computer-controlled cropping rooms. They failed to understand that the situation prevailing in temperate Europe is very different from that prevailing in tropical India: while the temperature needs to be increased under European growing conditions, the opposite is true in India. The job becomes more complicated when you have to manipulate other parameters like air speed, heat removal, and carbon dioxide and oxygen levels in the cropping room. All the above parameters are to be maintained at a certain level during various stages of crop raising.

Also, many raw materials that are used in Europe (for example, peat for casing) are not available in India, and we have to use alternative materials instead. The European grower is used to watering peat casing heavily, which will not apply under Indian conditions. Post harvest handling of fresh mushrooms in temperate areas is easier than in hot climates, where time for post harvest handling.

Foreign machinery sellers offered buy-back arrangements to most of the projects (EOU's); in many cases the arrangements turned out to be false guarantees. It became a fashion with financiers in India to ask for a buy-back guarantee from a foreign buyer, which in their opinion was nothing but a ploy to safeguard the interests of the financiers. The real guarantee should have been a clear picture of the domestic and international market. Every project entrepreneur should undertake a market survey on a realistic basis, and then give his projection of the market.

In spite of some negative experiences, India is a big market itself is a big market for future mushroom growers, especially for fresh mushroom marketing.

d) Varied availability of raw materials in India and lack of information on their optimal utilization: The raw materials available in different parts of India for mushroom cultivation are varied. In most of northern and central India, wheat straw is abundantly available, but prices are high. In the eastern and southern parts paddy straw is available in abundance, and at lower prices. Poultry manure is available everywhere at a very low price. Sugarcane bagasse is available in those areas where sugarcane is grown in abundance (Western parts of India, Central India, and some other places). The art of composting from wheat straw, paddy straw or sugarcane bagasse as base material will have different requirements. Limited information is available to the grower on the use of paddy straw and sugarcane bagasse as base materials for composting. Their optimal economic use for composting requires a specialized skill on the part of the manager/entrepreneur.

Casing is the second important input in button mushroom growing. Although not many casing materials are available for commercial growing in India, it is possible with either FYM (Farm Yard Manure), spent compost or composted coir pith. Each needs to be processed (water leached or steam pasteurised) before use, unlike the peat sold in Europe. (Peat is harvested from underground bogs deep down, is devoid of harmful microorganisms, and needs only a pH adjustment before use.)

The use of FYM, spent compost or composted coir pith in place of peat as a casing (in button mushroom cultivation) will also require experience on the part of the grower.

It remains to be seen whether mushroom productivity using these materials will be possible at competitive prices.

e) Absence of organized support to mushroom industry for processing and international marketing: There is no organized help available for marketing mushrooms abroad. Each export-oriented unit has its own arrangement for marketing. Mushrooms are preserved in brine and canned in large containers of 3-5 litres capacity, or even bigger, for export; it would likely be more profitable to sell in smaller units. Government support for mushroom marketing does not exist, nor is any special or preferential European Union quota available, as is available to other nations.

Direct export to the USA or Germany under some arrangement is one alternative that could be considered. For this the growers would have to form a marketing co-operative. There are no processing plants especially available as a support organization for this industry in India, except for a limited support by NAFED (National Agricultural Cooperative Marketing Federation of India) to seasonal growers in the

North Western plains. This type of support is available to mushroom growers in China, and they are able to can the produce on a large scale at rail-accessible points. Financing at lower interest rates, and inputs for infrastructure at fair prices, would also help to keep down the cost of cultivation. Reduced production costs, together with greater productivity per unit weight of compost, will help the industry to become competitive globally. A long-term strategy has to be planned to help the industry, including training, development of high yielding strains, better pest management programmes, and efficient post harvest mushroom handling and processing for added value.

Indian mushroom growers face unfriendly foreign tariff and quota, and capacity and technology issues. These problems currently pose more of a challenge than environmental barriers.

Tea

Background

Tea is one of India's oldest and most established export items. India accounts for about one-third of the total world tea production. The total tea export in 1998-99 was US $548.11 million, with a growth of 14% as compared to the previous year. The Tea Board is the principle agency for promoting tea exports. Two major research institutes are involved in this area, the Tea Research Association (TRA) in North-East India and the UPASI (United Planters Association of South India) Tea Research Institute in South India. They have their own well-laid out scientific departments for conducting applied fundamental and applied research in tea in the fields of agronomy, soil microbiology, plant breeding, physiology, biochemistry, plant protection, tea machinery, etc. There are about a dozen Government of India tea promotion schemes, ranging from technical assistance to subsidy and finance schemes.

Tea is mostly exported in bulk from India. The benefit of value added in consumer packaging is not available to Indian tea. Two important reasons are the 'brand–consciousness' of the western consumer, and the highly sophisticated packaging requirements in the sector. Many of the tea estates are owned or run by old and established western firms (mostly British) who have established brands in Europe and the US. They export bulk tea from India, and package and brand it in the consumer markets. Indian tea growers find it easier to send bulk consignments to these firms. Packaging laws, in Europe especially, are too strict for Indian firms. The German Packaging Ordinance and the European Packaging Directive, for example, require sophisticated machinery and skill.

In recent years, there have been increasing reports of pesticide residues in tea. These reports have an effect on market access. For example, Germany complained about high levels of ethion residues in Darjeeling tea. Complaints were also received about high levels of bicofol in Assam, Terai and Booras tea. In addition, the Government has banned the application of DDT, BHC, aldrin, aldrex, endrine, heptachlor, chlordane and tetradifon. Moreover, there are Government guidelines providing that if chemicals such as thjiomton, dimethoate, monocroptos, fenicyphermethrin, fenvalerate, phorat, phosphomodon, formothian, acephate and carboxin are applied during the plucking season, the plucking that immediately follows these sprays should be discarded.

Doubts were raised some time ago about the justification of some of the objections in the European market about pesticide residues. In 1995, the German limit of 0.01 mg of tetradifon and 2 mg of ethion per kg of tea were somewhat arbitrarily imposed because of lack of data from India on its pesticide safety limits for tea. Later, the Teekanne Darjeeling Gold brand of tea was rejected because it contained 0.24 mg of tetrafidon per kg, twenty-four times the limit set by Germany. The rejection was soon followed by a report by the German Institute of Environment Analytics, Messzelle, denouncing the brand as unsafe. On the other hand, there were no rejections from the UK. This led some to believe that the German ban was motivated by protectionism. An alternative explanation is that most of the Indian tea firms follow British practices.

The tea estates are largely well managed and employ sufficiently educated people to adhere to these guidelines. The production process is also sufficiently well oiled to ensure the meeting of these standards. However, there is a problem regarding testing and conformity assessment for these standards. Only one institute, the Pesticide Residue Laboratory, can test commercial samples of tea in India.

Another problem is the cost factor. It is reported that the test required to clear a consignment for Germany costs roughly US $234 per analysis. This is unaffordable, at least for the bulk tea exporters who get a much lower realization.

The Tea Research Association now monitors pesticide residues. Exporters apply the ISO 3720 standard. The Indian standards are even more stringent than ISO and all other countries' domestic standards, with the exception of Japan. The best tea is supplied to the UK and

Japan, while lower quality tea goes to countries like Russia, Poland, Iran, etc. The stricter EC standards apply to exports to the UK, while for Japan it is enough to get EIC (Export Inspection Council) inspection done.

Non-tariff barriers are still faced by exporters, despite improvements made in recent years. Child labour is a big issue. Buyers visit plantations to ensure that there is no child labour. However, some children may still be helping their parents in the plucking work. Plucking contracts are given on the basis of the quantity plucked, and plucking is not done by regular employees. Families come and do the plucking; the children also help and learn the trade. However, there is no bonded or forced labour. The pesticide issue still raises its head sometimes, and leads to lowering of the price of the consignment, and distress sales as a consequence.

Packaging and recycling regulations in the markets abroad are still a major barrier. Buyers ask the exporters to pay the recycling fees that they pay in their markets. Packaging was earlier done in wooden tea chests costing Rs. 120 for 40 kg. Now, buyers demand multiple-wall paper sacks, imported from Australia, Argentina and USA, and costing Rs 30 for 40 kg., that are suitable for recycling systems in the target markets. In Germany, for example, on some occasions buyers have refused to accept wooden boxes because of higher recycling costs. Unfortunately the shelf life of these paper sacks is much shorter than the tea chests. As a consequence, exporters cannot keep any inventories and are subject to the vagaries of the market place. For the domestic market, they still use jute bags that cost only Rs. 20 per 40 kg.

For tea destined for Australia, a radiation test requirement was imposed after the Chernobyl mishap, although there is no fear of radiation in the tea production areas. This test can be done only at the Bhaba Atomic Research Centre (BATC) at Mumbai. Such testing adds to the costs.

Concluding Remarks

Observations on HACCP

Theory and practice are both critical to the successful design and implementation of HACCP.

HACCP is a prevention process, not a detection process. It may be difficult for some processors to grasp the concept of process control, when the inspection system to this point has been focused on the detection of problems through various tests. But it is a valuable exercise. Microbial testing can be done as one verification step to help assure a HACCP system is working, but by itself it is a not a failsafe tool for use in monitoring or assuring a safe product.

HACCP is a process and production method; not all its critical control points (CCPs) are necessarily product related. While some CCPs would ensure that the process is safe for the environment in which production takes place, they may not be relevant to what gets finally incorporated in the product itself. Principle 6 of HACCP is an example at a broad level.

HACCP can be a profitable proposition for manufacturer and exporters, due to increased market access. HACCP is a process control and can help companies get a better handle on their operations. At the same time, good HACCP systems will improve the quality of product coming out of their plants.

Since no product can be guaranteed 100 per cent safe, HACCP should be considered on the basis that it promises checks and safeguards against safety problems.

HACCP is a dynamic system, and only good as long as it is maintained. The evolving nature of HACCP means that companies can't introduce the system and let it run by itself. Monitoring and verification are needed.

In spite of these benefits, HACCP standards were considered an additional cost by many of the respondents. Some even questioned the relevance of some specific elements of the standard to their product or to safety itself.

Conclusions on HACCP

- HACCP is a good concept and can be cost effective if there are economies of scale at the farm level as well as at the processing level. Of course, HACCP may not be suitable for all products. Mangoes, for example, are available for only two to three months per year, during which exporters have to implement HACCP, including training of workers and conducting certification assessment. As a result, the pressure on the units is immense, particularly because they also have to complete their production schedules in the same period. Perhaps HACCP should be reviewed and adjusted for products like mangoes that have a very short growing season.

- There are additional costs for adoption of HACCP, which would have to be borne by the exporters. Hence, special and differential treatment provisions of WTO Agreements available for developing countries should be utilized by India not only in seeking time for adoption, but also in getting technical and technological assistance commensurate with India's development, trade and financial needs.
- HACCP creates virtually insurmountable costs for the small and medium scale sector. Application of HACCP to SMEs needs to be preceded by capacity building measures, including national and international technical and technological assistance and non-actionable subsidies.
- Idle capacity, lack of finance, the nature and size of farms, land laws and family traditions, lack of trained staff, and cutthroat competition are some of the hurdles in effective implementation of HACCP.
- Government regulations are focused on economic offences rather than on food safety. This is a disincentive for adoption of HACCP and needs to be reversed.
- A careful analysis is required at the national level on the norms of HACCP that exporters find difficult to adopt, and the Government needs to take these up in the Codex so that the Draft Standard under discussion there can be better adjusted to India's needs. Application of HACCP by importing countries can be suitably discussed at the Government-to-Government level, so that no measures are applied that go beyond the legitimate objectives built into the agreements on technical barriers to trade (TBT) and sanitary and phyto-sanitary standards (SPS).
- The EC regulations on marine products need a closer look to identify their HACCP plus components, the compliance costs

arising therefrom and the assistance that could be sought bilaterally and multilaterally to save the SME sector in India, which appears to be dying in the process of complying with domestic standards based on EC regulations.

Conclusions on Other Environmental Requirements

Capacity-building measures are necessary for most of the environment and health related requirements faced by Indian exporters. While large enterprises and better organized sectors have been able to overcome these requirements through advocacy and efforts (*e.g.* pesticides in tea, azo dyes in textiles, effluent treatment plants for dye manufacturing units in Gujarat) even they have faced higher compliance costs, resulting in erosion of profits or loss of markets.

SMEs in particular need capacity support both from the Government and from industry associations, if they are to survive these requirements. Their case also needs to be taken up in multilateral agencies like the WTO, ISO, Codex, *etc.*

Solutions for capacity constraints may also involve subsidies or trade related investment measures (TRIMS). Multilateral effort, particularly in the WTO would be required to render such subsidies non-actionable, and such TRIMS compatible with WTO rules.

Capacity constraints requiring technical and technological solutions may not be overcome only by government efforts. International cooperation may be necessary in this area. The reviews of the TBT and SPS agreements should factor these constraints into the recommendations for changes or special and differential treatment.

Capacity building is also necessary to overcome market diversion or distress sales. Exporters need to be advised to shed their fears of market loss and report distress sales to the government, so that environment and health related requirements can be analyzed for possible disguised protectionism. Further, the relevant provisions in and enforcement of the Indian Export-Import Policy need to be strengthened in this regard.

Standard setting organizations in India need to be strengthened and brought under a common canopy for uniformity. The enquiry points for the TBT and SPS Agreements need to create institutional support for dissemination of draft standards notified in the WTO, and get exporters' feedback for sending comments to Governments abroad.

Where standards in India differ from standards in the buyer's market, equivalence may be attempted, particularly where harmonization is not possible because of domestic constraints, or where foreign standards are unsuited to local conditions.

Testing equipment and procedures and possibly, funding of laboratories, need greater attention at the national level. Mutual recognition agreements with important buyers may be necessary and should also be encouraged multilaterally.

Appropriateness of foreign standards to local conditions need to be assessed at the national level before applying them, as was done in the case of dyes and dye stuffs and the marine product sectors. Social costs should also be factored into this assessment.

It is important to examine the legitimate objective behind standards applied on India's exports, and to analyze the risk that non-fulfillment may create (consider the cases of marine products, peanuts, and spices discussed above). Such risks should be commensurate with the effort involved to meet the standard as well as the compliance costs. If not, equivalence or MRAs may be the answer.

Quotas (for example, on mushrooms) and price preferences to competitors are relevant issues for the Government to take up with concerned foreign governments for redressal, particularly where the export of environmentally friendly products could provide India a 'win-win' on environmental and market access gains.

Voluntary process requirements and other measures like eco-labels can act as de facto barriers to market access, and therefore may have become a necessity in the market place. Wherever significant market access effects are discernible, the matter needs to be taken up multilaterally by the government.

16

Sanitary and Phytosanitary Standards, Quality Norms and Complementary Agricultural Activity

SAMRAT BOSE

Introduction

A country that has sixty-five per cent of its population dependent upon the agricultural sector; an under-developed processed foods industry and fledging exports of agro-based commodities, should ideally consider see the Sanitary and Phytosanitary Standard (SPS) agreement of the World Trade Organization (WTO) as an opportunity to upgrade its skills and move up the value chain. In all the three segments, India has been wanting in its formulation of rules governing quality standards and its implementation. The signing of the SPS agreement in 1995 should be the external impetus required for the domestic transformation of the agro-economy of the country with the execution of more stringent standards.

Though the agricultural sector needs a structural change to come out of the morass of low productivity, the issue of standards for the allied sectors can address the problem of growth in the short run with a relatively painless transition. It is in this context that the SPS agreement can be the catalyst for progress as at its core are quality standards that need to be adhered to. In the process, the entire supply chain can move to the next level to attain these said standards.

The SPS agreement affects the finished product, but also encompasses process controls, quality benchmarks and packaging design, thus ensuring that the back processes too adhere to certain norms. It is this effect of the sanitary and phytosanitary standards (re-hauling the Indian processed food industry) that will necessitate improvements in the quality of the raw materials at the base of the pyramid *i.e.* the agricultural sector.

This paper traces the advent of the SPS agreement through its evolutionary history. It then goes on to discuss the core agreement as well as the adjunct treaties on Technical Barriers to Trade (TBT) and Pre-shipment Inspection. Subsequently, the mechanism of the agreement and the standardization procedures are presented. An overview of the Indian scenario is undertaken, which is finally followed by examples that have set the tenor for dispute resolution at the WTO.

Theoretical Underpinning

When consumers are provided complete information, given the price, they choose the quality and quantity of commodities that they think is optimum. In such a case there is no need for market intervention, as stated in neoclassical economics. A similar argument can also be given by incorporating the variable of food safety. Underlining this theory, however, is the assumption that all goods being traded are homogeneous and substitutable. But this is farthest from the attributes of commodities in the arena of international trade in agriculture products. In such a scenario, access to information becomes all-important with 'information' commanding an economic price rather than being freely available (Stigler, 1961). Thus the approach to solving the problem of asymmetric information in farm trade is one that is of importance to the political economy of nations, especially since it has a direct bearing on the way a major proportion of the population lives.

Against neoclassical tenets of complete information, consumers rarely have comprehensive knowledge about the prices and quality of products in real decision-making scenarios. This is particularly true of items associated with farm trade, as they form a quality continuum of minor gradation changes that command differential pricing. Traditionally products being traded can be divided into three groups – Search, Experience and Credence – according to the level of information made available to the consumer (Nelson 1970; Darby and Karni, 1973). Search goods are those where the consumers can inspect and research the commodities before making purchase decisions. For Experience goods, the buyers cannot determine the attributes of the commodity in question till after the purchase and its use. When a client makes repeated transactions or when the producer establishes a 'brand', signifying certain attributes of the product, this nullifies the effect of imperfect information. Credence goods are the last of the troika, where the consumer lacks full information of the product before as well as after the purchase.

In fact, the seller's choice of product quality in one time period affects the sales of subsequent generation of goods from the same marquee due to the establishment of a reputation (Shapiro, 1982). In this dynamic process of producing goods and selling them, there seems to be a need for institutionalizing the process of quality adherence by benchmarking product attributes to certain predefined performance indicators. Markets were unable to solve this imperfection independently, which led to a need for some sort of a standardization/certification mechanism. Nations were trying to solve the problem by having regulatory mechanisms to manage this asymmetry of information. But with the signing of the SPS and TBT Agreements, the first move to facilitate the conversion of this involvement (of regulatory bodies) into a worldwide rule-based system was made.

The signing of the Agreement on Agriculture (AoA) hoped that that the market for agricultural commodities would become perfectly competitive (as is generally toted in textbooks), because the products were assumed to be homogenous. AoA did succeed in reducing tariff across countries, but there arose a new point of contention in international trade – standards and quality norms. To tackle these, a new agreement was needed between all the members of the WTO, which finally resulted in the Agreement on Sanitary and Phytosanitary Measures and Agreement on Technical Barriers to Trade.

Tracing the Agreement on Sanitary and Phytosanitary Measures

Historically, trade in agriculture has a strong tradition of protection, particularly in industrialized countries. The Uruguay Round brought the movement of agricultural products into the discipline of the rule-based trading system, though it might not have led to the liberalization of the market to the extent the developing world would have liked. But there were three main components of the deal that ensured some semblance of stabilization in the market for agriculture products. These were - targets set for reduction of farm export subsidies, expanding market access for imported goods and cuts in domestic producer subsidies (Anderson, 1999).

Understanding the AoA is important, because the concurrent signing of the Agreement on Sanitary and Phytosanitary Measures was a result of the developing and the least developed nations realizing that the concessions gained in the AoA could easily be diluted with stringent quarantine measures. The SPS Agreement was conceived to block this design and bring these variable policies into the ambit of a rule-based process.

At this moment it would be prudent to take a few steps back and map the progression of the SPS Agreement. The General Agreement on Tariffs and Trade (GATT), 1948, provides the underlying base for discipline in national food safety and animal and plant health protection norms. Articles I and III ensure the principles of non-discrimination and national treatment in the overall trade of goods between the signatories.

But it was the specificity of Article XX on General Exceptions that necessitated the need for the SPS agreement in 1995. In this article provision (b) provides for governments to impose restrictive requirements on imported products if they were "necessary to protect human, animal or plant life or health".

The Tokyo Round of multilateral negotiations between 1973 and 1979 made the first attempt to address issues of non-tariff barriers to trade and farm trade. An important outcome of this round was the TBT agreement, which covered the technical requirements, inspection mechanisms and labeling relating to food safety and animal and plant health. The relevant standards were to adhere to the principle of harmonization and transparency, with the GATT secretariat acting as the notification body.

The agreement also had a dispute redressal mechanism for Member countries. However, this code was applied to only those countries that ratified the TBT agreement which ensured the need for a stronger enforcement mechanism in the run up to the SPS agreement in the Uruguay Round.

With increased pressure to expand negotiation into areas like non-tariff barriers, the Punta del Este Declaration, 1986, made a specific mention of "minimizing the adverse effects that sanitary and phytosanitary regulations and barriers can have on trade in agriculture" among other issues such as market access and direct and indirect subsidies. Elimination of all these impediments are required to unknot trade in agriculture, but the developing nations were the strongest votaries of removal of SPS as a barrier to trade.

To overcome their concerns, the touchstone for the Working Group established in 1988 was the harmonization of standards on the basis of accepted scientific principles, development of a notification process for regulations and transparency in dispute resolution to weed out arbitrariness. All these concerns were tackled in the final draft of the agreement, but at the time of its passage, key areas like domestic implementation of stricter norms than international standards, process of risk assessment and inspection mechanism remained in the realm of grey. The developing nations were also able to get a concession of five years in its implementation.

Constitution of the Agreement on the Application of Sanitary and Phytosanitary Measures

Since the paper undertakes an in-depth discussion of the issues associated with the Agreement, rather than the provisions contained therein, the original text has been added at the end of the paper. Particularly important are the sections on the definition of sanitary and phytosanitary measures, harmonization of international standards, equivalence, risk assessment and transparency. A brief elucidation of the seven disciplines and one exemption (Charnovitz, 2002) is given below.

The first discipline is the science requirement as stated in Article 2.2 of the SPS Agreement. According to this, all government sanitary and phytosanitary measures should be "based on scientific principles, and is not maintained without sufficient scientific evidence." The second is on risk assessment that has been defined in Article 5.1. The three case laws presented – Hormones; Salmon and the Agricultural Products - in the 'Case Studies' section have debated this clause. The third is the requirement for national regulatory consistency pointed out by Article 5.5.

Article 5.6 states that the SPS measures should not more trade restrictive as compared to their "appropriate level". This is called the requirement of least trade restrictiveness. The fifth discipline is the use of international standards, which has been explained in Article 3.1. Next is Article 4.1, which requires the importing country to accept the SPS measure of the exporting country if it provides the same level of protection. This is known as equivalence. The last is the transparency requirement that has been detailed in Annexure B of the Agreement, asking Members to follow certain procedures while making new rules or changing existing provisions in domestic SPS laws.

The only exemption in the Agreement has been provided in Article 5.7, which states that in case of insufficient scientific evidence provisional SPS measure may be adopted by governments. The conflict arising from this is based on the precautionary principle.

Reading SPS with the Agreement on Technical Barriers to Trade and Agreement on Pre-shipment Inspection

The Agreement on Technical Barriers to Trade covers trading practices for all consumer products so that standards do not become an obstacle in trade between Members (though Article I makes it clear that the provisions in Annex A of the Agreement on SPS are not to be covered). The demarcation between the TBT and SPS is that the former is related to non-content standards for food items, while the latter is responsible for the effect of the content on human health. Still there is a sphere of overlapping influence of both these agreements in food products, as seen by the requirement of process labeling by some members, which is governed by TBT, but the labeling directed at health protection is governed by SPS.

Another area of conflict is the emerging area of Genetically Modified (GM) food products. Issues like mandatory labeling of GM falls within the TBT purview, while the problem of protecting a country from importation of organisms associated with GMs is an issue that concerns the SPS committee. Broadly, it is the objective of the measure that determines the application of the SPS Agreement, whereas the nature of the measure details the requirement of TBT coverage (Stanton, 2002).

TBT allows the exception of not imposing technical standards in case of conflict with national security or for curbing deceptive practices. Governments are also not obliged to use international standards if they are inappropriate due to technological or geographical reasons. Under the SPS Agreement, the reason for divergence of domestic standards from international norms is scientific evidence. Only one exception is provided for in this agreement, Article 5.7, as discussed in the previous section. Thus the TBT and the SPS Agreements answer the question of adherence to standardization with the latter being a subset of the former, concerning just food safety. Also, substantive rules of implementation are different in the two Agreements, though the goals of non-discrimination, transparency, treatment to developing countries and dispute settlement are the same.

Another agreement that should be read in conjunction with the SPS is the Agreement on Pre-shipment Inspection. This Agreement also takes into account the concerns of the developing nations that verify the quality, quantity or price of imported goods. It details the mandate of the Obligations of User Members in terms of non-discrimination, site of inspection, standards, transparency, protection of confidential information, conflict of interest, delays, price verification, appeals procedures and derogation.

To maintain the veracity of claims made by exporters, pre-shipment inspections are increasingly being resorted to. This gains increased credence in agriculture and processed foods exports as the quality standards become more complex and herein lies the importance of the Inspection Agreement to streamline this process.

Points of Conflict for the Developing World

The ambiguity inherent in the manner in which the Agreement is worded, ensures that there is the necessary leeway given to the developed nations to align their quarantine policies in a way so as to impede the flow of agriculture goods from the developing Members. However it would seem unfair to carry this judgment too far, because there are caveats built in that provide the necessary protection—albeit in experience—by resorting to dispute resolution, which in itself is a time and resource intensive activity.

Though the transparency provision in the document is flagged as one of its most important achieved successes, but in its application a lot remains to be desired. When a change is made in the provisions of domestic standards, it has an impact on the export of the same products. But in such instances, the information on the need to change the standard and its risk assessment are not available. The multiplicity of agencies handling issues also compounds the time taken to assimilate changes. The provision of allowing sufficient time to Members to analyze the changes also has not been adhered to, with the result that there is little time lag between the proposed changes and its actual implementation.

As the SPS Agreement places importance on meeting the importing countries' sanitary protection requirements as such, rather than the means by which the standards are achieved, the concept of equivalence serves as the basis for Mutual Recognition Agreements (MRA) between Members. Because of the differential standards of the developing and the developed Members, the trend has been that MRAs have been signed only between the developed Members. Further, these MRAs will free sufficient resources of the developed nations for stricter enforcement of standards on imports from the developing nations (Jaiswal, 2003).

One solution to the above can be the upgradation of skills and infrastructure of the developing exporting nation as has also been envisaged under the technical assistance section. But as there is no time bound commitment, this provision of the Agreement has remained ineffective. The problem of implementation of standards and upgradation brings us to the core issue of setting standards. The inability of the developing nations to participate in the technical sessions of the CAC, IPPC and OIE because of the lack of capacity in this sphere, stands in their way of implementing the set standards as it does not take into account their specific needs.

The provisions of Special and Differential Treatment are not being fully utilized. Coupled with the adaptation to local provisions, the developing nations can influence many more changes on the restrictive trade practices of the developed nations. Yet there is hope, as was reflected in the Doha Round, where the developing country Members were able to address some of these issues. They are now allowed around six months to implement the new provisions and have been provided with an extended time frame (till 2005), to build capacities to meet all norms.

Dispute Resolution Structure

The following is the way in which the process of settling disputes is tackled between the Members of the WTO.

Step 1 A Member submits to the Dispute Settlement Body (DSB) that it seeks formal consultation with another Member, as the latter is not complying with its obligation under the SPS Agreement. Other Members having an interest may also be included as third parties.

A Member can ask for the establishment of a panel if no solution is found after 60 days. The offending country may not agree with the first request for a panel and suggest further consultations instead; however, it cannot block the establishment of a panel the second time it is considered by the DSB.

Step 2 Within these 60 days, the Member can request the good office of the Director-General for conciliation or mediation. The national can also directly move on to the next stage.

Step 3 DSB establishes panel at the latest at its second meeting. The parties to the dispute enter into consultations on the selection of panel members and on the terms of reference of the panel. Unless the parties to the dispute reach agreement within 20 days on specific terms of reference, the standard terms of reference for a panel apply.

The dispute resolution panel is normally composed of a chairperson and two members. Panel members serve in their individual capacity and do not represent their countries.

Step 4 The panel's working procedure involves the submission of written arguments and evidence by the parties, and two meetings at which the parties may present oral arguments and questions to each other. The panel also provides an opportunity for interested third parties to submit their written and/or oral arguments.

The panel may seek information from any source, which they consider pertinent including relevant technical and scientific experts.

Step 5 The panel prepares a report, which contains a factual description of the situation, a summary of the claims and main arguments of the parties (including the third parties), the panel's findings and conclusions. Advice received from experts may also be included in the report.

The parties to the dispute are then provided an opportunity to comment on the draft of the descriptive part of the report and the summary of their arguments.

Step 6 The panel then provides an interim report, including both the descriptive part and the panel's findings and conclusions, to the parties.

The parties may submit comments and request an interim review by the panel. The final report of the panel is normally provided to the parties shortly before it is circulated to all WTO members and submitted to the DSB.

At any time during the dispute resolution process, the parties may reach a mutually satisfactory resolution to their dispute and terminate the panel's consideration.

Step 7 Once the panel's final report has been submitted to all WTO members, there are two possible scenarios:

1. The DSB may consider the panel's report and agree to adopt it, unless there is a consensus not to adopt the report.

	2. Alternatively, the parties to the dispute (but not third parties) may appeal the panel's findings, to the WTO's Appellate Body.
Step 8	In case of the second case, the DSB has established a permanent seven-member Appellate Body, whose members have rotating 4-year terms. Any appeal is heard by three members of the Appellate Body, who have access to all of the submissions made to the panel, plus additional submissions by the parties to the appeal. The Appellate Body must submit its report to the DSB within 90 days. It can uphold, modify or reverse any or all of a panel's legal findings and conclusions but its review is limited to issues of law.
Step 9	The DSB must consider the Appellate Body's report within 30 days, and decide whether to accept it. The report will be adopted, and unconditionally accepted by the parties, unless there is a consensus not to adopt the report. Following adoption of the panel's report, as modified by the Appellate Body, a Member government has a legal obligation to bring its measure(s) into conformity with its obligations under the WTO. The agreement provides an unspecified "reasonable period of time" for compliance, noting that this should normally not exceed 15 months.
Step 10	If no agreement can be reached regarding acceptable compensation, the winning Member may request the DSB to authorize it to suspend concessions, that is, impose limited trade sanctions.
Step 11	DSB authorizes retaliation pending full implementation, 30 days after expiry of predetermined reasonable period of time.

Source: Stanton, World Trade Organization

Setting Standards: CAC, IPPC and OIE

The three sister organizations of Codex Alimentarius Commission (CAC[1]), International Plant Protection Convention (IPPC) and Office International des Epizooties (OIE) are the nodal technical bodies recognized by the agreement to formulate standards on food items, plant health and animal health, respectively. They are partly financed by the Food and Agriculture Organization (FAO) and the World Health Organization (WHO).

For dealing with food items, the Codex has two basic kinds of committees whose work is aligned across horizontal and vertical line. The first are the general committees that deal with all classes of food

1. CAC and Codex are alternatively used.

items while the Codex Commodity Committees deal with specific foods within a class or group.

Horizontal and Vertical Committees of Codex

The nine general committees share responsibility on the following:

- General Principles, hosted by France;
- Food Labeling, hosted by Canada;
- Methods of Analysis and Sampling, hosted by Hungary;
- Food Hygiene, hosted by the United States;
- Pesticide Residues, hosted by the Netherlands;
- Food Additives and Contaminants, hosted by the Netherlands;
- Import/Export Inspection and Certification Systems, hosted by Australia;
- Nutrition and Foods for Special Dietary Uses, hosted by Germany;
- Residues of Veterinary Drugs in Food, hosted by USA.

Similarly, there are twelve committees that look after particular food groups that described the métier of the CAC.

- Fats and Oils, hosted by the United Kingdom;
- Fish and Fishery Products, hosted by Norway;
- Milk and Milk Products, hosted by New Zealand;
- Fresh Fruits and Vegetables, hosted by Mexico;
- Cocoa Products and Chocolate, hosted by Switzerland;
- Sugars, hosted by the United Kingdom;
- Processed Fruits and Vegetables, hosted by USA;
- Vegetable Proteins, hosted by Canada;
- Cereals, Pulses and Legumes, hosted by the USA;
- Processed Meat and Poultry Products, hosted by Denmark;
- Soups and Broths, hosted by Switzerland;
- Meat Hygiene, hosted by New Zealand;
- Natural Mineral Waters, hosted by Switzerland.

Source: Codex Alimentarius Commission.

Despite the diversity of the food groups dealt with under the auspices of the CAC, there is a common format while suggesting standards. They contain information on the following: Scope of the standard and description of the product; essential composition and quality factors; food additives and contaminants; hygiene requirements; labeling requirements; and methods of analysis and sampling.

There is also the joint FAO/WHO Expert Committee on Food Additives and Contaminants (JEFCA) that carries out the toxicological evaluation of heavy metals, industrial pollutants, natural toxins and the veterinary drug residue levels. The committee defines the level of the Acceptable Daily Intake (ADI) of additives and contaminants that does not pose a health risk. The joint FAO/WHO Meetings on Pesticide Residues (JMPR) is responsible for defining the Maximum Residue Limits (MRL) for individual pesticides on specific food materials. The FAO/IAEA/WHO Expert Committee on Food Irradiation (JECFI) evaluates the level of irradiation in food products that is required to increase its shelf life. There are also two committees on risks associated with microbial contamination of foods (JEMRA) and GM Food Risk Assessment, that address issues associated with microbial risk assessment and viability of genetically modified micro-organism respectively.

Codex Procedures for Standard Setting

For making new standards or for revising them, the procedure detailed in the flow chart is followed.

Step 1	The Commission decides to elaborate a Codex standard and assigns the work to the appropriate Codex Committee.
Step 2	The Secretariat of the Commission arranges for the preparation of a proposed draft standard.
Step 3	The proposed draft standard is sent to Members of the Commission and interested international organizations for comments on all aspects including possible implications for their economy.
Step 4	The Secretariat of the Commission sends all comments to the secretariat of the concerned Codex committee. The committee compiles the comments and proposes amendments to the proposed draft standard.
Step 5	The proposed draft standard as amended previously is submitted to the Commission or to the Executive Committee for its adoption as a draft standard.
Step 6	The draft standard is sent to Members of the Commission and interested international organizations for comments on all aspects including possible implications for their economy.
Step 7	After compiling all comments with the secretariat of the concerned Codex committee from the previous stage, the comments and proposed amendments are considered at a session of the committee.
Step 8	The draft standard as amended previously is submitted to the Commission for its adoption as a Codex standard.

Source: Codex Alimentarius Commission

Codex has developed 237 food standards; 41 codes of hygiene or technological practices; evaluated 185 pesticides, 1,005 food additives and 54 veterinary drugs; set pesticide residue limits for 3,274 food items; and published guideline for 25 contaminants (Karki, 2002).

The internal processes of the IPPC and OIC are managed similarly with their mandate being more specific i.e. controlling plant pests and animal disease respectively.

India signed the IPPC in the April of 1952 and has followed international phytosanitary rules since by incorporating them in the domestic laws. The standards deal with plant quarantine related to international trade, pest risk analysis, eradication programs and export certification systems.

The OIC currently has four working groups – Biotechnology; Informatics and Epidemiology; Veterinary Drug Registration; and Wildlife Diseases – which review the progress being made in their respective fields. It also takes out two important texts called the International Animal Health Code and the International Aquatic Animal Health Code that apply science to animal husbandry practices. The OIE Manual of Standards for Diagnostic Tests and Vaccines describes the standards for laboratory diagnosis of diseases concerning terrestrial and aquatic animal life.

The Indian 'Standard' Scenario and Regulatory Framework

An entire gamut of laws deal with agriculture and its allied food processing activities with the purported reason of regulating the various aspects of this sector – technical and commercial. In this section we breakup the study of laws under three heads – sanitary, phytosanitary and commercial. These are dealt with in detail to offer a regulatory overview on this subject, to highlight especially, the complexity of operations entailed in order to run a legal agro-based business in India.

Sanitary Laws

The *Prevention of Food Adulteration Act (PFA), 1954* is the piece of legislation that formalizes the setting and monitoring of quality standards for raw and processed foods in India. Under this act, administered by the Ministry of Health and Family Welfare, the Central Committee for Food Standards advises the Central Government and the State Governments on matters of food quality standards. Members of this multi-departmental committee include the Director-General of Health Services as its Chairman; Director of the Central Food Laboratory; representatives from the Ministry of Agriculture, Commerce, Defense, Industry and Railways; nominees from the Bureau of Indian Standards and the Indian Council of Medical Research among others.

It is the *Prevention of Food Adulteration Rules, 1955* that provide a comprehensive framework for enforcing the law concerning agriculture and agro-based products. The Appendix B of this document contains the physical, microbial, packaging and labeling details of 30 groups that contain a total of 258 individual food and beverage items. Given below is the list of sections that quantify the presence of various foreign matters in the preservation of food.

Sections of Prevention of Food Adulteration Rules, 1955

Some important sections of the PFA rules are:

Part VI:	Coloring Matter
Part X:	Preservatives
Part XI:	Poisonous Metals (including Crop Contaminants and Naturally Occurring Toxic Substances)
Part XII:	Anti-oxidizing, Emulsifying and Stabilizing and Anti-caking Agents
Part XIII:	Flavoring Agents and Related Substances (including Carry Over Food Additives)
Part XIV:	Insecticides and Pesticide
Part XVI:	Sequestering and Buffeting Agents

Source: Prevention of Food Adulteration Rules, 1955

To differentiate agriculture produce according to its quality, the *Agricultural Produce (Grading and Marking) Act, 1937*, was enforced. The Directorate of Marketing and Inspection under the Ministry of Agriculture is the agency providing a Certificate of AGMARK Grading, which is the differentiator of products. This it does by comparing the product with its stated benchmark as laid out in the *General Grading and Marking Rules, 1988; Pulses Grading & Marking Rules, 1964; Cereals Grading Rules, 1966; and Vegetable Oils Grading & Marking Rules, 1955*. A list of 130 items is covered under this act that can go in for voluntary grading of quality. Penalties have been prescribed in this act for those products, which do not have the 'AGMARK' but fraudulently use it for greater consumer acceptance.

For the purpose of meeting the SPS norms, the European Commission has designated Directorate of Marketing and Inspection for conformity checking of marketing standards applicable to 25 fresh fruits and vegetables[2] prior to its import. Accordingly, the standards have been harmonized with the Codex Standards.

Two of the powers conferred on the State by the *Essential Commodities Act*, 1955, are:

a. Regulation by licenses, permits or otherwise, of the production or manufacture of any essential commodity;
b. Of bringing under cultivation any waste or arable land for the growing of specified food-crops.

It defines 18 commodities[3] that the Government considers crucial for the sustenance of the 'general public'. However, in the context of the state of domestic standards governing trade in food commodities, the following orders are of interest to us: *Fruit Product Order (FPO), 1955; Meat Food Products Order (MFPO), 1973; Vegetable Oil Products (Regulation) Order, 1998;* and the *Edible Oils Packaging (Regulation) Order, 1998*. The first order specifies the quality standards for fruit products and fruit-based beverages including the quality of water to be used; the second provides for sanitary and other requirements, limits of heavy metals, preservatives, insecticides, residue, etc., for processed meat products; the third outlines the norms for 25 varieties of vegetable oils; while the last order specifies the packing, marking and labeling of oils. Except for the FPO and the MFPO, the Act as well as the other orders are administered by the Ministry of Consumer Affairs, Food and Public Distribution while the FPO is under the jurisdiction of the Ministry of Food Processing Industries, and the MFPO is under the Department of Agriculture and Cooperation.

---

2. Grape, litchi, mango, pomegranate, guava, pineapple, banana, papaya, plum, shelling pea, sugar snap pea, ribbed celery, headed cabbage, spinach, Brussels sprouts, tomato, garlic, onion, pear, cherry, strawberry, melon, watermelon, beans and cauliflower.
3. Cattle fodder, including oilcakes and other concentrates; Coal, including coke and other derivatives; Component parts and accessories of automobiles; Cotton and woolen textiles; Drugs; Foodstuffs, including edible oilseeds and Oils; Iron and Steel, including manufactured products of Iron & Steel; Paper, including newsprint, paperboard and strawboard; Petroleum and petroleum products; Raw cotton, either ginned or unginned and cotton seeds; Raw jute; Jute textiles; Fertilizers, whether inorganic, organic or mixed; Yarn made wholly from cotton; Exercise books; Insecticides, fungicides, weedicides and the like; Seeds of food crops, fruits and vegetables, cattle fodder and jute; Onion.

The *Milk and Milk Products Order, 1992* was also promulgated under the *Essential Commodities Act, 1955*, and is administered by the Department of Animal Husbandry and Dairying under the Ministry of Agriculture. It seeks to ensure the observance of sanitary requirements for dairies, apart from regulating the production, supply and distribution of milk and milk products.

Lastly, for the purpose of regulating the process of irradiation in foods, the Department of Atomic Energy, Ministry of Science and Technology came out with the *Atomic Energy (Control of Irradiation of Food Rules), 1996*. Though the minimum dosage of radiation in food products is laid out in the PFA rules, the definition of standards and precautions to be taken by the units is under its purview.

Phytosanitary Laws

The *Destructive Insects and Pests Act, 1914* regulates the introduction into the country and the transport from one state to another of any insect, fungus or other pest, which might be destructive to crops. It empowers the Central Government to prohibit the import of classes of articles that are likely to cause infection to any crop with reference to the country of origin as well as the route of import. Further powers ordain that the Centre can charge a fee for making an application for a permit to import or for the required inspection, fumigation, disinfection, disinfestation or supervision of articles. This fee cannot be refunded if approval is not granted, as clarified by the *Destructive Insects and Pests (Amendment and Validation) Act, 1992*. The State Governments can also undertake to rules - for detention, inspection, disinfection or destruction of articles - and appoint officials to enforce the same.

Under the above act is the *Plant Quarantine (Regulation of Import into India), 2003*, which details the powers of the authorities associated with the regulation of phytosanitary measures in India and the regulation for import of plant and plant products. It specifies the type of information required for import, lists the plants that can be imported and those that are banned. The earlier *Plant, Fruits & Seeds (Regulation of Import into India) Order, 1989*, is replaced by this more extensive document, which is based on Pest Risk Analysis and has been aligned with the International Standards of Phytosanitary Measures of the International Plant Protection Convention.

Description of contents of the Plant Quarantine Order, 2003

The order contains the following schedules:

Schedule I:	Points of entry: airports (12); sea ports (34); land border stations (13)
Schedule II:	Inland container deports and container freight stations (60)
Schedule III:	Foreign post offices (11)
Schedule IV:	Prohibited plant species
Schedule V:	Restricted plant species permitted by authorized institutions
Schedule VI:	Restricted plant species permitted generally with additional declarations (74 commodities)
Schedule VII:	Plants and plant material permitted with normal PSC (83 commodities)
Schedule VIII:	Quarantine weed species (61)
Schedule IX:	Inspection/treatment and other charges
Schedule X:	Permit issuing authorities
Schedule XI:	Inspection authorities for Post-entry Quarantine
Schedule XII:	Seed quantities permitted for trial purposes

Source: Plant Quarantine (Regulation of Import into India) Order, 2003

The other piece of legislation that also concerns phytosanitary measures is the *Seeds Act* of 1966 and the consequent *Seed Rules* of 1968. A Central Seed Committee administers this act concerning the sale and classification of seeds. It defines the quality of seed of any variety to be sold for purposes of agriculture and can notify different kinds of seeds for different States or geographical areas. Marking or labeling that is required for transacting seeds in India too is encompassed under this Act. A Central Seed Certification Board is established with the express purpose of guiding the Central and State governments with matters relating to certification and to co-ordinate the functioning of the other approving agencies, which might have been granted permission to function by the government under section 8 (other certification agencies approved by the government) of this Act. A license is required for selling, exporting or importing seeds under the *Seeds (Control) Order, 1983*.

Apart from this, the *Protection of Plant Varieties of Farmers' Rights Act, 2001* and its Rules, 2003, provides the framework for farmers to register new plant varieties and extant varieties including those available in India which are notified under the *Seeds Act*, 1966, varieties about which there is common knowledge and is in the public domain. The Government of India also regulates the manufacture, sale, transport, use, import and export of pesticides through the *Insecticides Act, 1968* and its Rules framed under it in 1971. Accordingly, the Central Insecticides Board advises the Government on the technical matters for administering the Act. The Registration Committee is the nodal body, which approves the insecticide after testing for its safety towards humans, animals and the environment.

The above stated four acts are under the administrative charge of the Department of Agriculture and Cooperation, Ministry of Agriculture.

Commercial Laws

For the purpose of checking the export of sub-standard products from India, the Government passed the *Export (Quality Control & Inspection) Act, 1966* (amended in 1984). The Export Inspection Council enforces quality control and inspects commodities intended for export. This agency under the Ministry of Commerce provides five types of certification services: Consignment-wise Inspection, In Process Quality Control, Self Certification, Food Safety Management Systems based-Certification and Pre-shipment Inspection and Certification Schemes. It has also laid down plant approval norms[4], which has won it recognition from the European Commission, United States Food and Drug Administration and the Australian Quarantine and Inspection Service for certification of certain products for SPS approval.[5]

Enacted in 1976, the *Standard of Weights and Measures Act* was passed to establish standards of weights and measures and regulate inter-state trade of goods sold by weight, measure or number. According to the *Packaged Commodities Rules* issued in 1977, the identity of the commodity, net quantity, unit sale price, name of the manufacturer and origin of commodities in packaged form has to be declared. For retail sale of ready-to-eat food products and other processed foods in the

4. For Basmati rice; Black pepper; Egg products; Fish and fishery products; Honey; Milk products.
5. EU: Certificates of authenticity for Basmati rice; Approval of fish and fishery products' processing units. USFDA: EIC certification required by every batch of Black Pepper exported. AQIS: Random sampling of EIC certified seafood consignments.

domestic market, the *Recycled Plastics Manufacture and Usage Rules, 1999,* under the *Environment Protection Act, 1986,* specifies that vendors must use bags and containers made from virgin plastic only.

Tax and Cess on Agriculture Products

Apart from the *Central Excises and Salt Act, 1944* which specifies the rate of tax that a unit has to pay on the production of agro-based commodities, the following are some of the special cess that is charged according to various Acts and notifications:

Tobacco/Manufactured Beedis:	Tobacco Cess Act, 1975 / The Beedis Workers' Welfare Cess Act, 1976
Copra consumption:	Copra Cess Act, 1979
Cotton consumption:	Produce Cess Act, 1966
Coffee:	Coffee Act, 1942
Jute goods:	Jute Manufactures Cess Act, 1983
Paper:	Industries (Development and Regulation) Act, 1951
Exported marine products:	Marine Products Exports (Development) Authority Act, 1972
Oils extracted from oilseeds:	Produce Cess Act, 1966
Rubber:	Rubber Act, 1947
Salt:	Salt Cess Act, 1953
Tea:	Tea Act, 1953
Vegetable oil:	Department of Agriculture and Cooperation Notification No. G.S.R. 882 (E), dated 8-12-1983
Sugar:	Sugar Export Promotion Act, 1958; Sugar (Special Duty) Act, 1959; Sugar Cess Act, 1982

Source: Central Board of Excise and Customs, Ministry of Finance.

The *Solvent Extracted Oil, De-Oiled Meal and Edible Flour (Control) Order, 1967* and *Pulses, Edible Oilseeds and Edible Oils (Storage Control) Order, 1977* too are derived from the *Essential Commodities Act, 1955.* According to the former only those units registered with the Directorate of Vanaspati, Vegetable Oils and Fats, Ministry of Consumer Affairs, Food and Public Distribution can buy and use solvent extracted oils while the latter regulates the storage and distribution of edible oils and oilseeds.

Revisiting the Question of Unified and Harmonized Food Law

To simplify the existing *Food Adulteration Act* and to lay the foundation of a harmonized food law, a task force led by Justice ES Venketaramaiah was set up in 1995. Its main recommendation was a shift in the law from being regulator to one that promotes Good Manufacturing Practices (GMP). This would entail that the current rules be simplified and made uniform across the various Acts that govern the processed food industry in India. This can be seen from the divergence between the number of insecticides whose minimum pesticide residue levels have been defined in the PFA rules and the number of registered pesticide under the Insecticides Act. The former has specified the tolerance limit of 71 pesticides[6] in foods, while under the latter 1588 registration certificates were issued in the year 2000 alone. With the availability of newer and more complex insecticides, the PFA too needs to be parallely updated.

Also in the current regime most of the standardization norms (AGMARK, ISO 9000 certification *etc.*) are voluntary, and therefore, would require compulsory approvals. It is visualized that merit goods would be defined in terms of value addition and incentives for the production of such items will be provided within the proposed *Processed Food Industries Development Act* as mooted by the approach paper on it.

A comprehensive view on this subject was taken by the Subject Group on Food and Agro Industries of the Prime Minister's Council on Trade and Industry headed by Nusli Wadia. In addition to suggesting a host of measures to increase the productivity of the agricultural sector in India, in the present context it suggested three important measures. First, there is a need to consolidate the *Seeds Act, 1966*, and the *Plant Quarantine (Regulation of Import into India), 2003*. This would lead to balanced usage of available resources in agriculture as currently more stress is put on excessive input of water, pesticides and fertilizers because of the presence of a high level of subsidy. A reduction in subsidy and a unified phytosanitary code will increase the availability of better quality seeds, which would in turn lead to

6. The Ministry of Health and Family Welfare has notified draft minimum residue levels for 50 insecticides in Part II Section 3(i) of the Gazette of India vide notification GSR 768(E) dated 29th September 2003.

productivity gains. Secondly, a Food Regulation Authority should replace the Central Committee of Food Standards that manages the PFA and the harmonization of India standards with those of the Codex. Accordingly, all production units will have to qualify for GMP and HACCP. Lastly, all the developmental agencies like APEDA, MPEDA, *etc*. should be amalgamated into the Agro and Food Development and Export Promotion Council to be set up. This report lays down in detail the changes required in the PFA with regard to the way food samples are lifted, verified and tested as most of the cases in court get dismissed due to procedural flaws during sampling.[7]

Flagging Issues for India

Two important issues of the product versus the process debate and the labeling of food are dealt with in this section. The first issue has a regulatory import, because the manner in which standards would be defined and managed depends on this. The latter deals with the quality of information that the regulators and consumers would want access to. A discussion on HACCP is also undertaken under the first issue. The wider controversy of GM food products too has been touched upon. This section should be read with reference to the SPS Agreement and that is why topics like HACCP and GM are subservient to issues of product versus process and labeling of food respectively, which form the thrust of the controversy.

Product versus Process Debate

In trade two kinds of standards can be distinguished – product standards and process standards – that are used to ensure adherence to the attributes of a commodity. They are used to implement the stated health and environment policies of member states of the WTO. It is the difference in standards that leads to a conflicting situation in the context of trade and in the era of reduced tariffs, protect domestic players from outside competition.

Product standards are used as tools to restrict market access by invoking stringent health and environment standards for a particular class of commodities ensuring that the domestic players enjoy access

---

7. For detailed case law refer to Policy Paper No. 26 of Legal Adjustments and Reforms for Globalizing the Economy by Saleema Razvi.

to their markets. But under the WTO, these standards can be challenged on the grounds of either being too stringent without any scientific basis or because they hurt the trading rights of other member countries.

In contrast, process standards are used to target the lax standards that might be prevailing in the exporting nation. It helps to transfer the concern of the importing nation about the quality standard of the entire process being followed to the exporting nation and also enables it to change that procedure. For example, the EU directive[8] on importing milk that has been mechanically milked from cows can be called a process standard. Not only will this move impact trade between two nations, but it will also lead to structural change in the way the dairy business is carried out in the country from which the EU imports.

Thus in restrictive trade, while product standards serve as effective protection within the boundaries of a sovereign nation, process standards (though primarily serving the same purpose) also has a secondary externality. The exporting country has to align its own internal standards with that of the exporting nation while in the former there still exists a possibility of servicing the domestic market with lower standards. It is precisely for this reason that process standards have become a profound concern for the developing world for their targeting of internal change.

Within the context of the application of the above to the SPS, the WTO seems to be moving away from product standards and treading the middle ground between it and process standards. This shift is reflected by its handling of the earlier Tuna/Dolphin dispute and the more recent Shrimp/Turtle row, both involving trade restrictions based on environmental standards (Peel, 2003). In the first case the WTO Appellate Body rendered a narrow interpretation of Article XX of the GATT and found that the process standards having extraterritorial effect could not be justified. But in the Shrimp/Turtle controversy, the panel rejected the strict free trade position and became more accommodative to environmental concerns while interpreting the same provisions of the Marrakesh Agreement. A further elucidation on this is made in the Case Study section later in this paper.

---

8. (92/46/EEC).

Hazard Analysis Critical Control Point: 'Process Standard' Answer to the Quality Debate

The Hazard Analysis Critical Control Point (HACCP) approach is considered the panacea for unifying the standards code in the trade of agricultural goods with its underlying theme of adopting similar food safety assurance systems. HACCP is a process-based approach to ensure a certain minimum level of quality in the entire food chain resulting in the end product meeting the safety standards. With regard to the SPS Agreement, HACCP can provide three strategies for rapprochement between differential regulatory requirements (Jacob, 1994). From a conflicting position wherein there is no alignment between standards, the first step is towards coordination followed by mutual recognition and finally, harmonization. Seen as a continuum, the alignment process moves from one end of the spectrum of weak rapprochement to the other, which is the strongest level of rapprochement. Thus the success of HACCP will depend on the degree to which the various regulatory bodies coordinate their functioning as they move towards the stated aim of Harmonization provided in the Agreement.

But here too, the debate moves towards the process versus product controversy as HACCP provides the outline within which food safety norms are to be defined. This leaves enough scope to have variable implementation guidelines, which can further distort the regulatory systems that need to be aligned. Here performance standards are more conducive to the process of harmonization. But how will HACCP be implemented? And will it lead to a complete overhaul of the current Good Manufacturing Practices (GMP) or will it complement it?

Principles and Objectives of HACCP

Principles	*Objectives*
Hazard Analysis	Hazard Evaluation
Identify Critical Control Points Establish Critical Limits Establish Monitoring Indicators Establish Corrective Action	Risk Management
Establish Verification Procedures Establish Effective Record Keeping	Documentation Control

Source: Karki, 2002.

GMP, by definition, is a combination of technical and management practices that result in the meeting of predetermined specifications of the customer by the manufacturer. They include the regulatory mechanism already in place, which is purported to act as the base for HACCP implementation. The difference being that now the focus is on the critical points in the entire production chain rather than on the standardization of the end products that was earlier the case with most of the food laws. HACCP in its 'voluntary' avatar might have played a complementary role to GMP but its incorporation into the regulatory framework makes it subsume these practices. This leads to two problems – internally it runs the risk of a lack of complementarity between HACCP and the current GMP in the intermittent time when HACCP is being implemented. Externally, the divergence between the differing processes within HACCP once again brings about the dilemma of equivalence. As with any process standards, controlling the 'environment' within which production takes places is difficult to monitor as compared to scrutinizing product attributes.

The directive for implementing HACCP from the regulator could lead to a situation where public and private standards become interdependent. For example the ISO 9000 quality certification provided to food companies is complementary to the HACCP provision. Ultimately however the efficacy of HACCP in food trade will depend upon the willingness of various governments to engage in regulatory rapprochement (Caswell and Hooker, 1996). Thus the implementation of HACCP will shift the debate to the need to harmonize processes that are incorporated in manufacturing if it is brought within the gamut of national regulation.

Labeling and Traceability of food

Though labeling of food products does not fall within the jurisdiction of the agreement on SPS, it forms an important issue while implementing the same. It is governed by the TBT agreement of the WTO as it encompasses labeling of all products – food products constituting just a part of that purview. Technically, only packaging and labeling that relate to 'food safety' is covered under SPS. This particular point is being brought out as an example of the kind of barriers that manufacturers and traders will have to face in the near future if they want to tap the more developed markets.

Labeling programs can be positive, negative or neutral (Goodland, 2002). The first highlights the positive attributes of the product; the second warns consumers about the dangers of the hazardous ingredients in the product; while neutral labeling provides information to the consumer and can have a bearing on their purchase decision. The common thread between all the three programs is verification of claims that are made in the product labels, which can be undertaken by self, government or an independent organization. There are also Eco-labels that are granted by certification bodies (*e.g.* ISO 1400 which endorses certain environment processes) based on its life-cycle analysis. Sometimes the approval of such labels may take into account more conditions than those explicitly stated. For instance, in addition to the environmental impact of production, they may include other standards, which the developing world fears such as labour issues, working conditions *etc.*

An important reason for stringent labeling norms is the need for the tracking of food products. This record keeping helps foods with different attributes to be kept separately from one another as well as offer the agency responsible for public health an effective tool to follow the product through the supply chain.

Another major reason for putting so much stress on labeling, apart from meeting one's legal obligation, is the need for product differentiation. A case in point is the debate raging on the issue of the labeling of genetically modified (GM) food products in the US and European Union. The differentiation of GM based food products from traditional agricultural produce provides the consumer with not only product information through labeling instructions but also helps the producer to improve margins (in this case the consumer pays a lower price for GM products). This would not have been possible if extensive labeling information were not provided for.

With producers differentiating their products over a wide variety of attributes, some, which consumers can detect while others that go unnoticed; it becomes imperative to keep the end user informed about them. Such credence attributes can be defined either according to the content of the product or by the process of production.

Lighting the GM Controversy

The GM foodstuff controversy stems from the difference in the stated positions of the US and the European Community on this issue. The US sees this as a move by the EU to replace price support for its producers (as envisaged by the AoA) with technical barriers to trade, by not accepting biotechnology products as being proven to be safe. Similarly, the EU demands that they have the right to claim the precautionary principle as incorporated in Article 5.7, wherein, "in case of insufficient scientific evidence, Members may provisionally adopt international standards or those of other Member states", because the effects of genetically modified food products on human and animal health is not clear. This principle was also used to defend its stance in the Hormones case described in the next section.

From the perspective of informing the consumer, if GM and GM-free lines of agriculture production are established, there is a need for labeling requirements that point to this difference across the globe. But currently the US FDA does not differentiate between food produced from GM crops and those from crops developed by other technology. Consequently the labeling of transgenic[9] food requirements is the same unless it differs substantially from its conventional counterpart in product characteristics. In Europe the labeling[10] of foodstuffs that contain 1 per cent or more genetically modified material is required on the products that are identified on the basis of scientific evidence.

In fact, by providing detailed labeling information, there is a distinct possibility that the producers can differentiate their products from similar characteristic ones and charge a premium on its sale. This can certainly be the case for GM-free products, which might enjoy a higher payment as compared to its GM counter part if consumers are informed about them. Though the cost of compliance for non-GM processed foods might be more, consumer wariness towards GM foods could well ensure that the producers are not only able to recover the cost but also earn a profit on providing and certifying this information.

Apart from the above labeling issue, there is a wider ramification of the SPS Agreement that does not explicitly deal with the GM foods. The Cartagena Protocol on Biosafety signed in January 2000, envisages that once it gets ratified by the 50 signatories, governments can then

9. Transgenic and GM are alternatively used.
10. Regulation 1139/98 and 49/200.

decide whether to accept GM foods or not and define the conditions for imports. The precautionary principle in food trade gets enshrined with this treaty and provides governments with an opportunity to protect its citizens by allowing for an explicit identification of genetically modified organisms when introduced into the environment. Labeling requirements on final products must also carry a tag of "may contain" GM organisms. With the US not a signatory, an extreme situation may arise where the other party could ban GM foods altogether under the pretext of its effect on human health, as the process of production is different (in case of GM) from that of the conventional method. If in both cases the end product characteristics remain the same then it is compliant with the WTO rules but if some Members find the process of genetic engineering unacceptable, then it is a case of fissure within the Agreement. The labeling issues can be sorted out under the TBT Agreement with Codex trying to establish uniform standards for all Members (Nielson and Anderson, 2000).

Case Studies – Establishing a Precedence

A read through of two cases – Hormones and Shrimp/Turtle – will help us get a perspective of the type of the conflicts that international trade throws up especially in the context of the SPS Agreement. In the first case it was the US and Canada complaining against the European Union while the latter had Mexico requesting a consultation on the restrictive food trade practice of the US.

The EU had enacted a directive[11] that banned the use of natural as well as synthetic growth hormones in cattle for the production of beef. This edict was for both imported as well as domestic beef, which meant that under the GATT regime it adhered to both the national treatment and the MFN principles. But the US questioned the scientific basis of this ban as well as the timing of the same as there was a large glut of beef at that instance. On the first point the directive was violating Article 2.2 of the SPS Agreement and since the measure was not based on any international standard, it also did not follow Article 3.1. As there was no justification for this ban, the US and Canada termed it as a restrictive practice that was not following

11. (96/22/EC)

Articles 3.3, 5.1 and 5.5. It also provided an example of an additive being allowed in the production of pork and attributed this allowance to the relative competitiveness of the sector in EU.

On the part of the EU, they refuted the above claims on the basis that there was no scientific evidence on the long-term health effects of the consumption of hormone-treated beef. The SPS Agreement in such instances provided for a total ban under the precautionary principle. But this justification was not enough for the Panel and it upheld that the ban on beef by the US was a trade restriction measure. Though the EU went to the Appellate Body, it was in consonance with the Panel's decision and was followed by retaliatory trade sanction by the US and Canada on the EU.

The second case that I want to highlight here – the Shrimp/Turtle – brings our attention to the environmental concerns that have crept into the setting of standards. *The US Endangered Species Act, 1973*, prohibits the capture of endangered sea turtles. It was found that incidental catching of sea turtles by shrimp trawlers was the biggest reason for their declining population. A campaign was then started for the compulsory use of Turtle-Extruder Device (TED) and the US Congress enacted a law that called for negotiations with developing countries engaged in commercial shrimp farming to encourage the use of TEDs. The ruling went against the US and it changed the guidelines.

The above two cases were clubbed together to highlight the shift in the outlook of the Appellate Body which put trade concerns in the Hormone case in the forefront while in the Shrimp/Turtle trade conflict the environmental consequences were highlighted. Chronologically however, Hormones was followed by Salmon and Agricultural Products conflict.

In the Measures Affecting the Importation of Salmon case[12], Canada complained against an Australian ban, implemented from 1975, on the importation of uncooked salmon. Australia had implemented this fishery health measure to prevent the entry of exotic pathogens into the country. The Appellate Body ruled against Australia in October 1998 and in July 2000 it modified its regulations on the import of salmon. The Measures Affecting Agricultural

12. Referred to as the *Salmon* case throughout this text.

Products[13] followed this case. The US complained about a Japanese phytosanitary measure, in place since the 1950s, which banned the imports of apples, cherries, nectarines and walnuts due to the possible infestation with coddling moth. Japan lifted this ban in 1987 subject to a requirement of individual testing of each variety of fruit. The Appellate Body ruled against Japan in February 1999 challenging this particular condition. Subsequently, the regulation was brought in line with SPS rules.

The decision on the Salmon case led to a clarification, by the Appellate Body, on the definition of national regulatory consistency as underscored by Article 5.5. Accordingly, it consists of three parts – the level of comparable health protection should be the same across similar products; if there is a difference then it should not be arbitrary; and domestic health measure must not restrict international trade. Based on it, five reasons were put forward for the Australian ban to be a trade violation, in particular the existing internal controls were not equivalent to those imposed on foreign diseases. It also led to the interpretation of Article 5.1 on risk assessment. There should be evidence of "ascertainable risk" as against regulations based on "theoretical" risk that underlies all scientific uncertainty.

In Agricultural Products the science requirement was tested. There should be "a rational or objective relationship between the SPS measure and the scientific evidence." The Appellate Body concluded that Japan was violating Article 2.2 because it could not show whether the quarantine and fumigation used for one variety of fruit would be inadequate for other varieties or not. Japan was also the first country to invoke Article 5.7 but that too was struck down.

In Conclusion: Internalizing the 'Problem' of SPS and Suggested Solutions

Any impediment to trade is generally seen as having 'strategic implications' on a country's economy, and by an extension of this characterization, the barriers that the Agreement on Sanitary and Phytosanitary Measures throws up need to be tackled, and quickly. However, if this problem is looked at from another angle, SPS is not

13. Referred to as the *Agricultural Products* case throughout this text.

just a trade issue but constitutes a much bigger one – that of public health. While trade affects merely the economy of a country, health has much larger ramifications.

Much of the literature on SPS in India concerns trade and the influence that the developing nations need to wield at the WTO to break these non-tariff barriers. Such arguments, however, serve only to externalize the debate, taking away from us the onus of leveraging on these issues, with the result that the developed nations are left to take the initiative. An alternate approach could be an internal assessment of the standards that we have and its effect on our own citizens, with trade in commodities forming only secondary considerations.

Once such a stance is taken to solve the problem, the burden of SPS seems to rest on our shoulders. Yes, we do need to tackle the unfair trade practices that have crept in while implementing the agreement but a large swathe of the initiative to meet the quality standards should be our own. Underlying the SPS is a fundamental principle of quality standards that should address health concerns. Issues of cost and technology must take priority but only in the context of health and not market access.

One of the major impediments to fulfilling the potential that the Indian food processing industry possesses, has been the lack of post-harvest facilities. Whether it be the quality of storage space, the establishment of a cold chain for perishable items or basic value addition on the producer side, the facilities for the same are non-existent. The government should be the catalyst in the creation of such services, rather than the service provider, by following policies that induce investment in this sector. This approach will not only improve the quality of agro-produce but improve employment opportunities without the attendant baggage that direct government intervention brings.

To improve the quality of production and to verify the claims being made by the producers, a system of third party certification is a must. Herein lies the role of the government as a creator of such skills. Its role should be restricted to playing the regulator of such certifying agencies rather than being the authority that issues such clearance. Not only will the government be unencumbered from public dealing with the vast number of producers—thereby directing its resources elsewhere--it will also reduce corruption and improve the quality of verification services being provided. Thus by promoting more private sector participation, alternate extension service infrastructure and capacity can be created with the government being no more than the overall regulator.

As suggested in the above section, the documentation of norms required under SPS should be centralized with one agency (like the Bureau of Indian Standards) to handle all queries that arise from the implementation of sanitary and phytosanitary measures. One problem that is repeatedly stated is India's, (and the developing countries'), inability to find representation in the three sister organizations. As detailed in a section of this paper, the standards suggested by these organizations are all constructed in a rule-based manner, similar to the procedure being followed at the WTO for its dispute resolution.

Producers should be provided with the necessary support infrastructure to modernize the entire production process. Here the adoption of HACCP would be beneficial for the processed food industry. The technology needed to follow the processes outlined in HACCP is expensive but the government should provide the right incentive for indigenous technology and hence look to reduce costs. Traditionally, mechanization in the agriculture sector has been viewed with suspicion since this sector supports a large mass of population but the government should realize that the implementation of such technology would lead to the expansion of the food processing industry and help in transferring some of the labour force from agriculture to manufacturing.

The government can redirect the subsidies to research and developmental activities and capacity building initiatives in the agricultural sector to meet the challenges posed by SPS requirements. In fact subsidies in such activities will be considered under the 'blue box' of the AoA, which would not be considered to be trade distorting by the world community. At the same time due to enhanced skill levels, the quality and productivity related to Indian agricultural products will markedly improve. In fact Fen *et al.* have shown that in rural India government expenditure on roads and R&D have larger impacts on productivity growth than investment in any other sphere. Financial support to R&D in the rural sector must be pushed in the wider context of our ability to meet the stringent SPS requirements.

This strategy in the long term will help us achieve improved health standards as well as make us competitive in the international arena.

Also, as is reflected by the case studies on the disputes between members the jurisprudence established is veering away from the strict interpretation of trade law and is accommodating issues like environmental concerns. Here the developing world needs to take such changes into consideration and follow up the issues with the Dispute Settlement Body for incorporating their concerns while creating SPS case laws.

In the final analysis, the Agreement should still be held in good faith, as it is the implementation of the document that has lacked spirit. Though some of these issues were addressed in the Doha Round but they need to be further strengthened, the developing nations must open dialog to renegotiate parts of the Agreement that too can then be implemented as in the letter of the Agreement.

References

Anderson, Kym (1998). "Agriculture and the WTO into the 21st Century", CIES Policy Discussion Paper 98/03, University of Adelaide.

Caswell, Julie A. and Neal H. Hooker (1996). "HACCP as an International Standard", *American Journal of Agricultural Economics*, Vol. 78(3), 775-779.

Charnovitz, Steve (2002). Improving the Agreement on Sanitary and Phytosanitary Standards", in *Trade, Environment and the Millennium*, Second Edition, ed. Gary P Sampson and W. Bradnee Chambers.

Darby, Michael R. and Edi Karni (1973). "Free Competition and the Optimal Amount of Fraud", *Journal of Law and Economy*, Vol. 16, 67-88.

Deohar, Satish Y. (2001). "WTO Agreement on SPS and TPT: Implications for Food Quality Issues", Working Paper # 2001-04-05, Indian Institute of Management – Ahmedabad.

Economic Research Service/USDA (2002). "Traceability for Food Marketing & Food Safety: What's the Next Step?", *Agriculture Outlook*, January–February 2002.

Fen, Shenggen, Peter Hazell and Sukhadeo Thorat (2000). "Government Spending, Growth and Poverty in Rural India", *American Journal of Agricultural Economics*, Vol. 82(4), 1038-1051.

Henson, Spencer and Rupert Loader (2001). "Barriers to Agricultural Exports from Developing Countries: The Role of Sanitary and Phytosanitary Requirements", *World Development*, Vol. 29(1), 85-102.

Hooker, Neal H. and Julie A. Caswell (1999). "A Framework for Evaluating Non-Tariff Barriers to Trade Related to Sanitary and Phytosanitary Regulation", *Journal of Agricultural Economics*, Vol. 50(2), 234-246.

Jaiswal, Anand Kumar (2003). "WTO Agreement on SPS Strategic Implications", *Economic and Political Weekly*, November 8, 2003.

Karki, Tika Bahadur (2002). "Sanitary and Phytosanitary Measure (SPS) in SAARC Countries", Discussion Paper, v+43. SAWTEE, Kathmandu and CUTS, Jaipur.

Khan, Amir Ullah (2003). "Indian Agriculture and the WTO", IDF Working Paper No. 0301.

Nelson, Philip (1970). "Information and Consumer Behavior" *Journal of Political Economy*, Vol. 78, 311-329.

Patnaik, Gokul (2003). "Marketing, Storage and Extension Services: State of Agriculture in India", Bazaar Chintan – IDE India Working Paper Series on Agriculture and the Poor No. 9.

Peel, Jacqueline (2003). "Confusing Product with Process: A Critique of the Application of Product-Based Test to Environment Process Standards in the WTO", Research Paper No. 47, The University of Melbourne Faculty of Law.

Saqib, Mohammad (2003). "Setting the House in Order: A Study on Technical Standards that Affect Indian Agriculture Trade", Bazaar Chintan – IDE India Working Paper Series on Agriculture and the Poor No. 15.

Shapiro, Carl (1982). "Consumer Information, Product Quality and Seller Reputation" *Bell Journal of Economics*, Vol. 13, 20-35.

Srivastava, Jayati and Rajeev Ahuja (2002). "Shrimp-Turtle Decision in WTO: Economic and Systemic Implication for Developing Countries", *Economic and Political Weekly*, August 17, 2002.

Stigler, G.J. (1961). "The Economics of Information", *Journal of Political Economy*, Vol. 69(3), 213-225.

Storm, Servaas (1997). "Agriculture Under Trade Policy Reform: A Quantitative Assessment for India", *World Development*, Vol. 25(3), 425-436.

Unnevehr, Laurian J. (2000). "Food Safety Issues and Fresh Food Product Exports from LDCs", *Agricultural Economics*, Vol. 23, 231-240.

OECD, UN and WTO Documents

Food and Nutrition Division (2000). 'Agreement on TBT: An Overview', Multilateral Trade Negotiation on Agriculture: Agreement on the Application of Sanitary and Phytosanitary Measures and Agreement on Technical Barriers to Trade, Food and Agriculture Organization of the United Nations.

————. (2000). 'Introduction to Codex Alimentarius Commission', Multilateral Trade Negotiation on Agriculture: Agreement on the Application of Sanitary and Phytosanitary Measures and Agreement on Technical Barriers to Trade, Food and Agriculture Organization of the United Nations.

————. (2000). 'SPS Agreement: Provisions, Basic Rights and Obligations", Multilateral Trade Negotiation on Agriculture: Agreement on the Application of Sanitary and Phytosanitary Measures and Agreement on Technical Barriers to Trade, Food and Agriculture Organization of the United Nations.

Goodland, Robert (2002). 'Ecolabeling: Opportunities for Progress Towards Sustainability', The World Bank.

Griffin, R (2002). 'History of the Development of the SPS Agreement', Multilateral Trade Negotiation on Agriculture: Agreement on the Application of Sanitary and Phytosanitary Measures and Agreement on Technical Barriers to Trade, Food and Agriculture Organization of the United Nations.

————. (2002). 'Introduction to the International Plant Protection Convention', Multilateral Trade Negotiation on Agriculture: Agreement on the Application of Sanitary and Phytosanitary Measures and Agreement on Technical Barriers to Trade, Food and Agriculture Organization of the United Nations.

Jacobs, S.H. (1994). "Regulatory Cooperation for an Independent World: Issues for Government", Regulatory Cooperation for an Independent World, Organization for Economic Cooperation and Development.

Nielsen, Chantal and Kym Anderson (2000). "GMOs, Trade Policy and Welfare in Rich and Poor Countries", draft paper presented at the World Bank Workshop on Standards, Regulation and Trade.

Stanton, Gretchen H. 'Food Safety and Trade: Regulations and Transparency in the Global Market Economy', World Trade Organization.

————. 'The WTO Dispute Resolution System', World Trade Organization.

Welte, V (2002). 'Introduction to the Office International des Epizooties', Multilateral Trade Negotiation on Agriculture: Agreement on the Application of Sanitary and Phytosanitary Measures and Agreement on Technical Barriers to Trade, Food and Agriculture Organization of the United Nations.

World Trade Organization (1995). 'Agreement on Agriculture'.

————. (1995). 'Agreement on Preshipment Inspection'.

————. (1995). 'Agreement on Technical Barriers to Trade'.

————. (1995). 'Agreement on The Application of the Sanitary and Phytosanitary Measures'.

Government of India Documents

Agricultural Produce (Grading and Marking) Act, 1937

Atomic Energy (Control of Irradiation of Food Rules), 1996

Cereals Grading Rules, 1966

Destructive Insects and Pests (Amendment and Validation) Act, 1992

Destructive Insects and Pests Act, 1914

Edible Oils Packaging (Regulation) Order, 1998

Essential Commodities Act, 1955

Export (Quality Control & Inspection) Act, 1966

Fruit Product Order (FPO), 1955

General Grading and Marking Rules, 1988

Insecticides Act, 1968

Insecticides Rules, 1971

Meat Food Products Order (MFPO), 1973

Milk and Milk Products Order, 1992

Plant Quarantine (Regulation of Import into India) Order, 2003

Prevention of Food Adulteration Act (PFA), 1954

Prevention of Food Adulteration Rules, 1955

Protection of Plant Varieties of Farmers' Rights Act, 2001

Protection of Plant Varieties of Farmers' Rights Rules, 2003

Pulses Grading & Marking Rules, 1964

Pulses, Edible Oilseeds and Edible Oils (Storage Control) Order, 1977

Recycled Plastics Manufacture and Usage Rules, 1999

Report of the Subject Group on Food and Agro Industries of the Prime Minister's Council on Trade and Industry

Seed Rules, 1968

Seeds (Control) Order, 1983

Seeds Act, 1966

Solvent Extracted Oil, De-Oiled Meal and Edible Flour (Control) Order, 1967

Standard of Weights and Measures Act, 1976

Vegetable Oil Products (Regulation) Order, 1998

Vegetable Oils Grading & Marking Rules, 1955

APPENDIX A

Text of the Agreement on Sanitary and Phytosanitary Standards, 1995 of the WTO

Some minor changes have been made to make the text more reader friendly. The definitions in the text are written as paragraphs, which have been bulleted. Also, the Annex A, B and C have been incorporated in the middle of the text rather than at the end for the purpose of continuity.

Article 1 - General Provisions

It indicates that the Agreement applies to all sanitary and phytosanitary measures which affect international trade and informs that the definitions for terms used are provided in Annex A. Further, the rights of member states under the TBT Agreement that does not fall within the scope of the SPS Agreement remains unaffected.

Annex A - Definitions

1. Sanitary or phytosanitary measure is defined as following:
   - Any measure applied to protect animal or plant life or health within the territory of the Member from risks related to the entry, establishment or spread of:
     - Pests or diseases;
     - Disease-carrying organisms; or
     - Disease-causing organisms.
   - Any measure applied to protect human and animal life or health within the territory of the Member from risks arising from:
     - Food additives;
     - Contaminants;
     - Toxins; or
     - Disease-causing organisms in foods, beverages, or feedstuffs.
   - Any measure applied to protect human life or health within the territory of the Member from diseases carried by:
     - Animals;
     - Plants;
     - Animal/plant products; or
     - From the entry, establishment or spread of pests.
   - Any measure applied to prevent or limit damage from the entry, establishment or spread of pests.

Sanitary and phytosanitary measures include all laws, decrees, regulations, requirements and procedures related to:

- End product criteria;
- Processes and production procedures;
- Testing;
- Inspection;
- Certification and approval procedures;
- Quarantine treatments (associated with animal and plant transport and the materials required during their transport);
- Statistical methods;
- Sampling procedures;
- Methods for risk assessment;
- Packaging and labeling directly related to food safety.

2. Harmonization refers to the establishment, recognition and application of common sanitary and phytosanitary measures by Members.
3. International standards, guidelines, recommendations
   - For food safety, the terms international standards, guidelines and recommendations refer to those established by the Codex Alimentarius Commission relating to:
     - Food additives;
     - Veterinary drug and pesticide residues;
     - Contaminants;
     - Methods of analysis and sampling;
     - Codes and guidelines of hygienic practices.
   - For animal health and zoonoses, these same terms refer to the standards, guidelines and recommendations developed under the auspices of the International Office of Epizootics.
   - For plant health, they refer to international standards, guidelines and recommendations developed under the auspices of the Secretariat of the International Plant Protection Convention.
   - For matters not covered by these identified Organizations, standards, guidelines, and recommendations promulgated by other international organizations, open for membership to all WTO Members as identified by the SPS Committee, may be applied.
4. Risk assessment is defined as the evaluation of the adverse effects on human and animal health from additives, contaminants, toxins and disease causing organisms in food, beverages and feedstuffs, and/or the likelihood of entry, establishment or spread of a pest or disease and any associated biological and economic consequences.
5. Appropriate level of sanitary and phytosanitary protection is defined as the level of protection deemed appropriate by the Member establishing the sanitary and phytosanitary measures to protect human, animal or

plant life or health in their territory. This is also referred to as the "Acceptable Level of Risk".

6. Pest or disease free area is an area (entire country, part of a country, or all or parts of several countries), as identified by the competent authority, in which a specific pest or disease does not occur.
7. Areas of low pest or disease prevalence is an area (entire country, part of a country, or parts of several countries), as identified by the competent authority, in which a specific pest or disease occurs at low levels and which is subject to effective surveillance, control or eradication measures.

Article 2 - Basic Rights and Obligations

Members have the right to establish sanitary and phytosanitary measures at the necessary level of protection for human, animal and plant life and health as long as they are not inconsistent with the provisions of this agreement.

Only those measures that are necessary to protect human, animal and plant life and health are to be applied. They shall be based on scientific principles and shall not be maintained without sufficient scientific evidence. Measures are not to be arbitrary, discriminatory, unjustified, unnecessary or disguised barriers to trade.

Sanitary and phytosanitary measures which conform with the relevant provisions of the Agreement shall be presumed to be in accordance with the obligations of the Members under the provisions of GATT 1994 which relate to the use of sanitary or phytosanitary measures, in particular the provisions of Article XX (b).

Article 3 - Harmonization

This article requires Members to base their sanitary and phytosanitary measures on international standards, guidelines and recommendations, where they exist and if sufficient to provide appropriate level of protection. They can establish a higher level of protection if scientific justification is provided in accordance with the requirements in Article 5 (Risk Assessment).

It is further expected from Members to participate in the relevant international organizations to promote the development of sanitary and phytosanitary standards. The SPS Committee will develop procedures to monitor the process of international harmonization and coordinate efforts in this regard with the relevant international organizations.

Article 4 - Equivalence

The Members shall accept the sanitary and phytosanitary measures of other Members as equivalent, even when these measures differ from their own or from those of other Members trading in the same products. For this the exporting country should objectively demonstrate to the importing country that its measures achieve the importing country's appropriate level of sanitary and phytosanitary protection. Members shall also enter into bilateral and multilateral agreements on recognition of each other's sanitary and phytosanitary measures.

Article 5 – Assessment of Risk and Determination of the Appropriate Level of Sanitary and Phytosanitary Protection

- The measures are to be based on an assessment of the risks to human, animal and plant life and health using risk assessment techniques developed by international organization.
- Risk assessment must take into account:
  - Available scientific evidence;
  - Relevant processes and production methods;
  - Inspection/sampling/testing methods;
  - Prevalence of specific diseases or pests;
  - Existence of pest/disease free areas;
  - Ecological/environmental conditions; and
  - Quarantine or other treatment.
- In assessing the risk assessment for animal and plant life or health, SPS should take into account the relevant economic factors:
  - Potential damage in terms of loss of production or sale;
  - Costs of control or eradication of the importing Member;
  - Relative cost-effectiveness of alternative approaches to limit risk.
- The appropriate level of the sanitary and phytosanitary measures of the Members should take into account the objective of minimizing its negative trade effects.
- Arbitrary or unjustified measures shall not be considered.
- Protection levels shall not be more trade restrictive than the concept of appropriate level of protection against risks to human life or health, or to animal and plant life or health. A measure is not more trade-restrictive than required unless there is another measure reasonably available that achieves the appropriate level of protection.
- In case of insufficient scientific evidence, Members may provisionally adopt international standards or those of other Member states. A review of such measures will be taken within a reasonable period of time.
- Explanations of the reasons for measures may be requested by Member states.

Article 6 - Adaptation to Regional Conditions, Including Pest- or Disease-Free Areas and Areas of Low Pest or Disease Prevalence

- Measures shall be adapted to specific areas of the country to minimize the impact on trade.
- Pest/disease free areas and low prevalence areas shall be identified.
- Exporting countries shall provide information on pest/disease free areas.

Article 7 - Transparency

Members shall notify changes in their sanitary and phytosanitary measures and will provide this information in accordance with the provisions in Annex B of the Agreement.

Annex B

The requirements for transparency includes:

1. Prompt publication of regulations.
2. Provision of sufficient interval between the publication of regulations and its entry into force to provide lead time to producers in exporting Members to adapt as required by the importing Member.
3. Establishment of an enquiry point.
4. Notification procedures:
   - The Member must publish a notice at an early stage in such a manner as to enable interested parties to be acquainted with the proposal.
   - The Member must also notify other Members, through the SPS Committee Secretariat, of the products to be covered by the regulation with a brief indication as to the objective and rationale for the proposed regulation. Such notification is to be provided at an early stage to allow opportunity for comment.
   - The Member is also to make available, upon request, copies of the proposed regulation and if possible to identify the parts which in substance deviate from the international standard, guideline or recommendation.
   - The Member is to allow reasonable time for the other Members to comment in writing on the proposal and provide the opportunity to discuss these comments and then take into account the comments and the results of the discussions.
5. In the case of urgent or emergency circumstances related to health protection or the threat of a breach in health protection, then the Member may omit steps listed above, as long as they do the following instead.

- Immediately notify other Members through the SPS Committee Secretariat of the products to be covered including a brief indication of the objective and rationale of the regulation, and a description of the nature of the urgency. This eliminates the requirement to publish at an early stage.
- Provide to other Members, upon request, copies of the regulation.
- Finally, the Member must allow time for other Members to comment in writing and to discuss the proposed regulation and then take the comments and discussions into account.

6. All documents are to be provided in one of the three languages of the WTO - French, Spanish or English.
7. More developed countries are to provide copies of their notifications to those Members that request them or if too voluminous, they shall provide summaries in English, Spanish, or French.
8. The WTO Secretariat is required to promptly circulate copies of the notifications to all Members and interested international organizations.
9. A central government authority at the national level is to be designated as the responsible organization for the implementation of the prescribed notification procedures.

Article 8 – Control, Inspection and Approval Procedures

Members shall observe all the provisions in Annex C to ensure that their procedures, including approval of the use of food additives or for establishing the tolerance levels for contaminants in foods, beverages and feedstuffs, are not inconsistent with the provisions of this Agreement.

Annex C

1. Members are to ensure that:
   - Control, inspection and approval procedures are completed promptly for imported goods as is done for domestic products;
   - Standard or anticipated processing times are published or communicated;
   - Information required is limited to what is necessary for appropriate control, inspection and approval;
   - Confidentiality of information for both imported and domestic products is respected;
   - The number of product specimens is limited to what is reasonable and necessary;
   - Fees are equitable for both domestic and imported products;
   - Criteria for the siting of facilities for carrying out procedures or for the selection of samples should be the same for imported products as for the domestic products;

- Whenever specifications are changed, procedures are to be limited to those that are necessary to ensure the product meets the new specifications so that compliance with the other specifications, which have not changed, is not altered;
- A system is established to review complaints about the procedures; and
- This annexure also addresses the situation where a food additive is not permitted or its use is limited to the degree that it restricts access to markets by exporting Members. In this case, the importing Member shall consider the international standard for the additive as the basis for access to the markets until a determination is made.

2. In the situation where sanitary and phytosanitary measures are to be controlled at the level of production, the Member in whose territory the product is produced is to provide assistance to facilitate the control and the controlling authority.

Article 9 - Technical Assistance

Under this article the Members agree to facilitate the provision of technical assistance, especially to developing countries, either bilaterally or through the appropriate international organizations. Assistance can be provided, among other things, in the areas of processing technologies, research and infrastructure, including the establishment of national regulatory bodies. It may take the form of advice, credits, donations or grants, including, for the purpose of providing technical expertise, training and equipment to allow such countries to adjust to, and comply with, the sanitary or phytosanitary measures necessary to achieve the appropriate level of protection in their export markets.

If substantial investments are needed for an exporting developing country Member to fulfill the sanitary or phytosanitary requirements of an importing Member, the importing Member shall consider providing such technical assistance to the exporting Member. This would allow the exporting Member to maintain and expand its market access opportunities for the product involved.

Article 10 - Special and Differential Treatment

The special and differential treatment provisions call for the consideration of the needs of developing and especially the least developed countries when preparing and implementing sanitary and phytosanitary measures. Such considerations include providing longer time frames for compliance on products of interest to developing country Members.

The SPS Committee also has the authority to grant developing and least developed Members, upon request, time limited exceptions in whole or in part from obligations under the Agreement, taking into account their financial, trade and development needs. Developing and least developed country

Members are also encouraged in this provision to take an active part in the activities of the international organizations.

Article 11 - Consultations and Dispute Settlement

This article informs that the provisions of Article XXII and XXIII of GATT 1994, as they are elaborated and applied by the Dispute Settlement Understanding, shall apply to consultations and the settlement of disputes under this Agreement, except if stated otherwise.

In the case of a dispute involving scientific or technical issues, a panel should seek advice from experts chosen by the panel in consultation with the parties to the dispute. The panel may also, when it deems it appropriate, establish an advisory technical experts group, or consult the relevant international organizations, at the request of either party to the dispute or on its own initiative. Members also have a right to seek settlements to disputes through other international organizations or dispute mechanisms established under any other international agreements.

Article 12 - Administration

This article establishes the Committee on Sanitary and Phytosanitary Measures to provide a regular forum for consultations. This committee is intended to carry out functions that, in effect, implement the provisions of the Agreement and the furtherance of its objectives, particularly the objective of harmonization. The procedural requirements are spelled out along with the terms of reference in this provision. They encourage the use of international standards, guidelines and recommendations by all Members, including sponsoring technical consultations and study with the objective of increasing coordination and integration between international and national systems and approaches for approving the use of food additives or for establishing tolerances for contaminants in foods, beverages or feedstuffs.

The Committee is to maintain close contact with the three sister organizations (Codex, IPPC and OIE) with the objective of securing the best available scientific and technical advice for the administration of the Agreement and preventing duplication of effort.

The Committee shall also develop a procedure to monitor the process of international harmonization and the use of international standards, guidelines or recommendations. For this purpose, the Committee has adopted a preliminary procedure. This procedure encourages Members to identify where there are problems with existing international standards, or where an international standard is lacking. Other Members are then asked whether they share the identified concerns, and these are brought to the attention of the relevant standard-setting organizations.

For those cases in which a Member does not apply an international standard, guideline or recommendation as a condition for import, the Member is to provide an indication of the reason thereof, and, in particular, whether it considers that the standard is not stringent enough to provide the appropriate level of sanitary or phytosanitary protection.

If a Member revises its position, following its indication of the use of a standard, guideline or recommendation as a condition for import, it should provide an explanation for its change and so inform the Secretariat as well as the relevant international organizations, unless such notification and explanation is given according to the procedures of Annex B.

The Committee is to consider the use of information generated by procedures, particularly notification procedures, which are in use by the relevant international organizations in an effort to avoid duplication.

The Committee upon request of a Member can invite international organizations or their subsidiary bodies to examine specific matters related to acceptance or non-acceptance by their members of standards, guidelines or recommendations, and to provide a basis of explanations for the reasons for acceptance or non-acceptance.

Finally, the Committee is responsible for conducting a review of the operation and implementation of this Agreement to be undertaken three years from the date of the Agreement coming into force. The results shall be reported to the Council for Trade in Goods (WTO) with proposals to amend the text of the Agreement, if indicated by the review. The review is to take place thereafter as the need arises.

Article 13 - Implementation

National governments are fully responsible for observance of obligations under this Agreement. To assure this level of responsibility, national governments must formulate and implement positive measures and mechanisms to support the observance of the provisions of the Agreement by other than central government bodies. This includes:

- Local, regional and provincial governments;
- Semi-government, private sector organizations, commissions, committees or institutions;
- Non-governmental organizations;
- Any other organization with or without official sanction or recognition.

Article 14 - Final Provisions

The final provision of this Agreement allows the least developed country Members to delay application of the provisions of this Agreement for a period of five years following its date of entry into force with respect to their sanitary or phytosanitary measures affecting importation or imported products.

Other developing country Members may delay application of the provisions of this Agreement, other than paragraph 8 of Article 5 (providing a Member with information and an explanation as to the reasons for a sanitary or phytosanitary measure) and Article 7 (transparency, enquiry point and notification procedures, Annex B) for two years following the date of entry into force of this Agreement with respect to their existing sanitary or phytosanitary measures affecting importation or imported products, where such application is prevented by a lack of technical expertise, technical infrastructure or resources.

17

Are Subsidies in US Agriculture Justified?

An Economic Analysis

SHASHWAT MODY

Introduction

Agricultural markets across the world have observed significant change over the past fifty years. Supply has grown faster than demand, causing global prices to fall considerably, reducing food shortages that were a common phenomenon in the past. In a bid to increase food security, governments across the world have followed the policy of subsidizing agriculture to achieve self-sufficiency. However, with the vast base of resources that rich countries have access to, developing nations have often lost their competitiveness in world trade markets due to rock bottom prices, resulting in growing trade deficits for developing countries.

Until the 70s, developing countries experienced a net surplus in agricultural trade. Since then, falling agricultural prices, growing subsidies and increasing costs of inputs have forced many to become net importers. According to the Food and Agriculture Organization (FAO) of the UN, this trend is projected to continue and worsen by 2030, due to a rise in imports of cereals and livestock products. A continuing drop in prices of agricultural commodities may rob the very income source of the poverty-ridden population of the world, who are primarily involved in the agricultural sector. Contrary to the projections made by the World Bank, malnutrition may actually increase, leading to greater health, social and financial problems amongst the poorest section of the world.

Many cite East Asia as an example of how countries have transformed themselves through specialization in the non-agricultural sector, thus reducing their poverty levels. However, most countries in Africa and South Asia do not have the infrastructure or stability needed to encourage drastic reforms. Furthermore, even with low returns, many have no choice but to engage in subsistence agriculture, due to the fact that the industrial and service sectors are not developed enough to employ more people. Liberalization of domestic markets in developed economies is the only way of empowering the majority of the lowest-income groups in developing countries, which will provide them with the entrepreneurial flexibility through higher returns in agriculture. Access to foreign markets will result to greater incomes for the common masses, leading to the security needed to build a sound political and social framework, essential for sustainable growth and development.

According to the Agreement on Agriculture (AoA) member countries of the WTO have agreed to better market access, to reduce domestic support and to lower export subsidies, with greater commitments by developed countries than those by developing and least developed nations (Khan, 2003). Non-tariff barriers such as a ban on imports of certain products and quantitative restrictions have been eliminated, tariffs have been reduced and the Aggregate Measure of Support (AMS) through either price or budgetary support has been lowered. However, massive subsidization of agriculture continues to take place and dirty tariffs along with the misuse of various agreements such as the Sanitary and Phyto-sanitary Agreement (SPS) often make agricultural output unpredictable. The glut in prices affects developing nations the most as they lose the comparative advantage in their primary sector. Global trade welfare through liberalization of agriculture was projected to be almost $165 billion, of which developing countries were to get one third of the share; this is yet to materialize. Even though the WTO has moved in the right direction, proper safeguards are still needed to ensure compliance and predictability of nations in the future.

The magnitude of subsidies extended by developed countries to farmers often outweighs the returns. Using the justification that subsidies are essential to prevent agriculture from becoming vulnerable to global supply, Japan, US and other OECD countries provide close to $500 billion annually as support, six times the total amount of aid given to developing countries (Sharma, 2003). An average cow in the US and EU is given $2.70 a day in subsidies, while World Bank (2003) estimates show that close to 1.2 billion people in developing countries survive on less than $1 a day and 800 million people across the globe go without a meal everyday.

This report analyses the economic costs and returns from US agriculture and the trend of 'breakeven' subsidies that have been required over the years to sustain farming in rice, wheat and cotton production. A historical overview shows how the present day form of subsidies has evolved, and what impacts they have had on developing nations of the world. India has been used as an example of a developing country to compare with the US economic costs of production, and recommendations for future course of action have been made.

Overview of US Agriculture

Approximately 41 per cent of land area in the US is used for agriculture, with 931 million acres and 43 million people in farm and farm related jobs[1]. Ninety percent of farms are family or individually run, with an average farm size of about 491 acres. Sixty percent of all farms are under full ownership, giving farmers strong financial stability and access to financial markets resulting to an average debt to asset ratio of 15 per cent and a capital consumption of $20 billion annually.

Over the past 40 years, US agriculture has become highly dependent on exports, averaging about 20 per cent of total cash income (Fig. 1), and upto 70 per cent of total agricultural production for crops such as wheat, rice, cotton, oilseeds, tobacco, nuts and animal products (Fig 2). Japan, EU, Canada, Mexico and South Korea are the major markets for US exports, which have been growing steadily over the years. The greatest increase has been observed with trading partners Mexico and Canada, due to the North Atlantic Free Trade Agreement (NAFTA) which has liberalized trade between these countries (Table 1a, 1b). Significant imports include commodities in horticulture, fruits, vegetables, nuts, wines, coffee, cocoa and rubber (Table 2).

Since 1975, the US has maintained a trade surplus in agriculture, which according to the US Department of Agriculture, "helps counter the persistent deficit in the non-agricultural US merchandise trade".[2] Figure 3 shows that the surplus has been increasing over the past few

1. Economic Research Service & US Dept. of Agriculture, 2003a.
2. Economic Research Service & US Dept. of Agriculture, 2003b.

decades except for a few short-term dips. However, upon digging deeper it is seen that the trade surplus has been a direct outcome of the subsidies offered to farmers, enabling them to compete in world market at prices way below the cost of production.

Figure 1

Exports as a Percentage of Cash Income in the US

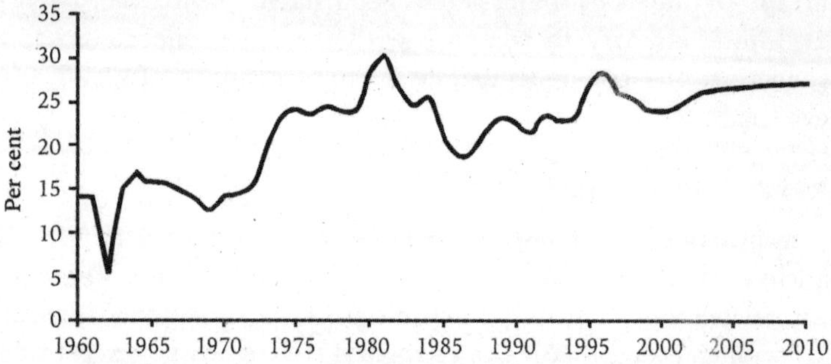

Source: USDA Agricultural Baseline Projection to 2010, Feb 2001, Economic Research Service (ERS), USDA.

* Excluding Direct Government Payments.

Figure 2

Export Share of Production in the US

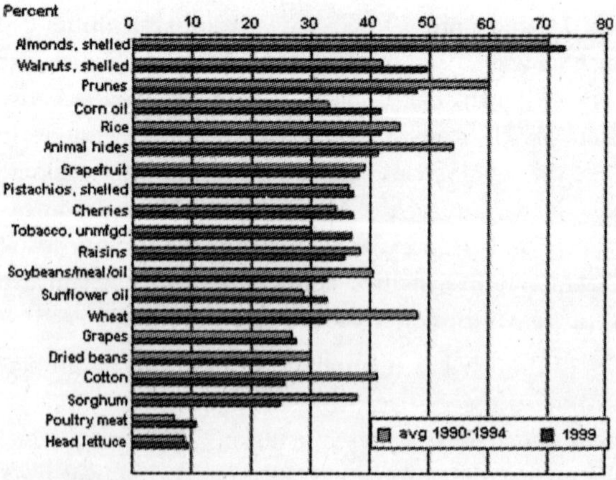

Source: Briefing Room, US Agricultural Trade, Economic Research Service (ERS), US Dept. of Agriculture (USDA).

Table 1a

US Agricultural Imports, Ranked by Country

(US $billion)

Country	*Avg. 1990-96*	*Avg. 1997-00*
Canada	4.6	7.9
European Union	5.3	7.5
Mexico	2.9	4.6
Brazil	1.3	1.4
Indonesia	1.0	1.3
Colombia	0.9	1.3
Australia	1.0	1.2
New Zealand	0.8	0.9
Chile	0.5	0.9
Costa Rica	0.5	0.8

Source: Briefing Room, US Agricultural Trade, Economic Research Service (ERS), USDA.

Table 1b

US Agricultural Exports, Ranked by Country

(US $billion)

Country	*Avg. 1990-96*	*Avg. 1997-00*
Japan	9.3	9.6
European Union	7.6	7.7
Canada	5.1	7.0
Mexico	3.7	5.8
South Korea	2.6	2.7
China (Taiwan)	2.2	2.2
China (Mainland)	1.1	1.4
Hong Kong	1.0	1.4
Egypt	0.9	1.0
Russia	1.0	0.9

Source: Briefing Room, US Agricultural Trade, Economic Research Service (ERS), USDA.

History of Subsidies in US Agriculture

Subsidies for US agriculture were first introduced in the 1920s, when severe price fluctuations along with a weak economy caused frequent national crises, subjecting millions to poverty.[3] A steep rise

3: 1upinfo encyclopaedia, 2003.

in agricultural supply during World War I caused overproduction in the post war period, plummeting prices of agricultural commodities. A bill was passed in the Congress, which led to the creation of the Federal Farm Board with a budget of $500 million to maintain stability through open market operations. However, with the guarantee of stable prices, farmers began to produce even more, leading to the failure of the board and a $200 million loss.

Table 2

US Agricultural Imports, Ranked by Commodity Groups

(US $billion)

	Avg. 1990-96	*Avg. 1997-00*
Horticulture products	10.9	16.8
Animals and products	5.7	7.1
Coffee, cocoa, and rubber	4.3	5.8
Grains and feeds	1.8	3.0
Sugar and tobacco	2.1	2.5
Oilseeds and products	1.3	2.0

Source: Briefing Room, US Agricultural Trade, Economic Research Service (ERS), US Dept. of Agriculture (USDA).

Figure 3

US Agricultural Exports, Imports and Surplus

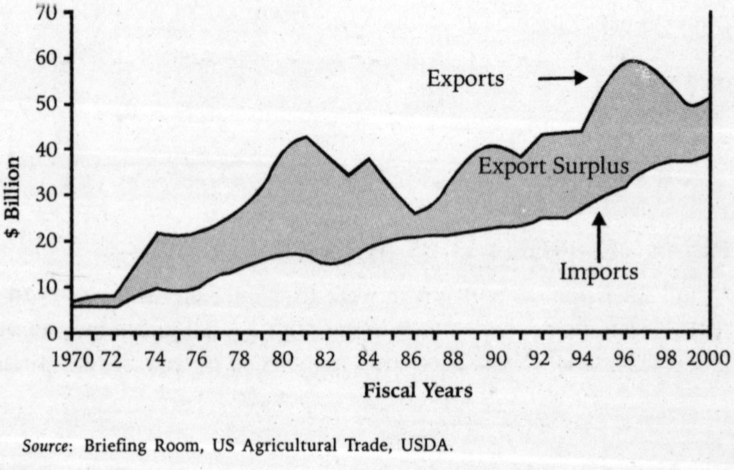

Source: Briefing Room, US Agricultural Trade, USDA.

Upon election, President Franklin Roosevelt then introduced the Agricultural Adjustment Act (AAA) in 1933, which controlled supply by providing payments to farmers to reduce production, with added incentives of loans to farmers who conformed to the government's guidelines. The programme worked successfully, and agricultural prices saw an increase by 85 per cent in the next 5 years. In 1937 the act had to be amended as the Supreme Court declared parts of it unconstitutional, leading to the Agricultural Act under which price support loans were made mandatory for the main products (corn, wheat and cotton), optional for all others.

During the 40s and 50s, price support levels varied significantly, as surpluses dried up quickly during World War II and the Korean War, and grew significantly otherwise due to rising productivity and lower demand in Europe and Asia. The introduction of a flexible price support programme and the Soil Bank Programme (which gave direct income support to reduce acreage) failed to counter supply, as yield continued to rise with better technology. From the sixties onwards, rising costs along with falling demand has lead to an overwhelming increase of direct payments to farmers mainly involved in grain, wheat and cotton production.

Subsidies in US Agriculture as they Exist Today

The rationale used to continue subsidies today, is that poor farmers are not able to sustain themselves without additional support. However, in a study done by the Heritage Foundation (Riedi, 2001), it was found that more than two thirds of all subsidies go to the richest 10 per cent of the farmers, whose annual incomes are well above $250,000. Subsidies in agriculture also throw the income balance off, with an average farm household in 1999 earning $64,347 (17 per cent above the national average), having a net worth of $563,600 (double the national average) and receiving $21,000[4] in direct income support. An average farm is projected to receive more than a million dollars in support over the next decade. Fifteen of the Fortune 500 companies are agricultural firms, and even though an average farm is one-sixth as likely to fail as a non-farm business, the US economy is still burdened with subsidies to agriculture.

4. Dept. of Agriculture and Cooperation (Agricoop), 2000a.

The US agricultural producer support estimate between 1985-2001 varied considerably, ranging from $22 billion to almost $56 billion annually (Fig 4). Even though subsidies declined in between the mid 80s to early 90s, they suddenly saw an enormous increase in the latter half of the decade. The average support increased from $34679 million between the period 1991-1994 to $50552 in 1998-2001. Amongst the OECD countries, the US accounted for almost one fifth of the total support.

Figure 4

US Agricultural Producer Support Estimates (PSEs)

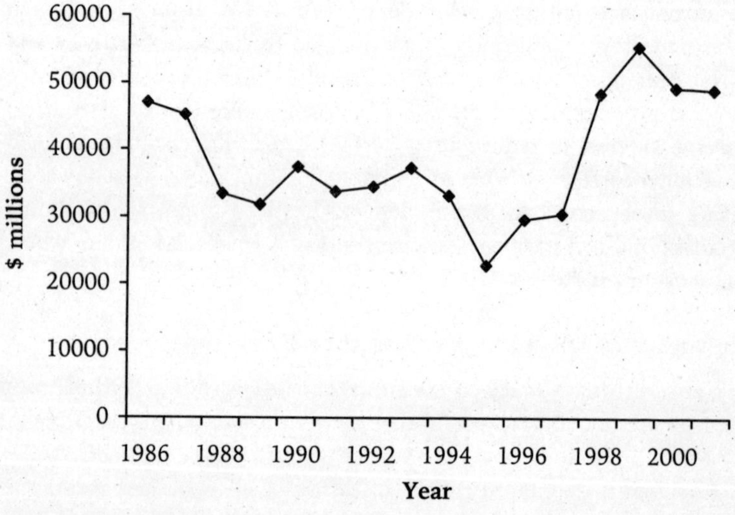

Source: Based on data from the World Bank on Trade and Import Barriers – Producer Support Estimates.

Analysis of Economic Costs and Returns from US Rice, Wheat and Cotton Production

Rice, wheat and cotton historically have been important crops for US farming and have been used as examples to illustrate the extent of subsidies needed to keep farm households in business today.

Over the past 25 years, variable cash expenses, capital replacement costs and the opportunity cost of land and unpaid labour more than doubled, while yield and the harvest period price experienced marginal changes. The yield (per acre) for rice, wheat and cotton grew at a slow rate from 50.73, 31.04 and 535.60 in the 80s to 57.23, 34.08 and 577.75 in the 90s (Fig 5a, b) and the average harvest period price during the 80s and 90s stagnated with rice ($/cwt.), wheat ($/bu) and cotton ($/lb) selling for $7.63, $3.34, $0.60 and $7.66, $3.26, $0.61 respectively.

Figure 5a

Yield of Wheat & Rice

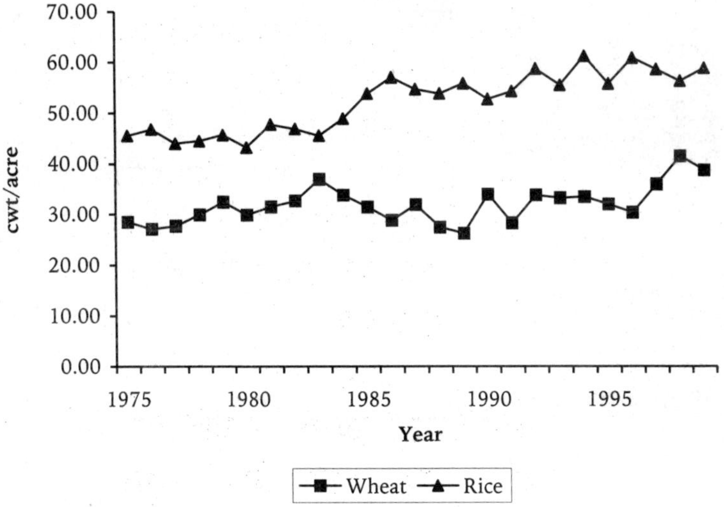

Source: Based on data provided by the Economic Research Service, USDA–Costs and Returns.

The economic cost of production has thus increased over the years, making it harder for US agriculture to sustain itself (Fig. 6). Between the 80s and 90s, rice has seen the largest increase in economic cost, almost 34 per cent, followed by wheat and cotton of 24.83 per cent and 16.03 per cent. This has caused immense losses to the US economy, with average residual returns per acre for rice, wheat and cotton falling enormously from -$74.55, -$23.79 and -$45.45 in the 80s, to –$167.99, -$47.95 and –$71.57 in the 90s (Figure 7). Since 1982, neither wheat nor rice has provided any economic gain while cotton has proved to be productive at only three occasions.

Figure 5b

Yield of Cotton

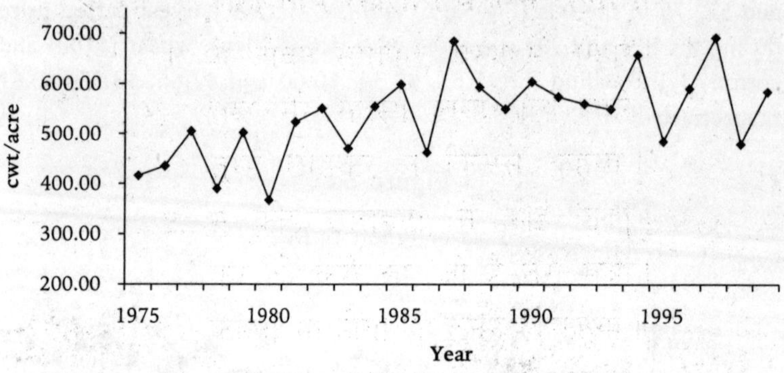

Source: Based on data provided by the Economic Research Service, USDA—Costs and Returns.

Figure 6

Economic Costs of Production (USA)

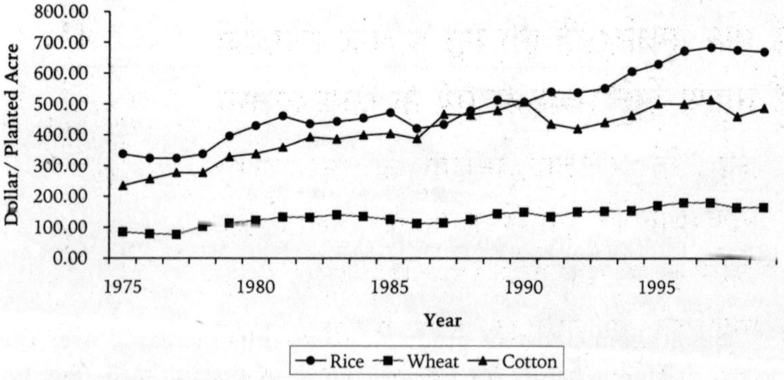

Source: Based on data provided by the Economic Research Service, USDA—Costs and Returns.

'Break-even' Subsidies in US Agricultural Production

The computation of minimum subsidies paid out by the government over the years to keep farming viable for households, has been made with the assumption that farmers would expect returns

Figure 7

Residual Returns (USA)

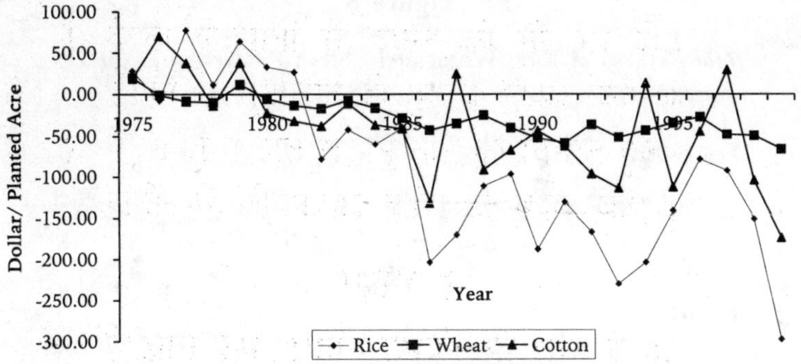

Source: Based on data provided by the Economic Research Service, USDA—Costs and Returns.

that would at least cover the negative returns from their farms; i.e. returns per acre sown extended to the total area for production. The total area sown under rice, wheat and cotton has fluctuated widely between 2833, 74900 and 9477.6 acres ('000) in 1975, to 3531, 62714 and 14873.5 acres ('000) in 1999. The trend shows that the negative returns for the 25 year period beginning 1975, peaked in 1999 at –$1.05 billion, –$4.22 billion and –$2.57 billion for rice, wheat and cotton, totalling a whopping –$7.84 billion (Fig 8). Considering that subsidies have covered almost a hundred commodities at some point, this figure looks like a realistic amount paid by the government for the three crops, as it came dangerously close to violating its commitment in the WTO of limiting subsidies.

The US government also provides direct payments to farmers in certain years to reduce acreage in order to prevent overproduction. This is not accounted for when calculating subsidies through economic returns per acre, as it only takes into account area sown, not area left fallow. Governments across the developed world often conceal this subsidy by calling it an expense for landscape beautification or soil conservation, which makes it difficult for countries to contest it at the dispute settlement court of the WTO. The Farm Bill of 2002 allotted a major part of the $17.1 billion towards various environmental programs[5], it is to be seen how this amount is utilized in the future.

Figure 8

Total Returns of Rice, Wheat and Cotton Production in the US

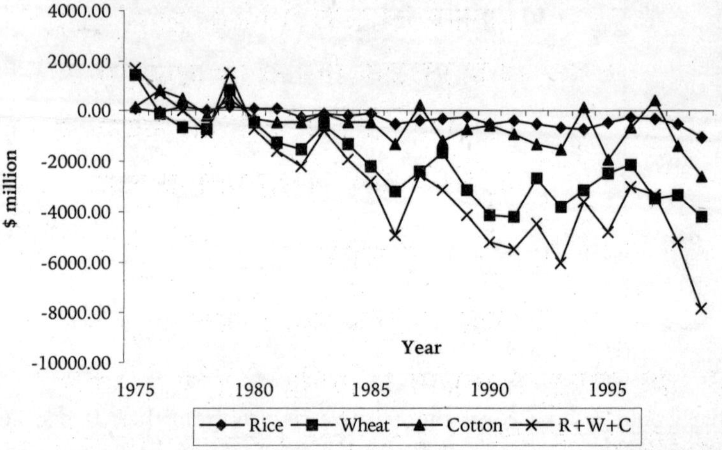

Source: Based on data from the Economic Research Service (ERS) - Costs and Returns, National Agricultural Statistics Series (NASS) - Historical Track Records, USDA.

US Subsidies and Its Impact on Developing Countries

Subsidies in the US from time to time have shown adverse effects on other developing economies. Having lost the comparative advantage in agriculture, many have become net importers of food. Taking an example of rice farmers in 1999, subsidies amounting to $1.3 billion were given for an agricultural produce worth only $1.2 billion (Sharma, 2003). In a collaborated study done by the World Bank and the International Cotton Advisory Committee (ICAC) in 2002[6] on the impacts of world cotton subsidies on West and Central Africa, it was found that even though this region has the lowest cost cotton production in the world, they were spending almost $60 million a year in subsidies in order to keep up with international competitors. The magnitude of subsidies can be imagined from the fact that if the US alone would reduce support by $2 billion, world

5. US House Committee on Agriculture, 2002.
6. Ghura, 2002.

prices would rise by 12 cents a pound, resulting to annual revenue of $250 million for this region alone. Other countries like India, that provides $1 billion support to its 550 million farmers, simply do not have the resources to subsidize agriculture further. In order to compare the economic costs of production in US agriculture with a developing country, India was the prime choice due to the fact that amongst all developing nations India collects the most up-to-date and relatively accurate set of published data and the diversity of Indian agriculture allows a comparison in a wide range of commodities.

Comparison of Economic Costs of Production in India and the US

India has the second largest arable land area in the world (after USA) and uses the seventh largest area for agricultural production, after Russia, Canada, China, USA, Brazil and Australia. After China, India has the largest number of people involved in agriculture (approx. 553 million), and has the largest irrigated area in the world. It ranks third after China and USA in the production of cotton (lint) and cereals and has the second largest produce of wheat and rice (paddy). India is also the second largest producer of oilseeds (groundnut & rapeseed), fruits, vegetables and tobacco, and the largest producer of tea, jute and pulses.[7]

When comparing the economic costs of two countries, it is important to realize that the calculation of data differs enormously between countries and exclusion of costs or hidden subsidies may cause inaccuracies. Costs included in India such as procurement, post procurement and carrying charges to state agencies are not applicable in the US scenario. Excluding these from the comparison of economic costs of production is not unreasonable, as it can be argued that if liberalization of agriculture were to occur, costs involved in procurement and post procurement of crops in India would be reduced heavily, as moving, storing and handling would become more efficient through privatisation. The elimination of the common market (*mandi*) system in India would reduce costs drastically as fees, taxes and 'middlemen' would be reduced. Thus, the pooled cost of production data has been used as the economic cost of production, as it takes into account the farmers' wages for unpaid labour, land and

7. Dept. of Agriculture & Cooperation (Agricoop), 2000b.

other interest and capital payments that are incurred in the production process. The comparison, however does not reflect quality differences between produce of different nations, which can cause differential pricing, resulting to some error.

Interestingly, the economic cost of production figures for rice, wheat and cotton in India show that the presumption that developing countries can produce commodities at a fraction of the cost required in their developed counterparts does not always hold true.[8] While crops like rice and cotton are produced in India at one-fourth the economic cost, wheat production has similar economic costs in India and the US (Fig. 9). According to 1999 figures, the economic cost of production of rice (in $/planted acre) was $145.42 in India, as opposed to $671.04 in the US. In Gujarat, India's largest cotton-producing state, the economic costs involved were $124.36 per acre, while cotton production in the US utilized $488.07 per acre. However, wheat could be produced in India and the US at similar costs per acre, $124.35 and $166.15.

Figure 9

Economic Costs of Production in US and India

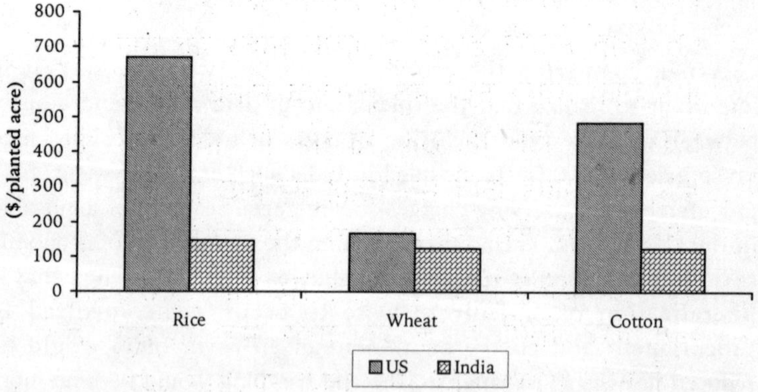

Source: Based on data from the Economic Research Service (ERS)- Costs and Returns, USDA, Commission for Agricultural Costs and Prices - Ministry of Agriculture (Govt. of India).

8. Economic Costs data for India have been taken from 'The Reports of the Commission for Agricultural Costs and Prices- 2003'. All conversions have been made to the US system of weight calculations, with the exchange rate of $1= Rs. 47.

Would Immediate Removal of Subsidies Solve the Woes of Developing Countries?

It is easy to blame the US and other developed nations for the glut caused in prices of agricultural products worldwide, and demand for immediate removal of subsidies in the WTO, but this move could have disastrous consequences worldwide. It is important to remember, that even though some developing regions of the world have lower costs of production, the overall volume produced by developing countries today is still not adequate to cover total world needs. Developed countries have far greater purchasing power, and a sudden decrease in agricultural supply could cause a shortage of commodities, inflating prices and resulting to mass starvation and unrest amongst developing economies. A further study could be carried out in this area in order to determine the possible effects of a sudden decline in supply on world agricultural markets.

Conclusion

The analysis of costs and returns from the production of rice, wheat and cotton has illustrated the fact that over the past few decades US agriculture has become highly dependent on government benefits. Subsidies and target pricing have helped the rich farmers get even richer, and have also prevented food prices from falling within the US causing consumers to lose out on both ends, bearing a considerable burden as taxpayers, and paying a higher price for agricultural commodities.

In world markets, US subsidies have caused a greater demand for its commodities, causing a false perception of a trade surplus. Developing countries have encountered considerable losses due to the glut in prices. From a development perspective, liberalization of trade and reduction of subsidies may not alone solve poverty issues in poorer countries. The US stands to benefit only through a gradual reduction in domestic subsidies coupled with a commitment of aid and infrastructure support to raise agricultural productivity in developing countries. The rise in income levels in lower income countries could spark a greater demand for US exports in other sectors, thus benefiting a larger section of the world through trade. This move would also ensure that sudden shortages will not occur, and with infrastructure growth predictability of global agriculture will be maintained, causing global stability.

Table 3

Area Sown under Wheat, Rice and Cotton, USA, 1975-1999

Year	Rice (000 acres)	Wheat (000 acres)	Cotton (000 acres)	Rice-Residual Retuns ($/acre)	Wheat-Residual Retuns ($/acre)	Cotton-Residual Retuns ($/acre)	Rice(R)-Total Returns ($ mill)	Wheat(W)-Total Returns ($ mill)	Cotton(C)-Total Returns ($ mill)	R+C+W
1975	2833	74900	9477.6	28.00	19.58	18.36	79.31	1466.54	174.01	1719.86
1976	2489	80395	11635.5	–8.11	–1.49	69.79	–20.19	–119.79	812.04	672.06
1977	2261	75410	13679.5	77.36	–8.94	37.42	174.91	–674.17	511.89	12.63
1978	2993	65989	13375.1	10.91	–10.37	–14.35	32.66	–684.31	–191.93	–843.58
1979	2890	71424	13977.5	63.90	11.53	37.71	184.67	823.52	527.12	1535.31
1980	3380	80788	14533.8	32.95	–5.77	–23.17	111.36	–466.15	–336.71	–691.50
1981	3827	88251	14330.1	26.67	–13.89	–32.74	102.06	–1225.81	–469.11	–1592.86
1982	3295	86232	11345.4	–79.39	–17.56	–38.95	–261.57	–1514.23	–441.86	–2217.67
1983	2190	76419	7926.3	–43.20	–7.81	–11.56	–94.61	–596.83	–91.60	–783.04
1984	2830	79213	11145.4	–61.30	–16.86	–37.55	–173.47	–1335.53	–418.50	–1927.50
1985	2512	75535	10684.6	–41.44	–29.26	–42.44	–104.10	–2210.15	–453.43	–2767.68
1986	2381	71998	10044.6	–203.16	–44.06	–131.49	–483.74	–3172.23	–1320.81	–4976.78
1987	2356	65829	10397.2	–169.88	–35.95	24.41	–400.25	–2366.55	253.79	–2513.01
1988	2933	65529	12514.8	–112.14	–25.65	–92.41	-328.91	–1680.82	–1156.43	–3166.16
1989	2731	76615	10586.6	–97.60	–41.08	–68.59	–266.56	–3147.34	–726.16	–4140.06
1990	2897	77041	12348.1	–187.31	–53.70	–44.85	–542.63	–4137.10	–553.83	–5233.56
1991	2884	69881	14052.1	–131.35	–60.07	–63.38	–378.80	–4197.75	–890.64	–5467.19

Contd. ...

...Contd. ...

Year	*Rice (000 acres)*	*Wheat (000 acres)*	*Cotton (000 acres)*	*Rice-Residual Retuns ($/acre)*	*Wheat-Residual Retuns ($/acre)*	*Cotton-Residual Retuns ($/acre)*	*Rice(R)-Total Returns ($ mill)*	*Wheat(W)-Total Returns ($ mill)*	*Cotton(C)-Total Returns ($ mill)*	*R+C+W*
1992	3176	72219	13240.0	–166.45	–37.18	–97.32	–528.63	–2685.10	–1288.58	–4502.32
1993	2920	72168	13438.3	–229.64	–52.87	–114.91	–670.54	–3815.52	–1544.20	–6030.25
1994	3353	70349	13720.1	–203.14	–44.43	13.13	–681.11	–3125.61	180.10	–3626.62
1995	3121	69031	16931.4	–141.51	–35.36	–113.28	–441.64	–2440.94	–1917.99	–4800.56
1996	2824	75105	14352.5	–79.64	–28.19	–46.01	–224.90	–2117.21	–660.29	–3002.40
1997	3125	70412	13898.0	–93.40	–49.45	29.28	–291.86	–3481.87	406.93	–3366.80
1998	3285	65821	13392.5	–150.33	–50.92	–105.06	–493.83	–3351.61	–1407.02	–5252.45
1999	3531	62714	14873.5	–297.20	–67.30	–173.27	–1049.41	–4220.65	–2577.13	–7847.19

Source: Based on data from the Economic Research Service (ERS)- Costs and Returns, National Agricultural Statistics Series (NASS)- Historical Track Records, US Dept. of Agriculture.

Index

C

D

K

L

M

N

O

S

T